ACCLAIM FOR DAPHNE DE MARNEFFE'S

maternal desire

On Children, Love, and the Inner Life

"This is truly one of the most extraordinary books I have ever read, as a professional, as a working parent, and as a woman. It is a brilliant, radical, and deeply poignant look at mothering and in particular *women's desire to care for their children* that I think should be required reading for all women. . . . The true beauty of *Maternal Desire* is de Marneffe's ability to consider theory and history against the backdrop of her own experience of mothering, and to consider its emotional depth and complexity in ways that are heartbreakingly simple and evocative. This beautifully nuanced, textured, and deeply accessible book helps put into words why it is sometimes so painful and difficult not to be home, but never succumbs to any suggestion that this complexity can be remedied by a simple, functional solution, such as staying home or not staying home."
— Arietta Slade, PhD, *Journal of the American Academy of Child and Adolescent Psychiatry*

"The notion that women want to be with their kids is crucial to the logic of de Marneffe's argument. . . . In de Marneffe's view, it is a mistake to equate staying at home with forgoing an adult identity, because it is precisely in caring for children that an adult identity is formed."
— Elizabeth Kolbert, *The New Yorker*

"*Maternal Desire* contains flashes of insight and expressions of deep sympathy, as when Ms. de Marneffe notes that our values inevitably determine what we consider to be our needs. She captures the exquisite conflicts that weigh on women, and . . . she writes movingly of the transfiguring effect of motherhood."
— Patricia Cohen, *New York Times*

"De Marneffe's book isn't so much about the desire to have children as the desire to spend time caring for them once they're yours. . . . Her radical move is to urge women to think hard about what they *themselves* want or need from mothering, not just what their children want or need, and not what women's rights activists or psychological experts or right-wing politicians demand that they want or need. . . . *Maternal Desire* interweaves feminist history, psychoanalytic theory, subtle analyses of the abortion and day care debates, and rich vignettes from de Marneffe's own mothering life."
— Laurie Abraham, *Elle*

"*Maternal Desire* is transforming in both a generational and political way. Sadly and ironically, the politicization and polarization of so-called women's issues has had serious stifling, counterproductive, and lasting consequences for both mothers and career women. Here is a book that gives a common voice to women on both the left and right; to women who work and women who don't. Having had my babies at forty-two and forty-five, and therefore able to compare that joy with work, even great life-fulfilling work, I am still amazed every day how there's just no comparison in terms of sheer aching love and exuberance.   — Mary Matalin

"In joining motherhood with desire and pleasure rather than obligation, *Maternal Desire* is a subversive book. It undercuts the opposition of self-development and emotional connectedness, and affirms a woman's right to choose to spend time with her children. That this right is currently restricted to the economically advantaged is one of the scandals in our society. *Maternal Desire* demonstrates why women in our society will not really be free until all women have more power to shape their maternal lives."
— Carol Gilligan, author of *In a Different Voice* and *The Birth of Pleasure*

"This is no sparkly-rainbow-and-dewdrop vision of mothering. De Marneffe, a mother of three, is clear-eyed about the demands of caring for small children. But as a clinical psychologist, she sees many women struggling to suppress a visceral ache to spend more time actively mothering. . . . *Maternal Desire* is an important addition to the literary canon on motherhood." — Stephanie Wilkinson, *Washington Post Book World*

"*Maternal Desire* is the most original and stimulating book on motherhood to come along in a very long while. De Marneffe makes fresh and moving use of feminism and psychoanalysis to explore an aspect of motherhood that is often, strangely, neglected: its pleasures. She nudges us gently but persuasively away from the competing clichés of mothering as either sacred duty or time-juggler's burden, and makes us think about why women want to take care of children in the first place. *Maternal Desire* is a pleasure to read and to think about, not least because it argues with equal power from both the head and the heart." — Margaret Talbot, staff writer for *The New Yorker*

"De Marneffe offers a fascinating analysis that's a welcome addition to the dialogues about motherhood." — *Publishers Weekly*

"Daphne de Marneffe has tapped into something powerful and true about motherhood. Rigorously intellectual, passionately researched, and above all enormously generous and inclusive of all mothers — this is a book that deserves to be a classic." — Dani Shapiro, author of *Family History*

"A work of personal conviction backed by scholarly research, sure to arouse controversy among feminists and psychologists." — *Kirkus Reviews*

"De Marneffe has a unique voice with an unusual capacity to hold the complexity of multiple perspectives. She speaks for and to an earlier feminist generation, and for and to the next generation faced with different demands and social-psychic realities. Recognizing the authenticity of different choices, she masterfully draws on current developmental theory to argue that women's subjectivity and sense of recognition can be found not only within the workplace but also within the mother-child experience. This remarkable, moving, and provocative book is about the passion of that experience, written by an important scholar in the midst of raising her own children."
> — Susan Coates, PhD, Columbia University Center for Psychoanalytic Training and Research

"Provocative. . . . Sure to spark debate at a playground near you." — *Parenting*

"A refined discussion of 'the eros of parenthood.' . . . De Marneffe elegantly summarizes a number of psychoanalytic views of maternity,"
> —Alissa Quart, *New York Times Book Review*

"De Marneffe embraces much of the feminist heritage, and she writes powerfully about the happiness that can be gained in integrating work and motherhood. But her case for 'maternal desire' is an important corrective to feminism and a must-read for anyone concerned with family and gender issues. . . . De Marneffe notes that for now, child-rearing is done primarily by women — and that is a reality our discussion of work and motherhood has to recognize, instead of imposing an abstraction of equality on everyone. Striving toward equality while recognizing reality, and seeking the best possible balance: That's a good prescription for change."
> — Cathy Young, *Boston Globe*

maternal desire

On Children, Love, and the Inner Life

Daphne de Marneffe

BACK BAY BOOKS
Little, Brown and Company
NEW YORK · BOSTON

For Sophie, Alex, Nicholas, and Terry
with love

Back Bay Books / Little, Brown and Company
Time Warner Book Group
1271 Avenue of the Americas, New York, NY 10020
Visit our Web site at www.twbookmark.com

Originally published in hardcover by Little, Brown and Company, March 2004
First Back Bay paperback edition, February 2005

Excerpt from Gwendolyn Brooks's "the mother" is reprinted by consent
of Brooks Permissions from the volume *Blacks* (Chicago: Third World Press,
seventh printing, 1994).

Library of Congress Cataloging-in-Publication Data

De Marneffe, Daphne.
   Maternal desire : on children, love, and the inner life / Daphne de
Marneffe. — 1st ed.
      p. cm.
   Includes bibliographical references and index.
   ISBN 0-316-05995-1 (hc) / 0-316-11028-0 (pb)
      1. Motherhood.   2. Mothers — Social conditions.   3. Mothers — Psychol-
ogy.   4. Feminism.   I. Title.

HQ759.D4 2004
306.874'3 — dc22   2003056812

10   9   8   7   6   5   4   3   2   1
Q-FF

Book design by Guenet Abraham
Printed in the United States of America

CONTENTS

ix PREFACE

1.
3 The "Problem"
of Maternal Desire

2.
23 Feminism

3.
57 Psychoanalysis

4.
90 Pleasure

5.
118 Ambivalence

6.
147 Child Care

7.
182 Adolescence

8.
211 Fertility

9.
237 Abortion

10.
255 Midlife

11.
280 Fathers

12.
312 Time with Children

337 ACKNOWLEDGMENTS

339 NOTES

371 BIBLIOGRAPHY

391 INDEX

IN OCTOBER 1997 I WAS a few weeks pregnant with our third child. The child was very much wanted, and planned, but the way I felt still surprised me. I had imagined that once I became pregnant, my spirit of welcome would be subtly tempered by an array of practical worries. Instead, though mindful of the challenges that lay ahead, I felt an almost giddy sense of freedom.

I remember walking along the bike path near our house, which borders an estuary. Egrets jabbed their needle-like beaks into the water, and ducks bobbed in the current. I felt poised at that moment of maximal clarity and alertness, that sliver of time between the discovery that one is pregnant and the descent into nausea and bone-tiredness. I knew that soon even thinking would exhaust me, so I was impatient to figure out what was making me feel so light.

A memory played in my mind. It was summer, and my father held my bike as I awkwardly tried to ride. I coasted alone only for brief stretches, and I couldn't imagine I would ever be able to pedal on my own. Yet miraculously, the next day I got on my bike and rode — unsteadily, but irrevocably. That memory evoked the sensation of being at the final stage of not knowing something, and tipping, overnight and without conscious effort, into the most elementary stage of knowing. It captured a transition I sensed was taking place in my life. I was moving from a shaky endorsement of a model in which children were fitted into my previous life to a desire for a life centered on mothering, from which other priorities flowed. Paradoxically, the outward complication of our lives was introducing a radical simplicity.

My feeling of freedom did not diminish, of course, the real demands we would face in having another child. We worried, as any expectant couple does, about whether we would have enough time and energy to give to each of our children. We worried about money. I worried about my psychotherapy practice. As I anticipated another maternity leave and a likely move of my office closer to home, I worried about the effect of these disruptions on my patients.

Still, I found the glimmer of freedom compelling, in part because its source — my shift of emphasis toward mothering — felt so transgressive. How was it that at the dawn of the twenty-first century, the ancient imperative that women mother their children felt somehow liberating and new? Those thoughts led me to reflect on the complexities of women's experience of mothering young children in America today. They stimulated me to reconsider intellectual questions I had long had about the place of motherhood in the psychology of women. And ultimately, they drove me to use my training as a psychologist, my sympathies as a feminist, and my experience as a mother to try to understand how we evaluate and live out, socially and individually, the desire to care for children.

Like some women and unlike others, I had always had the desire to mother. When I was young, my sister and I whiled away our afternoons in an ongoing saga of sisters with four kids apiece, each with a set of twins. We withstood car crashes, camping disasters, hurricanes, poverty — this was Motherhood as Adventure, the savory drama of mothers protecting their young. When I was growing up in Cambridge, Massachusetts, in the sixties and seventies, traditional notions of family were up for grabs, but I always knew that caring for children was something my own mother loved to do, and I intuitively modeled myself on her example.

In college, the philosophical questions I studied rarely bore on what was to me a central existential dilemma: how could one devote oneself to two vocations — in my case, intellectual work and motherhood — in a way that truly answered one's most deeply held values about both? Role models were hard to find. I sought out women mentors, few and far between, who combined intellectual achievement and motherhood in a way I wanted to emulate. I found beacons along the way: courses on human development that introduced me to the writings of Nancy Chodorow and Dorothy Dinnerstein; the mentorship of Carol Gilligan, whose pathbreaking book *In A Different Voice* was about to be published; and the work of Annie Leclerc, a French writer known to only a handful of American scholars, whose slim treatise *Parole de Femme* put the pleasures of motherhood in philosophical terms.[1]

The importance to me of my long-standing mothering wish was not that it necessarily made me fit for parenthood. I don't believe that early maternal feeling is a prerequisite for being a good mother. Rather, it was more like a placeholder, reserving space that would one day be occupied by caring for children. That day arrived with the birth of our first child when I was several months shy of completing my PhD. Overnight, motherhood became thrillingly and dauntingly real, filled with our newborn daughter's suckling, her startle, her drunken contentment after nursing, her nocturnal waking, her nerve-jangling cries.

As it happened, the beginnings of my maternal and professional careers coincided, but it was the space allotted to my professional life that was the more problematic. I loved my work as a psychologist and went about building a psychotherapy practice for children and adults. My research on childhood trauma and gender development I held in abeyance. I was fortunate to have a profession in which I could make my own schedule. But I found that whenever I was out of the house for more than a couple of hours a day, I felt an invisible tether drawing me home. I couldn't bear to leave our baby; when I was away, I

ached, and in her presence, I couldn't imagine a worthwhile reason for leaving her. And, rather than being a feeling I wanted to
diminish or overcome, it was one that I wanted to endorse and
embrace.

At 4 A.M. feedings, an hour ripe for morbid rumination, I
would wonder if my reluctance to leave my daughter was some
sort of weakness. Perhaps I was too driven by emotion or suffered an excess of sentimentality — a fault perennially attributed to women. Yet when I heard other mothers saying that
their day at work made them feel "fresher" to deal with the demands of their six-month-old babies, I experienced an almost
physical sense of disorientation. The incongruity between our
experiences made me want to understand more about the larger
issue of mothering and the desires involved. And it prompted
me to wonder, tentatively at first, whether the conversations I
was hearing might be part and parcel of a contemporary discourse defined by its very evasion of the whole question of the
desire to mother. Perhaps these mothers' comments, exchanged
almost as a currency in female bonding, were partly shaped by a
tacit agreement to steer clear of the messy passions toward babies that ensnared so many women, because the costs to one's
sense of personal achievement, and sometimes even to one's
sense of identity, were perceived to be so steep.

As my desire to spend time mothering gathered force within
me, I noticed how hard it was to talk about. Usually comfortable
expressing myself in words, I found myself strangely inarticulate
when it came to this topic. I avoided professional mentors because I was afraid they would ask what I was doing with my life.
The only time depression ever drove me to shop was after a respected colleague bemoaned over lunch my post-motherhood
lack of professional productivity. As if in a trance, I bought a
hideous mauve suit as a sop to my vanished professionalism.
Needless to say, I never wore it. My obstetrician genially asked
what I was up to, and I muttered something about having turned
into a fifties housewife. It was as if the moment words began to
form in my mouth, they instantaneously tumbled into the well-
worn groove of cliché. I was the site of colliding motives; my

wish to care for my child was something I felt both hesitant to admit and called to defend, and the conflict made it hard to utter anything genuine at all.

I knew that my conflict bore the stamp of my own idiosyncratic psychology. But in thinking it over during my walk that day in October, it struck me anew that this was not my unique problem. Every mother I knew, and virtually every mother I read about, grappled more or less explicitly with the same painful questions: Where should caring for children fit into one's life? What should one do with the desire to care for one's children? How should one understand it, think about it, or talk about it? No one expected to have easy answers, but it seemed that so often our culture's response was framed as a matter of how little time one could spend with one's children and not do them damage. So rarely did public discussion take account of the embodied, aching desire to be with their children that many mothers feel. What's more, the vocabulary for this desire seemed so limited, the language available for exploring it so constricted, that it was hard to get a grasp of what part the desire should play in one's decisions and in one's very assessment of oneself.

There is a complicated blend of emotions at the heart of these issues and a complicated overlay of social messages. They are a minefield, where we step gingerly around our own feelings and those of others, balancing self-revelation and self-concealment in an effort to respect others' choices, maintain friendships, not offend. Our reticence is not only personal but strategic and political as well, for we are acutely aware of how vulnerable the real gains women have made in the workforce can be. Women's desire to *have* children has survived the vagaries of feminist suspicion and is now fully respectable and in public view. Remote are the days when the radical feminist Shulamith Firestone identified childbearing as the root of women's oppression.[2] The ubiquity of fertility treatments attests to the lengths people are willing to go to have children. Competent women committed to their work passionately declare that whatever else they value, it is their children that they cherish most. But the territory that remains occluded, dogged with contention and strangely unspeakable, is the territory of *caring* for children — of spending one's hours and days with them, of "quantity time," and of its meaning and value not only to children but to mothers as well.

It seems that in our culture, the image of a woman who takes care of her children is not unlike the old psychoanalytic image of the "castrated" woman. Once upon a time, Freud suggested that women's penis envy was psychological bedrock; that it was women's fundamental condition to perceive themselves as lacking. The psychoanalyst Karen Horney pointed out that women did not simply envy an ostensible anatomical advantage; they envied men's participation in the public domain.[3] Today, women participate in the public domain, and the perception of lack once ascribed to women in general has been shifted to the figure of the caregiving mother. From the timeworn platitudes "I don't work" and "I'm just a stay-at-home mother" to the equation of mothering with martyrdom, there is an intransigent insistence that something is lacking in women who spend their time mothering.

In light of this cultural image, it is not surprising that some women contemplating motherhood fear that their agency, power, prestige, and their very identities are at stake. For them, the embrace of motherhood amounts to an agreement to become a social nullity, a consent to dissolve oneself into an atavistic state. In reality, becoming a mother does involve losses; but that fact does not fully account for the intensity and prevalence of women's fears. Over and above the concrete losses and trade-offs, women's fears are heightened by a rhetoric surrounding motherhood that conceptualizes mothering as antithetical to self. Women observe the absence of any satisfying formulation of why mothers might *want* to care for children — not as some sort of unthinking surrender to women's conventional or "natural" role, but as an actively pursued and authentic means of self-expression — and that very absence tends to confirm some women's suspicions that stepping into motherhood is like stepping into a void. Pieties about mothering, whether conservative or feminist, do little to help. Politically motivated descriptions of "stay-at-home motherhood," so devoid of imaginative reach or moral nuance, seem to support the notion that when a mother is home with her children, "nothing" is going on.

Yet within this stubborn self-effacement lies a more complex truth. As Horney herself said, female sexuality and mothering offer a cornucopia of pleasures. She expressed amazement that Freudian theory could have ignored or repressed knowledge of that reality. Embedded in the emphasis on the caregiving mother's nonentity status is a tendentious refusal to recognize the pleasures, the self-expression, and the moral fulfillment mothering can afford. Mainstream feminism, with its espousal of Western individualism as the basis of women's liberation, has been ill equipped to recognize, let alone critique, this limited view. Though feminist activism has helped secure for women the public power previously denied them, it has done little to challenge the assumption that women who spend their time caring for children are powerless, un-self-actualized, and at the margins of cultural life.

My goal for this book is to provide a framework for thinking about women's desire to care for their children in a way that is consistent with feminism and free from sentimentality and cliché. This aspect of mothering is relatively neglected in psychoanalytic, feminist, and popular writing, and it calls for serious consideration. But since the sense we make of motherhood has a powerful impact on women living their day-to-day lives, my goal is ultimately a therapeutic one. The creation and nurture of children transforms men and women alike. They provide a unique opportunity for reconsidering the premises of one's life. We live in a culture that enshrines acquisition but profanes care. When a person, still most likely a mother, feels the desire to care for her children, our tired cultural scripts shed little light on the profundity of her situation. This book offers a view of maternal desire — its qualities, its effects, and its pervasive devaluation and misinterpretation in our individualistic culture. I hope it proves useful to women reflecting upon their lives. More than that, I hope it frees them to tap into their own human happiness.

maternal desire

1

The "Problem" of
Maternal Desire

IT WOULD SEEM THAT EVERYTHING it is possible to say about motherhood in America has already been said. Beckoning us from every magazine rack, beaming out from every channel, is a solution or a revelation or a confession about mothering. Yet in the midst of all the media chatter about staying on track, staying in shape, time crunches, time-savers, and time-outs, there is something unvoiced about the experience of motherhood itself. It sways our choices and haunts our dreams, yet we shy away from examining it with our full attention. Treated both as an illusion and as a foregone conclusion, it is at once obvious and invisible: our desire to mother.

The desire to mother is not only the desire to have children, but also the desire to care for them. It is not the duty to mother, or the compulsion to mother, or the concession to mothering when other options are not available. It is not the acquiescence to prescribed roles or the result of brainwashing. It is the longing felt by a mother to nurture her children; the wish to participate in their mutual relationship; and the choice, insofar as it is possible, to put her desire into practice.

Maternal desire is at once obvious and invisible partly because it is so easily confused with other things. Those fighting for women's progress too often misconstrue it as a throwback or excuse, a self-curtailment of potential. Those who champion

4 / MATERNAL DESIRE

women's maternal role too often define it narrowly in the context of service — to one's child, husband, or God. What each view eclipses is the authentic desire to mother felt by a woman herself — a desire not derived from a child's need, though responsive to it; a desire not created by a social role, though potentially supported by it; rather, a desire anchored in her experience of herself as an agent, an autonomous individual, a person.

As common wisdom would have it, "mother" and "desire" do not belong in the same phrase. Desire, we've been told, is about sex. Motherhood, we've been told, is about practically everything but sex. A century ago, sexuality was repressed; blooming young women in Freud's day contracted odd symptoms — paralyzed arms, lost voices — as a way to adapt to social mores that inhibited women's awareness or expression of their sexual desires.[1] Today, sexuality is everywhere, and the desire to mother is more prone to obfuscation. Partly owing to five decades of feminist writing, women's sexual desire no longer comes as much of a surprise. Maternal desire, by contrast, has become increasingly problematic. It is almost as if women's desire for sex and their desire to mother have switched places in terms of taboo.

The taboo against wanting to mother operates as a strange new source of inhibition for women. Some try not to think about motherhood while they pursue more immediate professional goals. Others deny the extent of their maternal wishes, which become clear only after hard-won insight in psychotherapy. Still others try to minimize their desire to nurture their child, setting up their lives to return to normal after their baby is born, never fully cognizant that there may be no "normal" to return to. For one woman, wanting to stay home with her child is an embarrassing reversal of previous priorities. Another can't decide whether caring for children is a choice or a trap. Another feels she needs to maintain earning power and professional status if she wants to safeguard her self-esteem. For Freud's patients, sexual desire was frustrated by a restrictive model of decent womanhood, which emerged from complex social and economic forces. Today, maternal desire is constrained by a contemporary model of self that has developed in response to more recent economic and social realities.

Fifty years ago, women who wished to realize professional ambitions dealt with gender inequality by refusing or relinquishing motherhood. Twenty years ago, mothers evaded gender inequality by keeping up their professional pace and not letting motherhood interfere with their work. Women continue to recognize the impediments to earning power and professional accomplishments that caring for children presents, and some adapt by deferring or rejecting motherhood. But the problem remains that for many women, these approaches to attaining equality don't deal with the central issue, namely that caring for their children *matters* deeply to them.

What if we were to take this mattering seriously, to put it at the core of our exploration? Even to pose the question is to invite almost instant misconstrual. It's as if this would recommend to women to live through others, forsake equality, or relax into the joys of subsidized homemaking. But that reflexive misinterpretation is itself evidence of how difficult it is to think about maternal desire as a positive aspect of self. The problem is on view in the ways we talk about motherhood and work. Defenders of mothers' employment often begin by enumerating its benefits to children, families, and above all mothers themselves. Then they abruptly switch to the claim that mothers can't afford *not* to work, so we may as well spare ourselves the unnecessary pain and guilt of even examining its potentially troubling aspects. This rhetorical one-two punch appears designed to fend off a candid consideration of the whole complicated arena of mothers' competing desires, and especially the desire to care for their children. It is not the stay-at-home mother whom this evasion hurts most, but the working mother who longs to spend more time with her children. For her, the need for a frank, legitimizing public discussion of maternal desire is particularly acute.

I juxtapose "maternal" and "desire" to emphasize what we feel oddly uncomfortable focusing on: that wanting to care for children is a major feature of many women's lives. We often resist thinking through its implications because we fear becoming mired in clichés about woman's nature, which will then be used to restrict women's rights and freedoms. But if we resist thinking about maternal desire, or treat it as a marginal detail, we lose an opportunity to understand ourselves and the broader situation of women. To take maternal desire as a valid focus of personal exploration is not a step backward but a step forward, toward greater awareness and a truer model of the self.

THERE ARE MANY HISTORICAL REASONS why the desire to mother has rarely surfaced as a point of inquiry. For most of human history, women exercised relatively little choice about becoming mothers. "A woman can hardly ever choose," the novelist George Eliot, née Mary Ann Evans, wrote in 1866. "She must take meaner things, because only meaner things are within her reach."[2] In the nineteenth century, industrialization and urbanization irrevocably changed patterns of work and family. The work of production moved outside the home, and child rearing became mothers' dominant focus. This shift in maternal activity, prompted by economics, soon shaped standard ideology as well: raising her children was a good mother's sacred calling. If she wanted something different or something more, then something was surely wrong with her.

In the twentieth century, gender roles were transformed. Betty Friedan's 1963 call for women to become whole persons, actualizing themselves in public and private realms, catalyzed the expansion of opportunity that had begun earlier and spearheaded the feminist political movement that would begin dismantling gender discrimination. Although "glass ceilings" and insidious gender biases persist, educated women are omnipresent in the once male precincts of medicine, journalism, and law. Women at all class levels are out working, as sales reps, firefighters, and civil servants. Mothers work outside the home in record numbers.

Many would agree that the problems of access Friedan and

others decried — of admissions to schools, colleges, and corporations — have largely been redressed. Yet all the access in the world doesn't solve the difficulties that arise when women become mothers; for if a mother wants to spend time caring for her children, her relationship to work necessarily changes. In the 1960s and 1970s, spending time with children was viewed as a roadblock to pursuing personal aspirations. Today, women's successful integration into careers creates a roadblock to spending time with children. Regardless of the decade, it seems, "there is never a 'good' time to have a baby."[3]

In a 1999 *New York Times* piece, the feminist writer Naomi Wolf lamented the lack of political will among very bright college women. One Yale student was quoted as saying, "Women my age just have to accept that we can't have it all."[4] Wolf discerned in this young woman's attitude an apathy toward social change and an indifference to the history of women's hard-won struggles. Yet I suspect that if we delve more deeply into what young women like this one are saying, we will find a rather realistic appraisal of the ways that women's integration into the workplace has not managed to adequately address a fundamental concern. That concern is less whether one can squeeze procreation into one's life than how to be the *kind* of mother one wants to be.

The conservative critique of feminism has offered one perspective on the conflicts contemporary mothers face, questioning the benefits to mothers of egalitarian marriage, universal day care, and feminist-inspired ideals of self-actualization.[5] Too often, though, any useful observations they make are undercut by an urge to lay at feminism's door just about every problem women encounter. The French critic Roland Barthes decided to analyze contemporary mythologies because he "resented seeing Nature and History confused at every turn," prompting him to dissect the "ideological abuse" hidden behind the "decorative display of *what-goes-without-saying*."[6] Feminism's critics frequently settle for the "decorative display," the attractive but unfounded claim that nature is nature and always will be. They ignore the fact that feminism has inspired constructive changes in women's lives in areas that just a generation ago appeared as intractable "nature." Feminism, more than any other social force, has helped us question the view that our history *is* our nature.

At the same time, feminists concerned with the rights and opportunities of women can fail to appreciate the positive motivation — the authentic expression of self — that many women bring to the task of caring for their children. Some voice frustration at women's repeated "retreats" to the world of child rearing, seeing them as a personal or political regression. Others blame baby care experts who advocate spending time with children for trying to impose self-sacrifice on mothers.[7] These critics seem unwilling to apply their critical acumen to their own assumption that mothers *experience* caring for their children as self-sacrificing.

The view that caring for one's children amounts to self-sacrifice is a very tricky psychological point for women, and a confounding point for theory. It is confusing partly because the term "self-sacrifice" is potentially applicable to two different aspects of experience, the economic and the emotional. When it comes to their economic well-being, it is all too true that women sacrifice themselves when they become mothers. Time taken out of the workforce to nurture children, lost years accruing Social Security benefits, and a host of other economic factors result in unequivocal economic disadvantages to mothers. At the same time, from the point of view of emotional well-being, a mother often sees her desire to nurture her children as an intrinsically valuable impulse, and as an expression of what she subjectively experiences as her authentic self. This inconsistency presents contemporary women with one of the core paradoxes of their lives as mothers.

Considering for a moment the issue of self-sacrifice strictly from a psychological point of view, what is trickiest for women is the fact that some of what they find meaningful about mothering can be construed, from some vantage points, as self-abnegating. There are moments in the day-to-day life of every mother when the deferral of her own gratifications or aims is experienced as oppressive. But a narrow focus on such moments and the belief that they adequately capture, or stand for, the whole experience of mothering fail to appreciate the overall context in which those deferrals take place. When she relinquishes control over her time, forgoes the satisfaction of an impulse, or surrenders to playful engagement with her child even as she feels driven to "accomplish something," the surface quality of capitulation in these decisions belies their role in satisfying her deeper motives and goals. These deeper goals have to do, ultimately, with the creation of meaning. In the seemingly mundane give-and-take of parenting — playing, sharing, connecting, relaxing, enduring boredom, getting mad, cajoling, compromising, and sacrificing — a mother communicates with her child about something no less momentous than what is valuable in life, and about the possibilities and limits of intimate relationships.

This process can be one of extraordinary pleasure. There is the sensual, physical pleasure of caring for small children; the satisfaction of spending most of our waking hours (and some of our sleeping hours) with the people we love the most, taking care of their needs; the delight in being able to make our child happy and in being made happy by our child. There is the pleasure of being "alone together," of doing things near one another, feeling comforted by the presence of the other while attending to our own activities. There are also the enormous gratifications of watching children develop, grow, and change, and of being involved in the people they become.

Devoting time to caring for children is not, of course, all about pleasure and good feeling. It is also grounded in a sense of meaning, morality, even aesthetics. The choice to do so can express, for example, a value about time, having to do with the desire to create an atmosphere where time is not a scarce commodity and children's sense of time has a place. It can express an ideal about service, to one's immediate community and to a range of broader ethical and political goods associated with raising children well.

It can express a value about relationships. Managing one's rage, quelling one's desire to walk out the door on squalling children and dirty dishes, and feeling one is going to faint of boredom at the sheer repetitiveness of it all and yet continuing anyway are some of the real emotional and moral quandaries that caring for children routinely presents. Many mothers believe, for all their daily struggles with irritation and fatigue, that there is something intrinsically meaningful about managing and overcoming those states in the process of caring for one's children.

When the activities of mothering *are* interpreted as self-limiting, they tend to be treated dismissively. In Susan Faludi's book *Backlash*, the value of mothers spending time raising their children is articulated either by right-wing ideologues who are trying to suppress women's freedom and equality or by disaffected feminists lapsing into a defeated sentimentality.[8] Author Myriam Miedzian comments that life at home with children amounts to "shining floors and wiping noses."[9] Time with children is often framed in feminist analyses as a form of drudgery unfairly allotted to women, remediable through shared parenting or better day care. It is as if the day-to-day practice of mothering places unreasonable or unjust demands on mothers and is part of the oppression of women's gender-based role. Yet in an era of unparalleled choice for women, spending time caring for children cannot be glibly interpreted as a deficiency or inhibition.

One of the goals of feminism in the last twenty-five years has been to dismantle the ideal of the all-giving, self-sacrificing mother, an ideal with which previous generations of mothers did battle. But we can better understand the situation of mothers today if we don't view this image of the mother as an eternal ideal, because, in fact, for the current generation of mothers, the ideal has shifted. More recently, the ideal of the supermom has been by far the more vivid and immediate. This cultural ideal pressures mothers to perform excellently on all fronts, in a job, with their children, with their partner, at the gym, and in the kitchen, making those fifteen-minute meals.

The supermom ideal plays into people's fantasies that if they work hard enough to get everything "right," they will not lose anything, that nothing will have to be sacrificed. What we had in the previous ideal was a woman who lost herself to her children and her mothering. What we have in the supermom ideal is a woman who loses nothing. But in fact, the problem with trying to do everything is that it changes radically your perception of the time you have. Anyone who has tried to "fit everything in" can attest to how excruciating the five-minute wait at the supermarket checkout line becomes, let alone a child's slow-motion attempt to tie her own shoes when you're running late getting her to preschool.

Most women today are not struggling to break out of the ideal that instructed them to sacrifice everything for their children. They are more likely beset with the quandary of how to break out of the "do everything" model so that they will have more relaxed time for their relationships. Whereas the past ideal may have hindered women's search for autonomy and self-determination in the wider world, the current ideal makes it harder to express their desire to care for their children.

It may be the supermom ideal that Naomi Wolf's seemingly apolitical college women are rejecting when they say they can't "have it all." These young women may intuit, well before their mothering years, that life may require them to make a conscious and planned departure from the "do everything" model that preoccupied the generation of women that preceded them.

HUGE SHIFTS IN WOMEN'S LIVES — brought on by the availability of birth control, educational and economic access, and the possibility of diverse life choices — have finally created the potential for mothering to be a chosen activity in ways unimaginable for the vast majority of women throughout history and still in many parts of the world today. At the same time, the proliferation of choices presents new challenges, as it creates expanded arenas for conflict, indecision, and doubt.

In trying to understand our conflicting goals and desires from the inside, we might begin with that science of desire, psychoanalysis. The psychoanalytic method is a powerful means for understanding the desires women bring to mothering. It is, after all, a method designed to elucidate what we feel and what we hide from ourselves. It reveals to us that our desires, motives, and beliefs never have a single fixed meaning, and that they are not always what they announce themselves to be. Listening to patients in the clinical consulting room discloses the obvious fact that every woman brings to mothering her own personal history, temperament, and sense of herself. For any given woman, the desire to mother can be a heartfelt longing, a fantasy, an excuse, something to be denied — or all of the above, at different times. One woman extols the value of being an extremely attentive mother. She worries that if she doesn't make her kids' sandwiches every day and watch all their sports games, she's a bad mom. Meanwhile, her own work as a graphic designer languishes. At this time in her life, her notion of being a good mother keeps her from expressing other important aspects of herself. Another woman has little time to attend to her children's daily routines and takes pride in raising children who are as self-reliant as she is. For her, finding the time to help her children constitutes a healing liberation from her own exacting standard of self-sufficiency. Each of these mothers seeks a greater sense of vitality and meaning, but they differ in where they started and where they are going.

The personal meanings of mothering are endlessly complex, and the particular conflicts vary from person to person. Yet it seems that today, a mother's desire to care for her children is the side of the conflict that gets the most simplistic public airing, even by its partisans, and the side that mainstream feminism has done the least to support. Consequently, it is not uncommon for mothers to have a hard time seeing how their desire to care for their children is playing a role in their dilemmas.

For example, a thirty-five-year-old professional woman who was employed full-time dwelled on the potential inadequacy of her child care arrangement, worrying that her ten-month-old was unhappy, even though she could not think of any specific reason for concern. She attained greater clarity when she realized that the real issue was that she was *missing* her baby, and her sense of anxiety over child care then gave way to a more intelligible sense of yearning. It was hard to become aware of missing her baby, because she had operated with the assumption that if the baby was all right while she was away, she would — or should — feel all right about being away too.[10]

For this person, it took psychotherapy to make her aware that she was missing her child; but her quandary points to a more general cultural phenomenon. In the current milieu, women rarely perceive their desire to care for their children as intellectually respectable, and that makes it less emotionally intelligible as well. On a broader social level, mothers' need and desire to work and its importance to their self-sufficiency and self-expression get a strong public hearing, but mothers' needs and desires with respect to nurturing their children receive comparatively little serious discussion. Maternal desire tends to be treated as background noise or unspoken assumption rather than as something explicit, valuable, and important to include as an issue relevant to women's lives.

Our national discussion of child care, for example, understandably focuses on the reality that most parents need to work. Because the discussion appears to deal with an immutable fact of life, it is sometimes viewed as impractical, even elitist, to raise questions concerning the *feelings* of the parents and children involved. But progressive calls for universal affordable day care ignore a jumble of inconvenient emotions, including parents' desire to take care of their own children. Many mothers feel torn up inside being apart from their babies and children many hours a day, yet they feel realistic or mature when they are able to suppress those feelings. The terms of the discussion don't admit the possibility that pleasure is a reliable guide, or that desire tells us anything about truth.

Developmental psychology is one domain that studies the impact of pleasure on human growth. In the past two decades, it has undertaken an increasingly nuanced investigation of mother-child interaction, revealing the central role of shared emotional states and shared pleasure in healthy human development.[11] The research on mother-infant interaction teaches us about the making of mutual meaning, and about the roots of emotional complexity and richness. Yet, for the most part, these findings remain marginal to our public debates about day care. Their perceived irrelevance hints at our difficulty in making the *mutual* parent-child relationship a focal point in our reflections on child care.

The importance of the mutual parent-child relationship and a mother's desire to participate in that relationship are masked by the rhetoric of children's "needs." When exasperated callers to talk-radio shows insist on children's "need" to be taken care of by their parents, they are making a statement not primarily about facts, but, rather, about values. Children are not all alike; one two-year-old may happily trot into day care while another desperately protests. Children survive, and some even thrive, in a range of circumstances, including circumstances they wouldn't choose for themselves if given a say in the matter. The emphasis on children's "needs" represents an attempt to create a socially sanctioned arena for children's "wants" and what we want for them. In a sense, "needs" are a post-Freudian way to talk about values, a way to demarcate and honor those things we consider of greatest importance to human well-being.

The oft-heard question about day care — "Does day care hurt children?" — turns children into the repository of our *mutual* desire for human connection. If the studies show that children do fine in day care, we independent adults are supposed to go about our business without remorse. On this view, mothers' feelings simply aren't relevant; the only issue is day care's effects on children. But what is good for parents and what is good for children are equally relevant in a moral evaluation of day care. And adults' desire to nurture their children is much more passionate and complex than the opposition of dependent child and independent adult would have us believe.

■   ■   ■

MOTHERHOOD CALLS FOR A TRANSFORMED individuality, an integration of a new relationship and a new role into one's sense of self. This is a practical *and* a psychological transformation. It is screamingly evident that as a society we are grudging and cramped about the practical adjustments required by motherhood, continually treating them as incidental and inconvenient. Like an irritated bus passenger who is asked to move over and make room, we appear affronted by the sheer existence of mothers' needs. The disheartening, thorough analyses of this problem by feminist economists cannot be improved upon and are there for all to read.[12]

But these practical difficulties, not to mention the views that underlie them, also have far-reaching *psychological* implications. They affect how we appraise and experience the whole issue of inner maternal transformation, the "space" we will allow motherhood to occupy in our psyches. If everything around us seems designed to obstruct our integrating the full force of our maternal devotion into a life responsive to our prior commitments, our outlook and values about what we should "do" with our maternal desire can come to be subtly shaped.

This conflict is not lost on young women. Naomi Wolf's Yale student's "we can't have it all" response reflects one resolution among many to a question that confronts virtually every young woman at some point or another: namely, how she will integrate her maternal potential into her mature identity. The first stirrings of this question accompany a girl's sexual development in adolescence, for that is when she not only becomes capable of sexual and maternal expression but also meets up with cultural norms and ideals of successful adulthood. Cultural ideals about control, in particular, resonate with girls' psychological need for self-control at this stage, with both constructive and problematic effects. On the one hand, educated and upwardly mobile girls in contemporary society face a decade, perhaps two or even three, between their sexual maturation and childbearing, a span that gives them enormous opportunity for self-development and self-definition. Contemporary female adolescence is a time when a girl can optimally find a balanced perspective on the issue of self-control, one that will help her arrive at an integrated sense of herself as an individual woman and potential mother.

On the other hand, in our culture the very idea of control is laden with gender implications. Control, conceived as an aspect of adult autonomy, is at odds with our image of motherhood. The whole arena of pregnancy, childbirth, and the daily activities of mothering involve decreased personal control, and loss of control is among the cultural and personal anxieties that maternal desire raises. For some young women struggling toward a sense of identity, it is not surprising that motherhood comes to symbolize everything antithetical to the independent life they want to pursue. And the pressure on women to aspire to a certain model of control as a signature of adulthood is one of the social factors that can riddle maternal wishes with conflict.

It is true that the satisfying, somewhat predictable march of "progress" in one's life without children is replaced, when children arrive, by a messier, more ambiguous process of "becoming." In this sense, motherhood can seem an agitating distraction, even a threatening derailment. Yet the sense that motherhood robs us of individuality derives part of its power from a cultural definition of individuality that pits the "serving the species" script of procreation against the notion of giving birth to oneself. This definition asserts itself in adolescence, when girls observe the difficulty in integrating the desire to mother with the idea of a work life. It rears its head at the end of college, when it can be an embarrassment to admit that one would like children sooner rather than later. When women move into the workforce, they observe the correlation of motherhood with a loss of power, pay, and prestige. External conditions resonate with internal anxieties, making it difficult for many women to evaluate their own desires with respect to mothering.

The prevailing notion that motherhood and individuality are in pitched conflict may also play into what some women writers have described as their obliviousness to mothers and babies before they began considering motherhood themselves.[13] In the old days, women lived out their years in dense webs of female relationships, presiding together over birth, nurture, and death; women couldn't avoid children even if they tried.[14] But today, smaller families and freedom in charting our own course mean that women can choose to live in relative isolation from children. There are plenty of women, of course, who simply aren't interested in children, for a host of reasons. A friend spent her youth raising her siblings; she'd seen all the "becoming" she could take and was liberated by the prospect of living her own life. Yet, I detect in the obliviousness described in these writings neither a simple response to changed social realities nor a lack of interest in motherhood, but rather a motivated sense that preserving one's selfhood depends on shutting out an interest in children. That outlook can foster a kind of self-development, but it can also contribute to a deferral of childbearing that later, if it contributes to infertility, can be tinged with almost unbearable regret.

The incompatibility between motherhood and individuality has perhaps nowhere been more reflexively presumed than in the pro-choice rhetoric surrounding the issue of abortion. There, it has been perceived as dangerous to emphasize either the moral ambiguity of abortion or women's desire to mother, for fear of fueling a politically regressive view of women's place. The resulting approach has been to frame the issue almost solely in terms of a woman's right to govern her own body. But for many women, including many proponents of reproductive choice, the wrenching ambiguity of abortion has to do with how difficult it is to place in clear opposition one's interests as an individual and as a potential mother, or one's interests and a potential child's interests. Their intuition is closer to that which Gwendolyn Brooks captured in her poem about abortion, "the mother": "oh, what shall I say, how is the truth to be said?/You were born, you had body, you died./It is just that you never giggled or planned or cried./Believe me, I loved you all./Believe me, I knew you, though faintly, and I loved, I loved you /All."[15]

The tension between motherhood and individuality also surfaces in the seeming split screen between our cultural fascination with babies and the less articulated desire to care for them. Just as there are thousands of falling-in-love stories but many fewer tales of slogging to make a marriage work, there are countless media images of the miracle of pregnancy or the adorableness of babies but little that represents the day-to-day care of children. Perhaps it was ever thus. History provides a wealth of examples, from Cleopatra onward, of women who birthed babies, delegated caregiving, and emerged with their freedom of movement intact. And certainly from a psychological point of view, the desire to have a child and the desire to care for that child may coexist in the same person, but they are not the same thing. One woman captured the difference when she said, "My mother thinks I should try to spend more time with the children I already have, but I can't get the idea of having another one out of my mind."

Still, it is striking how the desire to have a child is today the object of such intense focus and, increasingly, extraordinary measures, whereas the desire to care for children is singularly unriveting, even a bit déclassé. A woman may believe that caring for children will express, rather than compromise, her individuality or her valued goals, but she regularly meets up with social and economic incentives that pull her in a different direction. In the course of educated young women's lives, for instance, it is usual to acquire training and jobs before children. A couple marries, both members work, and without giving it much thought, they develop a lifestyle predicated on two salaries. When they have a child, the mother may find that as her maternity leave draws to a close, she isn't itching to get back to work. Instead, she yearns to be with her child. Her change of heart presents the couple with the need to rethink their relationship and their decisions about lifestyle and money. They may conclude that it is going "backward" to give up one salary; and anyway, decisions made on the basis of two salaries, like buying a house, cannot be easily reversed. Rueful acceptance overrides her yearning: spending time caring for their children is a "luxury" they can't afford. Suddenly, like so many things in American life — health care, good schools, fresh air — motherhood has turned into something of a luxury. You have time for it only if you are very lucky.

Margaret, a lawyer, left a rewarding job at forty to stay home with her second son. She had worked fifty hours per week during her first son's infancy. Wisecracking by nature, she is uncharacteristically solemn when discussing her decisions:

> I'll never get over the regret I feel at missing my first child's babyhood. What amazes me still — you'd think I'd get over it — is how completely taken off guard I was by wanting to be with him. Before you have kids, you have the almost swaggering attitude that you won't fall into the mommy trap. You don't believe that once you're there, you'll genuinely *want* to be with your kids. Now whenever I'm in a position to counsel younger associates, I tell them, "Set up your marriage, finances and domestic life so that they don't depend on your continued wage earning, because hard as it is to imagine, once you have kids, you may not want to do what you're doing anymore."

Today's young women face a different social landscape from that of women a generation ago, and thanks to the struggle of the women who preceded them, they can take for granted access to work and public attention on work-family balance. The softening of rigid trade-offs has given younger women more latitude in assessing for themselves the relative satisfactions of work and family. To some older women, this can look like a regression to nonfeminist values. For others, it can lead to reflection on the choices they made and the social climate in which they made them. Elisa, a therapist with a college-age child, recounted that when she was a young mother, she left her child to go back to work with great sadness and trepidation, but she felt sure that it was the progressive thing to do. She and her friends "were looking at our own mothers as frustrated and depressed, and we had a clear sense of the importance of learning from their situation and making a life for ourselves. Now I look back with an incredible sense of longing; but I can't say I would do it differently, because that is who I was." Intergenerational discussions, potentially difficult as they are, can offer a rich opportunity for reflection to women at all stages of life.

I HAVE BEEN ARGUING THAT we do not know how to think about the desire to mother. We have trouble understanding it — within ourselves, in terms of our psychological and feminist theories, and in the public debates and institutions that structure our lives. The critical issue that has eluded theory and social debate is that caring for young children is something mothers often view as extraordinarily important both for their children *and* for themselves.

Reframing the mothering role in this way calls into question a number of views that hang in the cultural air. We are all familiar with these views: mothering is a sacrifice of the mother for the sake of the child; mothering will not be valued until it is paid work; careers enhance personal growth, while caring for children breeds stagnation; children disrupt, rather than foster, the realization of individual goals. Such views contribute to the emphasis some mothers place on "returning to normal" after children are born. They may also help to explain the surprise some women feel when they realize how much they want to spend time caring for their children.

In the popular American mind-set, there's always a second chance. So it comes as a shock to realize how fast children grow up, and how quickly they no longer crave your company or respond to your influence in the ways they once did. The time-limited nature of mothering small children, the very uniqueness of it, itself seems almost like an affront to women's opportunity, demanding as it does that mothers respond at a distinct, unrepeatable moment with decisions, often radical ones, about how to spend their time. Unfair as it may seem, the fleetingness is real. In that light, the fact that childbearing absorbs but a small portion of women's adult life span — often seen as a reason to "stay on track" — should point us toward prizing this brief period of our lives, and not just on a personal or individual level; as a culture, we need to express our recognition of its value through our laws, our policies concerning work and family, and our theories of psychological development.

Caring for one's children at home is sometimes dismissed as a choice open only to privileged women. But in fact, mothers at all socioeconomic levels face difficult decisions regarding the time they spend with their children. Moreover, the devaluation of mothering operates at various levels of social and economic reality and in many intersecting ways. If we open our eyes to the commonalities in mothers' experience, we might begin to develop some political consciousness, even solidarity, about the larger-scale problems that the devaluation of mothering inflicts upon everyone. It should not be acceptable to any of us, for instance, when politicians maintain both that middle-class children need their mothers at home and that welfare mothers should be joining the workforce when their children are four months old.

Economic necessity is always a fact of life, and economic privation affects those who suffer from it in every sphere of their lives. The mothers least likely to find fulfillment in their low-wage jobs are also those least likely to have time to enjoy being with their children. This group of mothers and children suffer a disproportionate negative burden. But for those people with some choice, an emphasis on economic necessity can itself be used to obscure the realm of feelings on which wise and satisfying choices draw. No one can banish economic need; but being aware of how we feel about time apart from our children, and being attuned to our children's feelings about it, are central to clarifying our priorities.

Why is this a book about mothers? Because caring for small children is compellingly central to many women's sense of themselves to a degree still not experienced by many men. If current research is correct, this may be changing, as more men place value on family time. From custody rights to employer policies, fathers are increasingly questioning the givens that have framed men's life courses in the past.[16] But for the moment, the care of children remains a predominantly female occupation. Some argue that this is a problem in need of correction — that true equality of the sexes cannot be achieved until child rearing and work responsibilities are equally shared. But whatever position one takes on this matter, and whatever one's social ideal for the division of labor, the idea that equality between men and women — or fairness between any two partners — can come about *only* through similar life courses and a parallel allocation of labor may constitute an abstraction by which few people actually want to live.

We need to speak accurately about the character of maternal desire, resisting its caricature either as sentimental false consciousness or woman's nature. Teasing apart the psychological and ideological strands of maternal desire can help individual women consider its role in their lives and make choices based on a conscious awareness of their own conflicts and wishes.[17] Maternal desire is not, for any woman, all there is. But for many of us, it is an important part of who we are. And among such women, it is time to start a conversation.

2

Feminism

EVERY WOMAN'S FEMINISM IS A love letter to her mother. "For my mother" is the most usual dedication at the start of a feminist book.[1] Each author offers, among other things, her own reading of her mother's life, and if the book is about motherhood, it grapples with her mother's choices and constraints in light of the author's own. This effort takes as many forms as there are feminists. For some, it is about defining oneself in contrast to one's mother. "As much as I loved my mom," writes the journalist Peggy Orenstein in *Flux*, "I knew I didn't want to be like her."[2] For others, it involves taking the measure of their mother's thwarting at the hands of male power, as Adrienne Rich does in *Of Woman Born*. For still others, there is the impulse to repair and redeem the limits of one's mother's life through achievement in one's own, as Betty Friedan poignantly described in *The Feminine Mystique*.[3] Even when a book grieves a mother's absence or betrayal, it is often a cry of pain about what could have been, were it not for the mother's own suffering in a sexist world.[4]

Whatever else feminist discussions about motherhood may be, they are passionate. The disagreements about children and work, the appropriate role of day care, and the needs of mothers, children, and families are not just glib debates or surface differences. They cut to the core of our values and the human purposes we hold dear. And because our ideas arise in the emotional atmosphere of family, from the wordless observations and lessons we take from our closest kin, we often experience our convictions as unformulated ("I don't know how I know it, I just do"). They can feel as close as our breath.

When feelings run deep, as they do about mothers and motherhood, the temptation to make extreme statements is high. Strong emotions have the singular capacity to polarize our thinking, to make us see the world in black and white. Motherhood is a raw, tender point of identity, and its relationship to other aspects of ourselves — our other aspirations, our need to work, our need for solitude — almost inevitably involves a tension. It is hard to sit with that tension, which is one reason discussions of motherhood tend toward a split view of the world.

Where we side depends on what we see as the most essential threat. For those working for gender equality over the past forty years, an enduring concern has been that women will be marched back home, restricting the exercise of their talents and their full participation in political and economic life. Efforts to mobilize public opinion against that regressive alternative have at times oversimplified women's desire to mother and assigned it to a generally backward-looking, sentimental view of women's place. When taken to the extreme, the argument suggests that women's care for their children, the time spent as well as the emotions aroused, is foisted on them by purely external economic and ideological forces. Locating the sources of the desire to mother "out there" may temporarily banish the conflict, but ultimately it backfires, alienating women who feel it does not take into account, or help them to attain, their own valued maternal goals.

For those who identify most strongly with their role as mother, the greatest threat has been that caring for children and the honorable motivations behind it will be minimized and misunderstood, becoming one more source of women's devaluation. Such women feel they suffer not at the hands of traditionalist ideology but rather from the general social devaluation of caregiving, a devaluation with economic and psychological effects.[5] At times, proponents of this position insist on the essential differences between the sexes and the sanctity of conservative-defined "family values." Such views end up alienating both women who question such prescriptive generalizations and those who feel their own sense of self or their aspirations are not reflected by them.[6]

Most of us feel ill at ease at either pole of this debate, because though the poles represent opposing positions, they both flatten the complexity of mothers' own desires. At the extremes, neither offers a way out of a stale and stubborn dichotomy: either mothers don't need (or shouldn't have) to spend their time caring for children, or mothers don't need (or shouldn't have) to pursue other goals and interests. The challenge instead is to formulate a way of thinking about the self that does justice to mothers' *range* of goals. And the particular facet of that challenge that concerns me is understanding mothers' desire to care for their children as a feature of their self-development and self-expression, rather than as its negation.

In my investigation, feminism has not always helped me. How many times I have encountered a feminist book filled with innovative ideas for changed gender relations, the acceptance of whose argument requires just one small price: that I relinquish my attachment to spending time caring for my children. The argument elucidates how that attachment compromises my bargaining position in marriage and in work; or it anatomizes the origins of that attachment in social ideology, the better to dispel it; or it intimates that in clinging to this attachment, I shirk painful psychological and political growth and prove myself less than rational or less than just. At that moment, I am struck with the feeling that the author and I inhabit truly different emotional worlds. What seems like a rational, sane, and humane solution to her seems like a Faustian bargain to me. The desire to care for children, which she sees as something of a detail or correctable condition, I see as the core issue that psychology and feminism needs to explore.

Feminism has understandably focused on loosening the grip of women's conventionally defined roles, working to secure the right *not* to have children (birth control, abortion) and the choice *not* to stay home caring for them (universal day care). But if feminism's broadest goal is to address problems that affect women as a class, to free them from unjust incursions into their bodies and psyches, and to lift restrictions on their opportunity, then there is every reason that mothers' desire to care for their children and the political mechanisms to help them attain that goal should also be on the feminist agenda.

In our effort to complete the feminist project by including maternal desire, the tried-and-true feminist adage "the personal is political" comes to our aid, suggesting that we take our ordinary experience as a starting point for questioning the culture. An ordinary experience in the lives of many women is the desire to care for children. To come to a useful understanding of our own needs and desires, and the cultural and historical forms that interpret, structure, and limit them, we must think through received ideas in light of our personal experience. We can begin that project by looking at some classic feminist stances on motherhood.

Foremothers

SIMONE DE BEAUVOIR's *The Second Sex*, the sprawling, exhilarating, and indispensable founding text of feminism's second wave, owes its enduring fascination not only to its analysis of women's condition but also to its relation to de Beauvoir's own life. De Beauvoir's choices emblematized one solution to the "problem" of being a woman: by evading all the traps associated with being a woman — financial dependence, marriage, children — one could effectively negate one's oppression as a woman. Observing de Beauvoir herself, many took *The Second Sex*'s main message to be that refusing traditional feminine roles was a prerequisite for "masculine" achievement. The seventies paperback edition of *The Second Sex* bears the almost quaint subtitle "The classic manifesto of the liberated woman"; and indeed, de Beauvoir's way of uniting art and life held particular power for women questioning the apparent givens of female existence.[7]

The impact of de Beauvoir's life on the interpretation of her work was nowhere more powerful than in the arena of motherhood. As the literary critic Alice Jardine wrote, de Beauvoir "provided what has remained, in spite of everything, *the* feminist myth: the baby *versus* the book. . . . In the classical feminist economy, you cannot have them both; you cannot have it all."[8] On careful reading, we see that de Beauvoir argues that women can authentically and freely choose motherhood;[9] but her most vivid descriptions paint a bleak picture of the mother's sacrifice of her individuality and freedom, and the inevitable limits of the mother-child bond. The child, for his part, is "an existence as mysterious as that of an animal, as turbulent and disorderly as natural forces, and yet human."[10] In the relation of mother and child there is "no reciprocity; the mother has to do not with a man, a hero, a demigod, but with a small, prattling soul, lost in a fragile and dependent body. The child is in possession of no values, he can bestow none, with him the woman remains alone."[11] When a mother finds pleasure with her child, it is because "being more or less infantile herself, she is very well pleased to be silly along with him."[12] The mother's satisfactions come across as little more than the titillation of her body and her narcissism, or the indulgence of her possessiveness; her frustrations, ascribed largely to her oppressed social condition, are rarely recognized as the inevitable — and often growth-inducing — byproducts of the messy business of human relationships.

For de Beauvoir, pregnancy is perhaps the paradigmatic instance of women's consignment to the status of object. Of the prospective mother, she writes: "The transcendence of the artisan, of the man of action, contains the element of subjectivity; but in the mother-to-be the antithesis of subject and object ceases to exist; she and the child with which she is swollen make up together an equivocal pair overwhelmed by life . . . she is a human being, a conscious and free individual, who has become life's passive instrument."[13] Sounding the opening notes of a refrain that will haunt subsequent feminist analyses of motherhood, this passage imagines motherhood engulfing a woman, drowning her individuality in the force of life. A woman's will is rendered precarious by motherhood because it pits her individual interests against those of the species. And in contrast to men, because of her life-giving functions and their bodily impositions, she is more vulnerable to a sense of herself as "done to" rather than "doing."

It is true, obviously, that childbearing and child care impose certain restrictions on mothers' free movement and that they can be, and have been, exploited by the larger society to deprive women of opportunities or power. And it is also true that the "drowning" of which de Beauvoir speaks portrays certain transitory emotional states experienced by some mothers; as in lust or illness, the body imposes itself peremptorily in pregnancy, a physical fact with which pregnant women must psychologically cope. But the problem with de Beauvoir's view, as well as the general feminist conversation that followed, is that it dwells almost exclusively on the limits this situation places on women — existential, political, economic, psychological — to the exclusion of its opportunities. These opportunities involve, above all, a new and different understanding of ourselves and our relationship to others.[14]

In an important sense, our difficulty in speaking about the subjectivity of mothers begins with this imagery of engulfment and merger, and its acceptance as a concrete reality rather than as a fundamentally psychological experience. Perhaps in the late 1940s, when *The Second Sex* was published, the constraints on women's reproductive freedom were still so vast and strict that it was hard to disentangle passivity and lack of choice from motherhood itself. But later, filtered through the heated climate of 1960s and 1970s feminist opinion, de Beauvoir's vision fed a sense that only through escaping the burdens of child tending could a woman hope to fulfill herself. For women like my friend's mother, who felt held back by motherhood, refusing to cook dinner for her children became a feminist act.

In contrast to de Beauvoir's lustrous philosophical distance, Betty Friedan's *The Feminine Mystique,* published fewer than fifteen years later, was a report from the trenches of marriage and motherhood. Starting from the assumption that "love and children and home are good,"[15] Friedan's quarrel was not with women's desire to marry or mother, but rather with the ideology that conferred upon these feminine achievements a mystical worth at the expense of women's vital participation in the larger culture. She particularly lamented the stretch of years after their children were launched, when mothers were expected to "try to make housework 'something more'" rather than using their potential to make a difference in the world. "Why," Friedan asked, echoing de Beauvoir, "should women accept this picture of a half-life, instead of a share in the whole of human destiny?"[16]

Friedan's book has been widely read and remains relevant because it offers a humane view of the needs and desires of many women — both for children and for vital participation in the larger community. Critics have decried as narrow in scope its focus on the mainstream American woman of the time — a white middle-class mother married to a wage earner but not one herself.[17] Despite that, Friedan's analysis remains surprisingly fresh partly due to her understanding of the internal struggles and choices of women as universal human dilemmas.

But Friedan's analysis was limited by her unquestioning acceptance of the values of the prevailing culture with respect to achievement.[18] For work to provide a sound basis for a woman's identity, Friedan argued, it needed to be "work that is of real value to society — work for which, usually, our society pays."[19] "Real accomplishment" is "achievement that has meaning to the culture," and motherhood's low standing hampered its ability to provide the psychological rewards gained from socially valued work. Friedan did not attempt to shift the framework to one where the activities of mothers were revalued on their own terms. While her view offered a galvanizing rhetoric to her audience in the mid-sixties, men and women, scholars and lay-people alike have become more skeptical of the definition of achievement that Friedan accepted so uncritically. Mothers to-day wonder whether what the culture rewards as "real accomplishment" is likely to satisfy their most valued goals. This question is not posed only by conservatives. During his 2000 presidential bid, Ralph Nader asked, "Who's standing up for a type of economy that allows one breadwinner to have a middle-class standard of living for the family?"[20] And the sociologist Sharon Hays found that mothers she interviewed saw their decision to stay home to care for their children rather than work outside the home as a moral choice involving the rejection of the impersonal values of the marketplace in favor of "lasting human connection."[21]

It was Adrienne Rich who took the crucial step of teasing apart the pleasures offered by mothering and its oppressive aspects. In her unsparing opus *Of Woman Born*, Rich distinguished between motherhood as an experience — an embodied field of relating between persons — and as an institution, which forced mothering practices into a strict mold designed to serve the interests of men. She argued that full-time motherhood in relative isolation was created and maintained by patriarchal priorities to the psychological, economic, and intellectual detriment of women.

The power of Rich's vision was that, by dividing the experience of mothering into the patriarchal overlay of oppressive ideas and the raw female potential for experience, she created a place for maternal passion. Her poignant account of a Vermont summer spent alone with her sons shows Rich at her most free to experience maternal pleasure.[22] Yet, within this division of patriarchal oppression and maternal expressivity also lay a problem. If, in Rich's view, the difficulties of motherhood were due to the effects of patriarchy, then what children — particularly daughters — need is for their mothers to stand up to patriarchy, to have the courage of their own convictions and desires. When mothers do not do this, according to Rich, it is the source of girls' greatest sense of woundedness and betrayal.

By emphasizing the daughter's need for her mother as a role model of resistance, Rich was able to align the mother's most important function with the most urgent political stance she could take toward society. It permitted Rich to demonstrate, among other things, that a poor or oppressed mother's fight for the sheer survival of her family through long hours of paid work away from her children was a positive expression of mother love, not simply an absence. But the problem in Rich's emphasis on the mother as a model of resistance is that emotional relationships, and especially the early needs of the developing child, rarely cooperate with political categories.

In other words, Rich does not flesh out fully what the little girl, or any child, might need prior to her needing her mother as a role model in the world. What if those needs depend on her mother's presence, and particularly her mother's delight at being present — her mother's desire to be, and love of being, *with* her? And more, what if a daughter needs her mother to honor what she cares about — even something as politically suspect as her barrettes or her Barbies — to feel recognized, valued, and loved? To acknowledge the importance of this kind of gratification to a young daughter's feeling of being loved creates complications, as it requires a deeper questioning of how a mother can exercise autonomy, choice, and political resistance while at the same time being truly responsive to her child.[23]

This difficulty in Rich's work brings to the surface a fundamental maternal paradox. She writes: "Women's lives — in all levels of society — have been lived too long in both depression and fantasy, while our active energies have been trained and absorbed into caring for others."[24] And yet, the energies trained and absorbed into caring for others are also the sources of the "trust and tenderness" that Rich affirms we need most "deeply and primally" from our mothers.[25] Rich thus recognizes the love that children need from us, even as she identifies what giving that love costs women. Posing the conflict this way raises a number of perplexing questions: Is action in the world — political, economic, and artistic action — of a fundamentally different character from action whose goal is the care of intimate others? Are our active energies rendered passive simply because they are directed at caring for others? Is there something about the care of others that is hard to conceptualize as a self-chosen, goal-directed activity, making it more conducive to states of depression and fantasy? And how might this vary among individual mothers?

These are questions that all of us deal with somehow or another, and the personal sense we make of them affects how we think about what our children need from us — economic support, emotional care, and moral and practical guidance — in relation to our own goals. But it seems to me that, despite the titanic changes in middle-class women's lives that Rich, Friedan, and de Beauvoir helped bring about, the basic conflict as they articulated it — between a woman's autonomous human goals and her motherhood — remains largely unquestioned in the ongoing feminist conversation. Further, the conflict continues to be routinely, reflexively discussed, as if the only issue were how to find a way for women to do less caring for children. Within that framework, it remains difficult to think about the possibility that mothers have experienced themselves vividly, even within the strictures of patriarchal society, as makers of meaning, sometimes more in their mothering than in other spheres of their life. Or, that mothering might be experienced as a goal-directed activity, as an accomplishment and contribution, at times even more than paid work. Or, that it might be in the act of the emotional responsiveness, the personal sharing of worlds called for by mothering, that mothers feel most alive, most authentic, and derive the most pleasure — *and* experience the most opposition to prevailing social values. To understand more about why these alternatives have been hard to find, we need to look more closely at some of the interpretations of motherhood that have grown out of feminism's second wave.

Feminist History of
Middle-Class Mothers:
Critiquing the Angel
in the House

I TALKED TO A GRADUATE student once who described to me her thesis on women's sexuality, a sophisticated analysis of the subtle interplay of psychological and social forces in women's perceptions of their own agency and desire. But when we began to talk about motherhood, she promptly recited a series of platitudes condemning it as a mind-numbing, self-sacrificing trap. It struck me that despite the ever-increasing diversity of writings on motherhood, belief in the inherent contradiction between motherhood and self-determination remained alive and well. And even for a woman who prized careful thinking, it appeared acceptable, in the case of motherhood, to hold an extraordinarily simplistic opinion. Her response made me curious about how it is that certain stubborn assumptions about the profound incompatibility of motherhood and selfhood continue to resurface, even when social conditions have vastly changed and scholarship is increasingly devoted to studying motherhood's complexity.

One place this shows up is in the divergence between research on the historical development of women's roles and the uses to which it is put by popular feminism. The past few decades have seen an extraordinary flowering of feminist historical scholarship devoted to understanding the lives of nineteenth-century middle-class American women and to tracing the emergence of a concept of domesticity that continues to influence us today. The Industrial Revolution in the early 1800s — of which the authors Barbara Ehrenreich and Deirdre English said that "'revolution' is too pallid a word"[26] — transformed the social conditions and dominant ideas that governed ordinary people's lives. Rapid economic growth, urbanization, a shift from subsistence to commercial farming, the replacement of home-based with factory production, not to mention developments in politics, education, and religion, all wrought profound changes in family life and the lives of women.[27] For married women and mothers in particular, daily life came to revolve less around the production of goods such as food, cloth, and soap, and focused more on the care of children and the upkeep of the home. Married men increasingly assumed the role of provider by making their way in the "cold world" of the capitalist economy. Out of these changes arose a new ideology of domesticity, which idealized women's domestic roles and made the rapidly evolving separate spheres of men and women appear natural and good.

Historians point out that the effect of these huge social changes on middle-class women's lives were mixed, neither pure victimization nor pure opportunity. Women, particularly single ones, gained unprecedented access to employment (albeit paid far worse than men's). Married women threw themselves into civic and religious causes, which at once gained them a public voice and confirmed their Christian (and domestic) values of love, nurturance, and good works.[28] The general evaluation of motherhood was high, some would say cloyingly so; but it meant that motherhood's civic and spiritual importance was continually acknowledged and amplified.[29] The "separate" sphere to which women were assigned contributed to the formation of emotional relationships between women, including mothers and daughters, of extraordinary richness and complexity.[30] And the sense of commonality among women that their separate sphere engendered, combined with women's belief in their unique strengths in child rearing and religious morality, fed both their activist participation for social betterment and a solidarity that would underlie their later calls for women's rights.[31]

At the same time, the high value placed on motherhood served to support rather than critique the impersonal values of the capitalist marketplace. Wives and mothers were enjoined to create a haven from the cruel world so that their husbands could function better within it. The whole posture of the middle-class woman in the mid-nineteenth century, especially her immersion in sentimental fiction and consumer culture, has been interpreted as a massive refusal of political consciousness.[32] The cult of "True Womanhood" by which women were judged and judged themselves offered an immensely constricting roster of virtues; piety, purity, submissiveness, and domesticity were virtues guaranteed, in their very nature, to admit no objection or rebellion.[33] And throughout this period, of course, opportunities in the new economy for risk or self-assertion, not to mention most educational avenues into the professions, remained virtually closed to women.

But though historians have emphasized women's gains and losses during this period, the rehearsal of their findings in works of popular feminism tells another, more one-sided tale. The Industrial Revolution, it is asserted, removed not only remunerative but *meaningful* work from the home. Deprived of meaningful work, women were left with what remained, namely child care and housework — thin gruel indeed. Such writings assume that the work of caring for children or tending a home was relatively thankless, devoid of any of the creativity that purportedly adhered to candle making, weaving, or any of the other "productive" activities from which women were now excluded. And viewing the past through a present-day lens, they tend to focus on what it meant for women to have to forgo employment in order to care for their children, to the relative exclusion of what it meant to women to have to forgo caring for children in order to work.

When the removal of production from the home and the high valuation of the mother-child bond are relentlessly cast as unjust limitations, it is difficult to ponder the positive meanings that being able to focus more on the care of their children might have had for mothers themselves. In reality, middle-class mothers were in no sense left idle when they stopped weaving their own cloth and tilling their own soil; rather, their activity was directed toward different ends, including the increasingly solicitous care of infants and children. That care included, then as now, pleasure and satisfaction. "That most interesting of all occupations is begun — the care of my child," wrote Abigail Alcott in 1831, "and delightful it is — I would not delegate it to an angel — I am at times most impatient to dismiss my nurse that not even she should participate with me in this pleasure." Then as now, mothers struggled. "My time is abundantly occupied with my babies," she wrote in 1833, soon after the birth of her second child (Louisa May). "It seems to me at times as if the weight of responsibility connected with these little immortal beings would prove too much for me — Am I doing what is right? Am I doing enough?"[34] Then as now, their self-doubts and struggles were not only, or simply, rooted in their position as mothers in patriarchal society; they were the struggles anyone assumes in trying to do meaningful work.

The idea that nineteenth-century mothers caring for children were left at home with "nothing" to do has been argued on the basis of the debatable claim that childhood itself is something of a modern invention. This interpretation dwells on how brutal parent-child relations used to be, and the absence of an ideal of tender affection in the family.[35] We are told, for instance, that before the sixteenth century in Europe, "parent-child relationships appear to have been much less emotional. What is seen today as a deep biological bond between parent and child, particularly mother and child, is very much a social construction."[36] Nurturing child-rearing practices spread during the eighteenth century, but by the nineteenth century, the account goes, this norm of nurturance had become something of a shackle for women. "The idealization of mother love, vigilant attention to the needs of children, and recognition of the unique potential of each individual came to dominate child-rearing ideology," writes the economist Juliet Schor.[37] We are left with the impression that whatever good resided in this ideology, it oppressed women by idealizing motherhood and pressuring mothers to devote their energy to their children. Although it is hard to believe that the earlier model of child rearing would induce feminist nostalgia, it is held up in many ways as preferable to what came after, the installation of middle-class women as "angels in the house" and the fashioning of child rearing by nineteenth-century ideology into an activity demanding of time, thought, and emotional investment.

There is a diverse body of scholarship that contradicts this version of events. It demonstrates that tender bonds between family members and between mothers and children were evident throughout the fifteenth and sixteenth centuries, though economic hardship and infant death sometimes made it hard to express them.[38] It also contends that, when seen in the context of what came before, the ability of middle-class women to oversee children's development was conceived as progress.[39] "There is nothing to wonder at," wrote the novelist and essayist Marilynne Robinson, "that the ideal of mother and children at home, and father adequately paid to keep them from need, was a thing warmly desired, and that for generations social reform was intended to secure this object."[40]

Perhaps the main source of irritation for today's critics of nineteenth-century domesticity is the latter's unapologetic, core belief in the indispensability of mothers to children, for it is this belief above all others that reverberates in our current conflicts and debates. In the nineteenth century, middle-class mothers began to take their work as parents extraordinarily seriously, and for better or worse, we are inheritors of that tradition. Whereas then the focus was religious character, now it is psychological health; but in Alcott's concern about her children's souls we can detect a spirit very similar to our own. Critics may charge that children's need for continual maternal attention is little more than a "social fiction."[41] But if we're honest, we can't leave it at that. Much as we may fear that an intensive model of mothering shackles women, or much as we may rail against today's overinvolved and overanxious ethos of parenting, we cannot dismiss the value to children of parental attention, or the sincerity with which many parents desire to give it. Certainly the lucky among us, whose parents helped them with their homework or spent time talking with them about their problems, can hardly scoff at its positive effects.[42]

The popular feminist renditions of the history of mothers suggest that what mothers want and need, what constitutes true equality, is to be freed from making the care of children central to their lives. Within this framework, it is almost impossible to understand the desire to mother as something more positive than fuzzy thinking, lack of self-knowledge, or weak politics. In other words, the popularized feminist conception of what mothers *want* is incomplete, and its biggest flaw may be its misunderstanding of maternal desire.

It's All Drudgery:
The Erroneous Collapsing of
Housework with Caring for Children

DE BEAUVOIR WROTE, "THE CHILD is the foe of waxed floors," and painted a grim picture of the housewife's losing battle against the grime with which her children besmirched her pristine home.[43] Betty Friedan diagnosed the problems of the mother who focused her considerable energies on getting spots out of her carpet rather than on larger social goals. But though the familiar feminist target of compulsive housekeeping has evaporated — largely because most mothers work and long ago gave up hope of a spotless house — Friedan's disdain for housework persists in the tendency to view child care and housework as sharing the dull repetitiveness of maintenance activities and to lump them together as one demeaned, poorly remunerated, and tedious task.[44]

When a mother staying at home caring for her children and keeping house is viewed in economic terms, the first thing we notice is that she is not paid for her work. We can respond to this obvious economic fact in a number of ways. Some believe that because home-based work is unpaid, it *is* of low worth. Some believe that if women are to act in their own rational self-interest, they should vacate the home and refuse to be stuck in unremunerated work. Others question how it is that women's work in the home has been "disappeared," redefined as non-work or economically worthless. Still others feel confused as to why economics should constitute the only legitimate measurement of what are obviously intrinsically valuable activities.

The first two of these views — the view that domestic work is inherently oppressive, and a sense of the injustice of women being stuck doing it — have dominated feminism, at least in its white, middle-class incarnation. An odd sleight of hand has pervaded this position. It is easy enough for anyone to concede the drudgery of housework; yet, because care of children also takes place in the home, child care is then tacked on, with hardly a thought as to the fundamentally different character of child care and housework for the mothers who perform it. The collapse of housework and child care into one blanket category of "domestic work" tends to obscure rather than clarify the character of women's work lives, since we cannot fully understand the nature of women's choices, options, and possible sources of oppression without taking account of the unique nature of mothering work.

Popular diatribes are a major source of this viewpoint — recall Myriam Miedzian's disdain for "waxing floors and wiping noses" — but academic studies are susceptible as well. For instance, within the economic formula for conceptualizing women's unpaid work presented in *The Overworked American*, the economist Juliet Schor does not differentiate the work of cleaning and the work of caring for children. Schor argues persuasively that in the nineteenth and twentieth centuries, housewives' workloads ballooned to fill the time available, not only because their forced absence from the workforce effectively cheapened their time, but also because as labor-saving devices proliferated, housekeeping standards rose. Curiously, though, the increasing standards for household cleanliness are treated as of a piece with rising standards for child rearing. "Once deflated," Schor writes of the value of the housewife's time, "the tendency to fill that time with household work was powerful. From the institution of the full-time housewife, it was but a short step to cleaning the floor a second time or *spending more time with the children*" (emphasis mine).[45] In this view, child care was "make-work," which, like keeping the floor clean, required a lot less time than mothers lavished on it. Why did women capitulate to these inflated standards? Not, by Schor's lights, because they had any motivation to spend more time caring for their children. Rather, she attributes it to women's fear that their husbands would resent their leisure, or to their feeling morally obligated to work as hard as their husbands did. Both housework and child care are understood as "services" that a housewife performs for her husband: "Men liked the fancy cooking, clean homes, *and healthier children* their wives produced" (emphasis mine).[46]

The lumping together of housework and child care expresses a bias toward seeing the care of children through the lens of housework, rather than seeing housework through the lens of caring for children. Caring for children is envisioned as a sort of extension of the tedium of housework, instead of housework being regarded as a workable way to be with children.[47] Even if we grant that housework can be tedious and dull, doing it is redeemed and its pain is lessened by the fact that it can be accomplished (with more or less success) while tending to children. The character of housework may be primordially suited to the hovering, background attention that children desire from their adult caregivers, and that adults often feel suited to provide. Whatever drudgery may be involved, housework meaningfully contributes to the overarching goal of creating a home. And as my children grow older, I even use it as an arena to teach the importance of cleaning up our own messes, on the living room floor and in life. Domestic work complements caring for children precisely because of the kind of work it is. If my work involves intense intellectual engagement or risky physical labor, tending children simultaneously can only result in frustration, distraction, and incompetence. But if caring for children is my priority, housework is not a bad companion activity.

A more positive slant on domesticity surfaces in the criticism of mainstream (white) feminism by those who consider the ways that class, race, and ethnicity affect a woman's experience of motherhood. The work performed by women of color has often entailed domestic service for others, and employing others to take care of their domestic chores has often enabled privileged mothers to enjoy greater freedom of movement.[48] From slavery times to the present, the family lives of minority women have been regarded as secondary to their usefulness as cheap labor. Slave families were broken up with impunity, and third world women today leave their children with relatives to work caring for the houses and children of first world families.[49] For a mother intimately acquainted with these realities, her own domestic sphere of child care and housekeeping may well represent greater potential for influence and creativity than does the sphere of paid work.[50] Without our quite realizing it, the pejorative feminist slant on domesticity has tended to reflect a certain blindness to the range of circumstances in which mothers of different class, race, and power positions find themselves.

The main problem with the collapse of housework and child care into one is that it misconceives, again, the meaning to mothers of caring for children. Charlotte Gilman Perkins was neither the first nor the last to compare the work of mothers to that of domestic servants. Certainly every mother has days when she feels her children treat her that way. But an equally relevant comparison might be between mothers and artists, or mothers and professors. Mothering is one of many kinds of work perceived as meaningful by its practitioners even when society doesn't reward them handsomely. Artists are rarely well paid, but people continue to make art because it has intrinsic value that is of greater meaning to them than the rewards of the marketplace. Professors might view their work as socially devalued because they are often paid poorly. Yet, though the study of scroll illumination in medieval France has negligible relevance to our market economy, an art historian impassioned by her subject sees her domain of scholarship as intrinsically worthy. No one lives on love alone, and love shouldn't be the only reward of motherhood. As Ann Crittenden observes, we don't insist that a professional ballplayer forgo pay because he loves his job.[51] But neither should motherhood's less quantifiable rewards be viewed suspiciously as sentimental or ideological sops to keep women in their place. The desire to care for her children can, and often does, motivate a mother to make choices she wouldn't otherwise make — not only to forgo income, but also to take on a larger portion of the household work necessary for family life.

To understand this latter motivation, especially among women with some degree of choice, it is important to understand the ways that goal-directed activity for a mother differs from goal-directed activity in most job situations. In order for a person to feel effective as a parent, and to engage in parenting more or less harmoniously, she needs to be in tune, at least some of the time, with the pace and rhythm of her children. Books like *The One Minute Mother* may imply that a mother's effectiveness and efficiency go hand in hand.[52] But in practice, the effort to tightly control the rhythm of young children's lives usually results in frustration and conflict, and a sense of inadequacy for both parent and child. For that reason, a parent will often intentionally seek to create an environment that fosters conditions different from those provided by most paid jobs, such as spontaneity, play, the injection of emotion, and a continually shifting balance of structure and flexibility. If these are the specific conditions I am after, I may take on the less gratifying chores of household management because they afford more potential, in comparison with other jobs, to create conditions conducive to parent-child harmony.

It's All Trivial:
The Erroneous Collapsing of
"Femininity" with Mothering

IN HER BESTSELLING 1991 EXPOSÉ *Backlash*, Susan Faludi catalogued feminists who retrenched in the 1980s. She criticized Sylvia Ann Hewlett for concluding that most women didn't even want feminism; Betty Friedan, for backsliding into a sentimentalization of domesticity; and Carol Gilligan, for developing a psychological theory that appeared to legitimize the notion of women's "special sphere."[53]

Yet in her portrait of the personalities contributing to the backlash, Faludi failed to consider the potential validity of Friedan's, Hewlett's, or Gilligan's substantive assertions. Each of them addresses the question of how women's motherhood might figure into the way we conceptualize equal rights, women's freedoms, and feminism's goals. In Faludi's book, it is hard to find a single thinking person who formulates this issue in a straightforward, reasonable way. When it does appear, it tends to be uttered by self-serving ideologues and opinion makers crassly commercializing backlash traditionalism for their own gain.

The reason the views of Hewlett, Friedan, and Gilligan receive such unflattering treatment is that Faludi, like other similarly inclined thinkers, rejects versions of feminism that accord any special consideration to women in their capacity as mothers. One impetus for that rejection is the perennial and perennially wrongheaded tendency to see women *only* in terms of motherhood. Being a woman doesn't boil down to being a mother, they rightly remind us, and the tendency to conflate the two has led to restrictions in women's opportunity and skewed theories about our psychology.[54]

Yet in spite of their legitimate concern with the tendency "to conflate 'mothers' with 'women,'"[55] they oftentimes counter with a troubling fusion of their own, treating motherhood as just one more socially constructed feature of femininity. "Femininity," when used as a critical term, denotes female-assigned characteristics, like compliance or wearing lipstick, that women are encouraged to value and yet signal their subservience. Too often, subtly or not so subtly, motherhood ends up tarred by the same brush. Women may vary in which features of femininity they adopt: "Women choose their face-lifts," lawyer and social critic Wendy Kaminer writes, "just as some choose to regard themselves as naturally better parents than men." But time spent on their faces or on their kids is seen as time spent capitulating to the same confining set of sex roles.[56]

Contributing to this point of view is the dubious assumption that any attempt to adjust our laws or economic incentives to account for the practical and psychological requirements of motherhood is no more than a flight from equality and a plunge into celebrating feminine "difference." When, for example, Kaminer writes of her own coming-of-age, she describes her pleasure at competing on an equal footing with boys while retaining the advantages of femininity. In her own "youthful desire for both equality and the pedestal," she detects hints of "the historic conflict between protectionist feminism, which emphasizes traditional notions of gender difference (the moral strengths and practical weaknesses of motherhood) and equality feminism, which challenges gender stereotypes and roles."[57] Here, the pedestal and motherhood are placed on one side of the ledger, equality on the other. Wanting "special" treatment as a mother, when stripped of its sanctimony, is really a desire to be worshipped for one's femininity or coddled like a pampered child.

This outlook may appear vaguely acceptable before you have children, but it becomes enormously confusing, even damning, once you do. Here you are, trying to care for your child, wanting the overwhelming importance of what you are doing to be acknowledged, yet simultaneously feeling that in leaving or cutting back on your job, you have relinquished all claim to adult respect. Yes, you want to feel valued, even special, amid the diapers and baby's spit-up and your exhaustion; but you cringe at the thought that devoting yourself to this not particularly easy role might be viewed by some as a demand for special treatment, as some kind of refusal to pull your own weight. And yes, admittedly, you occasionally crave a manicure or a new haircut; and though perhaps these are lame, socially engineered desires, you can't deny that they will make you feel better, maybe even *because* they carry a welcome whiff of femininity now that you are living in sweatpants. It turns out, then, you *do* want to be special and you *do* want to be feminine, and you *are* trying to enact, as Kaminer puts it, "the moral strengths" and manage the "practical weaknesses" of motherhood. In other words, you are guilty on all counts.

The way out of this morass may be to think more carefully

about the word "special." Special in the sense of "exceptional, primary, or esteemed" is expressed in the idea that women have unique propensities for caring, nurturing, and peacemaking, which emanate from their femaleness, their capacity for motherhood, or their experience as mothers. But special in the sense of "particular or distinct" is the relevant meaning when considering pregnancy, lactation, and parenting small children (the first two biologically limited to mothers, the latter empirically associated with mothers). These specific, practical, necessary activities are carried out by mothers for the continuation and flourishing of human life, and on that basis they deserve legal and economic consideration. That these maternal activities are sometimes viewed as "special" in the first sense does not delegitimate their "special" status in this second sense.

Yet the two senses of the word "special" are often blurred and treated as synonymous. Kaminer, for one, appears to see no meaningful distinction:

> Retreating from equality and questioning the efficacy of rights, feminists in the 1980s began demanding special protections for women. . . . Only women get pregnant . . . opponents of equality intone; so they demand laws that treat the sexes differently, in respect of their reproductive roles, as if the mere possibility of becoming pregnant makes women uniformly more compassionate, nurturing, cooperative, more sexually submissive, and more interested in family life than men.[58]

Kaminer dismisses in one broad sweep the particular requirements of mothering as just one more manifestation of "difference feminism," a perspective that focuses on women's qualities of empathy, nurturance, and relatedness, and their devaluation in male dominant culture. In so doing, she ignores the crucial issue: it is not a woman's abstract proclivity to nurturance and compassion that might legitimately serve as the basis for maternity leaves, preferences in custody disputes, and the like; rather, it is her actual participation in family relationships. Demanding laws to recognize and protect the value of a mother's emotional and economic investment in her family hardly seems like an attack on equality.[59]

It appears that thinkers like Kaminer worry that protecting mothers in any meaningful legal or economic way reduces women to child status. But their own language bears some responsibility for the equation of motherhood and its "practical weaknesses" with a childlike position. They cast it as a regressive flight from equality if mothers seek recognition in laws or social policies for the actual demands of motherhood. But in real life, any woman who risks losing her job because of a difficult pregnancy does not want extra time off or sanctioned leave in order to gain unfair female advantage or be treated as "special." Rather, she wants it in order to protect her status as an adult in the workforce, as well as her own health and safety and that of her unborn child.

Ironically, those who most vociferously defend women's reproductive rights with regard to contraception and abortion are often least forceful in defending women's reproductive rights as pregnant workers or new mothers. Abortion rights proponents quite reasonably affirm that just because sexual intercourse can lead to conception, it does not follow that a woman is responsible for bringing the conceived child to term; she should not have to "pay" for the first act with the second. And yet with respect to pregnancy, if a woman gets pregnant and her pregnancy happens to be difficult, it is rarely deemed unfair to expect a woman to "pay" for the undesired effects of her pregnancy by taking whatever the ostensibly gender-neutral policies of her workplace dish out. Witness an exchange between lawyer Anita Blair and editor Barbara Jones in a *Harper's* magazine forum on women in business:

> BLAIR: As a lawyer, what I find often happens is that somebody is pregnant, and she's having a terrible time of it and missing a lot of work. That person may be fired for missing work. That's not the same as getting fired for being pregnant.

JONES: But if we want a next generation, and if women are working, working women are going to have to have babies, right?

BLAIR: You've still got a job that needs to be done. The deal between the employer and the employee was not: "I'm going to pay you regardless of how many hours you come to work." The deal is: "You work, you get paid."[60]

In this particular version of equality, unequal burdens will fall on women who become mothers as a matter of course. But that particular inequality doesn't seem to bother Blair very much.

Inadvertently, the school of thought known as difference feminism may have contributed to the confusion of femininity, motherhood, and "specialness." In *In a Different Voice*, which offered the most powerful contemporary version of the view, author Carol Gilligan wrote: "The different voice I describe is characterized not by gender but by theme."[61] But in many less careful iterations, the connection between women and a general orientation to care is presupposed. My own guess is that when Gilligan wrote her book's first essay, "Woman's Place in Man's Life Cycle," or when the philosopher Sara Ruddick tried to systematize the discipline of mothering in her book *Maternal Thinking*, each was trying to articulate a perspective she developed in the course of maternal activity. In other words, each writer was trying to account for perspectives that emerged from concrete practice. It may be true that motherhood is a role for which some women feel they are preparing their whole lives, chiefly in identification with their own mothers; or, that when they become mothers, they begin to read their entire lives through the lens of that transforming experience. But even when such women are very "female-identified," the dispositions toward nurturing they have developed are instrumental capacities rather than passive "qualities of self."[62]

What is striking is that both equality feminists and difference feminists overlook how motherhood is often the first time women feel truly powerful in who they are, grounded in an identity mercifully free of stereotypical feminine concerns. Though it is elementally connected to body and to sex, in its most vital, useful, and responsive moments, mothering is not about *gender*. The novelist Toni Morrison eloquently described the experience:

> There was something so valuable about what happened when one became a mother. For me it was the most liberating thing that ever happened. . . . Liberating because the demands that children make are not the demands of the normal "other." The children's demands on me are things that nobody else had ever asked me to do. To be a good manager. To have a sense of humor. To deliver something that somebody else could use. And they were not interested in all the things that other people were interested in, like what I was wearing or if I were sensual. Somehow all of the baggage that I had accumulated as a person about what was valuable just fell away. I could not only be me — whatever that was — but somebody actually needed me to be that.[63]

This "falling away" that Morrison describes is one of the reasons why attempts to "feminize" women's experience of sex and motherhood so often miss the mark. Like soft-focus videos about labor and childbirth, they try to render tame and frilly the raw power of female sex and motherhood. "Most of the instruction given to pregnant women is as chirpy and condescending as the usual run of maternity clothes," writes novelist Louise Erdrich. "We are too often treated like babies having babies when we should be in training, like acolytes, novices to high priestesshood, like serious applicants for the space program."[64] When femininity and motherhood are spuriously linked, what gets lost is the character of motherhood as vividly self-expressive, and goal-directed. Equality feminists may treat motherhood as another feminine option, and difference feminists may imply that it expresses feminine qualities of self. But neither group fully communicates the ways that motherhood transcends the trappings of gender, putting us in touch with the deepest meaning of being human.

Connecting Motherhood
and Desire

AN ACCOMPLISHED FRIEND OF MINE once asked me, genuinely curious, "Why would you want another baby after you've already had one?" She couldn't fathom my wanting a second child; her wondering about it was equally incomprehensible to me. People really are different; they want different things. There are as many forms of feminism as there are feminists because what each of us wants bears the stamp of our unique history of relationships. Whatever understanding of the world we've created out of our experience of those relationships feels desperately central to who we are.

It makes sense, then, that the reigning imagery of mainstream feminism resonates more for some women than for others. But whatever our individual vantage points, mothers share a common predicament: we all deal in one way or another with the splits and conflicts in our lives, and we all struggle with the fact that when it comes to having babies and the daily activities of mothering, we need to figure out a workable solution. From time to time, we try to fortify ourselves in our choices by disowning our competing motivations: by elaborately insisting on our contentment at home with children, or our belief in the importance of mothers' work. But the reality for most of us is that we are torn, and we live with a sense of conflict, sometimes flickering, sometimes flaring, hour by hour, day by day.

The sources of our conflict are various, but Adrienne Rich put her finger on one important one: our ability to strive in the outer world for self-sufficiency, advancement, or self-expression usually entails our absence from daily stretches of interaction with our children and diminishes our in-person participation in the "trust and tenderness" that our children need "deeply and primally" from us. Historically this has been an unremitting reality for poor mothers; but today, though the stresses they endure are less extreme, many middle-class mothers share a version of this plight. The very structure of work, whether performed by necessity or choice, dictates ongoing dilemmas between providing material subsistence and tending to our children's emotional and psychological needs. Anyone who works to keep her health insurance or to make the rent or mortgage and leaves her infant or child at day care all day in order to do it is up against a situation where the contradictions between meeting the material and emotional needs of her child can be truly agonizing. When work is chosen or deeply satisfying, some things are easier, but it does not banish conflict or dispel the pain.

What is agonizing is not only our awareness that we might not be providing what our child wants and needs. It is also the experience of what might be described as a thwarting of self. Having a child creates not only a physical being but also a relationship between two people. The desire to mother is in part the desire to participate in that relationship and in the creation of another human personality through our unique capacities, through our own personality. It is often experienced as pain when that desire is insufficiently fulfilled. Like the artist or the poet, a mother can feel she is not truly living her life or being herself if she feels deprived of the time and emotional space to relate to her child. She can still nurture and support her children, still feed them and put a roof over their heads, but her sense of creative contribution can be diminished. To feel fully engaged in this creative process does not necessitate round-the-clock togetherness or perfect attunement. But it involves a physically felt need for time together in which each person comes to discover and progressively know the other.[65] This unfolding process can be harder to manage and sustain in the context of the rigid schedules that jobs often require. That incompatibility is at the root of some of mothers' most wrenching moments of frustration, sadness, and doubt.

In light of this last issue, namely, mothers' *own* desires to care for children, conventional feminist interpretations of women's work, motivation, and gender roles are wanting. Constructing women's equal participation with men in the workforce as liberation has entailed asserting an astonishingly depleted view of the world left behind: Children don't need "intensive mothering"; women's care of children is custodial drudgery, not meaningful engagement; motherhood is just another feminine "option" — all these arguments promote the conclusion that what happens in the daily transactions between mother and child is dispensable. Perhaps these arguments salve the potential pain of ambivalence by denigrating what is lost. Certainly they accurately reflect the views of a subset of women. I'll always remember the quote by radical feminist Ti-Grace Atkinson in my family's 1970 issue of *Newsweek*, "Women in Revolt": "Many women are not ready to give up [a personal life] yet. But when they see that they're not so much giving up something as getting rid of it, they will."[66] The problem is, arguments like this misapprehend the desires and intentions that fuel maternal motivation.

Part of the misunderstanding comes down to us from the tendency to assert that the practical realities of motherhood necessarily lead to one kind of psychological experience. De Beauvoir suggested that a sense of agency and free choice were rarely met in the circumstance of motherhood. Likewise, some feminists have erroneously identified the *content* of women's roles as the source of their oppression, treating housework and child care as in and of themselves limiting and thankless. They have failed to recognize that no one activity is intrinsically more oppressive than another; the meaning with which a person endows a given activity has a great deal to do with whether she inwardly consents to do it. Defining women's traditional roles as oppressive closes off our recognition of the variability of psychological and cultural experience and narrows our understanding of what mothering means to women.

Our circumstances today give us a sharply different perspective on the equation of women's traditional roles and oppression. For contemporary women in developed Western countries, who have access to birth control and a broad range of potential life paths, motherhood is more than at any time in history a self-chosen project worthy of de Beauvoir's criteria. What mothers today grapple with at least as vividly as the constraint of home is the constraint of work. Work was once idealistically vaunted as the royal road to meaning and autonomy. But for many mothers their jobs are what they feel compelled to do, not free to choose, and it is work rather than mothering that they experience as a repetitive necessity.

Even when the work is relatively rewarding, the conflict between doing it and caring for children can be powerful. One professional woman I know spends her Monday mornings in her office, like clockwork, crying over leaving her children for another work week. Another, who can't imagine staying home with her three children, took a rare morning off to take her toddler to a gym class. She was shaken by how much she enjoyed the time with him, because it put her in touch with a whole side of experience that she normally closed off. An acquaintance who loves her very demanding job took a vacation with her husband and two children, three years and ten months old. During their week together, she was astonished to see her baby growing up before her eyes. She freely admits she's "tortured" because she can find no way to put together doing her job with the knowledge that day-to-day she is missing her ten-month-old's babyhood. The models for a fulfilling life that these women grew up with helped them chart a course for developing themselves professionally. But these same models misjudged, perhaps even willfully ignored, the subjective sense of cost that they would experience once they had children.

Perhaps the most troubling legacy of a certain strain of anti-domesticity feminism is how it has affected women's self-evaluations. Women wonder what's wrong with them when they can't adjust to their conflicted situation. A professional woman with two small children feels lucky to have a great job, a great boss, and more flexibility than most other workers in her field have. Her job is interesting, but she doesn't want to be doing it. "I think I'm really just spoiled," she says. She knows her four-year-old daughter needs more attention, and she feels terrible she doesn't have it to give. She worries about the supervision of swimming lessons at her six-year-old's summer camp and regrets that she can't take her older daughter swimming herself. After all, summer, she thinks, should include lazy days at a pool. She attempts to resolve the conflict by buying a membership at an expensive health club nearby so she and her husband can take the kids swimming in the evenings. But she sees the irony of spending more money (further justifying their long hours at work) and keeping the kids up too late (ensuring that they'll be cranky and less resilient the next day) in order to approach more closely her vision of the kind of time she wants to share with her children. Is there a clear solution? No. But she is not "spoiled" to be pained by the conflict and her sense that things aren't working.

Working Mother magazine reports on a survey designed to determine what makes for a successful professional mother. It turns out that successful "fast-track" mothers "have done extremely well at setting aside guilt, regret, and ambivalence about the choices they have made."[67] Success, it appears, is synonymous with getting rid of your yearning to be with your children or your belief that they need you. Feeling conflict about leaving your children all day is a self-destructive hangover from the benighted past. Here we see a chilling confluence between a certain set of feminist ideals and the aims of corporate capitalism. And the net effect is to make mothers feel that there is one more thing to feel guilty about: their inability to banish guilt.

Rather than understanding our predicament in a social and historical context, we sometimes feel that the division within ourselves is something that we should just be able to deal with, through our own savvy or strength of character or streamlining of feelings. We drain ourselves by trying to cope with ever greater efficiency. *Working Mother* has more articles on efficient time management than any magazine in the history of the planet, purveying the subtext that if you are just efficient, energetic, and healthy enough, you can pull it off and "have it all." But the reality is darker and less tractable. Mothers are often the unwilling bearers of the burden of the home-work divide, and they end up making all sorts of adaptations to it. Self-respecting professional women routinely hide their commitment to their children at work, especially in corporate settings, in order to be "taken seriously." And it is not just working mothers who feel a lack of wholeness. The same friend who is crying Monday morning at leaving her children is told by her stay-at-home-mother friend that she is "bored out of her mind." A sense of integration eludes both women. And what makes it especially painful is that each sees it as some kind of *personal* failure; mothers' lives are divided, and they fear it is fundamentally a problem of *self*.

On a psychological level, we must look beyond a static appraisal of roles — "should mothers be at home or should they work?" — to investigate the inner terrain of mothers' lives, where values are negotiated and conflicts are felt and managed. It is not useful to side with one aspect of women's lives while devaluing another; characterizing motherhood as always oppressive is just as wrongheaded as claiming it is always a path to joy. What we need is a fresh look at maternal desire, in the context both of the practical conditions of women's current lives and in light of the powerful cultural ideas that contribute to women's perceptions of themselves. We need to develop a more satisfying, more complex understanding of what women *get* from mothering, not only the rewards of being responsive to children but also the ways in which mothering is responsive to self. What contributes to an authentically joyful experience of motherhood? What gets in the way of it? In exploring these questions, we will learn, I suspect, about the ways that maternal desire is fulfilled through a sense of wholeness and integration, and about the practical, ideological, and psychological pressures that can make that integration difficult to sustain.

Over thirty years ago, Germaine Greer argued in *The Female Eunuch* that women's power was drained by the inhibition of their sexuality.[68] Today, we might consider whether women's power is inhibited by impediments to their motherhood. No one in his right mind would suggest that a sense of power and effectiveness in the world is attained at the cost of lopping off one's sexual impulse; yet everyone takes for granted that we have to find a way to compartmentalize maternal desire if we want to achieve that same power and effectiveness. The very structures of work in our society encode the demand that mothers sequester their maternal desires in order to perform at their job or forgo their desires for the rewards of employment in order to mother. The question is not how to free mothers to go to work or how to free them to care for their children; it is how to deal with the demand for self-dividedness that is not only inherent in our structures of work but also permeates our psychological models of the autonomous self.

Insofar as feminism has valued lives framed by individual achievement at the expense of those framed by motherhood, it has had its own part to play in women's sense of dividedness. That dividedness cannot be addressed by endlessly reversing the hierarchy of value, but by finding truer, more complex stories. Gurinder Chadha's 2002 film, *Bend It Like Beckham*, starts out with what appears to be a straightforward feminist formula. Jess, the British-born daughter of Indian immigrants, is an enormously talented soccer player, pulled in two directions — by her traditional parents ("Who'd want a girl who plays football all day but can't make chapattis?") and by her love of the game. Jess's drive and seriousness of purpose glowingly compare to the stereotypic concerns of her marriage-bound sister, Pinky, and Pinky's like-minded friends. But at the film's climax, the director takes us in an unexpected direction. Crosscutting between the fever-pitch excitement of Jess's championship match and the orgiastic dancing and music of her sister's traditional wedding, Chadha points to the commonalities between different forms of human ecstasy, and in so doing implies an equivalent dignity between Jess's and Pinky's paths to happiness. Each woman, in her own way, fulfills deep aspirations through committed participation in community life. If at the end, when a pregnant Pinky proudly displays a photo of Jess's college soccer team, the resolution strikes us as a bit too neat, it still manages to communicate that there is room for many different roads to female fulfillment.

3

Psychoanalysis

CAROLINE, A THIRTY-YEAR-OLD professional, contemplated with some excitement a promising new relationship she was in. Though she occasionally confessed to fantasies of marriage and motherhood in therapy, she also talked a great deal about how getting married and having children were an escape from the "real world." She worried that pursuing marriage and motherhood was a kind of shrinking from challenge, an admission that she couldn't "make it." She dwelled on the fear that a child's dependence would cause her to lose her own hard-won independence. Over time, it became clear that Caroline harbored an intense desire to have children, which she was embarrassed about revealing. By emphasizing her fear of a child's dependence, she downplayed her wish for that dependence, as well as her even more self-incriminating wish to depend on a mate as she pursued motherhood. Her worry that motherhood meant "not making it" obscured a desire to feel permitted somehow to make mothering the center of her life. What was striking was how invested she was in hiding her wishes for motherhood and children, much as women of an earlier era might have hidden their sexual wishes.

One reason it is hard for Caroline, or any of us, to think about maternal desire is that the life changes implicit in those desires, the identity we will need to assume, seem radically at odds with the kind of goal-oriented activity that is commonly viewed as leading to success. To choose to redirect one's energies toward mothering means not only a change in one's use of time (not to mention one's economic standing or security), but often a drastic reformulation of one's orientation toward control, independence, and even one's prior identity. Caroline does not feel she is considering the difference between two paths to meaning, two kinds of aspiration, or two avenues to satisfaction; she feels, rather, that her dilemma involves mature, goal-directed activity (work) on the one hand versus an amorphous mass of feelings (motherhood) on the other. What's more, she feels this is a problem with *her*; she faintly worries she is too girlish, not ambitious enough, too passive. However, her problem derives part of its force from the more general problem we have with recognizing the kind of meaning-making activity mothering is, the aspirations at its heart. Caroline may feel, somewhere buried under her attention to her inadequacies, that the most direct way to do good in the world is to foster another person's happiness through devoting her energies to parenthood. But that seemingly sentimental belief is almost impossible for her to articulate or even acknowledge.

Most people today do not encounter psychoanalytic theories of human psychology in a therapist's office or on the analyst's fabled couch. We encounter them, rather, in the broader culture and in our own assumptions. In daily life, we tend to take for granted that we have desires and conflicts we keep out of awareness that have an ongoing impact on our feelings and choices. We accept that there are things about our current interactions that reflect aspects of the past; that we unconsciously expect our boss to act like our perfectionistic mother and find ourselves feeling a strangely familiar resentment toward him or her, or that we treat our child when he's naughty like our father treated us. As a therapeutic endeavor, psychoanalysis's unique contribution is that it explores the human psyche through the relationship of therapist and patient. In this way, it powerfully illuminates the nature of intimate relationships more generally.

Motherhood is, in the first instance, a relationship. And in or-der to explore mothers' experience of caring for children at a deeper level than social commentary, we need a psychology, like psychoanalysis, that takes relationships as its focus. Historically we find, as much in the work of the psychoanalytic dissenter Karen Horney as in the work of the orthodox Helene Deutsch, some of the same questions about motherhood that we are still asking ourselves today: What is the relationship between our in-dividual aspirations and our maternal impulses? How are we to think about and manage the conflicts between them?[1] The an-swers to these questions have changed with each generation and each wave of psychoanalytic thinking. At times, emphasis on women's maternal role has overshadowed attention to their other needs and desires; at other times, the reverse has been true. Today, we are able to reconsider the entire scheme that pits individual and maternal aspirations against one another. Aided by suggestive findings from mother-infant and attachment re-search, we can begin to think more clearly about the ways that caring for children satisfies mothers' *own* desires.

What Came Before

IN THE PREFACE TO HER 1951 BOOK, *Motherhood and Sexuality*, the Argentine psychoanalyst Marie Langer wrote:

> Does a woman engaged in a professional career experi-ence obstacles to her realization of motherhood, and if so, to what extent? . . . During my adolescence it was a frequent topic of conversation. . . . Later I had to aban-don the question at the theoretical level so that I might resolve it in practice. Only when I recently read a book with the alarmist title *Modern Woman, The Lost Sex* did I begin to think again about the possible incompatibility between motherhood and career. The authors of the book maintain that modern woman is losing her femi-

ninity because of changes in her role within the family and society. . . . I began to struggle with this question — to observe, investigate, and analyze — and I came to the conclusions expounded [in this] book.[2]

It is surprising to discover, though perhaps it should not be, how central the seemingly contemporary conflict between family and work was for early women psychoanalysts writing about the psychology of women. Even though she penned it over five decades ago, Langer's question is remarkably fresh, and even the scaremongering *Modern Woman* is not altogether unfamiliar, as such books still appear with cyclical regularity. Women psychoanalysts like Langer, and Helene Deutsch and Karen Horney before her, worked to find a satisfying synthesis of theories of female development consistent with their own subjective experience as mothers and ambitious women.

Helene Deutsch's interest in motherhood led to observations both poignant and astute, and her clinical writings bear the hallmarks of personal struggle. She believed breastfeeding to be an ultimate maternal achievement, yet she herself felt drained by it.[3] She deeply desired more children but had an avowed hatred of her own mother, which she felt hampered her own ability to care for her child.[4] As an adult, her only son, Martin, spoke resentfully of her absence and her tendency to fire caregivers to whom he had become attached.[5] One of her first psychoanalytic papers, "A Two-Year-Old Boy's First Love Comes to Grief," was about her son's loss of his beloved nurse Paula; in it, Deutsch offered an unvarnished portrayal of her son's mourning.[6] Deutsch felt keenly that mothering took her away from her work, yet she also felt that the child's inevitable developmental separation from his mother was "the tragedy of motherhood."[7]

These very contradictions formed the focus of Deutsch's analysis of motherhood. She took individual differences seriously and understood all human activity, including mothering, as inevitably characterized by conflict. Clear-eyed about the fact that being a mother involved conflicts between real and different desires, she also tried to articulate something about the mother's own desires *toward* her child. She addressed these desires in the concrete arena of the breastfeeding relationship (a biological trope usual in that era of psychoanalysis) but described them with reference to the overarching emotional relationship as well:

> In order to thrive, the baby needs his mother and the mother needs her baby. . . . Whenever [some women] are away from their children, they are seized by a peculiar and irrational feeling of restlessness and worry; sometimes they describe it as "longing." It is akin to the feeling in childbed that I describe as "listening"; it is the natural pull at the psychic umbilical cord. The younger the child, the shorter the cord, and the more the pull is burdened by neurotic additions and excessive dutifulness, the more painful it is.

"This kind of longing," she continues, "is not comparable to any other emotion; it is neither pure dutifulness nor love."[8]

For Deutsch, the difficulty for women in "our own modern society" was that the constellation of feelings she termed "motherliness" — "the mother's deep longing for a more intimate relationship with her child, her justified concern for his emotional development, and her feeling of guilt for neglecting him" — could be experienced as at odds with "the interests of her own individuality."[9] Deutsch offered a clinical approach characterized by a gentleness toward the conflict and a realism about the trade-offs:

> Very often the situation can be mastered only by means of a compromise. Women whose whole life has assumed certain forms and whose sublimations have become an irrevocable component of their psychic life, can be good and loving mothers only if motherhood does not become a danger to their solidly rooted life values. . . . The task of the psychologic adviser is to give these women

permission to compromise. . . . They themselves must accept as a necessary result of the compromise the fact that by reason of it they are missing something important.[10]

For Karen Horney, another early woman psychoanalyst, the crucial issue was not mothers' internal conflicts so much as the need to introduce a perspective informed by mothering into psychological theory. Unlike Deutsch, who idealized her father, Horney devalued her father, identifying with her mother's dissatisfactions with him. Horney's mother, whom Horney called "my great childhood love,"[11] died at around the same time Horney gave birth to the first of her three daughters, perhaps strengthening the intensity of satisfaction she felt in mothering her infant.[12] Although Horney "devoted a great deal of energy to trying to be one of the boys," according to her biographer Susan Quinn, and "felt trapped, in the beginning, by the undeniably feminine position in which pregnancy placed her," the experience of childbirth and mothering an infant compelled her, "for the first time in her professional life, to take an independent position." Her own experience convinced her of the inadequacy of psychoanalytic theories that saw babies as a substitute for masculine strivings, and "she was forced to propose an alternative theory."[13]

In her 1926 essay, "The Flight from Womanhood," Horney argued that Freud's assumptions about female development — that women's sexual impulse and having babies are "compensatory devices" for her lack of a penis — were tone-deaf to the actual experience of motherhood. Her view was captured in her famous lines:

> At this point I, as a woman, ask in amazement, and what about motherhood? And the blissful consciousness of bearing a new life within oneself? And the ineffable happiness of the increasing expectation of the appearance of this new being? And the joy when it finally makes its appearance and one holds it for the first time

in one's arms? And the deep pleasurable feeling of satisfaction in suckling it and the happiness of the whole period when the infant needs her care?[14]

Horney's experience and reflection on motherhood led her to frame an alternative psychoanalytic view, in which motherhood stood on its own as intrinsically rewarding. Her formulation of a different female line of development laid the groundwork for the feminist reinterpretation of psychoanalysis that followed.

The Feminist Turn
in Psychoanalysis

FOR THOSE OF MY GENERATION who read feminism and psychoanalysis as young women, it is hard to imagine life before books like Nancy Chodorow's *The Reproduction of Mothering* and Jessica Benjamin's *The Bonds of Love*. These were among the consummate feminist texts that took inner life seriously; and they remain richly generative of psychological theory, practice, and self-reflection. In my own training, I must have read each book half a dozen times, each time with a deeper understanding of the argument and a renewed appreciation for its elegance.

When I returned to these books after I became a mother and had experienced the relationship with my children myself, I found my respect for their contribution was undiminished but that my emotional reaction to them had changed. Aspects of their arguments, and the assumptions on which they were based, suddenly felt open to reconsideration. Their theories appeared to operate from the premise that there was something inherently disempowering in being a mother caring for one's children; that patriarchal society had instigated and enforced this disadvantageous position for women; and that it was a goal of theory to unearth the unconscious tributaries feeding this oppression. I became intrigued with the ways that this worldview, which I had begun to find increasingly dissatisfying, was woven into the very fabric of their arguments, at times obscuring what was most central to me about being a mother.

Quite obviously, my changing reaction to these books was the result not only of a personal evolution but also a social one. The medium in which their arguments grew was one of more limited prospects for women, a context that made it hard to perceive motherhood as intentionally chosen rather than passively accepted. Daughters of forties and fifties mothers, like Chodorow and Benjamin, were understandably motivated to analyze the problem of women trapped in a narrow domestic sphere by a society that believed that that was the best or only way to raise children.[15] But the daughters of sixties and seventies mothers, like me, needed to solve something different: namely, how to take advantage of the access women had gained in the workplace while not shortchanging their desire to mother. Upon returning to these books, I felt that although they acknowledged that women may find gratification in mothering, this gratification was never treated as a motivator or first cause; the desire to mother was not fully articulated, almost as if it were politically suspect or theoretically inconvenient. And yet viewed from today's perspective, this is exactly the matter we need to understand more fully.

Chodorow's goal in *The Reproduction of Mothering* was to explain why, generation after generation, women assume the role of primary caretakers for their young. By posing the question "Why do women mother?," she meant to demonstrate that mothering was not simply biologically determined, but also socially and psychologically created, or "reproduced." She argued that female motherhood, rather than being natural, was rooted in a gendered division of labor that promoted the development of a psychological disposition toward "maternal" qualities, such as empathy and nurturance, in girls and women. This division in psychological capacities contributed in turn to gender inequality in society and incompatible emotional needs in women and men.

Chodorow's psychoanalytic account began from the premise, thoroughly grounded in the clinical theory and infant research available at the time, that the earliest relationship of an infant to his or her caretaker — almost always a mother — is characterized by a sense of merger or oneness. The concept of merger captures the infant's utter dependence on the caretaker, and his basic need for human contact. But it also connotes that the infant is incapable of experiencing his mother as a separate being, or of distinguishing fantasy from reality.[16] In a 1949 paper, "Love for the Mother and Mother-Love," the psychoanalyst Alice Balint went further, not only describing the infant's incapacity to conceive of the mother's independent interests, but also suggesting that a mother's love for her baby was similarly "remote" from "reality." For, "just as the child does not recognize the separate identity of the mother, so does the mother look upon her child as a part of herself whose interests are identical with her own."[17] Chodorow rightly rejected the idea of perfect symmetry in the mother-infant bond, pointing out that a mother has an entire social and personal life and history apart from her baby. At the same time, she concurred that mothering depended on experiencing "the infant as an extension of the self," which arose from the mother's own experience of being mothered in infancy, and which, in her view, was basic to the capacity for empathy.[18]

This understanding of mother-infant merger was central to Chodorow's main thesis, which was that mothers experience more intense and long-lived feelings of oneness with their daughters than they do with their sons, resulting in the creation of stronger propensities for identification in daughters and for independence in sons. On the positive side, this meant richer capacities for empathy among women, and less conflict-laden individuality for men. On the negative side, it meant difficulties connecting for men and separating for women.

Chodorow's psychological theory joined with her politics in the solution she proposed to this gender asymmetry: to equalize male and female social and parenting roles to the point where there was not such a wide gap between the extended mother-daughter merger and the shorter mother-son one. Fathers and mothers should equally share parenthood, and mothers and fathers should assume similar roles in social and economic life. Thus, a particular developmental account of mother-infant merger, and particularly of mother-daughter merger, fed a feminist argument about the division of labor in society that advocated the importance of both mothers and fathers being models of independence and intimacy for their children. If mothers and babies had trouble disentangling themselves, and this was particularly intense for girls, then the path to greater independence and self-determination for women was for women to assume more of the separateness traditionally afforded men.

The premise that Chodorow's argument rested on — the idea that a mother and baby begin their life together in a state of complete identification or oneness — has come in for a thorough rethinking and revision since her classic work was published.[19] Mother-infant observation has greatly expanded in the last twenty-five years, and contemporary researchers view babies and mothers as engaged in complex interactions from birth. To begin with, scientists of infant cognition have demonstrated that the baby is able to perceive the caregiver's physical separateness from early on, and does so as a matter of course. Experiments have compared, for example, the baby's perceptual processing of stimulation that follows from its own actions (like putting its thumb in its mouth) to their processing of stimulation that comes from the outside (like their mother's cooing), and have documented that even very young infants identify differences.[20]

Beyond these capacities, infants even a few days old are strongly motivated to respond to social cues.[21] Mother-infant research has shown that the infant expresses his or her agency in encounters with the caregiver, and that the caregiver and baby are both extraordinarily attuned to their unique interaction from very early on. Offering a striking glimpse into the coordination of infant and caregiver, one study compared a group of newborns fed on an every-four-hours schedule for the first ten days with a group of newborns fed on demand. The researcher, Louis Sander, found that the demand-fed newborns prolonged one or two of their sleep periods at three or four days old; by a few days later, these longer periods of sleep were occurring more frequently at night than in the day, in synchrony with the mother's sleep cycle. Thus, even at the seemingly "purely" biological level of feeding, the infant's demands were influenced by the mother's pattern of responsiveness; their mutual attention to the other's "demands" allowed them to join each other in an increasingly synchronized (and less sleep-deprived) pattern of interaction.[22]

This mutual responsiveness of baby and caregiver, of self and other, runs throughout the baby's development. In the earliest weeks of a baby's life, baby and parent already relate to one another via exquisitely tuned interactions that are, to borrow from Sander, "little miracle[s] of specificity."[23] At three or four months, babies and parents engage in face-to-face play of extraordinary coordination and nuance that lay the groundwork for patterns of relating and intimacy throughout life.[24] The caregiver and her baby are increasingly active partners engaged in getting to know each other, continually and subtly shaping each other's actions to achieve a gratifying rapport. If the baby depends on the caregiver to guide and manage his level of excitement or settle his arousal through soothing, it is not because he has no experience of "self"; rather, it is because much of what he is able to feel at this age "is possible only in the presence of and through the interactive mediation of an other," in the words of the infant researcher Daniel Stern.[25] By nine months, babies deliberately seek to share feelings and intentions with others, for they now begin to grasp that other people have minds like their own. It is common for parents to talk about this as a "great age"; one reason is the feelings of delight, for the parents and baby, that accompany the baby's first awareness of sharing subjective states with others.

An important theme underscored by this mother-infant research is that human psychological experience does not follow a linear progression from fusion to autonomy; rather, feelings of oneness and separateness oscillate throughout life. A baby can first conceptualize and yearn for an experience of merger only in the course of developing an increasingly distinct sense of self. A mother with a mature sense of autonomy will at times experience with her baby the mingling of self and other characteristic of passionate love. At every stage of life, our separateness creates the potential for intersubjective sharing, while our experiences of oneness replenish and enrich our individuality.[26]

Taken together these research findings do not contradict how utterly dependent the baby is on the caregiver.[27] Nor do they undercut the reality of the transient states of melting into each other that mothers and likely babies experience.[28] Nor, obviously, do they undo the fact that an average mother is likely to feel at times as if her life has been taken over by her infant, and that she no longer has the same clear-cut experience of self. But they do help us make sense of our intuition that images of oneness or fusion do not adequately capture the interpersonal dynamics of mother and infant. And they help us create a narrative more true to our experience that in the interaction between a mother and baby, *both* parties express a great deal more individuality than the somewhat swampy metaphor of merger evokes.

This subtle point is crucial because it changes our picture not just of the baby, but also of the *mother*. Once we take account of the genuine relating that takes place between mother and baby, we begin to notice how the idea of mother-baby merger, when subjected to a certain feminist sensibility, tends to characterize mothers' experience of caring for babies as inimical to their individuality. To give one example of the problem, Chodorow argues that since the baby is completely dependent, he or she will "employ techniques which *attempt to prevent or deny its mother's departure or separateness*" (emphasis mine).[29] There are actually two critically distinct ideas here: the baby's attempt to "prevent departure" and her attempt to "deny separateness." These are starkly different goals, the fulfillment of which relies on two different kinds of techniques. The first requires protest and active efforts to get the caregiver to stay, while the second implies a mental act aimed at denying reality. Collapsing the two ideas into one distorts both the baby's intention and the mother's optimal response.

A baby's effort to prevent the mother's departure is about his *attachment* to the mother. This effort is carried out behaviorally, through crying and later through motor activity; it arises from the evolutionary need to maintain contact with the primary caregiver in times of danger or stress. The outward behavior and the inner feeling states associated with the goal of maintaining physical proximity, the interactions of parent and child with respect to this goal, and the psychological communication between them all have implications for psychological development and for both the infant's and mother's inner worlds. But they are part of a universal human and primate pattern, empirically observable and documented.

A baby's desire to deny the mother's separateness, by contrast, is highly conjectural, derived largely from the confluence of retrospection by adult patients in psychoanalysis and a particular set of theoretical assumptions about the baby's inner life.[30] The idea is that in the presence of frustration or intensely felt unmet need for the mother, the baby denies, wishes away, or otherwise alters in fantasy the reality of the mother's separate being. The theorists who elaborated this view believed that children engage in instinct-driven fantasy virtually from birth; that the denial of reality and hallucination of the absent breast or caregiver was a common method of adapting to painful circumstances; and that such fantasies were a normal and universal feature of infant psychology.[31] In this view, a baby expectably engages in a fantasy of oneness with his mother in order to defend himself against frustration or his mother's painful absence.

It is important to distinguish between a baby's desire *to maintain proximity*, on the one hand, and his desire *to deny that the mother is a separate person*, on the other (if he indeed has such a desire), because conflating them distorts how we see the mother's relationship to her child. If we imagine that the baby's wish to deny separateness is the same thing as his wish to maintain proximity, then we are likely to view it as healthy for the mother to have a certain dose of suspicion toward the child's bids for proximity and protests against separation. Indeed, we will see it as the mother's duty to frustrate the child in order to help her child develop a sense of reality. Mothers who "give in" to their baby's purported denial of reality in the service of merger are in danger of prolonging their child's refusal to perceive and accept separateness.

But this view risks misunderstanding, and invidiously pathologizing, a mother's own motives for minimizing separation from her child. Like her baby, who is bonded to her by a powerful attachment, the mother is bonded by a powerful motive to give care. Indeed, recent research has begun delineating the features of a parental caregiving system that complements the child's attachment system.[32] Though Balint was extreme in stating that a mother feels perfect identity between her own and her baby's desires, recognizing this exaggeration should not plunge us into the opposite one. It is equally problematic to characterize what a mother wants for herself as wholly distinct from what she wants with, and for, her baby. One of her most powerful desires *for herself* is often to care for and relate to her baby. When that desire is subsumed into a notion of merger, it gives rise to an image of mothering as passive, infantile, and depleted of agency and desire.

Fears about whether relating to an infant is regressive or engulfing can exert a lot of power over some women. A thirty-three-year-old marketing director who was planning her first maternity leave decided to take a minimal amount of time off and go back to work at full capacity, even though her job potentially allowed for more flexibility. Some of her concerns revolved around the pragmatics of getting back up to speed professionally if she cut back her work hours. But this realistic concern was also fueled by being afraid to think about how her feelings and her identity might be changed by a baby. Over the course of therapy, one of her tasks was to understand more about those aspects of her emotional history that motivated her fear, which allowed her eventually to question the dichotomies she previously accepted between women who "moved ahead" with their lives and those who became submerged in maternal preoccupation. This work allowed her to think about the previously avoided question of whether she might *want* to be with her baby and the ways that idea threatened her self-image.

JESSICA BENJAMIN'S BOOK *The Bonds of Love* was published ten years after Chodorow's, and it used newer infant research that cast the infant not as merged or symbiotic but as able and motivated to relate to others from birth. From the first days of her baby's life, a mother feels both a powerful sense of connection and a sense of the baby's otherness. She seeks to recognize her baby's feelings and intentions, and experiences pleasure at her baby's dawning recognition of hers. A mother is not, as previous thinkers implied, simply the connected "home base" from which the child grows independent. *Both* mother and child are powerfully motivated to assert themselves and recognize the other, to be separate and connect, and they must find a balance between those goals in their relationship to each other. When the balance breaks down — that is, when the tension between self-assertion and recognition of the other cannot be sustained — relationships of domination and submission result.[33]

According to Benjamin, mutual recognition — the child and mother's acknowledgment of each other as persons — is particularly vulnerable to breakdown during a developmental phase Margaret Mahler termed "rapprochement," beginning around fifteen months, because that is when the child most vehemently struggles against recognizing the mother's independent identity and goals.[34] Whereas Mahler portrayed the rapprochement struggle as involving primarily issues of separation, Benjamin emphasized the child's wish to control the mother's comings and goings.[35] For Benjamin, rapprochement is the birthing place — or at least the staging area — of the impulse to dominate. The toddler, she writes, "will insist that mother participate in all his deeds. He will tyrannically enforce these demands if he can, in order to assert — and have mother affirm — his will."[36] As the toddler becomes aware of his frustrating limitations, he tries harder to assert his control and independence. As he becomes more aware of his separateness and vulnerability, he strives to control his mother's every move and bend her to his will. He gains some temporary sense of mastery at forcing his mother to participate in his plans, but at the expense of recognizing her as a person with her own goals. As to the mother, "if [she] sets no limits for the child, if she *obliterates herself* and her own interests and allows herself to be *wholly controlled*, then she ceases to be a viable other for him" (emphasis mine). Recognition of the mother, seemingly an inevitably unfolding development in infancy, is resisted by the toddler, who now seeks "absolute assertion" of himself.[37] In this way, Benjamin links the genesis of human domination to the toddler's willfulness at rapprochement.

This view of the toddler's intentions has certain implications for how we view the mother's response. If the toddler's agenda is to control his mother, it is not surprising that the mother is understood to be maintaining her selfhood through asserting herself and not caving in to his will. A "sense of herself as entitled to a separate existence" is the crucial ingredient in the mother's ability to support her child's developing capacity for recognition and to wean him from his insistence on control.[38] How is this sense of herself expressed? Benjamin repeatedly exemplifies a mother's self-assertion in two ways: her ability to set limits with her child, and her ability to have independent aims, most often illustrated with the situation of leaving her child.

Setting limits for one's child and leaving to pursue one's goals are not in fact identical, but in Benjamin's account they blend together. Her examples imply that leaving to pursue one's own interests *is* a kind of limit setting. Choosing to illustrate the mother and child's clash of wills almost exclusively with examples of the mother's leaving the child — a "limit situation" that puts in boldest relief the reality of the mother's independent agendas and her child's passionate objection — Benjamin makes it hard not to infer that in her view a mother's ability to leave her child is the very thing that allows the child to recognize her subjectivity.[39] If a mother capitulates to a child's bids for her to stay, she risks depriving him of the opportunity to accept the subjectivity of others. Indeed she risks depriving him of the necessity of accepting reality itself. When the mother and child avoid separation, they risk remaining stuck in an omnipotent fantasy where each feels that to separate would be devastating. In this scenario, "neither [the mother] nor her child could tolerate the disillusionment of knowing that she exists independently of him. Mother and child must cooperate in the fantasy that he is the center of her life."[40] From that angle, the mother who wishes to minimize separation, either because that is what the child wants or because that is what she wants, or what they both want, ends up looking like a clingy saboteur of her child's healthy disillusionment. Benjamin does not explore the meaning to the *mother* of leaving her child, other than to focus on the extreme, pathological case of the mother who "can never leave" because of a fantasy of destroying her child.[41]

One might infer from the drift of Benjamin's argument that a mother who feels most entitled to a separate existence — most entitled, for instance, to hold an absorbing job — would also be the mother least likely to cave in to her child's bids for control. But in the real world, there doesn't seem to be much of a correlation between the ability to set limits with a child and the ability to leave to pursue separate goals. Leaving one's child does not necessarily solve, and in some cases may exacerbate, parents' inability to stand firm or to assert themselves. In her book *Spoiling Childhood*, the psychologist Diane Ehrensaft documented the effects of parents' not having enough time with their child, including overindulgence and giving in to their child's will, often out of guilt at their absence and wanting to please their child when they are home.[42] The tendency to cave in to one's child's will is as likely to show itself in the parenting of a person who is consummately able to be an "equal other" in the public world as it is in, say, a stay-at-home mother. And that is because having a "self," and being able to stand up to one's child in the necessary ways, does not have a direct relationship to what one does in the outside world.

In this respect, Benjamin's drama of a mother's assertion of autonomy in response to a child's controlling demands expresses a dominant image behind, and a reigning fantasy within, a certain strand of feminist thinking about mothering. In this picture, a good mother must hold fast to the ballast of her independent aims, not capitulating to the dominating child's insistence that she be "just his mother." The potential repercussions are momentous, for the very groundwork for the master-slave relationship is laid "in the mother's renunciation of her own will, [and] in her consequent lack of subjectivity for her children."[43] But the problem here is that a mother's "renunciation of her own will" is identified too closely with a mother's having "sacrificed her own independence," as if the two were synonymous.[44] Conditions of mothering where a mother hasn't insisted on her independence — presumably, conditions where a mother is at home spending her time caring for her child — "trap mother and child in an emotional hothouse and make it difficult for either one of them to accomplish separation."[45] Again, it seems that the only way for psychological separation to be accomplished is for the mother to insist on her independent selfhood, repeatedly operationalized by Benjamin as the ability to leave. But the kind of independence Benjamin is really getting at is an internal autonomy, a connectedness to one's own desire, a sense of authorship in one's life. And this sense bears no necessary or inevitable relationship to the mother's ability to pursue independent goals away from her child.

All this might remain a problem for specialists to puzzle over, except for the fact that Benjamin's argument has been translated in popular books about motherhood more simplistically as a mother's right and duty to avoid the perils of putting a child's needs before her own.[46] And even in professional journals where Benjamin's psychotherapeutic arguments are subtly debated, her feminist assertions go uncritiqued. They are still treated as an unquestioned reality: "At this point in cultural history," write three sophisticated clinicians, "the family context mediating the child's conflict [at rapprochement] still tends to be organized by the traditional, culturally determined scenario in which women mother, such that mothering requires a repudiation of true agency and desire."[47]

For the most part, Benjamin conceives a mother's independent identity in terms of those desires and aspirations that are distinct from her activities as caretaker for her child. She is not primarily concerned with how caring for children might express a woman's autonomous desires rather than thwart them. But that is our concern, and it is one that recent psychological research can help illuminate. From a variety of angles, studies on mother-infant interaction offer ways to think about how a mother *expresses* herself through her responsiveness to her child; and they suggest ways her responsiveness, particularly to her child's attachment needs, *contribute* to her child's ability to recognize her as a person in her own right.

Mutual Recognition
Reconsidered in
Light of Attachment

THERE IS AN ODD DISCONNECT in current psychoanalytic writing between the portrayal of motherhood as requiring the "repudiation of true agency and desire" and the burgeoning research pointing toward how centrally a baby's *and* mother's intentions and desires figure into their creation of mutual satisfaction and pleasure. Many extol the contribution mother-infant research has made in replacing the image of mothers as "extensions of babies," with a more accurate picture of mothers as full persons whose desires are not fully answered by motherhood or baby care.[48] But comparatively little has been said about the light this same research might shed on mothers' desire *to* care for children, let alone the meaning of that desire with respect to mothers' identity and goals.[49]

Yet, in minutely describing the processes by which mothers and babies together create a satisfying pattern of interaction, the research brings into focus some of the capacities that *mothers* bring to these interactions. And these capacities conform, in all relevant particulars, to the characteristics we commonly associate with a sense of self: the ability to reflect, to interpret, to enact goals, to respond flexibly and creatively, to share pleasure. It should come as no surprise, then, if a mother feels her *self* truly engaged in her relationship with her child; if the mutual growth she experiences with her baby is a source of profound gratification; and if this gratification transforms her self-image or affects her priorities and goals.

Attachment research is one domain that explores the relationship between a mother's capacities of self, her responsiveness, and her child's emotional well-being. Decades ago, the psychoanalyst John Bowlby conceived of attachment as a universal infant pattern of seeking proximity with a trusted caregiver in response to perceived danger.[50] Mary Ainsworth and her colleagues devised a systematic method to observe babies' separation and reunion behavior with their caregivers — known as the "Strange Situation" — and discovered that when babies are twelve months old, their attachment behavior conforms to one of a small number of typical patterns.[51] A securely attached child reacts with distress at being separated from his mother but is eager to greet her, able to be soothed, and soon returns to play or exploration. A child with an insecure-avoidant attachment may appear unaffected when his parent leaves, choosing to focus instead on toys or the physical surround; upon reunion, he may avoid the parent by moving or turning away, but without overtly expressing anger. An insecure-ambivalent child responds to reunions with an inconsistent push-pull, preoccupied with the parent but unable to be fully angry or fully soothed. Alternating between seeking and avoiding her parent, the child continues to cry after the reunion and does not return to calm exploration.[52]

These widely validated patterns of attachment arise in the interaction of parent and child, and they reflect the impact of the parent's responses to the child's attachment-seeking behavior. A baby is utterly dependent, of course, and to preserve her relationship with her caregiver, she will be highly sensitive to doing what is necessary to continue to elicit care. She will mold her emotional responses to the conscious and unconscious demands of the caregiver. When the caregiver's demands are in tune with fostering the baby's security and growth, things work out well for the baby. But when they require the baby to ignore or distort her responses in a systematic manner, the demands create obstacles to her healthy development.[53]

What is it about a mother's emotion and behavior that affects whether her child develops a secure attachment? Researchers asked parents about their memories of their own early attachment experiences, using the Adult Attachment Interview (AAI), and what emerged was very compelling. Parents of infants who are securely attached tend to be able to talk coherently about their childhood attachment experiences, even if very painful or confusing, in a manner that is both collaborative with, and intelligible to, the interviewer. These parents are able, in effect, both to value attachment and to view their own relationships with some objectivity. By contrast, parents of insecure-avoidant babies tend to offer responses that are dismissing of attachment. They may avoid discussing negative emotion or deflect introspection. They might claim a "happy childhood" or a "wonderful mother," but when asked to supply specific memories, they often give examples that frankly contradict their generic appraisal. Finally, insecure-resistant or -ambivalent babies tend to have parents whose interview responses display inconsistency, vagueness, and a preoccupation with early or current relationships that is marked in its lack of distance or perspective.[54]

Researchers have found, then, that the way in which parents *represent* their own early attachment relationships has a great deal to do with how small children *experience* their attachment to their parents. What appears decisive is not, as one might expect, the *actual* attachment experiences parents had with their own caregivers. Rather, it is how parents are able *to think and talk about* those experiences — in other words, their ability to reflect on and communicate about their experiences — that relates to the security of their child.[55]

This says something quite striking about the importance not simply of a mother's custodial care, but also of her subjectivity. Being able to take perspective on one's experience and develop a coherent, self-aware point of view is obviously integral to what we consider maturity, autonomy, or a sense of self; and it is these very capacities as expressed by the mother that foster her child's security. How exactly might this work? It appears that one crucial link between the mother's coherent narrative about her experiences and her child's security lies in the mother's capacity to reflect. If a mother can reflect, she can more accurately perceive and understand her own and others' thoughts and feelings. This, in turn, makes her more likely to be able to respond sensitively to her child. The researchers Peter Fonagy and Mary Target define a secure bond as "one where the infant's signals are accurately interpreted by the caregiver."[56] In other words, a baby develops a secure attachment *by virtue* of the caregiver's reliable recognition of his needs and desires, and her appropriate response.

A mother's responsiveness combines both her willingness to enter into emotional states with her child — what we commonly call empathy — and her ability to reflect and offer a *different* perspective. When a baby is distressed after an injection, mothers who are most effective at soothing their distressed babies typically do two things: first they mirror the baby's emotion, sometimes in an exaggerated way, by making a grimace or a sad face or by saying "ouch," and then they shift affective states, sometimes employing humor, skepticism, or irony.[57] In that reaction, the mother joins the baby's feeling (mirrors emotion), takes a perspective on it (exaggerates), and then says, in effect, "join me and let's shift to another emotional state." What is helpful to the baby is not simply that the mother shares his emotional state, but also that she "comments" on it. By momentarily feeling what her baby is feeling and then doing something different with it, she helps her baby gain perspective on his experience and learn to manage his own emotions. Thus, in the everyday act of comforting her child, a mother's very ability to help her child depends, fundamentally, on her having her own, different perspective. And for the baby's part, when he sees that his mother's response diverges from his own and gets a dose of her differing mental state, he learns something not only about his own inner world but about his mother's as well.

Obviously, not all maternal responses are as reflexive as soothing a baby, but this example serves to suggest a way in which a child's recognition of his mother comes into being in the course of her responsiveness to him. When the mother recognizes her child as someone with his own intentions, desires, and needs and responds to him accordingly, she creates the conditions for the child's reciprocal recognition of her intentions, desires, and needs. Though babies and mothers are partners who co-create their interaction, a mother's internal model of intimate relationships is extraordinarily powerful in shaping the baby's own. For this reason, valuing her child's inner life is what will most likely lead him to value hers.

In fact, when a child is unable to value his mother's inner life or recognize her as a person, his inability is likely to have been prefigured by his mother's lack of sensitivity to him, particularly to his attachment needs. According to the psychologist Karlen Lyons-Ruth, the ambivalence and conflict that Mahler (and Benjamin) regard as normal and universal in rapprochement actually indicate problems in the mother-child attachment relationship that predate toddlerhood. When a child attempts to feel all-powerful and minimize the mother's importance or autonomy, his behavior is not an expectable by-product of rapprochement; rather, the child's anger, distress, and ambivalence "appear to be rooted in the mother's much longer term difficulties in providing a responsive relationship, which includes genuine affective engagement and effective comforting and soothing of the infant at times of stress."[58] Securely attached toddlers with responsive caregivers also vigorously assert their needs and oppose their parents; but, unlike insecurely attached children, they are able to integrate their "initiatives into the social give and take while maintaining warm relatedness."[59] In other words, they assert their needs while staying in touch with, or recognizing, the caregiver.

It appears, then, that a child who is preoccupied with asserting power over his mother to the degree Benjamin describes is probably already enmeshed in a long-standing pattern of problematic relating, wherein his mother has not responded sensitively to his needs and desires. The problem such a child faces likely has more to do with achieving satisfying contact with his mother than with accepting limits or his mother's assertion of independent aims. By way of corroboration, we might note Lyons-Ruth's observation that "the ambivalence described [by Mahler] as typical of the rapprochement period is not centered around limit-setting situations but around desires for contact with mother."[60] Lyons-Ruth focuses on children with insecure attachments, but her work confirms the more general connection between our responsiveness to our child — particularly his attachment needs — and our child's security, flexibility, and happiness. As mothers, our awareness of this connection is one of the main reasons we try to be present with our children when we can, and try to balance spending time with our children and pursuing other goals separate from them.

Responsiveness to our child fosters his recognition of us not just in infancy or toddlerhood but throughout his development. Parents encounter this truth every day, particularly in those moments when we feel our relationships with our children are going right. We comfort our little girl when she has hurt herself, wash her cut, and kiss it and put on a Band-Aid. When she sees we are sad — even at age one or two — she hugs us or sings us "Happy Birthday." She feels secure and close when we accept and respond to her feelings; and when we respond, we confirm her view that "when I need or want something, Mommy understands and responds." This model of relationships in turn guides her interactions with us. Or, an older son uses his imagination to figure out the "exact right present" for us; he aspires to know us for who we really are, having so often experienced that same recognition from us. Such moments could be described as peak experiences of parenthood. They are fully saturated moments, bringing us satisfaction of two kinds: pleasure in our child's eagerness to know us and make us happy, and a sense of success in having nourished our child's own empathic capacities through our responsiveness to him. It is this very loop of empathy, I think, that is most likely to get parents and children through rough patches, be they the rebellions of adolescence or the storms of toddlerhood.

Of course, even in good relationships, empathy is rarely complete. Miscommunications and misattunements happen all the time. It should come as a relief to mothers to know that there is no such thing as the perfectly attuned caregiver; in fact, the inevitable moments of being out of tune give each person an opportunity to reach to understand the other's mind. Researchers have found that a baby's development into a happy, confident, curious child is likely associated not with a caregiver's perfect responsiveness but with her ongoing attempts to repair or self-correct after misinterpreting her child's signals, and to find ways to restore positive feeling after negative interactions.[61] The most detailed studies of mother-child interaction reassure us that our relationships to our babies are not about being perfect, knowing exactly what we are doing, or anticipating our baby's every need. The normal back-and-forth between two people who care for each other — the miscommunications, the repairs, the repeated attempts to connect and to elicit each other's interest or pleasure — these are the "stuff" of secure attachment and empathy.[62]

The very earliest roots of these processes have been studied by examining face-to-face interaction between four-month-olds and their mothers, a period in babies' development when, as researchers Beebe and Lachmann write, the only goals of the "infant's repertoire of interactive capacities . . . are mutual attention and delight."[63] Researchers studied the timing of vocalizations between mothers and their four-month-old babies, based on an earlier finding that a certain degree of coordination in the rhythm of dialogue of adults — neither too much overlap nor too little — contributes to their feeling in tune and understood. In some fascinating experiments, researchers have found that a middle range of adult-infant coordination of vocal communication at four months is related to secure attachment at one year, suggesting that the healthiest patterns of interaction are neither too tightly matched nor too mismatched.[64] Whereas disordered attachment relationships at one year are preceded at four months with a pattern of overly tight vocal tracking indicative of vigilance, wariness, and anxious monitoring, secure pairs are able to allow each other "more 'space,' more room for uncertainty."[65] In secure relationships, each partner is freer to apprehend and respond to her own and the other's affects and intentions. Even when baby is at the early age of three or four months, it appears not only that baby and mother are active partners in creating an experience of mutual engagement but also that, optimally, each makes room for the individuality of the other.[66]

In clarifying the specifics of early mother-child interactions, the research begins to illuminate a deeply felt but inadequately theorized aspect of a mother's experience: namely, that her ability and desire to respond to her child contribute not only to her recognition of her child but to her own sense of pleasure, effectiveness, and self-expression as well. In discovering who her baby is, in responding and learning to understand him, a mother also discovers aspects of herself. That self-discovery often leads to a sense of self-expansion or transformation, which she experiences as deeply gratifying and meaningful.

The research also implies that a mother's otherness is amply recognized by her child in the normal course of interacting. It does not require a dramatic demonstration of independence or assertion of autonomy. A mother is not at risk of being unseen as a separate person simply because she organizes her activities and her responses around what she perceives her child to want or need. It is neither pathological nor psychologically dangerous for her to feel that her child is, indeed, at the center of her life.

In light of these observations, we might consider whether the kind of assertion of self a mother needs to make to express herself in her relationship with her child need not necessarily be of the heroic feminist variety but can equally be in the more subtle communications of difference. These *also* have the potential to express and convey the mother's sense of self; these *also* have the potential to provide her recognition as a person in her own right. It is precisely this potential of seemingly "small" interactions to fully engage the personality of *both* baby and mother that has gotten lost in the broad-brush appraisal of caring for children as an abdication of self.

Balance and Flexibility, Love and Loss

MOTHERS EXPRESS THEMSELVES IN CARING for their children in ways that Chodorow and Benjamin may not have emphasized; but in a larger sense, each identified a facet of an enduring challenge all mothers face, namely our need to integrate love and loss, togetherness and separateness, and connectedness and autonomy in ourselves and in our relationships with our children. Chodorow explored how being mothered predominantly by women creates difficulties in balancing connection and autonomy for people of both sexes. Benjamin looked at how constraints on women's self-assertion feed social patterns of male domination and female submission. In their own ways, each theorist grappled with the problems created for women and for the culture when the image of motherhood is sequestered at one pole of experience, seen as all about connection, empathy, and nurturance and never about autonomy or assertion or anger. Both sought social solutions that would help foster greater balance in individuals and in our images of the two sexes.

For mothers today who are trying to figure out their lives, the general issue of balance is not most usefully characterized in the sweeping terms of society's denial of women's autonomy or the oppressive confinement of mothers to the domestic sphere. For individual mothers, it tends to arise in the emotional and practical question of how we walk the line of providing for the various needs of others and for ourselves, and how we manage the tension between love and loss in our relationships with our children. People cope with these issues in many different ways. Some try to soften the pangs of loss by trying to dodge separation. Mothers who feel a keen sense of loss as babies grow up, for instance, may deal with these feelings through outward action: "I'll have another child" or "I'll breastfeed longer." They may avoid letting go by staying perpetually confused about what they are doing for their child, and what they are doing for themselves. One mother, describing another's decision to continue nursing a three-year-old, concluded that the child was "not yet emotionally ready to wean. The comfort and closeness of nursing were still vital to the child's well-being." Framing the issue solely in terms of the child's needs, the writer did not consider what might have motivated the mother to continue to construct nursing as the best way to comfort her now-preschooler.[67]

Others find ways to circumvent feelings of loss by minimizing the importance of connection. A mother doesn't wake her thirteen-month-old son to say good-bye before she leaves early in the morning for her demanding job because she worries it will make him too sad. Reluctantly, she acknowledges that she avoids saying good-bye because it will put *her* in touch with her sadness at not sharing with him many of the moments of discovery and mastery he experiences when she's not there. Another mother misses her job and former identity intensely but believes she should be home with her young children. She cannot quite admit her grief at what she has given up; nor can she question her belief that she should be home. Because of her difficulty in facing how important her connections to colleagues and her work identity were to her, she has a hard time mourning her loss or deciding to return. That unfinished business makes it difficult for her to be fully present and vital in relationship to herself and her children.

Each mother, whatever her roles, must find a way to balance togetherness and separateness, and the feelings of love and loss that go along with them, in her own life and with her children. She must respond to her children in ways that are appropriate to their stage of life and her stage of motherhood, and find a way both to mourn the losses and embrace the opportunities that accompany her children's growth into more independent people.

A very bright woman with a two-and-a-half-year-old son is a stay-at-home mother, and she has gotten great satisfaction and joy from that role. Indeed, she feels that she was never so much "herself" or so happy with her life until she became a mother to this boy. Her son is curious, sweet, and engaging. However, the mother has arranged her life so that she virtually never goes out. The ostensible reason is that her son is still nursing; but it is obvious to everyone around her, and she herself on some level knows, that this is something of a fig leaf. She simply feels that his desire for her presence, and her desire to be with him, should trump all else. And her husband — though he knows their friends find it exasperating that it's possible to socialize only if they come over (and get babysitters for their *own* kids) — can't really find a reason to contradict her. After all, their son's well-being should be their most important priority.

We can certainly see here some of the omnipotence Benjamin spoke of, and the way this young woman's "hyper-maternal" stance allows her to control those around her. But situations like hers, which look for all the world like "excessive" maternal desire, have at their core a reluctance to face the inevitable losses that motherhood, and indeed life, presents us with. Her little boy's development from a babe in arms into a more independent child is one that she can't quite accept; the reality that he needs something different from her now — something equally essential — is somehow too painful to contemplate. She has her own reasons for being so sensitive to the losses, but not the gains, of each developmental achievement, perhaps having to do with her childhood experience. As a young child she remembers her own mother "never being around"; she may now believe that constant attentiveness to her son can heal her own wounds. But whatever her specific stumbling blocks, they keep her from progressing on the necessary path to fostering the degree of autonomy that would best nurture her child and aid in her own development.

One could glibly assert that this woman has no sense of self, or that a role in the outside world would help her deal with reality. But neither assertion captures the core issue. This woman's problem is not that she has no sense of self; what she considers her "self" is fulfilled by motherhood. Her problem, rather, is that she resists integrating loss into her experience of mothering. If someone told her what she needed was to pursue outside interests or get a job, she would feel misunderstood; her delight in, and attentiveness to, her child are qualities she rightly considers great contributions to his growth and happiness. In other words, it is not the fact that she has devoted herself to caring for her son that is her problem. Rather, it is her difficulty in finding a balanced approach, in achieving integration. The answer to her difficulty is not an outward change in role balance as much as an inward psychological one.

That said, there *is* a key social issue that relates to the maternal task of finding this balance, of managing to be connected and separate with one's child to the right degree at the right times, and that is the issue of *actual* flexibility in mothers' lives. One of the great difficulties many mothers face is that the emotional flexibility they draw on in relating sensitively to their child is interfered with by the inflexibility of their work situation. The yearning a mother might feel for a flexible work schedule is not only about the logistics of taking her kids to school or tending to them when they are sick, important as these are. It also relates to the reality that her children's needs are constantly shifting and arises from her desire to respond to needs as they arise. The problem would obviously be much alleviated by greater flexibility in the workplace, and a more humane national policy for longer maternity leaves. Greater latitude in practically combining work and motherhood would not only go a long way toward attenuating mothers' sometimes piercing sense of conflict; it would also create conditions for them to stay in better touch with their internal sense of what they and their children want and need, and give mothers greater freedom to act on that knowledge.

Maternal "Instinct" in a Different Light

THE PAST THREE DECADES HAVE seen an explosion of psychoanalytic thinking, much of it devoted to reframing our psychological understanding of women. Yet in spite of the important revisions by contemporary theorists, the idea that a woman expresses her subjectivity through caring for children and that there is a maternal desire that is as psychologically rich and potent as sexual desire has remained relatively unexplored. The field is awash with new visions of subjectivity, but scarce is the notion that a woman might find caring for children to be an authentic expression of her subjectivity. It is almost as if the view of motherhood as a place where women have been "stuck" for centuries has worked its way insidiously into theory, such that motherhood is a place where desire is not.

Going back sixty years to the work of Helene Deutsch, we find a surprising meeting of the minds on the very tributaries of maternal desire that mother-infant researchers are now identifying. Deutsch wrote, "The mother's task is to be constantly on the alert and to enter into her child's feelings, for only thus can she achieve the inner certainty that enables her to grasp the volatile expressions of childish life and to intervene now in a reflex manner, now with critical deliberation, to inhibit or to further. . . . The great 'wisdom' of mothers results from the blending of two functions, the affective-intuitive and the intellectual."[68] Deutsch's insights about the two critical components of mothers' response to children — empathy and reflection — are now being studied, and what has been found has implications for how we think about maternal desire.

The latest mother-infant research aids us not in the endless argument about why or whether a mother *should* be spending her time caring for her children but rather in thinking about the question of why she might *want* to be. It demonstrates an extraordinarily nuanced, though rarely articulated, awareness of self and other on which her activity is based. It illuminates her improvisational responsiveness and moment-to-moment appraisal of the child's and her own needs, desires, and capacity for frustration. It clarifies some of the mental, emotional, and intuitive challenges mothers work with in everyday interaction with their children, and the skills that are called upon and developed. Taken together, the research gives us more explicit knowledge about something that usually remains implicit: the activities of mothering can and often do contribute greater complexity of personality to both child and mother, and in that process mothers can and often do find enormous meaning and satisfaction. In these ways, the research helps us to describe more accurately what women who want to mother aspire to experience.

That description might help women like Caroline, considered at the beginning of the chapter, to look differently at the tension between her maternal and professional ambitions. In particular, it might help her disentangle her powerful desire to mother from a certain set of ideas she has about that desire. For reasons partly motivated by her own wishes and fears, she has espoused ideas, readily available in the culture, that wanting to care for children is regressive — politically, personally, economically. If she is ambitious or mature or truly autonomous, this story goes, she really "should" want something different. It might be a relief to her to consider that there is another way to look at her desires, one that does not eye them suspiciously as a retreat but rather permits her to imagine what, for her, would be the most satisfying way to express them.

Marie Langer's answer to her own question about how to reconcile mothering and professional life lay in the direction of recommending "educating women so that as adults they are capable of sublimating a part of their maternal instincts."[69] It has long been the fashion, for good reason, to object to the notion of "maternal instinct" as universalizing, overly biological, and unthought. And yet in the contemporary climate, what is refreshing in Langer's view is how she takes so for granted a notion on which we tend to heap anxious derision, that there is some sort of native wellspring of maternal pleasure that not only feeds the experiences of bearing and raising children but is a powerful source of energy for other pursuits as well. The world is not divided into the public world where we express ourselves and the private one where we care for others; our involvement in both worlds is equally fed by a passion to know and be known.

4

Pleasure

I AM IN THE SUPERMARKET, the one with natural foods and magazines about mysticism and yoga at the checkout stand. There is an issue of *Mothering*. On the cover is a chubby, delicious baby who has just raised his head from nursing. Next to his cheek is the answering curve of his mother's breast. I am transported to a time of life when my baby is about six months old; when, his tongue-lips-gums quivering, sometimes still latched on, sometimes taking a break, he looks up at me with sparkling, happy eyes. There is something impish in his breezy latitude, in his growing expertise at doing two things at once. In the picture, the camera is exactly where my eyes would be if I were the nursing mother; so looking at the baby's face tugs me into a physical moment of pleasure.[1] I feel it in my throat, in my belly, in my involuntary smile, and in a startling, ridiculous welling up of tears. It feels almost indecent to gape at the picture, not because it is prurient, but rather because I am not in command of my own joy. The delight I feel at being at the receiving end of those eyes is almost overwhelming, like a gush of uncontrollable laughter.

The photograph in itself was lovely, but what struck me was how ingenious it was to put it on the cover of a magazine that people would unexpectedly confront. Here I am, buried in my daily distractions, when I am suddenly put in touch with a reservoir of feeling, not in relation to my own baby or the baby of a friend, but out of the blue. There it is, that intense delight, that specifically maternal delight, there for all to see, and there for me to feel, sudden and unbidden.

It seems that on the simplest level, the desire to mother is rooted in this experience — the expectation of it, the living of it, the longing for it. It is a rush of connection, a feeling that both deepens and exceeds us. Nursing is one instance when we might feel it, but there are many. An adoptive mother may feel it when she first lays eyes on her baby. We may feel it when we hold our baby, or engage her gaze, or when she graces us with her first social smile. This delight, what the French writer Annie Leclerc called "the profound taste we have for children," surely encodes our mammalian heritage, the powerful evolutionary mechanisms that ensure that we will reproduce the next generation.[2] But it is our distinctively human awareness of this delight — the way complex emotion and memory interweave with it and the way it relates to the larger purposes of our lives — that expands our experience of intense pleasure to one of joy.

These experiences of connection are, by their nature, fleeting. The joy aroused by a baby or child so easily evaporates in the moment. It can become completely clouded under certain material conditions. Coerced motherhood, poverty, and the lack of social and emotional support are obvious ones;[3] painful family histories and depression are others. There are also certain casts of mind that seem to create barriers to pleasure as firm as external impediments. I have been struck at times, for example, by the stories of women I've known, each of whom anticipated a second child with something bordering on dread. One woman expressed concern about getting fat, another worried because she'd just gone back to work, another because she found days at the park frankly boring. Another became tearful because she didn't know if she could handle another child. Ambivalence plus hormones makes weepers of us all. But what was remarkable was that in each case, these otherwise supremely competent women, adepts at birth control for the better part of two decades, found themselves pregnant "by accident." Normally highly organized and proactive, they portrayed their pregnancies (to others and maybe even to themselves) as something that happened to them. Evidently, they were comfortable voicing their other motivations and desires, but their desire for the child was something they couldn't manage to articulate, let alone own.

The muffling of delight can take less drastic forms. One academic study argues, in prose assiduously pruned of emotion, that the ideology of intensive mothering is a social construction. The book is very scholarly, precisely written, and logically unimpeachable. In the author's acknowledgments, there is an unexpected eruption of mother-child pleasure: "I smother with kisses, shower with flowers, and promise an endless supply of frozen yogurt desserts to my beloved mother."[4] The contrast vividly exemplifies what we perceive as incompatible ways of speaking, in this case an incompatibility between academic seriousness and mother-child feeling. I wonder what it costs us to exert the necessary discipline to ensure that our gushing delight does not contaminate, or count against, our serious pursuits.[5]

Mothers have many legitimate, competing desires. It is understandable not to want to gain weight, to enjoy meeting the standards of one's profession, and to feel unstimulated spending hours at the park. It is not surprising that new or expectant mothers sometimes feel pulled to reconstitute their lives along familiar lines, even complaining about the costs of motherhood or feeling some relief at not being overly besotted by a baby. From the point of view of gainful employment, career continuity, and the opportunities work provides for satisfaction and personal growth, the efforts we make to stay on course professionally after we become mothers make sense. More, we intuit the importance of keeping alive what we value about ourselves as individuals as we enter into motherhood. At the same time, even in the face of these concerns, women continue to seek in motherhood both the opportunity to connect in a powerful, transformative way and the potential for growth, meaning, and joy that that connection offers. The adaptations we make, so necessary and reasonable within one framework of meaning, that of work, often cost us a great deal within another framework of meaning, that of caring for children.[6]

We can approach this conflict in different ways. We can deny or downplay our interest in motherhood's opportunities for self-transformation or connectedness. We can effectively fend off a shift in priorities with the birth of a first child, only to find ourselves yearning for — or dreading — such a shift with a subsequent child. We can find ways to distance ourselves from the feeling of connection because it is painful to be actively in touch with it. One woman related the experience of going back to work after vacation and not wanting to call her children because it was "easier just to block it out." "How," she asked, "do you keep the sense of joy going, and at the same time accept that you have to disconnect from a certain kind of feeling with them when you leave home every morning?"

When we are dealing with motherhood, we are dealing, on one level, with our relationship to our own human capacity for delight. What do we do with that delight? What place should it have in our lives? When it's not there, why isn't it, and what should we feel or do about it? Women's difficulty in taking pleasure in having or caring for children does not begin and end with the social pressures that "force" women into motherhood. It involves, among other things, the complex relationships we have toward our own potential for delight. And this relates, in turn, to questions of meaning: What makes mothering meaningful and pleasurable? What does time spent with one's child have to do with the creation of meaning? What does mothering have in common with other human meaning-making activities? These questions take us toward a more nuanced discussion of maternal enjoyment — what it is, what we seek through it, and what makes it hard to sustain.

In the Beginning:
Connectedness and Language

DESCRIBING HER FEELING AFTER HER first child's birth, one woman said: "When I saw him and heard him cry, I was overwhelmed with emotion, and when the nurse placed him in my arms I felt that I had *knowledge* of something very powerful that made life completely comprehensible. I remember feeling very light, as if every burden was lifted from me. It made me understand why some people search for ecstatic experiences of revelation in religion." Many women don't feel anything like this at the moment of birth (I was so traumatized by the pain of my first birth, I asked not even to be shown my baby for several minutes). But others do; and still others have it when they are holding their baby, biological or adopted, in the first few days, weeks, or months of life.

If we listen to what women say about this experience, we hear them using descriptions like "getting it," "waking up," or "being in touch with the meaning of life." They are moments when one's everyday perception is shot through with an awareness of a deeper connection to life and a deeper sense of meaning. In childbirth — where the physical changes produced are second only to those produced by death[7] — we experience this sense of a deeper reality physically and psychologically. In our unfolding relationship with our baby or child, we sense an integration among the various registers of our experience: the yearning for closeness, felt as physical; the desire to tend and nurture and satisfy; the aspiration to reach the depth beneath the surface, to be, as Robert Frost put it, "tripped into the boundless."[8] It is this quality of integration, of knitting together our physicality, our unconscious wellsprings of desire and need, and our conscious intention and awareness, that characterizes the most engaged, satisfying moments of caring for children. Like any creative practice rooted in human necessity, at its best, caring for a child involves physical engagement aligned with intention toward a valued purpose.

Perhaps the integration I am getting at can be best explored through the evocative role of language in mother-child relating. From the very first moments of contact, one of the ways we express our urge to connect is through our voice — human speech, its rhythms and cadences. We birth our babies with concentrated breathing sighs, with grunts, with shrieks of pain, sometimes with expulsive swearing at its surprising agony, and with occasional, truncated messages ("Don't push" "I can't not push!"), or perhaps, if we are medicated, with expectant, slightly distracted conversation. But when the moment of birth has come and gone, the gushing of our tears and our waters and our amazed, exhausted expressions of gratitude and joy have passed, we might begin, if we aren't too out of it, to talk to our newborn. "Hello," we might say, quietly astonished at how tiny her fingers look clinging to our own outstretched finger. "How are you? Where did you come from?" Our baby is exhausted too. But when she opens her watery, watchful, almost listening eyes, she seems to be trying to make sense of something. We might wonder if she is adjusting to the novelty of hearing our familiar voice for the first time outside the womb.

When we talk to a newborn, we have no illusion that she understands the semantic content of what we are saying. But our effortless patter feels "right"; we know intuitively that there is much more to speaking to our child than just verbal meaning. Research confirms that intuition. Newborns are extraordinarily sensitive to the nuances of maternal speech. They recognize and prefer their mothers' voices to all others, and the basis of that preference is laid in utero. Not only do they recognize their mother's voice, but their sensitivity is such that they recognize extremely subtle variations in her speech patterns. Researchers asked pregnant women to read a Dr. Seuss story to their fetuses in the third trimester. Once born, the babies paid more attention to a tape recording of their mother reading the Seuss story they "knew" than they did to one that they didn't know.[9] Even in the context of intrauterine life, a mother's vocalizations are part of the baby's bath of sensations, and a baby's dawning consciousness is shaped within an embodied experience pervaded by their quality and tone.

Until their babies are around nine months old, mothers tend to imitate their baby's behavior or vocalizations, modifying them slightly ("improvising") to add interest. Around nine months, mothers tend to add something new to these exchanges, what

Daniel Stern called "affect attunement," probably in response to their babies' growing ability to share subjective states. Rather than closely imitating her child, a mother begins to match more loosely the feeling state her child is expressing in one mode, for instance in physical gesture, with an action in different mode, for instance, vocalization. As an example: "A ten-month-old girl finally gets a piece in a jigsaw puzzle. She looks toward her mother, throws her head up in the air, and with a forceful arm flap raises herself partly off the ground in a flurry of exuberance. The mother says 'YES, thatta girl.' The 'YES' is intoned with much stress. It has an explosive rise that echoes the girl's fling of gesture and posture."[10] (The impulse to affectively attune continues in our relationships to older children. When my five-year-old sits with me at Fourth of July fireworks, we reflexively squeeze each other at the bursts of most spectacular brilliance. The squeeze both expresses and amplifies our delight.)

The way mothers tend to talk to their babies has certain widely observed features, leading scientists to name it "motherese." What is distinctive about motherese is that particular rhythmic and musical patterns of mother-infant vocalization are used to convey specific meanings. According to the linguist Steven Pinker, motherese "has interpretable melodies: a rise-and-fall contour for approving, a set of sharp, staccato bursts for prohibiting, a rise pattern for directing attention, and smooth, low legato murmurs for comforting."[11] The relation of certain meanings to certain vocalization patterns are widespread across cultures, and appear to be universal.[12]

In each of these cases — vocal soothing, affect attunement, and motherese — the mother's purpose is not to "teach" her child language. Rather, she intuitively knows that the meaningfulness of her communication depends on its emotional-vocal quality, and she attempts to communicate with her child through a sort of "feeling-drenched" language. The psychoanalyst Hans Loewald had a particularly compelling way of understanding this role of language in the mother-child relationship. Loewald saw people as beginning life in a "primal density," where all aspects of experience, whether physical, emotional, or relational, intermingle. Later, when a child acquires language, the semantic meaning of language becomes increasingly important, but never completely overtakes or replaces the richly affective earlier experience of language. In his view there is no such thing as a truly preverbal realm; rather, as the psychoanalyst Stephen Mitchell put it, "language is an intrinsic dimension of human experience from birth onward. The meaningful distinction is between a global, dense, undifferentiated experience, and a later era, when the semantic features of language have taken precedence over its sensual, affective features."[13]

Loewald questioned the psychoanalytic tendency to distinguish between the (earlier) "primary process" realm of unconscious drives, where fantasy holds sway, and the (later) "secondary process" realm, where ego, consciousness, and logic prevail. For Loewald, our early experience of wholeness is not illusory or "grown out of" with the advent of linear or verbal thinking. To the contrary, people able to experience their own vitality, their own inner richness, manage to "enchant" their conscious life with the emotional depth of their early experience. Optimally, a person remains in vital contact throughout life with the earliest feelings of wholeness, and with the vivid feeling tone of his first experiences with language. Indeed, for the psychologically healthy adult, "communication and interplay between the world of fantasy and the world of objectivity, between imagination and rationality, remain alive."[14]

In essence, Loewald described a kind of communication "midway" between the undifferentiated experience of language in infancy and the highly differentiated semantic meaning language eventually comes to have. Stern's affect attunement is one instance of a mother's feeling-laden use of language, residing somewhere between verbal representation and the "immersed, embedded flow of speech" that helps create the emotional climate of the mother-child relationship.[15] Motherese is similar. It combines words and intonation to communicate meaningful emotional messages, such as comforting or admonishing. It functions to demarcate and differentiate (the "secondary process" facet of language) through its emotional expressivity (the "primary process" facet of language). The apparent universality of motherese surely suggests that utterances paired with emotional tone will communicate best to the very young child. From the child's point of view, this creates a feeling-laden, relational experience of language.

Loewald's perspective on language and emotion captures something not only about childhood experience but also about *parents'* experience of meaning and satisfaction in relating to babies and children. Certainly, children's close connection to their emotional life endows their language with rich metaphorical possibilities. One little boy asked if "yesbody" would be there, meaning the opposite of "nobody." Another greeted his too-hot oatmeal with the exclamation "Very fiyaplace!" Children's creative, evocative use of language often breaks open our own habits of thinking. More generally, though, mothering a small child puts us in touch with our own embodied emotional life in a new way, through our own memory and empathy with our child. In interacting with our baby via language, we integrate various modes of human experiencing and relating. We help the baby to give form to feeling, translating feelings into the shared social realm. This is not some sort of didactic exercise; it is lived out intensely by mothers themselves in the context of a highly sensual, gratifying relationship. In relating to our child, we create a template for how to be in the world. In the best case, we offer a way of being in which emotion and intellect, nonverbal and verbal experience, fluidly communicate.

That our communicative exchanges with our babies and children feel so satisfying to us, so involving of our whole selves, has to do with the way they integrate multiple levels of our conscious and unconscious experience — physical, verbal, and emotional. Loewald described this integration with reference to emotion and language, but it has also been explored over the centuries by mystics and religious faiths. Among mystics of whatever tradition, we encounter the description of an unconscious level of experience that differs from the usual activity of our conscious mind, characterized by a sense of boundarylessness, eternity, oneness, and noncontradiction. In *The Symmetry of God*, the British theologican Rodney Bomford writes of the characteristic human search for meaning, be it for beauty, justice, forgiveness, peace, or being in harmony with one's self and the world — a sense of a true center.[16] Transcendent moments, or glimpses of "the center," occur when the unconscious awareness of oneness is apprehended by the conscious mind.[17] This feeding of the conscious mind by unconscious sources, this process of enriching, deepening, and rendering more resonant the acts and moments of lived experience, is what religious ritual, myth, and poetry are designed to do.

Though they are often fleeting, experiences of eternity or boundarylessness arise in the context of caring for an infant or child. Eternity itself, an ungraspable thing, is experienced by our conscious mind through a sense of the everlasting or momentary, the ancient or the new. When we gaze at our newborn, we are often struck with both her utter newness and her quality of being an "old soul."[18] Having and nurturing a baby, we are also aware of participating in an ancient practice, repeated seemingly endlessly across the generations, yet new to us. It is also not unusual to feel a changed sense of time, especially when caring for a newborn, with round-the-clock feedings and the repetitive cycle of feeding, wakefulness, and naps, but also when we engage in play with an infant or small child. The "nowness" of interacting with a child, or the absorption of looking into her face, can release us momentarily from our usual sense of time. Psychological writings most often focus on the problematic aspects when discussing a mother's feelings of boundarylessness — the baby's obliviousness to the mother's independent existence and its effect on the mother's sense of herself. Less explored but equally important is the way in which interacting with her baby provides the mother with an opportunity for experiencing a *welcome* relaxing of her boundaries.

In different ways, Loewald and Bomford both capture something central about what mothers find truly enjoyable — both pleasurable and meaningful — about the activities of mothering. They speak of an unconscious level of being, in which the laws of time, space, and contradiction do not operate. Human meaning comes about through the creation of forms of expression that use language and conscious thought but maintain their rich source in the feeling of earlier experience. Loewald focuses on the creation of interpersonal meaning, first between baby and mother and then between patient and analyst, whereas Bomford discusses the communal meaning created by religious myth and ritual. But both are interested in similar processes: the "translation function" of the mother, the psychoanalyst, or the religious story or text; the way each moves between primary and secondary processes and, through language, helps others to bring from unconscious, bodily sources the feelings that will make interpersonal and cultural forms and communication meaningful. This "translation function" is not intellectual or rarefied; it is basic to the human act of making meaning.[19]

When people have children, it is not unusual for them to feel the urge to extend the sense of connection awakened by the tender parenting bond to a broader connectedness to the world. The tendency of parents to return to the religious practices of their youth or forge new ones once they have children can be seen as a response to the impulse to place parenthood in a context of transcendent meaning. Religious traditions in no way exhaust the forms taken by this parental impulse. My husband likes to spend Sunday morning with our children in the sacred practice of looking at crabs at the beach; Louise Erdrich compares her children's baths to church.[20] Whatever form we give them, our sacred practices express the sense of integration and connectedness we feel with our children and extend it to our broader relationships — with others, with history, with the natural and spiritual world.

Mothering and the
Experience of "Flow"

MOTHERS OF BABIES AND SMALL children often perceive themselves to be in a different mental state than they are accustomed to. Some say, "I've lost my mind," while others talk about knowing what to do but not really knowing how they know. Mothers of babies can be uncharacteristically inarticulate when it comes to talking about their experience.[21] I think this has to do with having one foot in unconscious process and the other in conscious process. It's not that mothers of infants are merged, have lost their sense of self, their cognitive faculties, or their sense of boundedness. Rather, they are tuning in on the level of empathy with their baby in a way that is specific and nuanced but hard to articulate or describe. They are acting on what psychologists have called "implicit knowledge," a nondeclarative, nonverbal sensitivity to the interaction.[22]

This same access to the implicit, feeling dimension of communication persists once our children become verbal. When I step back to analyze what goes on when I try to communicate with my young child, I realize I am always seeking after some feeling of "rightness" or "fit" between how I express myself and how he will take in what I communicate. In daily conversation, my three-year-old asks a question or comments ("Mom, Mom, there are gray clouds! It's going to rain!"), and I am aware that in my response, I use intonation and quality of voice, in combination with words, to try to open up a new area of knowledge for him. Maybe I'll say, "Well, you know what?" — getting him positioned mentally to receive new information — "That's actually fog. And sometimes fog or clouds means it's going to rain, but sometimes it doesn't. Have you ever noticed that sometimes in the morning it's kind of cloudy but then it gets sunny?" He might say, "Yeah . . ." "Well, where we live we sometimes have fog in the morning, and then the sun comes out." As I explain, I am trying to communicate information; but I am also trying, not quite consciously, to create an *experience*, one that embeds the specific information in a particular kind of affective exchange where he feels his interest is shared and his curiosity is valued and where my response is adapted to his capacity to digest the information conveyed.[23] Seeking after this "rightness" is not always automatic or effortless. Particularly when I am tired, the feeling in these interactions is one of pushing against a slightly resistant medium to clear more area for sharing and communication. That quality of effort suggests one of the striking features of these interactions, whether they involve talking to a preschooler or comforting a baby: they require effort toward a goal, however dimly perceived and unelaborated, and satisfaction and pleasure result when the goal is met.

The kind of goal at issue is so different from what we commonly conceive of as a goal that it is almost unrecognizable.[24] Yet, we can understand it better with reference to the psychological notion of "flow." "Flow" is an evocative term for enjoyment, or "optimal experience," studied by the psychologist Mihaly Csikszentmihalyi among others.[25] We experience "flow" when we are able to put our energy into using skills that help us meet self-chosen challenges or goals. Flow experiences, regardless of whether they arise from a tennis match, meditation, or work, tend to have a number of things in common. Action and awareness become fused in a state of total concentration and involvement. People lose a sense of self-consciousness, and they experience a sense of heightened responsiveness to the task at hand. Flow experiences tend to occur within goal-directed activities where people have devoted themselves to developing skills, and they are often enabled in situations, such as games, that provide clear feedback.

Goals, challenges, and feedback are easily understood within the context of games and many work situations, but it takes a bit more unpacking to see their relevance to the activities of mothering. We can start from a fascinating observation by Daniel Stern regarding mothers' motivations for affectively attuning to their infants. The most frequent reason mothers gave for attuning to their baby was not communication (such as soothing, energizing, or changing behavior); rather, it was *interpersonal communion,* "'to be with' the infant, 'to share,' 'to participate in,' 'to join in.'" "Communion," Stern writes, "means to share in another's experience with no attempt to change what that person is doing or believing. This idea captures . . . mother's behavior as seen by experimenters and by the mothers themselves."[26]

Mothers are communing with their babies for its own sake, for the sheer mutual enjoyment of sharing the moment. It is an intrinsic satisfaction, an embracing of what unfolds between two people. But — and this is important — absorption in the moment also serves certain goals. They are not goals that a mother would name as such; somehow, to say that one is attuning to one's child "to enhance interpersonal growth" sounds woefully incomplete. Still, on an unverbalized level, what goes on serves goals of connection, growth, and happiness.

In communion experiences, growth occurs through enjoyment and the complexity that it engenders in the personality. Consider the nature of human growth as seen in terms of the concept of flow. An important way growth of the self occurs is through the mutual influence of enjoyment and complexity. An interaction is truly enjoyable when it entails a stretch toward something new, meaningful, or challenging.[27] The effort to stretch one's awareness or skills, the intention to share and discover something new, intrinsically involves seeking after greater complexity, which in turn contributes to psychological growth.

The happiness mothers get from moments of communion with their children is an example of the ability of flow experiences to contribute to a richer and stronger sense of self.[28] When I am absorbed in the moment, I am graced with self-forgetfulness. I am not preoccupied with myself, but in a state of keen responsiveness to the interaction at hand. After the experience of absorption and challenge is over and I am returned to self-consciousness, the self upon which I reflect is changed, "now enriched by new skills and fresh achievements."[29]

New motherhood clearly draws on new skills, requires a stretching of the self in the service of new challenges, and involves goals that matter intensely. But every stage of childhood and parenthood offers new avenues for growth. We intuitively grasp the way flow experiences add complexity to the personality when we spend the day building sand castles together, for instance, absorbed in the project of excavating a moat that will protect the castle from the encroaching tide. We return from the day tired from sun and salt, enriched by our shared absorption, and happy because those shared interactions harmonize with our larger goal of contributing to our child's enjoyment, creativity, and growth.

In the car, my now-school-age children and I listen to the Beatles. I love to have them guess who is singing lead and backup, to listen for the bass line, to discover the added instrument on "You've Got to Hide Your Love Away" (flute) or "You're Going to Lose That Girl" (bongos?). I like discovering which songs they really love, finding out what melodies move them. For me, our shared enjoyment connects backward to my early childhood, circa 1966, to my love for my older brother, to the whole feel of summer in my garden with "Day Tripper" wafting out the window. I bring all that intense emotion from my early life into the present interaction. They observe my enthusiasm, rooted in interest and memory, and they not only learn something concrete about the Beatles, but they identify with my process of loving something in the world. I experience delight in sharing what I love with them, and their own response to the music is enhanced by that fact. As I notice anew all the details I can teach them about, I find more facets to love. Between me and my children, between versions of myself, between us and the music, there is a flow back and forth, a sharing of love on many different levels.

Mothers' "Translation Function": The Case of the Virgin Mary

IN THE PROCESS OF RELATING to my children, I continually move back and forth, not quite consciously, between physical, emotional, and cognitive aspects of myself, and between past, present, and future. The process involves the communication between levels of experience that Loewald explored in terms of language, and that Csikszentmihalyi explored with respect to flow states. This maternal "translation function" has also been eloquently described by the French theorist and psychoanalyst Julia Kristeva.

Kristeva's writings offer their own idiom for describing primary- and secondary-process mental states: the "semiotic," rooted in an early time, when the music of language — its force, rhythm, cadence — is experienced in the context of the infant's relation to the mother, and the "symbolic," when language takes on declarative consensual meaning.[30] In considering the position of women in society, Kristeva invoked this distinction to reject what she saw as two alternatives feminism has offered to women: on the one hand, a "semiotic" retreat from participation in mainstream culture into visions of a self-enclosed female world, and on the other, a "symbolic" identification with the social and political power held by men. In place of these two extremes, she argues for a certain kind of philosophy of translation: "Let us . . . .refuse all roles to summon this 'truth' situated outside time. . . . But how can we do this? By listening; by recognizing the unspoken of all discourse, . . . by emphasizing at each point whatever remains unsatisfied, repressed, new, eccentric, incomprehensible, that which disturbs the mutual understanding of the established powers."[31] Kristeva's image assumes women's participation in the social order, but always with an ear attentive to other levels of experience, especially that which is forgotten, repressed, or marginal.

Kristeva is particularly interested in motherhood, because motherhood centrally involves dialogue, between self and other and between aspects of ourselves. Optimally, it involves maintaining access to all registers of our experience — the bodily, the intuitive, the rational — and not siding with one while pushing away another. One obvious instance is pregnancy, when we literally carry another within ourselves. We can go through pregnancy fairly oblivious to its implications, but it almost impels at least momentary glimpses of a different way of being ourselves, of being *in* ourselves. There is a vast and rich psychological literature brimming over with clinical vignettes about the bizarre dreams, intense fantasies, and subterranean psychic reworkings that accompany the body's toil at building a baby. I have paged through the journals I kept during pregnancies and postpartum and have been struck by their efflorescent imaginings, their depiction of mental states closed to me now. Kristeva speaks of it in more philosophical terms as the "redoubling up of the body, separation and coexistence of self and of an other, of nature and consciousness, of physiology and speech."[32]

When we are pregnant, the utterly novel condition of having another within us, a being that we slowly invest with subjectivity, potentially changes our relationship to our own unconscious. We exist in relation to something that is not a nothing and not a person. In this transitional space, we undertake mentally something akin to what our bodies do physically. We knit together a being, out of illusion, reverie, fantasy. When we are happy to be pregnant, we feel good things come from those parts of ourselves we don't control and that we can't directly see. That may be what the writer Faye Weldon meant when she said that having children gives a woman confidence in her creativity.[33] A pregnant woman perceives evidence from, and is in conversation with, primal sources of her being, her body and her unconscious mind.[34]

Pregnancy can also heighten a certain kind of multiple consciousnesses with respect to time. Kristeva contrasts *cyclical* time (of gestation, of biological rhythms) and *monumental* time, or eternity, with *linear* time, "time as departure, progression, and arrival — in other words, the time of history."[35] In pregnancy, all three ways of experiencing time are accessible in a heightened way. When we conceive children, history is in the making. Rarely do we feel so "up close" to a process that changes the course of things forever. One day we are not pregnant, the next we are; somewhere, sometime, as we browse the bookstore, buy the groceries, meet a deadline, sleep and dream, a vital connection is made, a journey is traveled, a zygote is implanted. All the while we busy ourselves, doing the things we always do. And yet, dimly we know that biology is launching, in its implacably repetitive and cyclical way, a unique human destiny. We are part of both the cycle of life and the march of history. This is an incarnation, and even as we stroll to the drugstore to pick up some toothpaste, it inspires awe — all the more so, perhaps, due to the contrast we suddenly perceive between the routine and the extraordinary. That sense of awe is often one adoptive parents express as well when evoking the experience of joining destinies with their child.

The figure of Mary, Mother of God has been so compelling over the ages in part because she captures mothers' simultaneous participation in cyclical, historical, and eternal time. In his article "Jesus Before He Could Talk," the theologian Jack Miles suggests that Mary's story is enduringly immediate because it conveys the multiple aspects of time experienced by individual women expecting children and expresses a sense of possibility, specialness, and duress with which mothers everywhere can identify.[36] I hung a print of Fra Angelico's *Annunciation* above the changing table as I readied a room for my first child. It was December, and as I looked at the picture, it struck me with stunning clarity, and for the first time, that Mary was not just a woman far away in time and space who was undergoing something magical. Though she was enshrined as extraordinary, a virgin attended by an angel, her sense of amazement was really not all that different from mine.

Besides holding in tension the various ways that mothers experience time, the symbol of Mary expresses and contains paradoxes in women's feelings about motherhood. Kristeva suggests that she does so partly by "striking a shrewd balance between" the female sense of power and specialness that arises from motherhood and the masculine power hierarchy of state and church.[37] The image of the Virgin Mary gathers to itself qualities of the maternal and the mother-child relationship; at the same time, this realm of feeling is incorporated within a largely masculine-inspired church dogma. In this sense, the symbol of Mary functions not only to reconcile competing and conflicting agendas within women themselves but also to represent maternal desire within the constraints of patriarchal structure. "The Virgin Mother occupies the vast territory that lies on either side of the parenthesis of language": on the one side, "high Christic sublimation, which she aspires to achieve and sometimes transcends," and on the other, access to the unrepresented semiotic, the world of the body, "the extralinguistic realms of the unnameable."[38] Mary suffuses the doctrines of the church with particular patterns of mother-child emotion, and the church fuels its own power through harnessing the energy and power of the maternal.

This very role for Mary was one the church sought. Orthodox Christianity "sanctioned the transitional function of the Maternal by calling the Virgin a 'bond', a 'middle' or an 'interval'"[39] "between the unnameable and the Name."[40] The figure of Mary mediates between language and nonlanguage, embodiment and spirituality, and in her role as intercessor, between suffering humanity and the heavens. Mary accomplishes on the level of symbol what a mother ideally accomplishes on the level of practice. The pregnant woman moves from singularity to carrying another within. The mother moves back and forth between her child's experience and her own, and calls on her own earliest bodily, emotional, and verbal relationships to do so. On the level of language and culture, symbol and metaphor integrate personal experience with shared cultural forms. The symbol of Mary translates our most basic maternal and infantile experiences into an intelligible network of narratives, myths, and cultural meaning, what Bomford called "mythic speech."[41]

Whereas at times Kristeva appears to contrast the "male" world of the symbolic with the "female" world of the semiotic, she is at other times concerned with the mother's *own* relationship to the symbolic order. Essayist Allison Weir endorses this latter project, arguing that "the mother does not exist outside the social order, as its support."[42] The mother's relationship to the symbolic realm of culture and language is characterized by her simultaneous participation in the body *and* language; the mother, like the poet, is ideally or optimally someone who can participate in the symbolic world of language and culture while maintaining access to multiple registers of experience. What her child identifies with is not simply the mother as representative of inchoate, preverbal experience, but with her "process of subjectivity" itself.[43] Weir captures the fact that a child identifies with the *process* of how his or her mother creates reality, how she lives the relationship between culture and her deepest wellsprings of feeling; in short, how she makes meaning.

This may sound abstract, but it can be illustrated concretely. On a small scale, it is what I was trying to do with the Beatles. But more broadly, think of the thrust of recent findings in attachment research. One of the most astonishing and generative observations in the study of attachment in recent years has been the robust connection between a child's security of attachment to a parent and that parent's ability to think and speak coherently about her own experiences of attachment, whether good or bad. When we look at those parents who demonstrate such coherence, we are seeing an example of what we might call "good translation"; that is, emotional and cognitive access to a full range of childhood experiences, whatever their quality, and an ability to make sense of them in terms that are coherent to others.

A research study that sheds light on this issue examined the relationship between a mother's observed behavior with her toddler, her perception of her relationship to her toddler, and her adult attachment quality. It found that those mothers who displayed "the capacity to flexibly access and integrate a range of thoughts and feelings relative to her relationship with her own parents" most often experienced joy in relating to their child. It is a bit of a shock to see the word "joy" anywhere in an academic study, but in this study of mothers of toddlers, there it is: "the [mother's] experience of joy and pleasure," and "joy, coherence, and richness of perception" in her relation to her toddler were correlated with her autonomous-secure status on the Adult Attachment Interview (AAI).[44] Recall that a mother's rating on the AAI is not based on her actual experiences, good or bad, with her own parents, but the *sense* she makes of them. Thus in a very real way, the way we translate our past emotional experiences into meaning in the present exerts a palpable effect on our reality. One could even go further and say it creates our reality. The autonomous-secure mother is able to transform her childhood experience into a mode of interaction with her child that does not systematically distort or suppress emotion from, and memory of, the past. When a parent is unable to do that — when their language is too cut off from their affect, as it is for dismissive parents, or their language is utterly permeated with stray affect, as it is for preoccupied parents — the child identifies with that "process of subjectivity" and develops an unsatisfying way of relating to others.[45]

What this joyful relating looks like is illustrated in a vignette by the psychologist Susan Coates:

> A young toddler, barely two, is playing in the backyard; he excitedly pulls at and sniffs some flowers while making excited but unintelligible utterances. His mother can see his pleasure, a pleasure that differs from her own, and smiles in recognition saying "You really love those colors, don't you? You are a guy who loves flowers." . . . The child looks at the mother, sees himself, and smiles; there is a recognition and a discovery of a part of the self held by the other. By virtue of being sensitively met, the child comes to experience loving colors and flowers as part of his notion of himself, and this notion has emerged in the transitional space created by the mother's attuned response. He has been met by his mother in an unobtrusive way such that her needs have not been imposed upon him; thus he has the experience of his own creativity.[46]

Here, the mother's ability to "meet" her son is rooted in her freedom to perceive and enter into his emotional state. Her freedom and flexibility are likewise the ground of her *own* ability to take pleasure and joy in their interaction. Her son's experience of the flowers is not completely captured by her words, of course, for experience always exceeds language. But her response brings into language, and into shared social and emotional reality, a maximally attuned understanding of the boy and his feelings, which he is then able to "easily and pleasurably integrate" into his sense of himself.[47]

Motherhood and Meaning-Making

THE QUESTION "WHAT WILL BRING me happiness?" lies at the heart of many women's desire to have children. Yet happiness, and the integration it implies, is what many mothers feel they lack. It surfaces in the feeling of being chronically torn, of never being able to feel they are doing any job well. The themes endlessly shift, rebalance, and shift again when one is in the course of raising children. I remember hearing a radio call-in show with the editors of the anthology *Mothers Who Think: Tales of Real-Life Parenthood*. A single mother whose children were grown called in. Impassioned, she said that what matters in mothering children is not whether you work or not, not whether you are baking cookies or winning court cases or driving a truck. What matters is whether you feel joy in being with your kids when you are with them. She said it had taken her twenty years to realize this. Then somehow, by the end of the call, she wound around to saying that motherhood is "hell."[48]

It can be both joy and hell at different times. Part of the hell is not being able to hang on to the joy and the insight about joy that occasionally refreshes and then slips through the fingers like water. It may also be brought on by the dissonance between one's awareness of the potential for joy and the complex personal and social obstacles to its fulfillment. The hell is also about the anxiety, so often expressed by mothers, that they are insufficient somehow, that they are not doing enough, or being enough, or giving enough to their children.

Statements like that of the single mother are shorthand expressions that we need to explore further. They draw energy from real conflicts between competing pressures and from the effect of such conflicts on our ability to enjoy mothering. We bring to mothering the illusion that we should, or could, do or be or give everything to our child, and when we fail, which we inevitably do, we either blame ourselves for our own inadequacy or search for social messages that have imposed unrealistic standards on us. But both attempts to lay blame fundamentally misapprehend what mothering *is*. The poet Jorie Graham said, "In poetry, you have to feel deeply something inchoate, something which is coming up from a place that you don't even know the register of."[49] All mothers may not be poets, but with her child, a mother necessarily engages in a similar process.[50] We can't know or be or do everything; we can only listen, notice, and feel our way into who our children are, who we are, and what each of us needs in order to become fully realized as who we are. Mothering is partly about improvisation, creativity, and an openness to discovering what is emergent. Kristeva captured the open-ended journey of mothering when she wrote: "The arrival of the child . . . leads the mother into the labyrinths of an experience that, without the child, she would only rarely encounter: love for an other. Not for herself, nor for an identical being, and still less for another person with whom 'I' fuse (love or sexual passion). But the slow, difficult, and delightful apprenticeship in attentiveness, gentleness, forgetting oneself."[51]

Motherhood puts women in a different relationship to themselves. It *really* does; not as some sort of pale "shifting of priorities," but as a new relationship to experience. As such, it can cause them to reopen themselves to forgotten depths of emotional experience, and to rethink their identity in light of what they discover. For many women who become mothers, the importance of finding a new relationship between different levels of experience is shocking in its peremptoriness. Kristeva writes that the artist's doing his art is necessary for "creating" the artist: "If he doesn't work, if he doesn't produce his music or his page or his sculpture, he would be, quite simply, ill or not alive."[52] Mothers can feel this way about mothering as well.

A mother's sense that caring for her children engages her at this level of vital meaning — that it is something, as my friend said, she "can't not do" — is a sense I've seen met with everything from joy to relief to resignation to outrage at the unfairness of it all. Whatever our personal reaction, the available cultural images of motherhood rarely help us to plumb its complexity. Mothers often talk about caring for their children in ways that feel strangely detached from the search for meaning. We put in terms of generic sentiment — "I just love being around babies" or "Work's a lot easier than being at home" — what we experience as deeper and more encompassing questions. We may adopt a well-worn story to account for a more complex array of intentions. Maybe we'll take the view that hanging around with children is akin to custodial care, numbing the mind and disempowering women. Or maybe we'll take the sentimental view, celebrating the "little things" — the scruffy little shoes, the worn teddy bear, the small acts of sacrifice — as tiny sources of big meaning. We may take these well-trod paths because it is so hard to communicate what matters to us most deeply. Perhaps we are embarrassed by the grandness of the aspiration or the delicacy of the process. Certainly, questions of ultimate meaning tend not to be part of polite conversation, especially in an arena as fraught as motherhood. Perhaps, to face our feelings fully would force us to confront choices that feel too difficult to make. But when we speak of our aspirations, we often substitute inoffensive clichés for a much more nuanced internal reality.

Many factors conspire to obscure the effort to make meaning that motherhood expresses. One factor is our confusion about what frame of reference to apply. In one sense mothering is work, but of what kind? Csikszentmihalyi remarks: "Work requiring great skills and that is done freely refines the complexity of self; and, on the other hand, . . . there are few things as entropic as unskilled work done under compulsion."[53] Mothering activity has often been lumped in with this second category, viewed as seldom freely chosen and not requiring special skills.

Certainly over the millennia, many women have not freely chosen motherhood. But the belief that it requires no special skills says more about how we conceptualize skills than it does about motherhood. What many mothers find satisfying in mothering is precisely such an exercise of skills, and the contribution that exercising those skills makes to the complexity and richness of oneself and one's child. Ironically, the skill set mothers draw on in nurturing their children is rarely identified as such. Using empathy and intuition to understand inanimate things — as does the repairman when he asks himself, "If I were that toaster, and I didn't work, what would be wrong with me?"[54] — has been held up as an example of transcendent "flow" experiences in work. But this same skill, when applied every day by a mother to the inner workings of her very animate child, tends to elicit neither wonder nor respect.

Another source of confusion about how to evaluate maternal motivation is that some of the conditions provided by work situations, including the sense of control and opportunities for clear feedback, promote feelings of effectiveness, growth, and "flow" in relatively unambiguous ways. Because of that, jobs can feel more satisfying, and mothering can feel like harder work. In our society, mothers themselves must create the context in which their mothering takes place; and both structuring the environment and directing the activities within it are indeed hard work. Further, the goals of mothering activity are more openended, and the application of skills less quantifiable and more improvisational, than those usually provided by jobs. This is one source of the "I'm so glad it's Monday morning" feeling of many working mothers. When your job gives you some control and measurable achievement, being with children can seem chaotic, exhausting, and Sisyphean by comparison. I once read that the journalist Meredith Vieira purposely kept her office messy so she wouldn't be tempted to spend too much time in it away from her kids. When work is a haven of order, the only place we can complete a thought, it is easy to see why we might linger.

Sometimes as mothers we find that the relative lack of structure inherent in staying home with a small child gives rise to frankly painful mental states. We may have counted on work to provide a sense of meaning and effectiveness, to structure not only our activities but our internal life. Left alone with children, we may feel anxious, sad, confused, or at loose ends. When I was at home with infants and small children, at times I noticed that my need to neaten the house would escalate in direct proportion to how little time I had to myself to read, think, or attend my own tasks. Aside from obtaining unexpected insight into the fabled compulsive housekeeping pathology of fifties housewives, I gained renewed appreciation of my own need for some domain of self-direction. We may want, in principle, to feel free to enjoy time with our children, and we may ardently believe in the value of doing so. But in practice, when tending them, we may feel troubled or unproductive. That dissonance can spiral into a general sense of ineffectiveness or even failure, which, depending on one's psychological makeup, can be tolerable or a feeling to be escaped at all costs.

The way that accomplishments are measured and rewarded, and their relationship to how our society structures work, means that many mothers experience themselves at the intersection of two competing and somewhat mutually exclusive reward systems. This can produce painful conflict, not least because it is hard to do two things well. Not only must we divide our energy and emotional resources, but from the point of view of happiness, there is no greater "flow killer" than conflict. When we interrupt our participation in a process, either at work or with our child, with a litany of doubts and concerns — "Should I really be doing this? Is this the best use of my time?" — we drain our experience of pleasure, cohesion, and depth. Some mothers feel that this level of conflict, particularly as it relates to their work and mothering roles, is a constant companion, detracting from the rewards of either role.

A sustainable and sustaining approach to this kind of conflict begins with respect for, and true curiosity about, our own inner lives. If we desire to draw on all levels of our personality, to be fully present and alive in relating to our children, we usually can't get there by suppressing one set of feelings or another; rather, we have to remain open to the multiple strands of need, motive, and feeling in our children and ourselves. If I feel guilty leaving my child, for example, and I simply suppress the feeling, I lose an opportunity for self-knowledge. If I can sit with it, I may learn something. I may notice that the guilt doesn't vanish when I see my child happily playing with the babysitter. I may realize that the knot of feelings I have labeled "guilt" also includes my own sadness at not being able to stay. It undoubtedly also includes my happiness at being free to leave. Whether I use this information to adjust my outward arrangements or not, awareness of my own feelings gives me a more complete picture of the emotional situation. Cultivating openness means I will feel my sadness, but it also gives me more freedom to experience my joy. I am then also more likely to be able to tune into my child's full range of feelings as well.

Openness also entails recognizing that we are entitled to our own complexity. When a friend arrived at work after a fight with her preadolescent daughter, she was racked with self-blame and stung by her daughter's criticism of her ineptitude over a trivial matter. Resisting the self-punitive rush to cast herself within the reductive Manichean framework of "working" versus "stay-at-home" mother, she instead sat with the fact that she, like her daughter, had a deep and complicated interior world, a history. She did not know everything, and it was all right to tolerate not knowing. By including herself in the circle of her own compassion, she could think more clearly about what was going on, in herself, her daughter, and their relationship.

As mothers we should give ourselves the room, the dignity, to discover what we think and what we want. Each of us must think through the issues for herself so that the life we live is a personal creation rather than a resigned-to reality. It is hard to hold on to all the threads of our lives while we are mothers; but at the same time, the actual practice of mothering carries within it an extraordinary thrust toward happiness. It is a happiness that we must find the words to articulate and that we owe ourselves the freedom to explore. We might then begin to envision maternal pleasure, not only as a fleeting accompaniment to the "little moments" of maternal connectedness, but also as a touchstone for a truer model of maternal motivation and identity.

5

Ambivalence

THE MEANEST I EVER WAS to any of my children was one evening when my husband was out, and I was ruminating about the success of a colleague. Something in the comparison of her professional jet-setting with my house-boundedness gave my life an almost suffocating sense of thanklessness. An unbridgeable divide opened between the seemingly simple tasks I was unable to accomplish (cleaning the house, washing my hair) and the seemingly difficult ones (getting promoted, fielding interviews) that she pulled off with ease. Had I been holding a vase, I'd have thrown it; as it was, I had a ten-month-old who was sitting on the bathroom floor crying because he couldn't see me in the shower. Pulling back the shower curtain, I yelled at him for crying. At that he only cried louder, his bereftness now compounded by terror. I must have looked like a drenched witch. I was in the grip of something on which I had no perspective. Having begun innocently enough as a bout of professional frustration, it was now a black hole sucking up any particle of my effectiveness as a mother, and even my sense of being a compassionate or reasonable human being. I finally collapsed on my bed in tears, holding my son close and saying I was sorry.

When I had calmed down enough to think again, this incident showed me something useful about the psychology of bad moments caring for children. The way we feel toward our child, and the way we behave, is shaped by the internal balance we are striking at a given moment between all of our own desires, judgments, expectations, and frustrations. That inner landscape — everything from wanting recognition to reliving painful events from our pasts to worrying about our job, marriage, or money — plays a big part in how we manage the ups and downs of mothering.

Something I read by the writer Anne Lamott gave me insight into this phenomenon. In a piece entitled "Mother Anger: Theory and Practice," Lamott articulates the mechanism behind our sudden, surprising bursts of rage. "When we blow up at our kids," she writes,

> we only *think* we're going from zero to sixty in one second. Our surface and persona is so calm that when the problem first begins, we sound in control when we say, "Now, honey, stop that," or "That's enough." But it's only an illusion. Because actually, all day we've been nursing anger toward the boss or boyfriend or mother, but because we can't get mad at nonkid people, we stuff it down; we keep going without blowing up because we don't want to lose our jobs or partners or reputations. So when the problem with your kid starts up, you're actually starting at fifty-nine, only you're not moving. You're in high idle already, but you are not even aware of how vulnerable and disrespected you already feel.[1]

Once you recognize the mechanism Lamott described, you begin to see it everywhere. You are getting ready to go out in the evening and your three-year-old keeps hovering around your legs. You feel dissatisfied with how you look and — boom — "Could you *please stop* getting in my way?" The kids are squabbling in the backseat of the car while you review an upsetting interaction with your employer, and — boom — "Stop it! You kids are *driving me nuts!*" You are stewing over a judgmental comment made by your husband or mother, your child upsets his cereal bowl, and — boom — that spilled milk on the floor suddenly feels like a completely justified focus for your rage. Medea, a woman so crazed by her husband's adultery that she killed their children in revenge, may be the ultimate exemplar of a mother for whom other preoccupations intruded on (and finally eclipsed) her ability to mother.

My own particular well of misery that night gave me renewed respect for the psychic conflict that is endemic to the lived experience of motherhood. It could not be otherwise, given all the elements that are constantly in play: inevitably conflicting goals and desires, our own childhood experiences, and the lack of self-control that arises in moments of frustration, ineffectualness, or fatigue. For me, at that moment, the focus was achievement, but the more profound issue was a sense of competence, value, and self-worth. It is hard sometimes to feel recognized for the value of our work in the day-to-day activity of mothering. And anything that makes our sense of competence more tenuous — like a baby who can't be soothed, or a preschooler who can't behave in public, or a school-age child who cannot learn — can evoke doubts about our effectiveness and worth in an even stronger way. Had I been able to step back, I could have reasoned that I was doing what I wanted to do, spending most of my time caring for my children. But in the moment, exhausted from endless bedtime demands, my self-esteem precarious, that knowledge was no bulwark against a whole different set of feelings. In that moment, the intrinsic rewards of mothering, usually palpable to me, felt invisible, lost.

What is remarkable about these moments is not that they are a rarity or a crisis, but rather that they are so routine. If there is any feature we can reliably assign to the experience of mothering, it is that it will encompass extreme states of feeling. Weathering and working with those states is not an incidental blip or exception; it is a central moral, emotional, and aspirational problem and opportunity that motherhood presents. Becoming a mother puts us into a new relationship with almost everything, not only our unconscious but also our bodies, our partners, our parents, our social world, our concept of self, and, of

course, our child. Mixed feelings about our children and ourselves are basic to what motherhood *is*. Childbirth expert and
anthropologist Sheila Kitzinger, herself a mother of five, wrote:
"If having children is all about love, it's also about passion, and
once you have passion, there's always this other side — of feeling desperately frustrated, perhaps feeling depressed, angry, all
the other side of the intensity of love."[2]

On the simplest level, we are susceptible to extreme states of
feeling because we are fleshly beings, with restless minds and
emotions, and the fact is, we get tired. A friend and her husband
tried for years to conceive a child. Finally they adopted a baby
boy, by whom they felt extraordinarily blessed. Later, after several miscarriages and untold pain and suffering, my friend found
herself pregnant. In her first trimester of pregnancy, another
baby became available for adoption, whom my friends also
adopted. I visited my friend, now the mother of a two-week-old,
when she was in her nauseated tenth week of pregnancy. She
and her husband were trying valiantly to curb the aggression of
their none-too-pleased older son. My friend was beyond exhaustion. There was no question that she felt a great deal of joy and
satisfaction in being a mother. There was also no question that
she felt awful, overwhelmed with being pregnant, caring for a
newborn, and dealing with her four-year-old. A sense of meaning, joy, and gratitude proceeded alongside abject fatigue, nausea, and a sense of ineffectualness as a parent.

Bone-tiredness, the endless round of viruses, or even the inability to make a dent in one's lists can dampen or temporarily
extinguish the pleasure to be had in mothering.[3] But often, the
greatest effect of such states is their power to intensify our existing conflicts. If our psychic equilibrium depends on orderly surroundings because we grew up in chaos, then fatigue and lack of
time to straighten up will tend to make us more on edge with
our children. If we are mourning lost professional status, a sense
of ineffectiveness can only make our resentment of our child's
demands more extreme. If our self-esteem comes from doing our
job well, then the taxing demands and divided attention moth-

erhood introduces can make us feel like we do everything badly. I was astonished to find, when I had infants, how closely the state of extreme exhaustion resembled depression, with all the feelings of inadequacy, irritation, and lack of energy that go with it.

Ideally we want to find a way to accept and work with whatever mental states motherhood throws at us, to try to find a balanced, centered place in ourselves where we can make sense of what we are feeling, forgive ourselves for lapses in self-control, and move on. Often, that is more easily said than done. In *Flow*, Csikszentmihalyi observes that the people most able to maintain a sense of equilibrium, flexibility, and flow in the face of obstacles are those who have a sense of inner confidence.[4] But that is exactly what is often in short supply in new mothers, or in any mother in the grips of work-family conflict, parenting challenges, or troubling childhood memories of her own. Old family patterns can reassert themselves with such force, and with so little rational consent, that often we must struggle with having our best intentions upended by our unwitting repetitions of them. A friend of mine felt undone by the way she was harshly judging her preadolescent daughter's neatness and grooming habits. She could literally hear her own mother's criticisms of her, as if she were channeling her. For weeks she felt that her relationship with her daughter was "horrible," which also made her feel very bad about herself. Fear of "becoming like one's mother" is so intense for some women that they are reluctant to have children.

But it is important to recognize that the ability to achieve a balanced, forgiving perspective on the roiling feelings aroused by motherhood is affected not only by our physical limits or family histories, but also by the larger context of social values and how we perceive our place within it. For all of us, irritation, boredom, frustration, and ineffectiveness are inevitable passing states in a day of mothering. But how we *interpret* these states is not simply personal; it is influenced by the social values and life choices of our peer group and the larger social surround. Depending on my interpretive framework, for instance, I could have decided that my fit of temper with my ten-month-old "meant" I should change my life and get a job with more extrinsic gratification; that it "meant" I should get over my attachment to recognition in the world; or that it "meant" I should somehow try to accept the inevitability of conflict and stay clear on my overarching goals as ballast against discontentment or rash action. I could attempt to "resolve" my ambivalence in the direction of one or the other role; I could try to live with a certain degree of ambiguity; I could even try to deny that any conflict existed.

Much has been written about how social taboos against expressing "the dark side" of motherhood get in the way of mothers' constructive acknowledgment of their own ambivalence.[5] Exacting ideals, it is argued, pressure mothers to aspire to continual availability, devotion, and patience, and to feel ashamed if they can't achieve it. This is certainly one side of the problem. But in my "drenched witch" episode, I felt more pressure from almost the opposite ideal: a newer ideal that urges mothers not to be emotionally susceptible to, or professionally derailed by, the inconvenient passions or practical exigencies of hands-on engagement with children. Although I'd blown my top, the locus of my sense of failure was not that I was inadequately devoted. Rather, I had a self-flagellating, if fleeting, sense that I was weak or overly emotional because I was unable or unwilling to delegate more of the care of my children to others and invest my energy in professional achievement like my colleague.

In a more reflective frame of mind, I could recognize the value in what I was doing, even when it included anger, which it inescapably did. And I could also reaffirm that I generally wanted to do and believed in what I was doing, and that a momentary state of frustration and longing didn't cancel all that out. (A mother at work all day, incidentally, is in a different situation but faces a similar psychological task. A sad day of missing one's child at work, even if compelling, does not imply that one should instantly quit work and go home.) Yet in the moment, my conflict was between how affected I felt by my children, how emotionally invested I was in caring for them, on the one hand,

and how frustrated I felt about the change it had wrought in my universe of choices on the other. I don't think I am alone in this. A focal point for maternal ambivalence today is the underlying tension between the reality that motherhood has the potential to transform us, to change everything, and our complex reactions to that fact. Women today struggle with wanting to let their relationship with their child teach them something new and to be able to rethink their life choices in light of what they learn. Yet they also want and often need to continue their previous commitments and interests. That tension, between openness to the possibility of letting motherhood radically reorder one's priorities and continuing with one's other valued goals relatively unaffected, contributes to the inchoate sense of inadequacy or confusion that can abruptly emerge on any given day.

People deal with that tension in different ways. I have known mothers who seem to have set up their lives quite successfully to minimize the practical adjustments and emotional upheavals of motherhood. As I talked with one woman, it dawned on her that she virtually never got angry with her kids. The few hours they had together in the evening were so precious that somehow anger just didn't "come up." Another woman worried before having children that she would be prone to short-temperedness, so she arranged her life so that she had copious nanny coverage and few waking hours with her children. She professed to love being a mother, but to me that feeling seemed predicated on shielding herself and her children from any possibility of disharmony, anger, or flaring conflict.

Though these mothers found a way to minimize the unpleasant feelings that come up with our children, one could argue that the price they paid was too high. We all wish we could sometimes be a little less involved, a little less pulled by our children, but that is also where the real human work gets done, where the emotional action is. These mothers, it seems, shied away from letting themselves be changed, letting their kids get under their skin. They seem to have sacrificed intimacy for the sake of predictability and emotional control.

At the same time that I see the downside of these mothers' approaches, I have occasionally felt oddly impressed that they seem so *unaffected*, either by their child's wish for their attention or their own desire to give it. I am impressed, I think, because from a social point of view, there are legitimate reasons for, and benefits to, why a woman might not want to be too affected by motherhood. On virtually any measure of outward achievement — pay, power, prestige, even job satisfaction — investing time and energy in motherhood is a recipe for marginalization. For mothers up and down the socioeconomic ladder, this fact gives rise not only to practical conflicts but to internal conflicts as well. The rewards of work — making a living, contributing to society, exercising our skills — often compete with the rewards of attending to our children. It is understandable, then, that we sometimes cope by obscuring one side of the tension we feel. We might "pretend" publicly that our job remains our chief concern, even when children have changed our priorities. As Allison Pearson's heroine Kate Reddy put it: "The old Kate, the one Before Children, never returned. But she did a great impersonation of being back, and maybe only a mother could have seen through her disguise."[6] Or we may try to reduce a sense of conflict by minimizing our own or our children's emotional needs, thereby turning the pragmatic necessity of "staying on track" into a psychological goal.

Whereas the ideal of maternal self-sacrifice used to obscure mothers' desires for things other than motherhood, today's ideal of "staying on track" obscures mothers' desires to be transformed by motherhood. Just like the old ideal, the newer ideal has begun to seem "just the way things are." In that context, a woman who yearns to make her new relationship with her child her central focus may feel her wish is subtly devalued, dismissed as at best impractical, at worst as a failure of imagination or nerve. That, in turn, makes it harder to understand the ways we struggle with the conflict, not only in relation to ourselves and our children, but also with our husbands, with our mothers, and even in dealing with the question of whether to have children at all.

Becoming a Mother
and Ambivalence About Roles

BECOMING A MOTHER INVOLVES LOSSES and gains, and the question for any given woman is whether the losses outweigh the gains or vice versa. There are any number of things that a woman might imagine losing if she becomes a mother, from her "little tummy," as the film star Julia Roberts put it, to her life. But present-day worries among most educated women cluster around the loss of autonomy, economic independence, opportunity, and the sense of equality in relationships and the world of work.

The economic costs of spending one's time mothering have been carefully documented by the economic journalist Ann Crittenden in her book *The Price of Motherhood*. Women who drop out of the labor force to spend time mothering lose Social Security benefits, seniority, and pension plans. Those women who stay in the workforce are also penalized simply by virtue of the lack of workplace policies that acknowledge the demands on parents of small children.[7] As corporations increase their efforts to create family-friendly policies, those hardest hit are the low-wage workers and welfare mothers.[8] Among highly educated women holding responsible jobs who become pregnant, there are routine stories of being forced out due to pregnancy even when the ostensible reason isn't pregnancy. A friend who edited a newspaper was asked to leave when she became pregnant. Another was told by the president of her company, after she returned from maternity leave, that he didn't like "her style," though he had voiced no previous complaints. The list of injustices, subtle and blatant, is long and grim.

But there is another level to this, and that is how a woman imagines or anticipates having a baby will change *her*. It is one thing to battle inequities in the workplace; it is another to hash out the conflicts within oneself as to how much weight and meaning to give one's identities as worker and mother. One solution to this question of balance was offered by sociologists in the 1970s and 1980s: mothers and fathers need to equitably divide the duties of child rearing for the sake of their own, their children's, and society's health.[9] Today there are many couples who combine mother and father care in a highly workable and satisfying system. There are also couples who both pursue work at a similar level of involvement and delegate the care of their children during work hours to paid day care or nannies or relatives; still others arrange their lives so that the child rearing is done primarily by fathers. In her book *Kidding Ourselves*, attorney Rhona Mahony suggested that women actively seek men who will be househusbands if they are serious about pursuing professional careers.[10]

But the recommendation for equally shared care has also proven more complicated than it appears at first glance, and one reason has to do with desire. A problem many couples confront is that partners have differing levels of desire to care for the children, and differing levels of perceived deprivation when they do not. One mother complained how easily her husband could go to work, without suffering the pangs of longing and guilt that she did at leaving their child. She felt that sharing care "cost her" in ways it didn't cost him and that in that sense, being with the children was more important to her well-being than to his. Sometimes a mother may wish for her partner to feel the same way as she does to create a kind of "emotional equality." A man I spoke with said that his wife, an academic like him, wanted him to *want* to be with their young children as much as she did. She wanted to be the one who spent more time caring for the children and did not want her husband to replace her. But the injustice that galled her was that because she wanted to care for the children more, she lived with a greater amount of internal conflict than her husband did. She wished that he felt the same degree of conflict about work and family; that was the equality she sought.

Mothers' simultaneous wish to be the central figure in their children's lives and their fear or resentment of the "one down" position it puts them in plays out in various ways. There is the exasperated superiority with which some mothers shoulder the burden of child care responsibility, the "it's easier to do it myself" school, where one's partner cannot be trusted to screw on the top of a sippy cup or buckle a car seat. A sense of burden exists alongside the wish to be indispensable in one's children's lives. By donning a patronizing attitude, a mother consolidates her centrality while attempting to equalize the power stakes.[11]

The fear of losing power as the price for caring for children can also surface in the subtle negotiations that take place between members of a couple about whose work is more "important." A wife and husband both worked in business, but the wife's job was the more high-powered. The couple was engaged in chronic simmering conflict, each vying to prove that the demands of his or her work required that the other pick up the slack in caring for their child. At first, they added more and more paid child-care hours as a way to soften the conflict between them. Later, the husband, whose work was less demanding, began to take over more of the child care. At that point, the mother began to feel jealous and sad when she saw that her child always called for her father when she needed comfort. After much back-and-forth, the mother ended up working out a less demanding work schedule.

Even if a mother derives satisfaction from taking care of her children, it is hard for her not to feel ambivalent about having rearranged her life to take it all on, especially if her partner doesn't acknowledge or value the effort involved. One friend admitted to having intentionally shut her husband out of caring for the children because she became enraged at how he would read one bedtime story or change one diaper and then talk to their friends as if he were doing half the work. Another loved the activities of mothering and domesticity but began to feel so resentful that her husband was absent most of the time and helpless the rest of the time that the activities were drained of their satisfactions. She even began to feel she was abetting his exploitation of the status quo by continuing to do it all herself.

For women contemplating motherhood, such concrete issues as the division of child care can seem a long way off, too abstract to think about in the particular. But in a way, the inability to think about them is itself a sign of the specific form of maternal ambivalence to which women today are, it seems, particularly susceptible. The quandary that fuels this ambivalence is how to reconcile the pressure to sideline maternal activity in order to establish one's mettle as a serious worker, as mistress of one's destiny, and as an agent unweakened by receptive, "waiting" femininity, on the one hand, with the desire to mother, on the other. One of the strategies by which young women cope with the potential pain and anxiety of this dilemma is by denying its existence.

The economics professor Nancy Folbre asked her undergraduates to fill out a questionnaire estimating future earnings. She found:

> The overwhelming majority of women express no doubt that they will, at age forty, earn the same amount of money as men with similar education credentials. Yet they also plan to have two children, and (unlike the men in the same class) they plan to take time out from their careers in order to raise them. When I point out that something is wrong with their calculations they aren't entirely surprised. But they seem almost embarrassed by having to consider the issue.[12]

These otherwise intelligent, thoughtful young women are embarrassed because Folbre's questions force them to look directly at their own irrationality; and specifically, at the vague, unstable story they tell themselves to obscure the conflict between maternal desire and their other aspirations. That story effectively keeps maternal desire from figuring into planning or thinking, even as it upholds the image of self-determination and independence they wish to endorse.

Social mores encourage this denial. Vanessa Grigoriadis writes in a *New York* magazine article entitled "Baby Panic":

> I'm 28 and grew up in Manhattan, attended a competitive private high school and a liberal-arts college, and at no point did anyone bring up the notion that the sexes

were anything but equal. To me, it seemed like ideology was going to triumph over biology. . . . It was just a matter of steering clear of bathetic girly pathologies — following the Rules, jettisoning a man after a couple of dates if he didn't show husband potential, making time-sensitive "life plans" that revolved around a phantom boyfriend.[13]

The pressure to deny maternal desire is obvious in the caricatured image of the woman who lets it affect her thinking or actions. Clearly, there are costs to your self-image if you reveal yourself to be desirous in a maternal way. Desiring sex, of course, confirms one's standing as an independent woman; but desiring a child, or worse, a husband, reveals one to be pathetically contingent. A refusal to countenance inconvenient realities, obscured by the idiom of "girl power," excludes from serious consideration the ways that motherhood might transform one's outlook and priorities.

Part of the problem is that before we have children, it costs us very little to minimize motherhood's potential effects. Indeed, it is hard even to imagine them. The psychoanalyst Nancy Chodorow commented on the pressure she felt writing *The Reproduction of Mothering* "to choose between one position that seemed biologically determinist and entrapping of women" — mothering as biological destiny — and another that claimed women's feelings about mothering were the product of "social structure and cultural mandate." "On a more personal level," she continued, ". . . I, along with many feminists of my generation, did not in our twenties and early thirties adequately understand how mothering is actually experienced . . . and many of us were ourselves not prepared for the powerful, transformative claims that motherhood would make upon our identities and senses of self."[14] For young women today, imagining the changes wrought by motherhood is not simply difficult; it is filled with conflict. And two of the most anxiety-ridden questions are how to think about and how to manage the powerful, transformative claims to which Chodorow alludes.

Maternal Ambivalence
and Relationships to Our Mothers

WHETHER BY POSITIVE OR NEGATIVE example, we look to the way our mother lived her life and interacted with us to map our own maternal course. Her own idiosyncratic pockets of ambivalence often determine what we most passionately want to avoid. If our mother was often enraged, we wish to exude calm. If she was cavalier about leaving us, we are fanatical about finding the best care. A friend's mother was chronically torn about work and family; she has carefully crafted her life around stay-at-home motherhood. A colleague remembers her mother as depressed; she bends over backward to convey joy. We have a powerful desire to mend our relationship with our mother through our relationship with our own child.

Our mother's lessons shape us in ways that are often difficult to subject to rational scrutiny, perhaps nowhere more than in the area of her relative investments in work and caring for her children. Some women feel the choices their mothers made were right for their mothers but are not right for them. Some women feel that their fathers exerted the primary influence on their work choices or life goals, and they are drawn to revisit their identification with their mothers only when they become mothers themselves. A woman's work life can be a way of surpassing or vindicating her mother's life, or a means of feeling truly independent, mercifully freed from the ancient mother-daughter cycle. Resistance to a mother's example or influence is relevant not only to women who have pursued professional lives their mothers have not. Expressing exasperation at her enlightened author-mother's urging that she settle down and produce grandchildren, the author Katie Roiphe wrote: "Could it be that lurking inside all the feminist mothers of the 70's is a 1950's housewife who values china patterns and baby carriages above the passions of the mind?"[15]

Identification and difference take on added intensity when we are faced with concrete decisions about how to care for our children. How we were raised can be an example to be followed or avoided; most often, there are some aspects we want to repeat and others we want to discard. "My mother's idea of good management was that if a child became too attached to a nanny, it was time to hire a new one, lest maternal control be diminished," wrote the primatologist Sarah Blaffer Hrdy. While Hrdy wanted, like her mother, to be unfettered by infant care to pursue her work, at the same time she worried, "If I delegated care to others, wouldn't that mean reverting to the ways of my mother's generation, before we understood the attachment needs of infants?"[16] For most women, their mothers not only exist in their memory but also often have a strong voice in the present. A woman I know remembered her own mother as "miserable" caring for children and knew that she herself would be a more patient mother if she had a job. But my acquaintance's mother did her best to instill guilt in her for even considering working while she had small children, in effect visiting on her daughter the same guilt-ridden self-inhibition she had visited upon herself as a young mother.

Some professional mothers find that they enjoy being home with their kids and decide to work less. They may then find themselves unexpectedly discomfited by identifying with their child-focused mothers. In deciding to spend more time with their children, in becoming "more like" their mothers, they may even need to mourn a sense of self-worth that rested on a feeling of having surpassed their mothers.[17] For one psychotherapy patient, healing involved discovering the ways she actually admired her mother. For her, competition with her mother remained relatively covert as long as she made different choices. But when she became "more like" her mother, her rivalrous feelings came to the surface.

This tension is visible, in even more dramatic form, in the dynamics of envy that can play a part in mother-daughter, and woman-woman, relationships. The psychoanalyst Carolyn Ellman writes of a patient, a thirty-year-old lawyer, wife, and mother of a young child, who spent a great deal of time trying to induce envy in her analyst, telling her how wonderful her own husband was and making a big point that she could still have babies while the analyst could not. At the same time, she hid a second pregnancy for fear that the analyst (now past her childbearing years) would be envious. The push-pull of wanting to induce envy while at the same time fearing it echoed a struggle the woman had had with her mother. She had felt her mother to be extraordinarily powerful and unable to "allow her to truly value her own independent identity as a girl,"[18] particularly by interfering with her love for her father by belittling him. The patient's anger at her mother, especially when she reached adolescence, led to an intense wish "to destroy her mother and have all the babies and goodies that her mother had. She then found it very difficult to truly enjoy the things that she obtained and achieved as an adult without feeling a profound sense of destroying someone (or something inside) to get them."[19]

This woman's conflict rested on a sense that she and her mother were locked in a zero-sum game in which if one of them had "something," the other was doomed to have "nothing." She had an intense wish to have everything herself and deny her mother any riches, as a response to what she perceived as her mother's similar motive toward her. But the very aggression that accompanied her envious wish to deprive her mother fueled her own fear that others felt similarly voracious envy toward her.

For anyone embroiled in this painful cycle, the only way out is to recognize that we will feel free to have "something" only if we allow the other person to have "something" too. The wish to deprive the other and the fear of being deprived ourselves are two sides of the same coin. In order not to feel so susceptible to others' envy, Ellman's patient had to understand her own desire to induce envy. And to do that, she needed to experience her analyst as someone who was trying to help her understand, rather than punish her for, that desire. In that safe context, she could gradually get in touch with enjoying what she had with less guilt, and appreciating what others had with less envy.

The patient's challenge is akin to the challenge that Jessica Benjamin described as at the core of mutual recognition: in order for one to feel recognized oneself, one must recognize the other. For a woman to break free from a cycle of envy, she must recognize her mother (or other women) as having something if she is going to have something too.[20] In any relationship, there is the potential for the breakdown of mutual recognition, where one person aspires to assert herself at the expense of another's will or autonomy. But there is a particularly keen potential in the mother-daughter relationship for the breakdown into the psychological roles of the "have" and the "have not," a drama of who will command the riches — whether beauty, power, or food — that is reiterated in countless fairy tales.[21] And this drama of the "have" and the "have not" plays out nowhere more passionately than in the arena of procreational prerogative, since it is an arena where specifically female capacities are so vehemently prized and treasured. This is the matter that Ellman's patient enacted in her relationship with her mother, and then her analyst, whose bygone fertility she demeaned as she vaunted her own. It emerges, more or less innocuously, in everyday interactions as well. A pregnant woman I know was in a standoff with a good friend, also pregnant, because each felt the other owed her a call to acknowledge and congratulate her on her pregnancy. Each subtly vied to be acknowledged as the queen her pregnancy made her feel she rightfully was.

A particularly feminine form of the fantasy of having "something" while others have "nothing" organizes itself, then, around fertility and motherhood. This competitive theme plays out on a cultural level as well, with social values and their ongoing shifts affecting whether motherhood is treated as a plenitude or a lack. Grigoriadis writes of some women's thinly veiled contempt for those intent on a mate and motherhood; more adventuresome spirits have something over these mildly silly women. But then, true to the theme of punishment that hovers in this narrative, the high are brought low. Those whose busy jobs and buying power leave no room for babies suddenly fear they may end up the losers. They ignored motherhood as long as there was nothing in it they wanted, or wanted to want; but now, suddenly, they are pursued by a fear of lack, as they find themselves wanting exactly what mothers (that previously denigrated class of women) have: namely, children.

Culturally, the theme of superiority and inferiority also plays out in the predictable pendulum swings of public opinion about the "right" kind of mother to be, as well as in the undercurrent of punishment that threatens to strike those who "fail." If one generation trumpets the value of stay-at-home motherhood, the next generation casts off its narrowness, while the next resents their mothers' absence. (One book on women's roles was even entitled *What Our Mothers Didn't Tell Us*.) Attached to evaluations of the previous generation's choices are the reparative and accusatory longings of the daughter toward the mother. Women also make earnest, constructive attempts to learn from their mothers' struggles and mistakes and mother differently, or better, than they did. But whatever the reason, when we strive to outdo the mother who has preceded us or the generation of which she was a part, a fear may lurk that we will be proved "all wrong," chastised and humbled. This dynamic of triumph and comeuppance fuels the vociferousness of the "mommy wars," which play themselves out not only intergenerationally but also between individuals and — most importantly — as a conflict within each of us. A professional colleague of mine says that every time she sees a new book about mothers, she feels mingled dread and hope as a question instantly pops into her mind: "Is it for me or against me?" She experiences these books not on the level of reasoned argument, but on the level of primitive attack.

Women today face a tension between the desire to become absorbed in mothering and go with the changes in priorities that might lead to and the desire to continue reaping the rewards of their professional commitments and former identities. In response, the recurring themes of superiority and inferiority, competition and envy, victory and defeat, latent in mother-daughter relationships and relationships between women generally, have found forms of expression adapted to this dilemma.[22] One way mothers attempt to master the conflict is by assimilating the new experience of motherhood into the familiar framework of competitive achievement. If fertility provides a sprinkling of competitive opportunities ("when I meet someone older than me, maybe even a year older, I somehow can't help but feel a little superior — I've got more eggs than she does!"[23]), motherhood produces an even greater bounty. Birth weight, Apgar scores, milestones, preschool admissions, academic precocity, and musical aptitude can all be co-opted for the purpose of establishing one's mothering "success," for structuring motherhood as an achievement that offers clear-cut measures of one's value and self-worth.

But this two-for-one gambit of trying to eke out the satisfactions of mothering in the mode of competitive achievement doesn't address the underlying problem or resolve the basic ambivalence. Neither does the alternative strategy of proclaiming one's passionate devotion to motherhood while spending little time with one's actual children. And that is because the conflict women feel is between two quite distinct ways of being in the world, each worthwhile but fundamentally different. The kind of "being with" that grounds our deepest moments of joy in connecting with others can't be done with an eye to the outside, or while looking over one's shoulder to see who is winning. Letting the relationship with one's child truly affect and change one is an internal, creative process that in its essence is inimical to a model of child rearing as "Mommy Olympics," in Wendy Wasserstein's apt phrase.[24] A common contemporary maternal conflict is how to find a way to both create a psychological and temporal space for a relationship with one's child that follows its own internal rhythm and direct one's energies toward achievements in the world that benefit from one's competitive spirit.

The Creative Potential of Maternal Ambivalence

THE BRITISH PSYCHOTHERAPIST ROZSIKA PARKER, who wrote the definitive book on the subject, observed that maternal ambivalence tends to provoke "a profound need to reassure and dampen down anxiety about the very existence of ambivalence." Instead, she suggests, it should arouse "a recognition of the creative potential of the ambivalent state of mind for maternal development."[25] The notion that powerful negative feelings toward our children might exert a creative force rather than a destructive one is quite alien to our usual way of thinking. Our first impulse is usually to try to get rid of our negative feelings, whether by denial, projection, or going to the gym. But these strategies attempt to banish or disown bad feelings rather than putting them to use. In Parker's view, ambivalence can prompt mothers to know themselves and their child better; it can encourage them to grow. She writes:

> It is in the very anguish of maternal ambivalence itself that a fruitfulness for mothers and children resides. . . . The conflict between love and hate actually spurs mothers on to struggle to understand and know their baby. In other words, the suffering of ambivalence can promote thought — and the capacity to think about the baby and child is arguably the single most important aspect of mothering.[26]

The hardest part of being in a rage with my child or feeling resentful toward him is that in the moment I can't really think. In my shower episode I was completely gripped by emotion. But Parker suggests that if our ambivalence has not already become utterly unmanageable, our feelings of resentment, frustration, failure, impatience, or ineffectiveness can goad us to think about what is going on, about how our buttons are being pressed. And that thinking is likely to result in a fuller, more compassionate view of ourselves and of our child, as well as a more constructive understanding of what might need to change.[27]

Parker and many others have written about how important it is to recognize the *cultural* ideals of motherhood that intensify our self-doubt as mothers.[28] The most exhaustively examined such ideal, that of the all-giving mother, puts pressure on mothers by minimizing how hard maternal giving can be, especially when there is little family or social support. Yet, though much has been written about the tendency to paper over the negatives of motherhood with what writer Anna Quindlen called the "Hallmark card version,"[29] it is worth noticing a countervailing set of social ideas that dispose us to see mothering in a negative light. Take, for example, the characterization of caring for small children as "boring." Everyone has bored moments, of course, but what fuels the blanket appraisal? According to psychologists, boredom crops up when people feel that a task is below their skill level.[30] Although scooping baby food or changing a diaper may not call on highly sophisticated skills, the more menial tasks of child care take place in a complex interpersonal context with plentiful opportunities for genuine relating and learning something new about self and other. Feeling unable or unwilling to find interest in caring for a child is not "natural," then; it is fed by the bias that there are really no skills involved that matter. If we convince ourselves that hands-on parenting is a kind of make-work, or if intelligent women complain that they "go out of their minds with boredom" from tending to kids, these social stories come to shape the norms to which we compare our choices and by which we evaluate ourselves.

Both the idealization and the devaluation of the rewards of motherhood tend to distract us from the much more individual and creative process of finding a way to live that is true to ourselves and responsive to our child. That process involves connecting to our private experience, as opposed to the clamorous other-referencing of the "Mommy Olympics." The pediatrician and psychoanalyst D. W. Winnicott suggested one way to think about how living creatively begins in a private experience of self. As babies, relaxed and purposeless in the presence of a trusted caregiver, we are free to discover an impulse of our own. We discover what we want and how we feel from the "inside out," rather than in reactive compliance to the external world. Psychologically, we make use of a "transitional space," where the fluidity between what is me and what is not me, what is illusory and what is real, is allowed to stand. In this "intermediate area of experience" where paradox is "accepted, tolerated, and not resolved," we experience ourselves as creative.[31]

Experiencing ourselves as authentic and creative depends on what Winnicott calls the capacity to be alone, which, paradoxically, only develops through the presence of a loving other:

> It is only when alone (that is to say, in the presence of someone) that the infant can discover his own personal life. . . . The infant is able to become unintegrated, to flounder . . . to be able to exist for a time without being either a reactor to an external impingement or an active person with a direction of interest or movement. . . . In the course of time there arrives a sensation or an impulse. In this setting the sensation or impulse will feel real and be truly a personal experience.[32]

Winnicott's observation that we discover our true impulses in the presence of a loving other, which he described as part of a baby's development, can be seen in a mother's development as well. We discover who we are as mothers partly through our own "floundering" in the presence of our baby. When we accept ambiguity and fluidity, when we manage to stay open to new experience and relax our need for certainty and control, we discover a place of initiative within ourselves out of which we can creatively respond to what we perceive as our own and our baby's needs. Attuned to our own experience, we are also less oriented to complying with external pressures, standards, and ideals.

The same possibility exists while mothering older children as well. I think of that archetypal parent-child battleground, homework, in response to which, I've noticed, I operate in two distinct emotional modes. Sometimes, if the older children are not getting it, or dawdle in doing it, the specter of failed standardized tests and bad character looms, and I become irritable and demanding in response to my own anxiety about their ability to perform. At other times, I enjoy getting "inside" their thought process and empathizing with their individual emotional and cognitive styles. If they need help, I connect to my own enjoyment in thinking and share that. When I am open to their process of learning and offer my own, I tune in to a level of experience very different from my fretful and judgmental overconcern with results. The less judgmental approach is, not surprisingly, much more helpful to them.

Winnicott's evocative image of a transitional space where paradox is tolerated can help us think about how to work with the range of feelings, pleasurable and difficult, that arise in the course of our own mothering. Rather than swinging from pole to pole, buffeted from love to hate, from feeling like the "right" kind of mother to the "wrong" kind, we can accept, even embrace, the contradictions, as the soil from which creative understanding and constructive action can grow. Whatever the conflicting pulls on us as mothers, we want to be able to ride the disorder and uncertainty with a sense of give, of play. We want to acknowledge our whole range of feelings, not siding with one and rejecting the other, but accepting that we contain them all. If we can accept their contradictions, and use that to initiate creative thinking, we can ultimately understand ourselves and our children better.

Sentimentality, Masochism, and the "Perfect Mother"

EACH OF US TRIES, THE best we know how, to manage motherhood in a way that keeps open the avenues of maternal gratification and clears rather than clouds our access to maternal pleasure. We are continually challenged in that attempt by our reactions — to our child, spouse, parents, other mothers — and the ways they affect our daily experience of caring for children. Our equanimity is also vulnerable to cultural norms and ideals about what kind of women and mothers are "successful."

Previous psychological and feminist writings on maternal ambivalence have argued that social taboos against maternal hate and unhappiness pressure women to dampen down their ambivalence and insist on an overly sunny, even sentimental, view of motherhood. These writings have tried to surface the full range of emotions that women feel in the course of mothering and remove the stigma associated with maternal frustration, anger, and boredom. They have shown how cultural ideals of the "good mother" can lodge in mothers, intensifying their guilt and anxiety, heightening their self-doubt, and draining them of confidence.[33]

But the social analyses aimed at exposing the ideals or idealizations of motherhood have at times failed to sustain the necessary tension between decrying the destructive effects of the ideals and recognizing the positive aspirations embedded within them. It is easy enough to agree that a sugarcoated image of mothering obscures a darker reality; but we must ask also what the elaborate attention to that darker reality might itself obscure. Critiques of sentimental images of devoted motherhood or the "perfect mother" appear disdainful, and at times almost phobic, of the notion that women might seriously aspire to the connection, fostering of growth, and shared pleasure that are also at the heart of those images. In a strange way, in our effort to free women by bringing to light the oppressive aspects of maternal experience, we have to some extent mischaracterized its opportunities for enjoyment.

It is not uncommon, for instance, to hear the charge that stay-at-home motherhood is sentimentalized; that this sentimentalization downplays what is difficult about caring for children, and even that the very role of stay-at-home motherhood relies on squelching the full, honest range of a mother's capacities. But what is sentimentality, really? Winnicott thought sentimentality contained a denial of hate. James Joyce wrote, "The sentimentalist is he who would enjoy without incurring the immense debtorship for a thing done." Literary theorist Camille Paglia wrote, "In the sentimental mode, too little is asked to bear too much." According to the critic Roger Kimball, sentimentality is "feeling unscrutinized by doubt."[34] Each alludes to the fact that sentimentality, in art or life, leaves something out, usually something construed as negative, at the cost of integrity, fullness, complexity, depth, or truth.

The critics of sentimentalized motherhood and the literary analysts agree: sentimentality involves an attempt to deny the negatives of existence and a refusal to integrate them into a truer, deeper picture of reality. But what family environment is most likely to foster this denial of the negative? Those who recoil at the sentimentalization of stay-at-home motherhood assume no woman could consent to it without suppressing half of herself, her negative emotions as well as her autonomous goals. But that view ignores the fact that mothering at home, when undertaken as a choice, usually has something to do with the aspiration to create an environment that will foster a child's fullest experience of self. In other words, it is usually founded on a mother's belief that her presence will help, rather than hinder, her child's ability to feel and acknowledge his full range of feelings. And in creating that environment, she is enacting one of her *own* most valued goals.

The novels and essays of the Czech author Milan Kundera contain a sustained attack on sentimentality, an attack the critic Roger Kimball understood as "only the other side of [Kundera's] defense of individualism. For it is just this — the lonely and irreducible *privateness* of experience — that sentimentality promises to dissolve. The essential appeal of the sentimental is precisely that it relieves one of the burden of individuality and the responsibilities of adult experience."[35] The "privateness of experience" is also what Winnicott saw as most deeply necessary for the individual. "At the centre of each person," he wrote, "is an incommunicado element, and this is sacred and worthy of preservation."[36] As we have seen, if a mother is present and available to recognize a baby or child's impulses in the context of their ongoing loving relationship, that interchange helps the baby form a sense of his "true self." A false self, in Winnicott's terms, is one that has been made to respond to another's needs too early, where the self is organized around reacting to others (particularly the mother) and taking care of them. In that light, a relationship between a mother and small child in which the mother is around, occupied with her own things from time to time but available to respond, would seem to promote something like the opposite of sentimentality; it would foster a climate that permitted the full range of emotional experience and thereby nourished the development of a child's true self.[37]

If the charge of "sentimentality" all too often becomes a way of dismissing the complex arena of maternal devotion, the view that consenting to care for children is somehow masochistic functions in much the same way. Mothers sometimes feel confused about whether their daily run of child-centered activity shades into doormat status. Even for the most self-assertive mother, it is always a balancing act. But when we eye suspiciously the orientation of service, undertaken willingly toward our children, as one more pathological or socially engineered manifestation of female submission, we overlook what it shares with the aspiration of what the psychoanalyst Emmanuel Ghent called surrender, the "liberation and expansion of the self as a corollary to the letting down of defensive barriers."[38] Ghent's notion more accurately characterizes the active desire to invest oneself in the care of one's child than does the image of abdication of will or resigned submission. Yet in the absence of another framework to put it in, mothers often fear that their very wish to care for their children is somehow masochistic; they wonder if something is "wrong" with them, or criticize themselves for not having enough "self esteem" to have dodged the chronic, unpaid role of putting others' needs first that mothering often demands.[39]

Finally, there is the stubborn image of the "perfect mother." In a 1976 article, "The Fantasy of the Perfect Mother," Chodorow and Susan Contratto argued that many feminists tended to buy into the broader cultural fantasy that mothers should be perfect. Society's tendency to blame and idealize mothers, they observed, is rooted in childhood fantasies about mothers' enormous power and limitless resources. Feminist accounts that blame mothers for disappointing daughters, or suggest that mothering either "destroys the world or generates world perfection," have at their base this same fantasy of maternal perfectibility.[40]

Since the mid-1970s much has changed, yet the same dynamics Chodorow and Contratto identified are still in play. As feminist daughters have become mothers, they no longer espouse the fantasy of maternal perfectibility. More frequently, they excoriate the cultural version of that fantasy, "the myth of the perfect mother," criticizing it as a larger-than-life, persecuting mandate that makes mothers feel chronically insufficient. *Leave It to Beaver*'s June Cleaver, trotted out as the ultimate avatar of the "perfect mother," is regularly blasted in popular writings as a retro focus of misplaced nostalgia. Now, criticism once directed toward mothers themselves takes aim at the "myth" that someone like June Cleaver might have valuable qualities worthy of emulation.[41]

Psychologically sophisticated versions of the critique of the "perfect mother" declare that ideals of maternal devotion are the product of primitive fantasy, which have no place in adult relationships or adult theories. The message is that women and men should "grow up" and recognize that at the heart of their nostalgia is a regressive longing for an irretrievable mother-infant union. But the adult reality to which they insist we should adjust is actually two "realities" merged for polemical effect. The first reality — the psychological truth that people are separate and perfect gratification is not possible — is treated as if it necessarily entailed a second reality, namely, mothers' absence from the home, the parental time crunch, and the negative effects (little homecooking, lots of TV) that follow. If we lament this second social and economic reality, it is treated as no different from an immature refusal to accept the first psychological reality. The whole notion that people expect or demand the "perfect mother" is itself used as an exaggeration to embarrass people out of the quite reasonable hope and aspiration that childhood include not "perfect" gratification, but a great deal.

When the wish for more maternal presence in children's lives, or *to be* more present as a mother, is characterized as a futile hankering after a lost world, a world created by fantastic infantile wishes, we lose an opportunity to rationally assess our current social reality. If some speak longingly of the days when children were let out the back door to play in the neighborhood till dinner (allowing mothers, it would seem, amazing amounts of time free of children!) or wonder whether we haven't lost something in replacing Saturday morning hanging out in pajamas with competitive soccer leagues, it is not simply a sentimental idealization of the past but a response to real changes, changes that can be evaluated, mourned or celebrated, and even resisted.

The noisy extremism of building up and shooting down the ideal of the perfect mother may, in the end, be little more than a diversion from the hard, undramatic choices involved in providing enough for our children, in being good enough. Being a good enough mother is, finally, not about image but about process. In her novel *Still Life*, A. S. Byatt gives a beautiful fictional rendition of the contrast. Elinor Poole, a graceful Bloomsbury matron with three charming children, has every appearance of being the perfect mother. She bakes scones, she makes her own yogurt, her children are well behaved. She and her children create things together: a dragon collage, a cake, a papier-mâché dolphin. She decorates the walls of their bright playroom with an alphabet frieze, the letters carefully crafted by the children each at his own easel: "E is for egg. F is for flower. S is for snake." Observing Elinor, Alexander, a houseguest who becomes her lover, finds he begins "to feel sometimes as though these careful surfaces, like the unbroken shell of the riddling egg, like the silk balloon with no door in which spiderlings live and grow, were impenetrable."[42] It is ironic, though not surprising, that in the novel's sequel, Elinor abandons her family altogether. Unsurprising, because we sense that although she has done everything "right" with her children, she has never really let them in.

Another of the novel's characters, Stephanie, has recently given birth to a son, William, when she tentatively tries to resume her scholarly work on Wordsworth. Though she "seemed to hear, to feel, to smell, powerful calling sounds, rufflings of the air, odors, which wanted her back, insisted that she must return," she manages to "put down rational foot after rational foot, with difficulty" on her way to the library.[43] Once there, she attempts to read the immortality ode:

> It took time before the task in hand seemed possible, and more before it came to life, and more still before it became imperative and obsessive. There had to be a time before thought, a woolgathering time where nothing happened, a time of yawning, of wandering eyes and feet, of reluctance to do what would finally become delightful and energetic. Threads of thought had to rise and be gathered and catch on other threads of old thought, from some unused memory store. She had snatched from Marcus and Daniel's mum, worse, from William, whose physical being filled her inner eye and almost all her immediate memory, barely time for this vacancy, let alone the subsequent concentration. She told herself she must learn to do without the vacancy if she was to survive. She must be cunning. She must learn to think in bus queues, in buses, in lavatories, between table and sink. It was hard. She was tired. She yawned. Time moved on.[44]

Stephanie's child has changed her utterly; he fills her time, "her inner eye and almost all her immediate memory." She has also, "with some pain cleared this small space," to allow for the vacancy, the "woolgathering" (what Winnicott might call floundering) that precedes the creative moment. Her son's need of her, her preoccupation with him, has made it very difficult to work; yet *at the same time* his birth triggers her growth as a reader, giving new depth to her perspective on the poem ("Now, feeling old at twenty-five, she was more interested in the distance and otherness of children, having a son").[45] Stephanie is like a new story whose cadences draw on an ancient text; she must find a way to carry forward who she was before, in a totally new way. "It is hard." She is torn. But she keeps faith with herself, her son, the poetry, by letting it all in, and not letting any part of it go.

Child Care

ONE MORNING AS I WAS writing this chapter, our babysitter came downstairs and said that she was moving to Florida in a month. Her new husband was having trouble finding work, and they could no longer afford to live in the San Francisco Bay area. At first the tears rolled silently down my cheeks; then I started to sob. I felt bad for my children, my littlest boy particularly, whose mornings were spent in her company. I felt heartsick and anxious for myself — how was I going to find a good new situation? I was pained by the irony that what suited her so well to the job — her empathy, her responsibility, her fun-loving nature — was exactly what made her leaving so stinging.

These dramas of separation have been a huge issue in my experience of child care and in the experience of many others I know. One of the most difficult moments in my life as a parent was when I decided I had to fire a caregiver whom the children loved but who was chronically late. She adored the kids, she was helpful to me, but she was rarely on time. First I tried to work around it. Then I tried to talk with her about it. Things improved and then got worse again. I began spending the first hour of my day trying to overcome my anger, sometimes calling my sister in Washington, D.C., to have her talk me down. Finally I knew I couldn't manage the lateness or my feelings about it anymore. The day I told her was one of unmitigated dread. I took a long walk. I came home and showered and dressed. I ritualistically applied makeup, thinking of the Sioux applying war paint, of Crazy Horse saying, "It is a good day to die." I tried to be rational, but I was helpless to control the power of my emotions. After she left, I didn't look to hire any help for several months. I felt, melodramatic as it sounds, that I needed time to heal.

When child care arrangements work, life feels like it makes sense, even sings with balance and purpose. When they don't, we are pitched into a sense of desperation, where the very foundations of life feel askew. When it goes well, we easily, even sometimes a bit smugly, take credit. But when it goes badly, the precariousness of the entire system is revealed, and we often want more than anything not to have to deal with it anymore. In almost nine years of motherhood I hired eight part-time caregivers; three were unequivocal shining successes, three were mixed, and two were downright bad. In-home child care has its own risks and benefits, but problems can arise in any arrangement. My friend Sarah, a college professor, was thrilled by the university child care center's care of her two-month-old daughter and felt her whole family was supported in their parenting by the collaborative relationship they had with their daughter's main caregiver, Lynn. When Sarah's daughter was twenty months old, Lynn left the center, and Sarah told me it took both her and her daughter "months to recover." A colleague of mine employs au pair after au pair, as one after another leaves or is let go. Each hire is as difficult and wrenching as the last, but she takes it on each time with the stamina of a long distance runner. Another friend, whose children are past the early child care stage, descends into an uncharacteristically dark mood whenever one of her children stays home from school sick and she has to resort to "Second Moms," the local temporary nanny agency. The wellspring of emotion in this normally unruffled person gushed forth when I heard her opining to a pregnant acquaintance that dealing with child care makes you want to kill yourself.

One could view these stories as exceptions, as a kind of heretical overdramatization of the difficulties of child care. But they bedevil practically every mother I know. The problems of continuity and reliability may be lessened by a national system of child care centers with well-compensated staff, as in France, or in individual cases by high pay, great benefits, good in-home working conditions, and pleasant children. But they are not problems that can ever be completely controlled or solved. One day, most parents come face-to-face with the fact that even the most dedicated, well-compensated, loving child care workers in the world can, and often do, leave. And so do most others, at their initiative or ours. In the realm of child care, disruption is the rule rather than the exception.[1]

Although this often masquerades as a minor detail, it is actually experienced as a recurring and central dilemma in mothers' lives. As child care arrangements fall apart or fall short, we repeatedly confront the same round of painful questions: What does it mean to our children when their caregivers leave? How does it affect their emotional life? Should the fact that caregivers leave affect our own life choices? How? How can we disentangle the effect of these ruptures on us and on our children? Should we even try? These dilemmas, born of happenstance, are so important because they cut to the heart of maternal self-esteem. Our sense of being good mothers *depends* on providing good care for our children, and on taking their well-being to heart, feeling it to be inextricable from our own. The problems presented by the run-of-the-mill unpredictability of child care land us, over and over, smack-dab in the middle of this significant, troubling domain.

The Central Role of Caregiver Turnover in the Work-Home Conflict

IT ALMOST BREAKS ONE'S HEART to read Sylvia Plath's letters to her mother only months before her suicide, with their repetitive allusion to her need for help with her children. "I got this nanny back for today and tomorrow. She is a whiz, and I see what a heaven my life could be if I had a good live-in nanny" (September 24, 1962). "If I had time to get a *good nanny*, possibly an Irish girl to come home with me, I could get on with my life . . ." (October 16, 1962). "I adore the babies and am glad to have them, even though now they make my life fantastically difficult. If I can just financially get through this year, I should have time to get a good nanny . . ." (October 21, 1962).[2] Plath's need was larger than most; her husband had left her, she was broke, and she was inwardly compelled to express her poetic gift. But any of us who have been unable to afford or find the help we need to do our work can resonate with Plath's note of desperation.

At the most basic level, child care is about whether you have coverage or not; whether you are gripped by panic that there is "no one," or you are flooded with relief that there is "someone." If we were to put it in terms of Abraham Maslow's hierarchy of needs taught in Psychology 101, the need for coverage might be likened to the basic need for food and shelter.[3] Once that need is met, however, we very quickly move to a concern about how good the care actually is. That appraisal strongly affects our effectiveness, concentration, and satisfaction at work. Any formulation of day care policy that urges us to still our anxieties on this score is at cross-purposes with our inclinations as parents. Our unwillingness to engage in a dispassionate cost-benefit analysis, trading off our own welfare against our child's, is one of the things on which people base their parental self-esteem. When we feel our child is not in good care, we feel horrible. We sometimes do what we can to deny it, not to see it, or put the most positive spin on it we can. (How often I've run into a friend at the dry cleaner, praising her new caregiver to the skies, only to run into her at the supermarket three months later and hear her explain that the caregiver had worked out terribly but had luckily been replaced by someone new and equally wonderful.) When we admit or discover that things are not going well, we are likely to try to look for alternative solutions, including rethinking the whole question of work.

When we find a good child care situation, though, our concern shifts to having that good situation continue. Whether one is dealing with hiring an in-home caregiver or with a child care center, the reality is that turnover is high.[4] Everyone, including day care advocates, agrees that high staff turnover, other things being equal, is not good for children.[5] A prerequisite of continuity is often reliability. As I found with our good but chronically late caregiver, at a certain point unreliability can become almost as stressful as no care at all. When laboratory rats receive electric shocks at random intervals they become more stressed out than rats that expect shocks on a more routine schedule. Not knowing when and if the babysitter will show up is sometimes more nerve-racking than knowing she will not show up at all.

The ongoing vicissitudes of child care availability, quality, consistency, and reliability play a much more basic role in mothers' conflicts between work and home than we usually acknowledge. The ups and downs, and our luck in avoiding them, often have far-reaching effects on how we decide to arrange our lives. Their practical and emotional effects bear directly on how we think about the issue of work. For a mother with the economic latitude, the unpredictability of child care may mesh with her ambivalence about how much her job keeps her away from her children and tip her toward finding a way to spend more time caring for them herself. She might decide that the potential emotional toll on her baby or child of having a full-time caregiver leave is a risk that she will rearrange her life in order to avoid. For others, no matter how much difficulty and unpredictability child care arrangements add to their lives, the alternative is worse. Working is something they need to do, or are completely committed to, and they do what it takes to make it possible.

At any level of the hierarchy of child care needs, differing individual pressures cause people to opt in or opt out of work at different times. That is one reason why dichotomies between "working" and "stay-at-home" mothers often don't ring true. And the ironies proliferate when we notice women asserting a "stay-at-home-mother" identity at odds with their own "working mother" behavior. Conservative spokeswomen in particular seem prone to adopting the role of "faux stay-at-home mom," to use Katha Pollitt's mordant expression.[6] Though they voice a common enough sentiment among women — that being a mother is the identity they most value — they tend to scold feminists for promoting the very thing they themselves engage in: work. One gets a whiff of a peculiarly female form of muscle flexing, a sort of "my maternal devotion is bigger than yours," but without the attendant time commitment one would expect from someone asserting that superiority.

In reality, the self-designation as "working" or "stay-at-home" mother is subject to change as mothers continually evaluate the economic, practical, and emotional dimensions of family life. Mothers often find rigid role descriptions superficial because they so often find themselves on both sides of the issue. One book group in Brooklyn became exasperated by the pile of books on working mothers that a *New York Times* reporter asked them to read, because they felt the categories offered were polemical constructions irrelevant to their lives.[7] The women moved between roles, always with an ultimate focus on what worked for their children and what didn't. In other words, they identified themselves less as "stay-at-home mothers" or "working mothers" than as mothers who tried to find ways to respond to the needs and desires of their children and their entire families.

The Child Care Paradox

WHAT IS STRIKING ABOUT SO much public discussion of mothers' work and day care is how rarely it grapples either with the ways that maternal self-esteem is entwined with the quality of care we can provide our child or with the inextricability of the emotional realities of parents and children. In proposed solution after proposed solution, some part of this is missed. Turning the care of our newborn, baby, or small child over to another, nonfamilial person, someone we often have known only briefly, is a momentous emotional and psychological act, even if we pretend that it isn't. It is fraught with an ongoing combination of relief, fear, hope, and sadness. That web of emotions not only affects our own day-to-day comfort and sense of success as a mother but also plays into hidden but powerful themes in the larger debate about day care policy.

On a societal level, there is the ongoing question of how to reduce the overall incidence of caregiver turnover so as to protect more children and their families from the turnover's practical and psychological effects. The solution generally advocated is a sound one; namely, better work conditions, education, pay, and benefits for child care workers. The point is repeatedly made that the people caring for "our nation's most precious resource" should not be in low-wage, dead-end jobs. The best way to confer respect on these jobs and make them attractive as long-term, stable career options is to reward child care workers with higher pay, better benefits, and attractive career paths.

This is an urgent and necessary goal, and virtually everyone can agree that on the face of it, the solution makes sense. But Americans remain curiously intransigent about improving the child care system. What accounts for this paradox? Though we can easily point to a host of reactionary reasons for it, we also need to factor in a basic conflict at the heart of the child care dilemma, a conflict that is fueled by maternal desire.

Consider the situation of a mother who is well paid and professionally committed and who wishes to continue working while her children are little. For her, the benefit of a stable, highly trained, well-remunerated child care force is clear. She will outearn hired child care workers by a decisive margin, and greater stability in her child care arrangements and better training of staff can only work to her benefit and to her children's. If we consider a mother lower on the socioeconomic scale, however, who receives relatively lower gratification, prestige, and pay from her job, the cost-benefit analysis may be quite different. She may feel that as child care workers' wages increasingly approximate her own, the added benefit that her income provides is eroded, and the incentive to earn money at the expense of time spent caring for her children is decreased. Scholars have described a preference among many working-class mothers, both white and minority, to care for their own children at home.[8] According to Ann Crittenden, "Uneducated married mothers are the least likely to be employed, having the least to gain from a job. They calculate, quite correctly, that as long as there is one breadwinner in the family, their presence at home can create more value, and be more satisfying, than much of the (under)-paid work they could find."[9] The family that ends up keeping only a sliver of the mother's salary after it has met its child care costs is likely to feel doubly penalized by their position: victimized by the high cost of child care, and deprived of the ability to care for their children themselves.

The seemingly obvious solution to these inequalities is for the government to subsidize day care or provide a day care system that lowers the financial burden on individual families. But that goal meets with an ambivalent response for a similar reason. Given how enormously expensive a government-funded day care system of highly trained, well-paid staff would be, many people would rather put their money toward funding their own "high quality" care of their children than toward a publicly funded system. Though our national stubbornness about funding a child care system looks from one angle like an attempt to keep women in their place, frustrating their ability to achieve social and economic parity, from another angle it expresses something about the value people place on caring for their own children, and their desire to do it themselves if they can.

Another facet of the child care paradox is revealed if one imagines the "best case" day care scenario, where mothers have access to impeccably consistent, reliable, loving caregivers. From one perspective, this is an answer to a mother's prayers; yet from another, it too meets with some ambivalence. Such a world has been envisioned by the primatologist Sarah Blaffer Hrdy, who offers a utopian solution to the day care issue in her call for day care centers to employ "well-paid and highly respected 'allomothers,' a cadre of 'as-if' mothers, who can be either male or female, so long as they are stable, conscientious, and treat the children like their closest kin."[10] There is, of course, the obvious question of where day care centers might locate a population of "as-if" mothers who hadn't already decided to deploy their energies caring for their own "closest kin." Certainly no longer, as the economist Shirley Burggraf has observed, from the huge population of gifted women teachers, nurses, and other caring professionals that previous generations could draw upon, a population that existed precisely because women were largely excluded from most "masculine" professions.[11]

Apart from these recruitment difficulties, however, there is the question of *who* would be amenable to funding this well-paid cadre. And herein lies the rub. In order for a mother to be able *and* willing to pay for a surrogate as good as herself, she would have to be not only sufficiently well paid but *also* sufficiently unambivalent about trading the rewards of caring for her children for the rewards of paid employment. This is a situation in which a subset of mothers, like Hrdy, find themselves; but the relative rarity of this confluence casts doubt on the viability of allomothers as a society-wide solution.

Its rarity involves, again, the dynamics of maternal desire. The main weakness of Hrdy's well-meaning proposal may not be its impracticality but the assumptions about maternal motivation on which it rests. In *Mother Nature*, her exhaustive book on the evolutionary biology of motherhood, Hrdy turns to her own area of expertise, primatology, to put forth a model for understanding mothers' competing goals. Among chimps like Jane Goodall's Flo, Hrdy argues, a mother's ambition — to command resources, territory, and power — is not at odds with, but is instead an inherent part of, good mothering behavior. Flo combines nurturing and ambition, and her ambition is also a kind of nurturing. In Flo, Hrdy sees something like an inspiration for how to think about our own motherhood.

But between Flo's situation and our own, as Hrdy acknowledges, there is a crucial difference: Flo has the advantage of being able to maintain proximity with her offspring *while* she pursues her ambition. By contrast, the specifically *human* conflicts about mothering and work arise largely in response to the spatial split between places of work and home, as well as the kind of focus required for mental work. Human mothers of young offspring today, unlike their primate and Pleistocene-era counterparts, have to make various trade-offs between ambition and proximity because of the absorbing nature of both work and child rearing.[12]

The virtue of the idea of allomothers is that it allows mothers facing a conflict between ambition and proximity to imagine a situation where they can side with their ambition without sadness or guilt. It suggests that if one has solved the problem of providing a consistent loving caregiver, then one has solved the problem of maternal proximity and freed maternal ambition. But for many mothers, the problem is a prior one; it is the very giving up of their *own* proximity to their child, *regardless* of how loving or consistent their replacement is. This aspect of maternal motivation, women's desire to care for their own children and their ambivalence about structuring social life in a way that decreases the possibility of that care, continually and quietly undermines their support of large-scale day care solutions, even idealistic ones, of the sort that Hrdy proposes.

Even when mothers forgo proximity and adopt a solution like Hrdy's, maternal desire expresses itself in the fact that mothers feel fiercely protective of, and deeply invested in, their central importance to their children. "Despite parents' worries," Susan Chira writes, "the results of studies are virtually unanimous: Children's relationships to other caregivers do not surpass the one with their parents in emotional intensity or influence. Study after study has found, with only rare exceptions, that children overwhelmingly prefer their parents to their caregivers."[13] Chira notes that in the words of one psychotherapist, the "housekeeper [by which she meant the nanny] never shows up in the material" that patients discuss in therapy.[14] While reassuring to parents in one way, this finding can be troubling in another. Not only is one reassured at the expense of the value of another woman's work (the caregiver who "never shows up in the material"), but one also knows that one's own relief says nothing about the experience of the child. It may be a comfort to a *mother* that she is more beloved by her child than is the caregiver; but what is she to do with the child's "overwhelming preference" for her? It is precisely this "overwhelming preference" that plays a role in finding a balance in work and family time, because it is often in the act of responding to this "overwhelming preference" that we feel best about ourselves as parents.

The Absence of Maternal Desire in the Day Care Debate

WHEN THE DISCUSSION OF CHILD care fails to recognize what it means to mothers to care for their own children and to relinquish that care, it misses the impact of maternal desire on the process of finding day care solutions. For the psychologist and day care advocate Sandra Scarr, for example, anything that interferes with women's equal participation in the workforce operates to the detriment of gender equality and women's interests. She rejects the advantages of family-friendly policies such as those in Sweden that "help mothers to balance work and family life by granting paid, job-guaranteed maternity and parental leaves, child allowances to supplement family income, and part-time work for mothers when their children are young," because they "support maternal absences from the labor force" and thus have negative effects on women's *careers*.[15] Scarr implies that such arrangements are put in place by outside forces that have nothing to do with women's own desires. "Unequal child-care responsibilities lead mothers to be less invested in career development and less motivated to maintain continuous, full-time employment," she writes.[16] These innocently declarative phrases, "lead mothers to be less invested in career development" and "less motivated to maintain continuous, full-time employment," treat the mother as a completely passive actor, somehow "led" to certain courses of action by her "unequal" time caring for children. Her own desire is entirely erased. There is no place to introduce into the equation the evidently less palatable possibility that the mother may *want* to shoulder greater responsibility for her children's care.

Operating from the assumption that the key to gender equality is the remediation of women's unequal child care responsibilities, Scarr proposes that child care center standards should be relaxed somewhat to make the price affordable for working parents. The regulations as they stand increase child care costs, with the danger of "driving most families into the underground market of unregulated care."[17] This shadowy, gray-market imagery may reflect in part Scarr's commitment to day care center care; she served as CEO of the for-profit day care chain KinderCare Learning Centers, Inc.[18] But again, this formulation takes into account only one aspect of mothers' interests, namely their interest in maintaining employment. It avoids confronting the fact that the "logically obvious" question Scarr attributes to fiscal conservatives — "What is the minimal expense for child care that will allow mothers to work and not do permanent damage to children?"[19] — is one that most mothers will only reluctantly entertain. Psychologists may make recommendations from a public health perspective, but any individual parent considering options for her own child's care is already in a position of passionate self-interest. Avoiding "permanent damage" to one's child is not the standard most people consider adequate when they are seeking child care. The point at which they feel their children are in substandard care is the point at which parents, and mostly mothers, feel compelled to try to rearrange their lives to try to do more of the care themselves. Contrary to Scarr's conceptualization of women's freedom solely within the framework of paid work and unequal child care responsibilities, for many mothers, leaving their children in even less good care than they already do is a recipe not for maternal freedom but for maternal despair.

Neglected in all of this is how interdependent a mother's and child's well-being are. One day care advocate entitles her book *Children's Interests/Mothers' Rights*, as if the agendas could be so cleanly counterposed.[20] Of course parents have important interests distinct from their children's, but they also take their children's well-being to heart in a way that really does overtake self-interest. (My children are fond of asking me, "Who would you rather have die first, you or me?," and I respond without a moment's hesitation, "Me." Never mind that now they've added the cat to the list, and they want me to account for why I'd save myself before I'd save her.)

Once when I looked into family day care for my youngest son, I visited a nice woman in my town who had six two-year-olds under her care, including her own. She had a lot of neat toys and some fun activities, but the kids kept having little accidents. One kid fell out of his booster seat at snack. There was relentless fighting over toys that ended in fisticuffs and hair pulling (two-year-olds aren't into sharing). Her own daughter was whiny and aggressive toward the other kids. She seemed angry that she was sharing her mom all day with so many same-age children. I may sound like a perfectionist, but in fact, I don't believe children need "perfect" environments, and I even think a little boredom and adversity are good for kids. If my two-year-old boy had spent his mornings at that family day care, I know he would have adjusted, that he would have been neither completely miserable nor emotionally damaged. But in the end, I didn't feel it was a place I wanted him to have to adjust to.

Was it him or me? Would he have been unhappy, or was it my problem? Where day care is concerned, the reality is that the two cannot be easily distinguished. They can't be easily distinguished because how you feel as a parent affects how your child feels; because whatever makes you uncomfortable has a good chance of affecting your child somehow too; and because when you are unhappy, the whole purpose of day care, to allow you to accomplish your work, is marred by your discomfort and preoccupation with how your child is feeling and doing. On top of all this, the hugely meaningful issue of how good one feels about oneself as a mother is deeply entwined with how well one is able to care for and provide for one's child. Just as poverty makes people feel worse about themselves, putting one's child in a substandard care situation makes mothers feel worse about themselves.

In the current climate, one reflexive reply to these emotional concerns is that they are the luxury of the few; for most, economic realities preclude such subtle objections. Economics are of course always central to needing to work and paying for day care. But one sometimes gets the sense that economic "reality" is invoked to shut us up. Its oppressive message that we "can't afford" to feel what we feel, so we might as well corral our feelings into existing categories and arrangements, seems driven to monolithically impose itself, to deny that "reality" is partly something we create for ourselves, both individually and socially. As the writer Marilynne Robinson remarked in *The Death of Adam*, "We act as if the reality of economics were reality itself, the one Truth to which everything must refer. I can only suggest that terror at complexity has driven us back on this very crude monism."[21] When mothers' interests are defined solely in terms of their economic interests, it tells us less about "reality" than about values, values about money and time that define away much of what is emotionally important to actual mothers.

Mothers' "Choice"

ONE REASON PUBLIC DISCUSSIONS OF day care seem so studiously to avoid the issue of maternal desire is the fear that once we start talking about what women want, we will stop paying attention to what they need. All sorts of ungenerous attitudes toward mothers are rationalized through the contemporary rhetoric of "choice." Since it is a woman's choice to have a child, the reasoning goes, it is her responsibility to bear all professional and economic costs associated with that choice. In response to this rhetoric, and in order to safeguard whatever gains we have made, women may find themselves observing a code of silence regarding the positive emotional motivations we have for mothering, lest the pleasure we derive from it be marshalled as further evidence of the purely voluntary and personal nature of the enterprise. In a weird way, our cultural eagerness to treat maternal desire as a manifestation of purely personal "choice" recapitulates, in a new key, the punitive attitude society has always taken toward women's desires.

The issue of "choice" with respect to work and mothering is also a lot more complicated than our sunny American view of self-determination would suggest. In her book *Unbending Gender*, the legal scholar Joan Williams offered a cogent rethinking of what it means to be a parent and a worker in our society. She argued that in the American workplace, the "ideal worker" is someone who can work long hours, conform to inflexible work schedules, and relocate if necessary. All these characteristics, Williams points out, require the background presence of someone who takes care of the "flow of household work." The norm of the ideal worker discriminates against women because it imposes requirements that most women are unable to fulfill; by virtue of their role as family caregivers, they themselves are usually responsible for "the flow of family work." The norm of the ideal worker tends to draw men disproportionately into the ideal worker role and women into lives framed around caregiving. As a result, men overwhelmingly miss out on time with children, and women are marginalized in the workplace for fulfilling their parental obligations.

Williams is particularly interested in how mothers' decisions not to perform as ideal workers, or to leave the workforce altogether, get construed as personal "choice." She reminds us that all choices come about within an economic and ideological force field. In particular, mothers' "choice" to care for children is affected by norms of domesticity that sanction fathers' consuming jobs and mothers' orientation around caregiving. Working mothers who quit and stay home because "'it just wasn't working,'" are not simply making a personal decision; they are yielding to an ideology of domesticity characterized by a sharp, and highly gendered, split between home and work. In her view, "women's sense of relief when they give up trying to perform as ideal workers reflects the fact that they no longer have to fight the stiff headwinds from domesticity. . . . Many women find that ceding to the demands of domesticity is the only way to have their lives make sense."[22]

Williams intends not only to show that the ideology of domesticity permeates what we consider our most private, personal decisions but also, and thereby, to weaken domesticity's powerful emotional appeal. Yet recognizing the ideology of domesticity does not necessarily undermine its appeal, for even if we grant that the "expectations and institutions of domesticity" influence our personal choices, few of us would affirm that they completely determine our choices. Most of us feel we have some portion of freedom, some room to authentically desire. The choice to care for children (and to put up with the losses and trade-offs associated with it) is certainly affected by the available social options; but it also connects to deep feelings we experience as truly personal, feelings we may see no virtue in weakening or dismantling.

"Ceding to the demands of domesticity" is not the only, or even the main, reason underlying mothers' feeling that "their lives make sense." Whatever role mothers assume — marginalized caregiver, ideal worker, or worker/caregiver — their feeling that "their lives make sense" tends to hinge, rather, on a feeling of connection to their children. Mothers vary in how much time and hands-on attention they need to give to their children in order to achieve a sense of connection; but this connection is often the single most decisive issue in whether they feel their situation works. An employed mother may well declare, "It just wasn't working," because she realizes she can't handle both being an ideal worker and accomplishing the flow of household work. But she might also come to that same conclusion when performing as an ideal worker works "too well"; when, for example, she has the thought "*I'm* the mother, *I* want to give them a bath" when she comes home and sees her children all toweled off by the nanny and readied for bed.

The strong identification of self with mothering is one reason why Williams's formulation of what prevents mothers from functioning as ideal workers is incomplete. She lists their impediments, including an inability to work long hours or relocate. Elite jobs require very long hours, and "few mothers can do this because few women have spouses willing to raise their children while the women are at work."[23] If it were simply a matter of resistant men, women would begin taking Rhona Mahony's advice and marry men with lower earning prospects or with less career focus than themselves.[24] These men would then be more available to provide the flow of family worker necessary to a person in an elite job. Yet this solution hasn't even approached 50 percent, in part because many women identify with their desire to mother as central to who they are. Even if they also identify strongly with their professional side, and even if they dream of an alternative universe where they could spend all their time as a mother *and* all their time as a worker, they are still reluctant to relinquish the central role of caretaking. This is not simply due to territoriality or wanting control; it has to do with what they subjectively perceive as meaningful. Williams notes that "two-thirds of Americans believe it would be best for women to stay home and care for family and children. In significant part, this reflects a paucity of attractive alternatives."[25] In part it does. But in part it reflects a positive wish.

One risk of not accounting for this desire fully enough is that the solutions offered to soften work-family conflicts will be ineffective. Williams rests her solution to the split between male ideal workers and female marginalized caregivers on establishing "a norm of parental care." On her view, a first step is to reach a social agreement on the amount of parental care children need. Once we agree on this, child care can and should be divided equally between partners. Although a social norm of parental care has virtues — chief among them the agreement on a minimal level necessary for children of *all* backgrounds — at the very heart of some of the most divisive disagreements among feminists, mothers, and people in general is the question of what kind of parental care children should have. People can even espouse the same goal but believe that it is best met in different ways. Some conceptualize the amount of parental paid work they do as the only, or best, way to give their children advantages, whereas some see their continuous availability at home as conferring these same advantages. A therapist colleague said that among her urban professional patients who are mothers, one of the most consuming dilemmas is whether it is better for their children if they work in order to provide them a private school education, or stay home in order to offer their children their own guidance and companionship.

To arrive at a social consensus about the amount of time children need, a logical starting point might be to consult the opinion of people who have spent their lives studying children and families. The pediatrician T. Berry Brazelton and the child psychiatrist Stanley Greenspan collaborated on a book called *The Irreducible Needs of Children*. Regarding infant care in the first year, they wrote: "We do not recommend full-time day care, 30 or more hours of care by nonparents, for infants and toddlers *if* the parents are able to provide high-quality care themselves and *if* the parents have reasonable options."[26] Yet with respect to a different aspect of Greenspan's child rearing philosophy, Williams regards his recommendation that parents spend a half hour per day per child playing on the floor as extravagant.[27] Agreement on a norm of parental care is severely hampered by the fact that even educated, thoughtful people vociferously disagree on these emotionally charged decisions.

Williams focuses on the rhetoric of "choice" with respect to women's participation in domesticity, though she might just as well have focused on the rhetoric of "choice" women use to support their participation in the workforce. As she would be the first to observe, both rhetorics of "choice" mask the same structural demands of the workplace that create the family-work divide in the first place; both shape a set of dispositions and beliefs into a worldview.[28] Certainly, mothers on any side of the work-family dilemma may interpret as choice a decision influenced by prevailing ideologies. Yet it is important to remember that although no choice is immune to ideological pressures, no choice can be reduced to those pressures either.

One of the more perverse aspects of the contentious "working versus stay-at-home mother" debate is how often people on one side of the issue discuss the motivations of their "opponents" in reductive, dismissive terms, treating what they say they think or feel as "really" about something else. In the benighted fifties, this took the absurd form of therapists solemnly pronouncing that ambitious women "really wanted to be men." Today, we're more likely to hear it assumed that mothers devoting their time to caring for children have been beguiled by a "cult of domesticity"[29] or brainwashed by the media or by attachment research. Chira, for example, reports on a mother of three, formerly on welfare, who says, "'a child's most important year is the first year. You build a bond with that child. To force a mom to go back to work, it's kind of hard.'" Chira then interprets the woman's sentiment as the sorry result of indoctrination rather than authentic opinion: "That's what we tell mothers they are supposed to feel. [This mother] is just one example of how propaganda about attachment has misfired. She's been convinced by the very arguments aimed at working-class and middle-class mothers."[30]

The biggest problem with these sorts of glosses is not their simplistic conclusions, but the habit of mind that produces them. In presuming to know what "really" underlies a person's self-declared beliefs or motivations, they display what the philosopher and psychoanalyst Jonathan Lear has called "knowingness." For Lear, "our contemporary culture's demand to already know" the basis of others' motivations and the solution to their problems is a way to deny the mystery and complexity of each individual, as well as the role of unconscious motivation in human meaning-making.[31] The effect is a lack of openness to unpredetermined outcomes, "as though there is too much anxiety involved in simply asking a question and waiting for the world to answer."[32] "Political correctness" has entered the common lexicon as a way to refer to this demand that any point of

view, even if arrived at through genuine curiosity and honest reflection, must end up in an approved-in-advance, thoroughly
predictable place.

The stance of knowingness pervades the cultural back-and-
forth on child care and work, but it even creeps into our most
commonplace interactions. I remember the first Halloween my
work prevented me from engaging in the admittedly enjoyable
but overly sacralized rite of the homemade Halloween costume.
As I casually chatted with another mother about what our kids
were going to be for Halloween, her homemade Robin Hood
was met with my Ninja from Target, and she became distant, nod-
ding her head distractedly as if her appraisal of my maternal
character was now concluded and there was really nothing more
to say. I had the sudden feeling she wasn't seeing *me* anymore,
but rather a whole constellation of ideas about me (lazy? too
caught up in my work? not in touch with the important things
in life?) set in motion by my Ninja from Target. It felt odd to be
on the receiving end of those projections.

Because our concern for our children is so strong, and the
stakes of uncertainty feel so terribly high, we are often anxious
for the world to tell us unequivocally what is right, especially
where our children's care is concerned. And there is no shortage
of experts willing to proffer ready-made formulas. You should be
at home, you should be at work, day care is bad for children, day
care is good for children. In our insecure, uncertain moments, it
is so easy to hang on others' advice about the right way to do
things, and to feel something is wrong with us if we don't want
to or feel we can't. We are constantly tempted to rely on an
outer index rather than an internal state. And the flip side of
others' being entitled to tell us what we "really" feel is that we
feel unentitled to either discover it for ourselves or treat intimate knowledge of ourselves and our children as a reliable basis
for action.

Regrettably, where mothers' work and child care is concerned,
statistics too often function like modern-day tea leaves, providing inconclusive information that we overinterpret in our anx-

ious need to know *something*. And it doesn't take a literary critic to notice how the ostensibly objective reporting on these topics tends to interpose a specific worldview to guide our interpretation of them. The *New York Times*, for example, reported 1998 census statistics showing that two working married parents had become the majority, edging out families with one working married parent by one percentage point (51 percent versus 49 percent). This was quickly couched in the rhetoric of progress and self-actualization: "Women are in the workplace to stay," said the president of the National Partnership for Women and Families, "and there's no telling how high the numbers could go; it'll be as high as women want it to be." Of all the aspects of the study it could have focused on, the *Times* chose to highlight in bold print the observation that "the stay-at-home mother has less and less company."[33] This interpretive frame says less about the import of the findings than it does about the ideology most acceptable to the *Times*'s educated readership. That ideology insists on relentlessly aligning women's employment with women's progress, in this instance citing the trajectory of diminishing interest in stay-at-home motherhood, even though, as a letter to the *Times* correctly observed, the statistics *also* demonstrate that "nonworking mothers are an amazingly large group."[34]

The rush to construe women's progress, as well as their needs and desires, in such deceptively straightforward terms contributes to the general spirit of flattening the psychological complexity of mothers' dilemmas about work and family. Ironically, this flattening prepares the soil for a backlash biologism and its reductionistic understandings of motherhood ("Women are meant to mother"; "It's in the genes") as people seek to offer *some* account of why motherhood feels so central and so compelling to many women. It seems we can't manage to conceptualize the interdependence of mothers' and children's well-being in a way that feels respectable or consistent with women's progress. Where there is a vacuum of awe for the complexity and depth of maternal motivation, it is no surprise, perhaps, that the inexorable forces of nature are invoked.

Child Care, Mothers' Work, and Mothers' Sensitivity

ONE PLACE WE LOOK FOR information to guide our thinking about our child care decisions is psychological research. Our collective hunger for evidence meets its match in the vast National Institute of Child Health and Human Development (NICHD) Study of Early Child Care, which has followed 1,364 children from diverse families in ten locations up to age seven and beyond, tracking a host of variables related to child, family, and child care characteristics. The study's goal was to move beyond the simplistic question of whether day care "hurts" children to consider the interaction of factors in children's lives. The study's overarching message is one of complexity: no one factor causes any one effect.[35]

But perhaps the aspects of the study that have been most gripping to mothers have had to do with variables that involve the quality of mother-child interaction, specifically attachment and maternal sensitivity. That is where a lot of the "heat" seems to be, because it is where we learn most about the emotional texture of the mother-child relationship.[36] What light does the NICHD study shed specifically on that relationship? Concerning attachment, it has shown that infants who have had extensive child care experience in the first fifteen months of life are no less securely attached, on average, than children who have not. Time spent apart from parents does not in itself appear to affect the security or insecurity of the mother-infant bond. What can make a difference is the sensitivity and responsiveness of the mother. Low sensitivity or responsiveness, when combined with more than minimal amounts of child care, poor-quality child care, or more than one care arrangement, is related to less secure attachment.[37] And more time spent in child care for children ranging from six months to three years has been found to correlate with less maternal sensitivity.[38]

The press release announcing these findings took pains to underscore that the correlation between hours spent in child care and maternal sensitivity was small; smaller, for instance, than the correlation between mothers' level of education and her sensitivity to her child.[39] All told, however, though the effect was relatively small, the NICHD study demonstrated that the more hours of child care a child received from infancy through age three, the less sensitive the child's mother was. In interpreting these findings, the *Wall Street Journal* columnist on work and family issues, Sue Shellenbarger, wrote: "Here's a twist: Childcare use affects parents. . . . Tuning in to a child is a skill that takes practice, time and effort, a process parents need consciously to safeguard when using lots of childcare."[40]

In a 2002 research study presented in the journal *Child Development* and much covered by the media, the authors reported that when mothers worked thirty or more hours by a baby's sixth or ninth month, there were negative effects on the child's school readiness at age three, keeping all other factors constant.[41] In some ways, the study could not have been calculated to cause more concern among members of the demographic group most volubly fretful about these issues: married mothers of European background who work more than thirty hours per week were the population identified as most at risk when controlling for the quality of day care, and the outcome measure — school readiness — is among the more highly valued criteria for parenting success in this group. To figure out what might contribute to the correlation between mothers' work hours and school readiness at age three, the researchers looked at the quality of child care and home environment, including maternal sensitivity. They found that the negative effect of early, full-time maternal employment on school readiness was exacerbated when quality of child care and maternal sensitivity were low. Children whose mothers worked more than thirty hours weekly when they were nine months old tended to be in lower-quality care at thirty-six months than children whose mothers worked less, and to have mothers who were rated as less sensitive than did children whose mothers did not work in their first year.[42]

A question these findings prompt is whether the mothers' insensitivity was more situational, having to do with the amount of time they spent working and that their children spent in child care, or more dispositional, having to do with their personal care-giving approach.[43] When trying to determine what accounted for the lower sensitivity among mothers who worked more than thirty hours per week by their child's ninth month, the research-ers found that even when mothers' prior level of sensitivity was held constant, these women *still* had significantly lower sensitiv-ity scores at thirty-six months than mothers who did not work when their child was nine months. In other words, their lower sensitivity could not be explained only by personality characteris-tics or prior behavior; the fact that they were working more than thirty hours in their child's ninth month appeared to have an in-dependent relationship to their sensitivity in interactions with their child.

This finding gives us a perspective on what can be so painful to a mother about being apart for significant amounts of time from her infant and small child. Being apart from her child for long stretches can make it harder to read him, to respond aptly, and to have a mutually satisfying interaction. Over and above the sadness of missing her child, and even the pain about the ways her absence creates stumbling blocks to knowing him as in-timately as she might, she may also feel anxious about whether she is able to give him what he needs. A friend of mine has a tod-dler who is frustrated easily and often inconsolable. My friend can always provide a reason ("She's hungry," "She needs a nap"), but privately she fears that she doesn't know how to comfort her daughter as well as the full-time caregiver does. Even more painful to her, she thinks that her daughter's inconsolability would diminish if she were around to console her more. Stress, fatigue, conflict, and simple lack of time diminish her sensitivity in ways that are hard for her child, painful to her, and eroding of her maternal self-esteem.

In our understandable focus on children's welfare in our dis-cussions about child care, we rarely explore what it costs moth-ers in terms of their *own* sense of sensitivity and effectiveness to be away from their babies and small children. A strong public voice affirms the importance of mothers' needs and desires with respect to working, but a fear of backsliding keeps us from having a similar kind of discussion about mothers' needs and desires for relating to their small children. Yet such a discussion is critical to moving our workplaces in a more family-sensitive direction.

Working, Not Working, and Maternal Intentionality

THERE IS ANOTHER KIND OF insensitivity, distinct from the situational one just described, a more intractable, dispositional insensitivity. In *The Nanny Diaries*, the protagonist "Nanny" gives a taxonomy of jobs: "There are essentially three types of nanny gigs. Type A, I provide 'couple time' a few nights a week for people who work all day and parent most nights. Type B, I provide 'sanity time' a few afternoons a week to a woman who mothers most days and nights. Type C, I'm brought in as one of a cast of many to collectively provide twenty-four/seven 'me time' to a woman who neither works nor mothers. And her days remain a mystery to us all."[44]

The novel's authors McLaughlin and Kraus convey with heartbreaking precision the world of a neglected child, Grayer, who with trusting eagerness, tries to make use of any drop of attention his parents give him. Like any child, Grayer is always ready to be nourished by parental love, to turn his face toward the sun and to conserve and use every last bit of its energy to help him grow. If a parent knows how to give love, if she earnestly tries to understand her child's feelings and needs, then that intention is felt by the child, and the child makes use of it; even when the parent is away, he carries it around inside. But Grayer's parents are impossibly self-centered; they don't see what he needs, and they have no interest in finding out. Grayer's problem isn't that he has parents who work too much (they don't); it's that he has parents who are blindingly insensitive.

We all know mothers who work a lot and are connected to their kids. And we know mothers who are around their children a lot and not attuned to what their children need. There are sensitive mothers who work a lot and insensitive mothers who don't. This mundane observation makes clear that we are not *simply* talking about employment status when we enter the fray of comparing "working" and "stay-at-home" mothers. When we make these distinctions, the value we are really trying to get at has to do with something deeper: a certain kind of *awareness* about what is important about being around one's children, even if one is not. We use the "marker" of mothers working, not entirely consciously, as an external indicator of the presence or absence of an inner state that we deem important in human terms.

There is a genre of article that shows a woman who has succeeded to the hilt in her career; she has broken glass ceilings, forged ahead under incredible odds, and shown other women they can do it too. There are often also hints that she has sacrificed her family life to her achievements. Such morality tales pull for certain conclusions about mothers' work. But if we look more closely at what is really bothering us, it is something about how she relates to those she is closest to. In one case, what came through in an article about a supersuccessful executive was an ongoing lack of insight into the developmental needs of her children. When she "couldn't make it home in time to help with homework, her two daughters would fax her a copy of their papers, and she would edit them while still at the office."[45] Or when her son was failing at boarding school, she swooped in and wrote his papers for him. Efficiently dispatching answers to one's children's problems (in this case, editing and writing their papers) without awareness of the importance of process is generally seen as problematic mothering.

While it may be that insensitive maternal behavior is associated with hours spent at work or degree of professional responsibility achieved, that is an empirical question that has never been directly studied. And we know enough counterexamples in our own lives to cast doubt on the existence of a clear correlation. The reason the executive manages her children the way she does or *The Nanny Diaries'* "Mrs. X" neglects her son, Grayer, has to do not with their specific activities but rather with something more fundamental about their posture toward the world. In both cases, though in different ways, that posture is problematic not only because of how much time it leads them to spend away from their children; but also because of how it leads them to relate to their children *when they are present*. Since they don't understand what their children need — the executive thinks they need her paper-writing skills; Mrs. X thinks Grayer needs organic oatcakes and admission to a prestigious kindergarten — their time together is starved of a nourishing connectedness. Of course, the tragic irony is that the parents most in need of observing their own insensitivity are least able or willing to do so. By contrast, the core of loving, responsible, interested intention that most parents direct toward their children encompasses their intuitive understanding of both what is hard for their child about their absence *and* what is valuable to their child about their presence.

The whole question of mothers' work and its effects is in part a question about mothers' intentions. The terms of our current debate suggest we are confused about what it is we are talking about when we talk about working mothers. We look at mothers' work in a crude iconographical way, almost to avoid looking at subtler movements of the soul, of the inner psychological world, that tell us more about the real effects of a given woman's employment on her relationship with her children. Some, particularly conservatives, try to compel intentions with the blunt instrument of moral judgment. Advocating the sacredness of a mother's commitment to her children, they then turn this value into a prescription that eagerly presents itself as the *only* analogue, the *exact* translation of this maternal commitment into action — stay-at-home motherhood for instance, or traditional gender hierarchy in the family. Yet, insisting that a certain type of behavior is the only way to express care has the effect of actually impairing some mothers' best expression of their love toward their children. For example, a mother who truly feels she is sacrificing herself if she stays at home but does so anyway may end up adopting a depressed self-abnegation or hypercontrolling demeanor at home.

Acknowledging the importance of maternal intentions helps

us understand the ability of parents who are away most of the day to connect and nurture their children even in their absence. It also helps clarify what might matter about parental presence. A friend of mine ruefully observed that when the family was on vacation, spending all their time together, her preschooler's vocabulary expanded exponentially. She knew there were a number of reasons that probably contributed: the child care person's English was limited, she didn't talk as much to the child as the parents did, and the child happened to be going through a developmental spurt. But my friend also felt she was noticing something less graspable about the kind of energy she and her daughter put into their communication because they were engaged with *each other*. There was a passion and interest that each brought to the interaction; their intense shared involvement was pursued for mutual enjoyment, but like most such enjoyment, it also set up a receptivity, a dispositional state conducive to learning. Parental involvement and interest give a fullness to the feel of life for children, encouraging them to experiment, risk, and reach, to take the next step.

If we end up discovering that the hours a mother spends away from her small child actually do have something to do with that child's readiness for school or ability to handle aggression or complexity of thinking or anything else, I think the reasons for it will lie in this direction. It will not be that mothers at home are holding up flashcards or teaching their kids conflict management skills or chess; rather, it will have something to do with the way their presence facilitates aspects of relating — shared positive feeling, moral conversation, relaxing — that *themselves* contribute to the child's development of a flexible and empathic approach to understanding the world, which *in turn* affects measurements of school readiness, self-control, and the like. Research suggests that a mutually responsive relationship between mother and child, characterized by secure attachment, shared positive emotion and experiences, and conversation about the child's behavior and feelings, contributes to the child's willingness and desire to embrace maternal values and to the development of conscience. Similarly, parents' discussion with their children about their feeling states contributes to children's later understanding of the emotions of other people.[46] These express in experimental terms what Winnicott long ago observed about the development of a child's moral sense: "In these matters the answer is always that there is *more to be gained from love than from education*."[47] The nuances of these processes still far exceed the scientific tools we have for studying them, but the studies we have do begin to get at the "stuff" of intentionality that we intuitively know underlies good parenting.

Time with our children is obviously a necessary condition for sharing these types of interactions. The question in the back of many a mother's mind is whether she and her child have enough of it. That question never goes away because, while being away from our kids doesn't necessarily cause problems, there are few problems that being around more wouldn't help solve. But the faulty inference that only certain roles — stay-at-home motherhood, for instance — allow for that time disregards many individual differences. A mother who is apart from her child many hours a day may strive to be particularly conscientious about tuning in to her child at the end of the day, precisely because she was away so long.[48] A mother who is home, whose paramount concern is getting through the day with her young children without completely losing it, or without letting the house degenerate into complete chaos, may find that her sensitivity to the nuances of her children's desires and needs (let alone her own) is not exactly finely tuned. One of the difficult aspects of stay-at-home motherhood can be knowing how precious your children are and how fleeting this bit of life is but being unable to feel appreciative because you feel too overwhelmed. This is an occasional lament of mothers who have stopped working to stay home with their children and who find that, instead of reveling in the slower pace, smelling the roses and responding to their child, they are caught up in an endless round of needs and chores, with little ready relief.[49]

I can honestly say I've been on both sides of this dilemma. The feeling I need more time with the kids is usually accompanied by sadness or shocks of pit-in-the-stomach grief. Feeling I don't have enough time for work is usually accompanied by a sense of frustration and anxiety. At different phases of my own life as a mother I have had startlingly different realities. When my first child was a baby, I couldn't bear to leave her. When my second child started preschool, I felt I wanted to stay for all of "circle time," to really know what school was like for him, to feel connected to his new world. My third child had more child care than the others and developed a very close relationship with his babysitter. When he was two, I began to become more involved with my work. It was the first time as a mother that I had allowed myself to be carried away, to feel sometimes that I could happily have stayed in my office all day. He was a very happy, outgoing little character, but sometimes I'd feel a sharp sense of loss that I wasn't sharing certain experiences with him.

The reality is that I was at a different point in my own development as a mother when this youngest one was two, five-and-a-half years after my first child was two. And though I could both relish what was exciting about this phase and regret what I was giving up, I couldn't turn back the clock. It seemed the best I could do was try to take the long view, to look at the big picture of what mattered, to each of us individually and as a family. I had, quite consciously, decided not to let work occupy a large emotional space for several years because I knew it would take on a life of its own and risk crowding out the priority of time with my children. I also knew I was at a time in my own life when I was ready to start letting some of that back in. In doing that, I began to reflect on some of my assumptions about how much my children needed me, and to ask myself hard questions about which desires of my own, and theirs, I would satisfy.

The Pursuit of Happiness

WHEN WE HAVE CHILDREN, WE sometimes crave freedom of movement, and we may even want our old selves back. But what we have to do to simulate that freedom — relinquish the care of our child to another — is something to which we may remain stubbornly unreconciled. Like Lamott's portrait of maternal anger, we are not always aware of how ambivalent we are; after all, the relief at having the help we need can be so palpable. Then, suddenly, some emotional line that we didn't even know existed is overstepped — perhaps the babysitter has everything taken care of and we can't quite find where we fit in — and we are returned to an almost primal possessiveness, an agitated sense that we are not where we most want to be. In those moments we are put in touch with our desperate desire to *live* our child's "overwhelming preference" for us, to drink it up through every pore of our skin and aperture of our soul. What we felt constrained by a moment ago is what we yearn for now. Even mothers who experience their baby's dependence as a kind of prison grieve for the lost singularity of that early bond. "The storm of emotion, of the new, that accompanied her arrival is over now," writes Rachel Cusk. "In her growing up I have watched the present become the past, have seen at first hand how life acquires the savour of longing."[50] Women who experience the immersion of motherhood as nothing short of cataclysmic are often astonished to find, once that immersion is over, that they yearn to have another child and live it all over again.

Child care is about social priorities and policy options and the needs of our children and the needs of working parents. But it is also about so much more than the practical problems. It is about purpose, and human limits, and happiness. Its fraught, politicized nature stems from these deeper emotional roots. We can't possibly understand what stands in the way of what every well-meaning policy recommendation says families need — reasonably priced, reliable, high-quality day care — without at least looking at some of the emotions that fuel our stasis and our disagreements.

Our whole discussion of day care says next to nothing about the mutual happiness of parent and child, and yet that may be the one true measure of its success. Perhaps we don't talk about happiness because individuals can differ so drastically in their views of what brings it about. On the one hand, the psychologist

Sandra Scarr appears unable even to perceive the possibility that a woman would be made happy, rather than dejected, by staying home with her children:

> I'm really amazed at the number of young women today who are graduating from a very good university and who feel very strongly that they want to stay home with their own children because they are irreplaceable. That tells you the culture's still out there telling them it's really better if you could stay home, and they feel guilty if they don't want to. You need to say, why, why would children be better off if you stayed home and were miserable?[51]

In a scientific review article on working mothers, the only examples Scarr and her colleagues gave for why mothers might want to "remain in close contact with their newborns" were needing to rest after childbirth and wanting to establish a nursing schedule.[52] On the other hand, the baby care manual author Penelope Leach assumes complete symmetry between a mother and a baby's happiness: "Your interests and his are identical. You are all on the same side; the side that wants to be happy, to have fun."[53] Scarr treats a mother's and baby's happiness as completely separate; Leach treats them as completely fused. But the reality for most mothers is somewhere in the middle. They are acutely aware of the inextricability of their own and their child's happiness, and that is a fact that can arouse everything from claustrophobia to ecstasy.

Differences between people's visions of happiness also account for some of the contentiousness surrounding the study of mother-infant attachment. Facile and ill-informed critiques of attachment theory abound, often carelessly confusing it with a short-lived, somewhat fanatical school of thought extolling the crucial importance of mother-infant bonding right after birth.[54] The note of indignation that so often accompanies these critiques suggests that it is not so much the merits of the attachment paradigm that are in question as it is the implication that women should embrace their primacy as attachment figures, that they should, in effect, enjoy their enslavement.

But the fact is that even among themselves, attachment theorists don't agree about what their theory implies for mothers' behavior, and these differences themselves reflect different visions of happiness. "Ultimately," said the attachment researcher Erik Hesse, "the most liberating piece of information a woman could have is that her infant can attach to anyone"; mothers are not indispensable attachment figures, as long as there are others who are able to fill the role.[55] Conversely, the founder of attachment theory, John Bowlby, said, "Just as the baby needs to feel that he belongs to his mother, the mother needs to feel that she belongs to her child and it is only when she has the satisfaction of this feeling that it is easy for her to devote herself to him."[56] Depending on one's view of happiness, Hesse's comment may be enormously relieving or a bit depressing; Bowlby's might represent a lucid statement of the rewards of caregiving or a straitjacket of prescriptions.

Diverging visions of happiness also play into how mothers perceive baby care manuals. Baby care books by experts such as Brazelton, Leach, and Spock would seem to constitute a mild, inoffensive genre, but critics detect amid the tips and bromides a velvet-gloved enforcer of maternal right conduct. They object that these books urge mothers to sacrifice themselves for the sake of their babies; and that in their multifarious suggestions for attentive care, for ways to spend time together, for toys to make, they deliver the oppressive message that it is good for a mother to live a life centered on her baby.

Indeed, Leach and Brazelton specialize in taking the baby's perspective. But their philosophy, their map of the psychological world, conceptualizes that perspective in a particular relation to the mother's own. In her book *Your Baby and Child*, Leach does offer, it is true, a compendium of homemade toys that only the most craft-oriented mother could love. But far from recommending "joy in submission,"[57] as one critic put it, Leach is trying to describe something about a mother and baby's interdependence. "Taking the baby's point of view does not mean neglecting yours, the parents', viewpoint. . . . If you make happiness for him he will make happiness for you. If he is unhappy, you will find yourselves unhappy as well, however much you want or intend to keep your feelings separate from his."[58] To the extent that they "advocate" stay-at-home motherhood, or have an "obsessive" fascination with babies, Leach and Brazelton try to articulate a point of view that embeds a mother's caregiving within a frame of existential and psychological meaning. They are looking to describe the way in which a mother's effort to make her baby happy is a way of connecting to herself. The anxiety point for any given mother in reading their books will come when their suggestions appear to presume a level of pleasure and satisfaction in caring for children that she does not feel. But for every mother they unsettle and offend, there is another to whom they offer comfort and confirmation. Whether the vision of happiness they offer resonates with our own will affect whether we experience them as sympathetic or sinister.

These books may at times irritate, but they raise the same issue we all are dealing with: the interdependence of our own happiness and our children's. Like the NICHD study, they try to capture the ways parents and children mutually influence each other's well-being. When this mutuality is missed, our thinking about child care can sink to Big Brotherish depths. Witness, for instance, a truly creepy "solution" to the problem of parental anxiety while their children are in day care, parent access to real-time video of their children. Here is a method ostensibly designed to make you feel "more in touch" with your child during your hours apart, and yet your child doesn't know you are watching him and you are unable to interact with him. Your sense of distance and alienation is not bridged, but rather reinforced, by watching him like a spy. Parental paranoia is the only problem this technological innovation addresses; on the level of intimate relationship, the video simply makes us more acutely aware that we are *not* connecting with our child.

The compartmentalization that defines our contemporary approach to work and family cannot help but permeate the way we think about child care. And our American love affair with results meshes with our proclivity for research methods that yield "hard facts" to produce neat categories, such as "attachment security" and "school readiness" for measuring child care's effects. These are worthwhile objects of research, and the rigor with which they are studied is beyond reproach. But although such categories codify what we agree to be important childhood indicators for future success in love and work, they inevitably leave out the quicksilver, disobedient current of happiness. Happiness isn't captured directly within these empirical categories, so its importance can't be "counted" either.[59]

And yet, happiness is the entry point of the territory we need to explore. Susan Chira described in her book a moment of sublime integration: "Cradling my nursing baby in one arm and the phone in my ear, conducting an interview with some serious personage, I could hardly contain my happiness. I don't really advocate trying to interview with a baby on one arm. But that one moment, ridiculous as it sounds, stands out because it was the first time I felt both my selves fit together with an audible click."[60] Notice the self-consciousness, almost the embarrassment ("I don't really advocate," "ridiculous as it sounds") with which Chira shares having lived such a moment — its raw power makes her bashful or afraid she will not be understood. But these moments are not simply a relief or convenience; they are moments of profound integration. When we have these moments, our "lives make sense." Maybe everything suddenly fits together when our children are in a day care center downstairs from work, where we can visit them, instead of across town; or when the fretting over our schedule pays off, to the point where things really are in balance; or when we realize the work of caring for our child is the work we want to do. However it appears to us, this experience of wholeness is a thread to follow, to observe and describe. It may hold a key to what Annie Leclerc called "the archeology of our affectivity";[61] it may teach us something new about maternal potential. Becoming intimate with these experiences of happiness and figuring out what they mean for our own lives, and even the life of the culture, is our child care dilemma's private face, its personal frontier.

7

Adolescence

IN THE EARLY WINTER OF eighth grade, my sister and mother and I visited some friends at a farm they had rented in Vermont. I can't remember if my older brother came too; by that point he had launched himself into music, friends, and who knows what else (one was afraid to ask). I made the first entry in a new journal while there — like adolescent girls everywhere, I was in constant dialogue with my journal — impelled in part by the familiar discomfort I felt in the midst of a happy intact family, while I was in the company of my father-subtracted one. It began with a declaration of what a good mother my mother was, how really guiltless and well meaning and wonderful. From there, I ventured a small, highly tentative, heavily censored, supremely tactful, exculpatory little criticism of her, having to do with what I don't even recall.

For a long time I felt something was wrong with me for never having properly embraced the stereotypical path of adolescence, the conflict, the moodiness, the rages, the remorse.[1] I felt my mother needed, more than anything, my support, which aroused in me a sympathy about her challenges and a boosterism about her good points. In one way, what caused me to censor my angry thoughts toward her was quite simple: I didn't want to hurt her feelings. But in another way, I was afraid that my impulse to criticize her signaled a new, uncharted phase of our relationship.

What I grappled with in not revealing my anger, even to myself, had something to do with the life of my relationship with my mother, and how it was beginning to undergo new changes.

A girl entering adolescence is aware, as I was, of growing beyond her former relationship with her mother. Her feelings about what she needs from her mother change in ways she can neither foresee nor control. When my daughter was ten, she began criticizing me with a low-level, thrumming persistence. Was this, I wondered, a premonitory symptom of the headache of adolescence to come? Though there was sometimes a note of superiority in her voice, I could see that finding fault with me pained her. It occurred to me that she was growing out of her ability to look at me as someone who could make everything all right. The world was becoming much bigger than her home, her parents, her brothers, and she was beginning to sense our limitations, with an aching sadness that mystified her. Development was demanding her, even before she felt entirely ready, to grow beyond us.

If adolescence pushes us into a new relation with our family, the arrival of puberty confronts a girl with two new potentials in herself: the sexual and the maternal. For girls, a basic task of adolescence is to figure out how to integrate these potentials into a maturing identity. In different eras, one or the other potential receives greater emphasis. Look at Tolstoy's *War and Peace* and you will find that the vivacious Natasha transmogrifies into a little mother with hardly a detour into full-fledged adult sexuality. Even in the twentieth century, Erik Erikson's nuanced psychological writings listed toward portraying adolescent girls as mothers in waiting, seeking intimacy before identity and emotionally organized around their "inner space."[2] Today, we recognize girls as driven sexually, just as boys are. As one woman put it, "You can't tell breasts not to grow; you can't tell the period not to come. Young girls' bodies are yearning for sex — to link up, to connect, to mate."[3] To some extent, we tend to view sexual discovery as part and parcel of the larger search for meaning and commitment that defines adolescence.

The contemporary purpose of adolescence for middle-class Americans, to become educated and form long-term goals, means that although girls may be driven to explore their sexuality, they are emphatically not ready, by and large, to deal with motherhood. From a social point of view, adolescent girls today, unlike their ancestors, are looking at a stretch of at least a decade between the advent of their fertility and their childbearing. Caring parents do their best to reward and enforce this waiting period, with obvious benefits to girls' development as educated people, members of the workforce, and mature mothers. But for girls themselves, the potential coincidence of the sexual and maternal can be troubling for reasons that are distinct from the educational or moral or contraceptive issues it raises. For, just at the moment a girl is growing out of her utter dependence on her mother and discovering her independent subjectivity and sexuality, she can feel a kind of inherent constraint in growing into the reproductive capacity she identifies with her mother. Her mother's reproductive, maternal role can represent a life of being for others at just the point a girl is trying to figure out how to be for herself.

In her effort to discover her own desire, a girl may cast her mother as a formulaic, two-dimensional mother-person, investing her with all the powerlessness, servile people pleasing, or lack of personal aspiration that the girl herself swears she will avoid. Characterizing — or caricaturing — her mother as devoid of autonomous desire is one way of managing the momentous task of constructing a desiring self independent of her. It is an attempt to differentiate from one's mother by distancing oneself from "motherness."

This is clearly only one among many possible strategies a girl may employ to deal with the contradictory pulls to differentiate and identify with her mother. As the British psychologist Terri Apter pointed out, girls continually use their mothers' choices as a sounding board for their own: "They will either do as she has done, or not do as she has done. They will not try to combine a career and motherhood because she has worn herself out doing so. They will not depend on a man for economic support because she has, and has either learned that such dependence is unreliable or has resented it or simply regretted it."[4] Yet, though it is obvious that rejecting "motherness" is not an end point but a way station in a girl's search for identity, a strange thing happened when it came to theory: this moment of rejection became ossified, hardened into a sort of Eternal Now in our thinking about girls' development.

In book after hand-wringing book, we find that a girl's need to distance herself from her mother's way of living the maternal role is treated as an essential step in becoming her own person. In a slightly different version of the same theme, the daughter can't get help in formulating her desires because the mother is so out of touch with her own. Even when the problem of female adolescence is identified as the culture's inability to value relationships, the mother herself is often portrayed as collusive. Society, we learn, makes teenage girls get thin, get fat, lose their voice, swallow the beauty myth, and otherwise destroy themselves; but society's messenger, often enough, is the "self-sacrificial wife and mother," or the mother blindly co-opted by society's obsession with beauty, thinness, or a narrow definition of feminine appeal.[5] These books insist on the trapped nature of motherhood, but this insistence is not without irony. For even while they blame patriarchy for consigning women to the role of "just a mother," the more heartfelt target of complaint appears to be the mother who didn't mother well — who wasn't attuned enough, either to her child or to her own desire. The manifest solution proffered is that the mother should be freer from her stultifying maternal role; but the underlying wish is that she might have been more desirously involved *in it*. And more — perhaps too much to hope — that her involvement might have been something she felt to be a source of effectiveness, self-expression, and self-worth.

The usual discussion of female adolescence, pitting the freedom-seeking girl against her mother as an exemplar of the inhibiting, desexualized maternal, suffers from its inability to recognize both sexual *and* maternal desire. In terms of adolescent development, it fails to consider that disowning the maternal while vaunting the sexual is not a permanent position or resting point, but a moment in a fluid psychological process. There are moments in the life of every girl, and in the construction of every theory, where motherhood can seem like a route to non-self. But like children who were once told to avoid getting dirty and then, forgetting why, cling to elaborate avoidance rituals into adulthood, our theories superstitiously retain our fear of the self-annihilating costs of the maternal without appraising the transitory developmental moment on which it is based.

Ironically, or homeopathically, sometimes it takes motherhood itself to cure us — to reveal caring for our child as one of the most potent infusions of meaning and value we could have imagined. We may only then come to see how nurturing our child directly connects to our deepest desires and, even in its difficulties, represents one of the fullest, most passionate uses for our attention. That realization may prompt us to reevaluate motherhood generally, and to question its image in the wider culture. But however we acquire this perspective, it can encourage us to question the ways we have come to view female adolescence. In particular, we should take another look at the importance to daughters of their mothers' emotional investment in mothering, and reconsider the all-but-neglected development of maternal desire in the girl herself. Those intertwined issues shed light on some of the specific risks in girls' teenage years, including sexual choices, preoccupation with eating and weight, and pregnancy.

The Sexual, the Maternal, and Ideals of Control

SEXUAL AND REPRODUCTIVE CONTROL HAS been a perennial concern for adolescent girls and society, but the targets of our efforts at control have changed. The main project of contemporary adolescent girls, as the historian Joan Jacobs Brumberg sees it, is the management, control, and adornment of their bodies.[6] Unlike girls of a previous era, who were socialized to engage in self-control in the service of moral development, girls now fastidiously attend to their surfaces: skin, hair, and weight. These attempts at self-control, reinforced by advertising and the packaging of teen celebrities, aim to enhance girls' sense of value in the sexual marketplace and their status among peers, two consuming adolescent preoccupations.

Considering how enormous the freedoms are that today's American adolescent girl enjoys in comparison to practically every imaginable counterpart, it is not surprising that girls are preoccupied with self-control. What vigilant parents and town gossips used to do, girls increasingly do for themselves. What used to be a concern to the larger community — is this girl a virgin? is she contributing to the group? — have become largely personal decisions. Girls still have huge forces to contend with in managing their sexual and maternal potentials. Understandably, perhaps particularly in the absence of ironclad social taboos and predetermined social roles, girls devote a great deal of energy to their attempts at self-control.

But what is striking is the emphasis on surfaces that characterizes the socially desirable image of self-control espoused by today's teenage girls. Certainly, as Brumberg points out, the rise of visually oriented consumer culture has a considerable effect on girls' preoccupation with monitoring and controlling their surfaces. But girls' attention to their surfaces also relates, I think, to our collective confusion about control, freedom, and femaleness. As a society we have a love affair with control, seeing it as the means to our ultimate values of freedom, autonomy, and self-determination. We also feel a slight revulsion from anything that might mire us in dependency, and anxiety about the value of private experiences that can't be quantified or shown off. Motherhood, of course, instantly connects us to others in a dependent relationship, and it is all about private experience. In this sense, it represents a kind of demeaned culmination of just those things that adolescent girls are encouraged to ignore. Girls fixate on their surfaces in part to signal their participation in a social club — the social club of their peers, to be sure, but also the larger social club that demands, as the price of membership, a turning away from the mysteries of the internal and relational toward a more gleaming, assertive, successful model of self.

Body management is one arena where girls express their aspiration to control; another is the domain of relationships, where girls place a high value on sexual assertiveness. Offering teenage girls a tough-minded solution to the "problem" of being female, that is, the problem of caring about relationships when caring too much makes one look ridiculous, popular culture commends turning what have traditionally been understood as bids for sustained love — wanting to look nice and sex — into vehicles of self-empowerment. Examining this trend, the reporter Alex Kuczynski quoted one eighteen-year-old girl: "I think with feminist thought being pushed upon girls from a young age, that some people put a premium on girls' dominating different areas of life. So girls may now feel that it is also important to dominate in a sexual relationship. This allows the girl to have more control." A male college student saw the issue in darker terms, as girls' effort to "transform sex into something as meaningless as they believe it is for boys." "Our parents are all divorced, and we have never seen a successful long-term relationship," he said. "Girls don't want to think of sex as something which is about love because that will just come back and bite them later. The sex thing is just the most visible sign of the disconnectedness we feel."[7]

The ideal of sexual assertiveness and control is linked explicitly by one teenage girl to the rejection of a traditional maternal role: "No one is a stay-at-home mom anymore. Women don't have to wear skirts. We are empowered and we can do whatever we want."[8] Her idea of empowerment comes to life through its contrast to the static, skirt-wearing stay-at-home mother. And in this, she assents to a thoroughgoing and broad refutation of any connection between girls' and women's "active" desire for sex and "passive" desire for motherhood, an idea obsessively re-inforced throughout popular female culture. One glance at the supermarket magazine stand and one is deluged with the mono-maniacal attention women's magazines lavish on attracting a man and maximizing sexual pleasure. Lust and magazine sales go some distance toward explaining the phenomenon, but the sheer, unceasing repetition almost makes one wonder what is being avoided or drowned out. Certainly, women's magazines could not possibly utter the opinion that having children is one of the goals to which many women hope catching a man and making things sizzle in bed will eventually lead.

The general view of sex as self-actualizing and maternity as self-annihilating, taken to cartoonish lengths by popular maga-zines, is one that permeates the outlook of some thoughtful young women as well. In interviews with young women about their sexuality, the sociologist Leslie Bell found that women in their early twenties tended to have little interest in being teth-ered to a relationship, preferring wider sexual experimentation instead. Women in their later twenties were more sanguine about long-term relationships but felt a sense of trepidation at being forced to think about motherhood by the exigencies of the biological clock.[9] Sexual partnering is obviously a key task of young adulthood, and figuring out who you like and why in-volves sexual discovery. What is striking is the way in which the young women represented that task as detached from questions of fertility, marriage, or childbearing, a detachment fed by a more general social bias. Whereas we tend to see it as horrify-ingly reductionistic to imply that many or even most women seek self-fulfillment in motherhood, we all but demand that they seek it in sexual activity.

Contrast our contemporary emphasis on what the sexual, adorned, controlled female body can strive for to a model of *internal* female self-development that seems hopelessly quaint. When I read my then-nine-year-old daughter Louisa May Al-cott's coming-of-age novel *Little Women*, I looked much more closely at the figure of Marmee, and her daughters' relationships with her, than I had when I encountered the book as a child. As I did so, I was amazed to discover a complex description, an entire vision, of a mother's impact on her daughters' ongoing struggle to develop and hone their characters. Over and over, whether it is finding a way to overcome lassitude and boredom through work, or curbing one's covetousness toward a pretty ball gown, or refusing to marry a man one does not passionately love, Marmee directs and supports her children in the task of inner discernment. She accords supreme importance to internal work: to the understanding of one's feelings and to an increasingly refined knowledge of their intimations of meaning and implications for action.[10] The depth of the human soul is not only presumed; it is treated as *what is real*. Every time one of the girls works her way through a challenge or difficulty, she can be found throwing herself on Marmee's lap, unspeakably grateful to have a mother she can lean on for tenderness and compassionate wisdom and look to for moral guidance — confirming, it would seem, the view that in the matter of the moral sense, as Winnicott said, "there is *more to be gained from love than from education*."[11]

Today, it sometimes seems as if the importance of this vision — the value of a loving maternal presence to the child's development of a moral sense, self-discipline, and the ability to tame impulses for the sake of a greater good — is notable mostly in the effects of its absence. One New York psychologist interpreted girls' growing tendency to see their success in sexual terms as directly related to a lack of parental attention. "One of the ways we learn about relationships is by being in them and seeing them at work. . . . Today, kids come home from school and the parents or parent might not be home. They watch MTV and talk shows and cruise the Internet, and that is where they are learning about relationships."[12] A young person's difficulty in valuing her inner life, her anxious deflection of her energies into the question of whether she looks good enough, may even align with a habit of not looking inward for fear of encountering her own loneliness in the face of parental absence or distraction.

As one counselor of adolescents saw it, "Girls now see themselves as sexualized and approach men with pretty much the attitude, This is all I have to offer."[13]

A girl's sense that she doesn't have anything inside, no rich or meaningful inner life that a prospective sexual partner might value, is grimly complemented by mothers' doubts about whether what they have to offer their child, their human presence, might be a waste of time. Moaned one stay-at-home mother in an article about Manhattan's unusually byzantine "Mommy wars": "My kids came home and shunned me [after Take Our Daughters to Work Day]. They said 'All you're good for is schlepping us around in the Navigator.'"[14] That this woman neither despaired at her children's disrespect nor took them to task for their status-mongering appraisal of her value says something about the ashamed, apologetic stance we've been reduced to in talking about what might be worthwhile about being home with children. The mother seems to have bought into the wholly inadequate dichotomy of disempowered connectedness and invincible autonomy that characterizes our discussion of women's lives more generally and that her own daughters had clearly absorbed.

Stories like *Little Women* are scorned often enough as examples of Victorian sentimentality, certainly not worth serious attention unless it is to damn the cozy, if threadbare, privilege they exude. Yet as the novelist Paul Auster put it, "Victorian sentimentality is something we all sneer at now and find very funny. But I think people will look back at us and sneer at the way we've looked at the world, too. Because cynicism and sentimentality are just two sides of the same distortion."[15] The novel captures something about which we've become, if not cynical, at least dismissive: the connection between a mother's vital involvement with her daughter and a girl's proclivity to value the internal and relational in herself. We see all around us a pervasive disregard of these two thoroughly entwined issues. Yet, while we may try to swallow the theory that children don't really need their mothers and mothers don't really need their children, we don't really believe it. Likewise, adolescent girls may muddle through by adopting the stance that they aren't after care or affection or fidelity, yet a barely concealed hopefulness lingers. "Make him say 'I Love You'" reads one article title on the cover of *CosmoGirl*, couching, in a language of control familiar to young girls tutored in female empowerment, the most vulnerable of wishes.[16]

Eating, Weight, and Ambivalence About the Maternal

WHEN I WAS AN ADOLESCENT, my physique made me suffer, though perhaps not in the statistically usual way. I was gangly, I was flat-chested, I wore a size ten shoe, and I didn't get my period until I was sixteen and a half. Because of my own specific sources of misery, I never quite grasped the complaint of excessive curviness; I always yearned for a little more of my friends' fat. Perhaps it was a holdover from my "the more weight the better" days, but I was unfazed by the weight gain of pregnancy. There doesn't seem to be any typical attitude toward this; for every woman I know who started out thin and fretted about those extra pounds as pregnancy progressed, I know a woman who started out ample and welcomed the license to enjoy her food under pregnancy's cover. Still, I've always had a problem with the preoccupation with gaining weight in pregnancy. I'll never forget my annoyance when my first, birdlike obstetrician insisted that twenty-four to twenty-seven pounds was the desired norm. Beyond the obvious issue of maternal and child health, it seems oddly, ascetically preoccupied with self-control at just the moment when one should have the freedom, the joy, the permission, finally, to feed one's baby and to feed oneself.

This is not to say that I have been exempt from the occasional fantasy that getting thinner would give me more power or control. When my children were tiny, if I was feeling irritated or inadequate in some conflict with my husband, I was not above indulging the thought, "OK, I'll get really thin and always look great and I'll be busy and not be home to cook dinner and I'll be totally self-sufficient, and then he can see how he likes it." There were times, in other words, where I co-opted thinness into an illusory project of perfection and control. These "I'll show you" fantasies always include a strong dose of anger. They are fueled by the wish to establish one's superiority by being impervious to attachment or need. The problem, of course, with fantasies of control is how unrealistic they are, especially when there are children. You can maintain the illusion for a day or two, but then something happens. Your child gets sick. Your babysitter quits. The washing machine overflows. You have worrisome medical tests. And you have the choice of escalating and becoming a control freak of truly disturbed proportions or loosening up and finding a way to peaceably live with unmatched socks, green phlegm, and life's inherent entropy. Perhaps most central, you find a way to live with all the ways your attachment to others — your partner, your child — completely condition your life.

In our society, perhaps especially among those who have been groomed for achievement and success, women really need to work at not developing a controlling attitude toward their eating and their weight. Scholars and mental health professionals have tried to make sense of this preoccupation, particularly when it takes a pathological form, as it does in eating disorders. The philosopher Susan Bordo, an extraordinarily nuanced theorist of eating disorders, sees the social significance of young women's obsession with thinness in terms of "contradictory ideals and directives" in "the construction of contemporary femininity." On the one hand, the ideology of femininity "requires that women learn to feed others, not the self," and "construe[s] any desires for self-nurturance as greedy and excessive." On the other hand, women see that to succeed in the terms set forth by the culture, they must "also learn to embody the 'masculine' language and values of that arena — self-control, determination, cool, emotional discipline, mastery, and so on."[17]

Yet the problem for women struggling with the symbolic meaning of weight, of which eating disorders are an extreme case, is not only that the culture purveys an ideology of femininity that demands that women sacrifice themselves to care for others, an ideology at odds with achievements coded as masculine. It is also that the *real needs and goals* inherent in the "feminine" activity of caring for children are both pragmatically difficult and psychologically conflicted for women for whom other (so-called "masculine") ambitions matter a great deal. That the conflict between "feminine" and "masculine" ends is played out by a woman on her reproductive body ("for many anorectics, the breasts represent a bovine, unconscious, vulnerable side of the self"[18]) is not incidental. Young women have to grapple with conflicts about the desires and needs presented by their own reproductive biology, and the practical implications of those desires and needs for their success within the culture. They are caught, in other words, on the horns of the familiar dilemma of how much to allow the maternal potential for transformation (physical and spiritual), "in" and how much to keep it "out" in order to pursue more socially rewarded ambitions.[19]

What are at issue, then, are the *actual human needs* that certain psychological capacities deemed "feminine" respond to, and women's feelings about those. Much as they may have been oversimplified, mythologized, reified, and gendered, these so-called "feminine" capacities of self — love, interest, flexibility, attunement, receptivity, teaching, sympathy — are basic to creating the kind of relationship we value as important between a parent and a child. These are also, not coincidentally, the very qualities that the anorectic is most likely to have excised as the project of complete and punishing self-control takes hold. There are certain physical and psychological situations in which the capacity to mother is foreclosed. One is insufficient body fat. Others are the need to be in control, to have a taut body envelope, and to not be "soft" or "weak," pejorative terms for being flexible or emotional. Body fat and eating take on meaning not only through their relationship to femininity but also through their relationship to reproductive and nurturing femaleness.

In her book *The Hungry Self*, the writer Kim Chernin also saw eating disorders as an expression of young women's conflicts between the maternal role and their other ambitions, though she offered a different perspective on the reasons. Why, on the cultural threshold of unprecedented levels of opportunity and fulfillment, did girls retreat to a preoccupation with food that left them ineffective and self-absorbed? Arguing that it was a way for young women to manage their guilt and fear about surpassing their mothers, Chernin drew on the psychoanalytic theory of Melanie Klein to make sense of the deeper forces at work. Klein postulated a kind of normative greed in infancy, expressed in fantasies of scooping out the mother's insides and sucking her dry. A psychologically healthy mother communicates to her baby that she has survived her baby's "attack" by being loving and constant in the face of the baby's inevitable greed. A girl with an eating disorder, in Chernin's view, likely never felt that her fears and fantasies about her own damaging greed were disconfirmed by her mother. In fact, something about her mother's way of being in the world, perhaps her depression or self-preoccupation, communicated to the girl that her desires actually *were* destructive and depleting.

The aspect of the mother's position that Chernin deemed particularly decisive was the mother's sense of dissatisfaction and defeat that resulted from her constrained social position. With respect to the daughter's reaction to her mother's predicament, Chernin wrote:

> It is worth considering what it means to a woman putting food into her mouth that she must immediately fear this food will turn her into a woman whose life is without ambition, who married and had babies and feels so ashamed that she does not dare to leave her house. . . . With every bite she has to fear that she may become what her mother has been. For here is a woman who cannot receive directly from her mother . . . the privilege of self-development. She cannot take as a personal inheritance those years of wisdom and study the profes-

sor in the book-lined study is handing down. A handful of cherished recipes, perhaps, a lifetime of broken dreams and disillusion — *that is what most women alive today can receive from their mothers*. [emphasis mine][20]

In an artful compression, Chernin suggests the equivalence of a slew of qualities — marriage and babies and lack of ambition and shame and agoraphobia and broken dreams and the failure to give daughters anything they can use. Her list evokes the familiar dichotomy between the mother who is a wife and mother and has "nothing" and the mother who has something (learning, a profession, the strong sense of self presumed to go with them) that fosters her daughter's growth. The agoraphobic, ashamed wife and mother is Chernin's paradigmatic figure of failed self-development, and it is a failure she explicitly links to the oppressions of patriarchy.

In Chernin's account, the mother is unable to contribute creatively to her daughter's development due to her own social oppression, particularly her misfortune at having been steeped in misogynistic ideals of self-sacrifice that left her unable to fulfill herself. This line of argument has a latent emotional purpose; for if sexist society is to blame for a mother's failures, the mother herself is exonerated, rendered guiltless, and thus protected from daughterly rage. Yet this formulation also replaces with social critique the painful recognition that it was an alive *maternal presence* that one yearned for and didn't have. For, if we stay close to the emotional situation of the girl with a depressed or self-hating mother, the daughter's struggles with eating or self-esteem are likely to have more to do with a failure of sensitivity, attention, and care than a failure of professional mentorship or role modeling. The daughter may come to see "a handful of cherished recipes" as symbolic of her mother's broken dreams; she may come to view "marriage and babies" as the stumbling block to her mother's ambition. But this particular construction, this particular interpretive choice, derives its force in the first instance from trying to make sense of the mother's emotional insufficiency *as a mother*.

By highlighting the uselessness to the daughter of her mother's specifically maternal activity, Chernin leaves essentially untouched the dichotomy that presents such problems for girls' development between disempowered, ambitionless maternal caretaking and self-directed public achievement. The situation Chernin poignantly grasped, as Jessica Benjamin did years later, is how hard it is for a girl to go further than her mother, if her mother cannot recognize or enjoy her daughter's exploration or delight in the world. Yet Chernin builds her argument on the premise that there is a basic conflict between self-development and motherhood, thus leaving to the side the decisive matter of how an individual mother might *realize* her own desire through maternal activity.[21] In reality, the mother's unique self is more significant to her child's development than any generalization one can derive from her social condition. If she is emotionally cut off from her child, perhaps because of her own depression or trauma, it is not explained by her social consignment to the "void" of marriage-and-motherhood. What contributes to the mother's self, to her capacity to relate, is much more individual and complicated than that.

Writings that portray the role of caring for children and home as destitute of self-chosen goals seem to suggest that the best way to help a woman to mother better is to get her out of the house. Certainly for some mothers, including those portrayed by Chernin, this may be true. But when it is assumed that marrying and having babies and shame and lack of ambition all operate together as evidence of the culturally blank, disempowered, or unself-actualized character of maternal activity, an ironic thing happens: maternal desire as a value — the importance of what a mother actually gives a child through her desiring, interested, vital presence — is rendered absent on the level of theory in much the same way as it eludes the troubled, hungry daughter in life.

What Use Is a Mother?

SEXISM, DENIED OPPORTUNITIES, AND ABUSIVE marriages may each contribute to certain climates of feeling in a woman, which then affect her relationship with her daughter. But mothers from all strata of society and all kinds of adverse conditions manage to give their daughters a strong, loved sense of self, even as other mothers from the same variety of circumstances do not. Chernin, who wrote of her own struggles with anorexia, had a mother who was the immigrant daughter of a violent father and his abused wife.[22] Margaret Bullitt-Jonas, in her memoir of her compulsive bingeing, *Holy Hunger*, describes her mother as the daughter of extraordinarily wealthy, privileged civic leaders. But both authors' emotional experience was equally characterized by a painful lack of connectedness with their mothers. "What I *did* know, as a child, was that I couldn't find her, couldn't touch her, couldn't feel her touch me," writes Bullitt-Jonas of her mother. "She was absent, elusive, gone. I knew she loved me. Even so, when she was with me she was not fully there. It was as if something essential in her was shielded from me, guarded, hidden under lock and key."[23]

Such heartrending descriptions only fortify our awareness that a child needs not just her mother's presence but her vital participation in their relationship as well. This is true throughout development. Contrary to bygone theories of adolescence as a time of rupturing family ties, adolescent girls are directly aided in their struggle for autonomy by their mothers' ability to stay connected and engaged. In her study of mother-daughter relationships in adolescence, Apter found that separation, disagreement, and conflict are not aimed at breaking the bond but are part of an ongoing effort to continue and transform the relationship to take account of changes on both sides. A teenage girl's frustration with her mother is often about her mother not seeing who she is *now*, and many of her fights are attempts to get her mother into a new kind of relationship with her. If a daughter feels her mother has never seen her as her own person, only as an extension of herself, then this process will be problematic and the outcomes uncertain; but ideally, adolescent development involves *both* figuring out who one is distinct from one's mother *and* maintaining a connection with her.[24]

For the mother, her vital participation in her growing daughter's care involves her ability to connect with her child — to be emotionally present, to share pleasure, to help — while feeling alive in herself and her own difference. Parenting well requires a sense of inner autonomy, a balance of separation and connectedness that we achieve through a continuing reworking of our relationships to others in the outer world and our internal representations of them. As Hans Loewald saw it, the critical issue is how open we remain throughout life to the fluid communication between levels of our experience; how well we manage to "enchant" our increasingly differentiated existence with the emotional richness of our earliest intimacy. Julia Kristeva evoked the ways in which conversation between levels of our own experience is central to maternal activity, constituting something like a maternal "translation function." As her daughter grows, a mother's ability both to claim her own autonomy while not defending against closeness and to be close while maintaining a sense of difference provides a girl with a model not only of how to be a person in the world but also of how to be a mother in the process of being herself.

On closer view, the necessary balance between separation and connectedness relates, again, to the capacity for reflectiveness so basic to satisfying relationships between children and caregivers. The core of reflectiveness is the capacity to perceive the difference between one's own mind and another's, and ultimately to be able to think about, and respond to, one's own and others' needs and desires. For both parent and child, being able to reflect on difference can take on new proportions in adolescence, as the need to recognize and allow for difference becomes more obvious and the accompanying conflicts potentially more intense. Girls who become mothers as teenagers, as we shall see, have often had trouble developing appropriate independence, remaining psychologically confused about what is their mother's desire and what is their own. Girls with restrictive eating disorders, on the other hand, appear to adopt a rigid and disconnected independence partly to defend against closeness and its potential enmeshment. An inability to reflect — akin to Bordo's description of the anorectic taking her body's contours as a "literal text" — characterized the approach of a twenty-four-year-old bulimic patient who spent most of her sessions venting anger at how often work situations required her to attend lunch meetings and how much other people ate. I tried to suggest that perhaps we might understand the problem better if we looked at her struggle with her own temptations and restrictions; no, she would impatiently insist, if *only* people would learn to stop getting together around meals, *especially* at restaurants that cooked with too much fat, her problem would be solved. My patient couldn't see her feelings as something internally created, so she couldn't get interested in how they influenced her perceptions about what was real.[25]

Is this kind of literalism so different from what we see in unresponsive mothering? The mother who swoops in and solves her child's problem by writing his term paper, Mrs. X in *The Nanny Diaries* who can only see her son through the lens of her own status-seeking — are these not examples of the mother who fails to see her child as a unique person with a genuinely different perspective that she, the mother, must seek to elicit, know, and understand? The bulimic girl tells her body, as the insensitive mother tells her child, Because I am a hammer, you *must* be a nail. In neither case is there the interpretive space, or the room for surprise, or the discovery of the other, that is the heart of true relating.

Parents who cannot reflect on their children's difference or experience the satisfaction of relating to them are more likely to raise children who suffer from feelings of emptiness or disconnection, and who fall prey to various psychological problems, eating disorders among them. When this parental insensitivity seamlessly blends with cultural values of external success and the comparative "nothingness" of motherhood, an individual girl's experience of maternal deprivation may fuel her view of motherhood as an empty, useless enterprise, an emotional vacuum that sucks up self, leaving nothing in its place. When a mother is incapable of nurturing, her daughter may envision a stark trade-off: care for self *or* care for another. She may have no experiential template of someone who was able to care for herself in the context of caring for another.

The Wish to Bear Children and Teenage Motherhood

EACH YOUNG GIRL WHO GETS pregnant does so with her own individual mix of volition, intention, and luck; the motives are rarely clear-cut. Perhaps she is prone to fantasizing that pregnancy or motherhood will give her things it can't possibly give her — a magically repaired childhood or an enduring sense of specialness. Yet however fatuous her hopes, her motives are neither utterly deluded nor solely an outgrowth of limited opportunity. There is often a powerful core of feeling there, an actual albeit problematic "yes" to motherhood, as unthinking as it is intense.

The unthinking intensity of the desire for a child is not only the province of impulsive, confused teenagers. I remember a version of that intensity myself. When I was a graduate student in clinical psychology, a classmate introduced me to Buddhist meditation. I tried to meditate every day, I attended a retreat, I read books by Joseph Goldstein and Jack Kornfield. I felt a particularly urgent need to understand what they were teaching me about desire. Although I could observe and let go of many thoughts once I noticed I was having them, there was one thought to which I was so attached that no amount of self-observation seemed to help me: the desire to have a child. Rationally, I knew that even if I did manage to have children, it would not put me beyond doubt or pain or satisfy my desires, which I accepted were endlessly regenerating. I read what Goldstein and Kornfield wrote about sense desire, the pursuit of pleasurable things in the vain hope they will bring us enduring happiness, and their suggested techniques for working with it: "One antidote is to resolve to practice moderation with regard to the object of desire. Another antidote is to reflect on impermanence, even on death. How much will fulfilling this desire mean at the end of our lives?"[26] I felt fulfilling my desire for a child would mean next to everything at the end of my life. "Through cultivating their opposite states as a balance or remedy, we can help weaken the hindrances and unhook ourselves from our strong entanglement with them."[27] I couldn't imagine what such an opposite state might be: despising children, rehearsing the gruesome possibilities of childbirth? I knew I was distorting the teachings, understanding them too superficially for them to do me any good. Yet I kept coming back to the feeling that the desire for children was one I wanted to have, and one I should be "allowed to keep." It was something, in other words, I felt hard-pressed to reflect on and entitled simply to feel.[28]

The intense desire for a child is one of the key challenges in addressing teenage pregnancy, as Judith Musick, a psychologist and counselor to poor, pregnant teenagers, has pointed out:

> If adolescents did not want babies, they would not have them. But they do want them. Indeed, many seem to fear infertility, craving pregnancy and motherhood. . . .
>
> The desire to be pregnant and to have a child makes the prevention of adolescent childbearing a formidable task. . . . And so the questions become: What is available to disadvantaged young women that is as emotionally satisfying as the idea (if not always the reality) of motherhood? What is worth the struggle and risks entailed in trying to be something else?[29]

The problem, as seen by Musick, is not only that girls desire motherhood and entertain idealizing fantasies of pregnancy and childbirth; it is also that pregnancy is a uniquely female oppor-tunity to act instead of think.[30] Of course, even educated people sometimes feel that pregnancy is something about which they shouldn't have to think, that it should be as natural as breathing or eating. People feel enraged at being infertile partly because they feel entitled to this natural human function. But, whereas people with opportunities and education generally have power-ful interests and goals that compete with childbearing, it is a particular challenge, as Musick stresses, to make other effortful activities look worthwhile to girls who have had little in the way of educated role models.

Significantly, though, some very poor and disadvantaged girls *do* find goals other than motherhood in which to invest their energies. What makes them different from the girls who don't? In a remarkable study of childbearing among unwed, poor African-American teenagers in rural Louisiana, the psycholo-gist Anne Dean showed that one important difference was the way that themes of individuation and ongoing connection played out in the mother-daughter relationship. In particular, whether a girl became pregnant or not had a great deal to do with her mother's sense of self and the mother's relationship with her teenage daughter.

Dean identified among the girls she studied three kinds of in-ternal working models of attachment relationships, which she termed deprived, competitive, and mature. "Deprived" girls ex-pressed a yearning for closeness, trust, and care, and wished for emotional sustenance they had not been given freely. Con-sciously they wanted to be good mothers, but they struggled un-consciously with impulses to harm their children and get back at their parents. These girls were highly likely to become pregnant. "Competitive" girls were slightly more likely to get pregnant than not. They tended to be focused on the triangular family re-lationships (father-mother-daughter), and consciously wished to escape from controlling or hostile mothers. Less consciously, they wanted both to win out over mother in their relationship with father and to atone for this wish by sharing their baby with her. Finally, "mature" girls were unlikely to become pregnant. They tended to identify with their mothers' skills, values, and ways of relating, and to have internalized their mothers' aspirations for their development and accomplishment.[31]

One deprived teen recounted her childhood interactions with her mother:

> Whenever I needed something, you know, she was, she'll be right in the kitchen, and I just call her, she'll come when I call her. Anything I needed she'll get. Like if she needed, if she had to talk about something, she just sit down and talk to me like, you know, like, if I could, you know, really give her an answer for anything. I hardly didn't know what to do, but she talk to me more or less like she talk to my, you know, [older] sister, I guess.[32]

Strikingly, midway through, this girl reverses roles with her mother, blurring the boundaries of who is needing and who is responding. Girls with deprived models tend to be confused about whose thoughts, feelings, and needs are whose. Unlike girls with mature models, they lack clarity about "what comes from within and what comes from without."[33]

Problems in early attunement and communication between child and caregiver create systematic distortions in how we see others, ourselves, and our relationships. As children, girls with deprived or competitive models tended not to have received the responsive care that helps a child build a differentiated, complex sense of self and other. As a consequence, these girls remained enmeshed and dependent on their family of origin, continually trying to get things from them that they never got or to work out conflicts with their original love objects instead of progressively looking outside the family to make their own lives. Having a baby as a teenager was one way to remain dependent on one's family of origin.

Consider, in this connection, the meanings of "having" versus "caring" for a baby. When a baby is a "production" that serves various unconscious goals within a relationship between mother and daughter, whether placation, union, or competitive victory, the baby's real needs for care and an ongoing empathic relationship can be overshadowed by his function as a means of communication between the mother and daughter. And precisely because the mother and daughter in such a relationship have trouble recognizing whose feelings are whose, the baby smoothly takes his place within a psychological matrix that fails to recognize difference.

Among girls with mature working models, by contrast, Dean found the same balance of autonomy and connectedness that Apter identified as basic to healthy mother-daughter relationships in adolescence. These daughters, Dean noted, "describe themselves as becoming more and more like mother at the same time that they are becoming more and more emancipated from her."[34] The contrast between the "deprived" girls who often became pregnant and "mature" girls who did not, brings us back, again, to the *self* of the mother. Mothers who raised daughters with mature models of relationships were devoted caretakers of their daughters. They were able to reflect on who their daughters were; to foster separation and individuation and aspire for their daughters' increasing maturity and independence; and to welcome identification and tolerate difference in the context of emotional nurturance, support, and respect.[35] Having achieved autonomy themselves, they were able to view their daughters as individuals as well. And in these pairs, more than in the others, the relationships with husbands and fathers were also more highly valued, an indication of the mothers' ability to engage in meaningful adult relationships of their own.[36]

Late Adolescence, Early Adulthood,
and Women's Self-Definition

FOR POOR GIRLS WITH LIMITED opportunities, like those studied by Musick and Dean, it takes enormous fortitude, support, luck, and courage to pursue one's own education and advancement. It is only rarely that aspirations for motherhood and for professional security are both realized in teenage mothers. Women with a college education, on the other hand, have a huge advantage starting out as workers or mothers. They tend to have not only economic advantages but also a certain level of familial support for their development and aspirations, and they have usually been encouraged to plan for their futures.

In the 1980s, the sociologist Anne Machung studied graduating seniors' future plans and found that, in contrast to men, women projected that they would move in and out of the workforce due to family responsibilities, and that their income and advancement would be lower as a result. They did not make this same projection for their prospective mates; indeed, 70 percent expected their partners' jobs to take priority over theirs. Thus, Machung's college women, though they were often vague about the particulars, factored time spent parenting into their vision of their future lives.[37]

Interestingly, though, when educated women plan to integrate motherhood into their adult identity — conveying a thoughtfulness so poignantly lacking in the pregnant teen — it is at times treated as a kind of thoughtlessness. Interpreting Machung's findings in her book *Flux*, for instance, the journalist Peggy Orenstein assumes that the women's decisions will affect their lives *negatively*: that constricted career options will work to their overall disadvantage, and their lesser earning power will mean less clout in family decisions. "Well before they enter the adult world (and, perhaps, long before they'd entered college)," Orenstein writes, "young women were making decisions that would virtually assure that their careers would be secondary to men's and that their incomes would be lower —

decisions that would, in the future, profoundly affect both their options and their leverage in organizing their family lives."[38]

If we were to start from a different premise, namely that these women wanted to take a central role in child rearing, we would see that their lesser earning power and the lower priority they placed on paid employment actually served an important goal. But because we are so reticent about looking squarely at young women's maternal desire, we misinterpret their behavior. We end up trying to explain why women are still, after all this liberation, unable to take care of themselves, illogical in planning their own futures, and shooting themselves in the foot. Women are making a calculation that when it comes time for one parent to assume the bulk of the child care in the family, it will be economically more feasible for them to do so; but rather than seeing this as an attempt to act in their own rational self-interest, we continue to construe it as self-destructive.

Is it a problem when young adult women, intentionally or quasi-intentionally, design their adult lives with motherhood in mind? One could certainly make a case for it being a problem that *men* do not feel similarly entitled or inclined to design their lives around fatherhood. The woman's prospective self-positioning as the lesser breadwinner makes her the obvious person to cut back on work when children arrive; it also makes the father, in most cases, the less obvious person to cut back on work. Though we tend to focus on the cost to women of staying home and caring for children, we should also keep in mind the cost to fathers of not having the time to nurture their relationships with their children. The structures of work, the ways careers are antagonistic to family life, the disappearance of the family wage, all conspire to marginalize fathers as parents.

For women themselves, the problem is not planning life with their desire to mother in mind but rather inhibiting thoughts about the impact that desire might have on their goals, values, and ambitions. College may be one point at which achievement-oriented young women begin to intuit that their desired future involvement in motherhood clashes with norms of academic and professional comportment. The psychologists Elizabeth Lloyd Mayer and Carol Gilligan taught a course to undergraduate women at Harvard, about which Mayer observed:

> We received a large assortment of e-mails afterwards, most of which described how these young women felt they had to excise certain things from what they said in class and what they wrote in papers. In particular, knowledge that was too "personal," too "subjective," too "focused on feelings" or — most of all — "too much about relationships instead of logic" wasn't knowledge that counted. They described being painfully aware of how editing that kind of knowledge out of their work was costing them passion, originality and authenticity.[39]

These students were likely responding not only to an external constraint but also to an internal conflict. They worried, no doubt, that approaching knowledge through their feelings would be viewed as incriminatingly feminine. But beyond that, they may have intuited that the current pressure to edit their feelings was but the front edge of the pressure they would feel later to downplay their desire to mother. In other words, presentiments of maternal desire and its "personal," "subjective" importance may have figured into their current sense of inhibition.

ADOLESCENCE CHALLENGES GIRLS TO DEVELOP an orientation toward their own maternal potential. But the values and pressures of contemporary society are not conducive to the development of the qualities on which good mothering draws. Our ideals of the successful student or professional, just like our ideals of female "empowerment," reiterate endlessly the pressure we feel to somehow graft female functions onto traditionally male structures, not unlike the strangely muscular statues by

Michelangelo that signal they are female only through their un-convincingly affixed breasts.[40] Signs of this pressure are appar-ent in the efforts girls make to trumpet their invulnerability through meticulous control of their surfaces. They are visible in the sought-after credential of well-controlled weight, which communicates our allegiance to the "masculine language" of self-mastery and emotional discipline. They are even evident, in a negative form, in the way we view teen pregnancy. Teen preg-nancy is disproportionately prevalent among girls of lower so-cioeconomic status, whereas anorexia nervosa has appeared, at least until recently, to be more common among the privileged.[41] It may be a stereotype, but it's still true that the gaunt figure of an anorectic is more likely to stroll the ivy-covered halls of a prestigious college than is a rotund pregnant (or obese) teen. The cluster of affluence, high achievement, and the overcontrol of the female body is only a pathological extreme of the gene-ral importance of female body control to success and social acceptance.

Contemporary accounts of women's psychology affirm that girls' relationships with their mothers in adolescence are deci-sive, crucial. But rarely does the mother's desire to nurture her daughter, and its role in a daughter's orientation to motherhood, figure into the narrative. Here, as in so many other places, ma-ternal desire seems strangely absent. We often hear the convic-tion expressed that what a daughter needs most is for her mother to be a role model in the public world: the more women in boardrooms, the more professors in their book-lined studies, the better for daughters' self-esteem. But what seems to dimin-ish girls' susceptibility to the standard pitfalls of adolescence — sexual acting out, eating issues, teen pregnancy — is almost sub-versive in its apparent traditionalism: having a mother who de-sires to nurture her daughter and is passionately concerned with her growth. Such a mother can certainly also be a CEO, but it is not her CEO-ness that is essential. What is essential, rather, is her ability both to be intimate to and respect difference, her ca-pacity to reflect on herself and others, and her commitment to seeing through the daily challenges of caring for her child. A mother's involvement and concern, her satisfaction in connecting, her freedom from preoccupation with her own disappointments, anxieties, or shaky sense of self — these are a constant maternal good throughout development, constantly needed and constantly desired. And it is probably these qualities, more than anything else, that will help a girl value her own maternal potential and infuse her view of the mother-child relationship with a spirit of creativity, purpose, and delight.

8

Fertility

ONCE WHILE VISITING SOME FRIENDS, I spied a book on their shelf called *How to Get Pregnant* by Sherman Silber, M.D. In it, I came across a statistic that astonished me. In any given month of trying to conceive a baby, a normally fertile couple has a 20 percent chance of success.[1] That meant that in a group of one hundred women, twenty would likely get pregnant the first month of trying, and eighty would not. The next month, sixteen of the remaining women would likely get pregnant, leaving sixty-four who did not, and so on, until after one year, six women would not have conceived due to chance alone. The 20 percent statistic surprised me in two ways. First, I hadn't realized that the probability of a healthy woman getting pregnant in a given month was so *low* — a fact that could not help but reassure if one were, say, in the fourth month of trying to get pregnant. Second, I was taken aback by my own ignorance; how could I not have had even a ballpark sense of these rates of conception?

My reaction took me back nine years to when I was first planning to try to become pregnant myself. I thought I would take the opportunity to educate myself a bit about the biology of conception, so I bought a slim book called *The Fertility Question* by Margaret Nofziger. Graphing my temperature on my ovulation chart was one of the more exciting and nerve-racking science experiments I'd ever conducted. As luck would have it, my temperature stayed elevated at the end of my cycle for the requisite number of days and I learned I was pregnant. But the entire process of temperature taking, graphing, and noticing changes in cervical mucus (learning there was such a thing as cervical mucus!), even as it made me marvel at the workings of my female body, also left me with a feeling of feminist irritation. How could it be that these basic facts of my biology were *new information* to me at the age of thirty-three? Had I been actively avoiding knowledge that was readily available in the world around me? Maybe when I'd read *Our Bodies, Ourselves* at the age of thirteen, the topic of conception had seemed too remote. Still, I felt wronged somehow not to have been thoroughly tutored in these aspects of the female reproductive cycle in my high school biology class. The immediate, observable monthly cycles of our own bodies, their day-by-day correlations with our fertility and even with our moods, were surely as worthwhile an object of study as the ecology of a nearby creek.

I suppose I took an odd discoverer's pleasure in happening upon a pocket of sex that I had not even known existed. But my stronger feeling was that there was something weird about my ignorance of my fertility, and something askew about the fact that most women seem to learn about their fertility only when something goes wrong. Visit the websites of the InterNational Council on Infertility Information Dissemination (INCIID.org) and the National Infertility Association (RESOLVE.org), a couple of the very few places where women's detailed scientific knowledge of human reproduction is dazzlingly on view. There's the "Beta Board," "where to wait for those betas to rise," information on BBTs, OPKs, and HPTs, and an abundance of medical forums on tubal surgery, ovarian abnormalities, and causes of male-factor infertility. Women discuss their in vitro fertilization (IVF) cycles in great detail and exchange notes about the side effects of their progesterone treatments.

Websites like those of INCIID and RESOLVE embody a feminist ideal, turning the tools of technology to women's ends. Via the Internet, we harness the latest fertility science and offer each other community and support in the service of the self-chosen goal of motherhood. This is true empowerment. Yet betwixt and between the fact sheets on infertility medications and the INCIID Miracles and Success Stories, in the precincts of despair where women confide their miscarriages, their failed IVF cycles, their grief and loss, it is hard not to feel that there is something backward about our before-the-fact ignorance of our fertility and our after-the-fact expertise. In one way, of course, it makes perfect sense; after all, we don't think much about our intestinal tract until there is a problem, either. But still, our general lack of before-the-fact knowledge seems to be motivated by something more. I think it is motivated by anxiety, at least in part. Thinking about our fertility is hard, because it makes us aware of both how deeply valuable and important it is to us and how uncertain we are about when and if we will ultimately actualize it. And even more particularly for girls and women today, thinking about fertility can put us in touch with momentous and often anxiety-ridden questions about life choices and identity.

If there is one place where these anxieties converge, it is in the fraught issue of fertility and age. Many women and men are infertile for reasons having nothing to do with age, and they are understandably offended by the implication that their infertility is somehow "their fault." In 2001, the American Society of Reproductive Medicine (ASRM) launched an ad campaign featuring a baby bottle in the shape of an hourglass with the caption "Advancing age decreases your ability to have children."[2] INCIID objected to the campaign, saying it propagated a "blame the victim" stance on infertility, overplaying the role of preventable causes of infertility and ignoring the higher percentage of medical, nonpreventable causes.[3] The possibility of "blaming the victim" is inherent in any public health campaign, yet people are not so touchy when they are warned against other known risk factors for infertility, such as smoking, exposure to chemical toxins, or sexually transmitted diseases.[4] Whereas people tend to approach somewhat rationally the need to get treated for sexually transmitted diseases, refrain from smoking as a matter of general and reproductive health, and assess their exposure to environmental toxins, their reaction to the issue of age is a far more complex, conflict-laden one.

I think one reason age and fertility is such a sensitive issue is that it cuts to the heart of female development. Age is like a seemingly innocuous thread that, once pulled, begins to unravel a skein of issues in women's lives. Women are aware of the extraordinary opportunities — educational, professional, creative, and sexual — that can be realized in a life unencumbered by children. With life spans hovering around eighty years, it is no surprise that people might wish to delay the parenthood phase and explore other interests and challenges first. In our culture, women aspire to a self-sufficient adulthood — educated, employed, and economically independent — and we struggle to mesh that goal with our decisions about when to have children. Our ideas of what is necessary to become a self-sufficient adult bear on how we go about finding partners. Our notions about what it means to be an autonomous individual affect how we view motherhood. As we age, of course, we change and develop psychologically. At one point in our own development we may feel that having a child holds little interest or will impede our productivity or growth; at another point, we may feel it will enhance our growth, and the idea becomes enormously compelling.

This web of social and psychological forces reveals how simplistic it is to tut-tut young women about waiting to have babies, telling them in effect to "just say no" to complicated relationships, conflicting ambitions, or internal doubts and fears. This is not, as the newsweeklies would have it, all about the fallout from women growing up with the expectation of "having it all."[5] It is about difficult choices, and trying to realize various important, and sometimes conflicting, human goals. It is about meshing our individual psychology with the timetable of our bodies and the structures of social life. It is about finding a way both to embrace possibilities and accept limits.

Caring for children remains a troubling, contested area for

women's identities, and that is one reason that fertility and questions of when to have children can be so complicated. Though both men and women cope with difficult choices in balancing conflicting commitments to work and family, fertility and childbearing tend to be more loaded issues for women, not only because they give birth to babies but also because they generally spend more of their time nurturing them. Society, and men, often expect women to devote more time to child rearing. But also, many women anticipate that they will want to.

In taking on the caregiving role, women make changes in their priorities, their jobs, and their relationships, and the positive motives underlying these changes are not always well understood or valued. At times we fear that caring for a child means an abdication of self-development or a demotion from full adult status. At other times, we fear that not spending our time caring for our child will hurt our child or hinder our own happiness. We struggle both with our own conflicting desires — to nurture children, to be employed, or to participate in the adult world — and with the ways that the rigid separation of workplace and home heightens that sense of conflict.

In the area of fertility, practical pressures and cultural ideas meet up with what people experience as the deeply meaningful personal decisions. By examining this meeting point, we discover ways in which the structure of work, our psychological ideals of self-sufficiency, medical technology, and even materialistic values, influence women to feel we should somehow "fit in" our maternal desire around the edges, and discourage us from thinking deeply and unashamedly about the role we want mothering to play in our lives.

"Why Did We Wait?": Wanting Babies and the Fate of Ambivalence

EAVESDROP IN THE WAITING ROOM of a fertility clinic or read the exchanges at an online infertility chat room and the message often heard, even from the most committed professional, is "motherhood is all I really want from life." When a woman contends with infertility, the desire to have a baby can become clear and keen and depthless; ambivalence about motherhood recedes until it is some distant and barely recognizable part of oneself. A vortex of yearning opens up at one's feet that suddenly, plainly, has been there forever. Gone is one's perspective on one's emotions, one's sense of the relative value of things, ambiguity, shadings. Wanting a baby becomes the truest thing one has ever known about oneself.

We tend to ascribe the all-encompassing force of the pain of infertility to the body's convulsion of protest when its species script is thwarted. Certainly the drive to have a baby feels as powerful as some of the other impulses to which we've given that name, like sex. As one woman said, "Our bodies were made to have babies, and it takes a long time for the body to get over not having them."[6] But this undeniable force in wanting a child, rather than deciding the issue, leads to more questions. Clearly, human appetites are not expressed in pure form but rather are inflected by the intimate relationships and larger culture in which they are expressed. As with hunger and sex, the drive to have a baby bears the complex imprint of the context in which it arose.[7]

These considerations in no way minimize either the longing to conceive and birth one's own child or the actual sense of loss, pain, and grief in relinquishing the hope of it. But they do offer a chance to reflect upon the ways our experience of our longings is affected by the values and arrangements of the society in which we live. Many of us cannot help feeling that a woman's pain at infertility is "bedrock," and yet it is worth being curious even about this. How does this particular pain get articulated, evaluated, and understood? How is it affected — even exacerbated — by social conditions such as lack of access to extended family or the premium we tend to place on individual accomplishment? And, specific to the matter of childbearing and age, by what process does some women's ambivalence about childbearing give way to such a painful sense of lack? What might that trajectory say about how contemporary women see their lives?

It seems that indifference or confusion about wanting a child, followed by a searing, tortured quest to conceive, has become an increasingly common developmental narrative. In *Crossing the Moon*, a memoir about her infertility, Paulette Bates Alden wrote: "For most of my adult life I've behaved as if mothers and children had nothing to do with me, which, on the whole, they haven't. But lately I can't take my eyes off them. I'm in the process of making (for me) a mind-boggling discovery: women have children. It's what women *do*. A lot of them."[8] As she pursues infertility treatment and ultimately makes peace with childlessness, Alden wonders, "How was it . . . that I had arrived at this point in my life: almost thirty-nine years old, no child?"[9]

In piecing together an answer, Alden finds clues in her traditional Southern upbringing, her mother's controlling and sometimes punitive ways, and her own core identity as a writer. Her story captures a conflict in the lives of some women between a certain kind of self-development — in her case, as a writer — and the role of mother, perceived as at odds with that self-development. Alden's frank account of her conflict illuminates how facile it is to treat the desire for a baby as the pure form of human instinct, and the equivocations as some sort of superficial overlay. For her, the desire to be a mother is not simply denied but deeply conflicted, which is why, perhaps, she remained unaware of it for so long.

It is obviously not a problem when women know they do not want children. The trend of women remaining childless has increased in recent years, suggesting that those with doubts about becoming mothers may feel less of a need to bow to social pressure.[10] A problem only arises when a woman feels that the choice not to have children is a settled one, only to find, too late, that her feelings have changed. In her younger years, such a woman may feel more kinship to women for whom motherhood has never held any appeal and who will remain contentedly child-free. In her later years, the same woman may find she deeply wishes to become a mother. Psychological development clearly plays a role in this shift. "I never thought I wanted children," wrote one woman who later desperately wanted a child. "My mother died when I was 13, my father when I was 17. The idea of 'family' for me was linked to the terror of loss."[11] This woman had no expectation of feeling maternal wishes; but later, when she was in a secure relationship and had resolved some of her feelings about past losses, these wishes came to inform her hopes and goals.

The question this trajectory raises is not so much why women have conflicts about having and caring for children — the reasons are as numerous as they are obvious — but, rather, what accounts for the developmental surprise of the desire to mother. Here, internal, psychological dynamics are joined by cultural pressures. Whatever a woman's personal reasons for putting children out of her mind, society colludes by making it hard to envision how to reconcile autonomous ambition with nurturing relationships. The time demands of work feed into women's worst fantasies that their identities as workers and mothers are incompatible. Simplistic notions of autonomy mistakenly suggest that women undertake motherhood only at a cost to their personal development.[12] When a woman's own emotional history and current desires align with this view, she can feel it costs her little to operate in a smoothly compatible way with it. But if her desires or priorities shift, this model may no longer serve her purposes. She may become more attracted to caring for a child. She may find herself interested in the ways parenthood enables access to new aspects of experience or new forms of creativity.

Deference to the hard-won nature of women's freedom, belief in the value of desired motherhood, and a respect for women's other aspirations all contribute to the gingerliness with which some sensitive men urge children on their spouses. The writer Philip Lopate admitted that one of his wife's many attractions when he married her was that she was of childbearing age. When she said she wanted time alone as a married couple before having children, he responded: "A reasonable request, I thought. I could wait. Not indefinitely, but . . . 'What if I *never* want to have children?' she asked. 'Would you still love me? Stay married?' I swallowed hard, said yes, and meant it. In the back of my mind, though, I gambled that she would come around eventually."[13]

In a more painful example, the writer Bob Shacochis chronicled his wife's and his efforts to conceive in a haunting essay, "Missing Children." Early in their marriage, when he raised the issue of children, his wife let him know that, "more than wanting the freedom to anchor herself in a career, she simply didn't wish to be pregnant, she told me, ever; pregnancy was synonymous with trauma, perhaps even self-destruction. And although I was alarmed by her rhetorical absolutism, I was also willing to tell myself that this was not her final word on procreation."[14] Further on in his account, we learn of his wife's traumatic second-trimester abortion at the age of sixteen, waiting alone for three days in a hospital room until her "womb evacuat[ed] its voluminous contents onto the tile floor."[15] Decades later, after numerous fruitless attempts to conceive, his wife is almost prostrated by grief as it becomes virtually certain she will never be able to become pregnant with her own biological child.

If a woman swears off sex after being raped, we think she needs help. If a woman swears off pregnancy after a traumatic abortion, she also needs help. The many feelings that play a part — self-punishment, wanting never to go to that unbearably painful place again — can seem to close the door firmly on babies when what a woman most needs is to find some way to reopen the door without dying of grief or self-blame. If her desire to forgo children or pregnancy is respectfully unquestioned as a matter of her right to self-determination and she realizes only later that her rejection of motherhood was self-protective, she stands to lose twice over. Yet, to ask whether a desire to mother is being deflected, suppressed, or ignored, even to wonder aloud about this possibility, feels strangely forbidden, as if one is committing a sin against the selfhood of women, tantamount to claiming that women are happy only if they are barefoot and pregnant.

The Subtler Reasons
We Delay Having Children

A FRIEND ONCE COMMENTED WHAT a huge job it was to manage to find a partner, get a career going, and have a child by the age of forty. It sounded a bit extreme, until I thought about how many people I knew who hadn't managed all three to their satisfaction. The conservative journalist Danielle Crittenden says women could solve their problems if they married and had children earlier.[16] But for people like me, whose mother married at twenty-two and divorced at thirty-four, that recommendation does not inspire much confidence. One of the major challenges for young women, along with becoming educated and gainfully employed, is sorting out all the emotional effects of their own childhoods enough to make a wise choice in a partner. The fact is that women who marry young divorce at a higher rate than others. Even if one's own parents didn't divorce, the high rate of divorce, not to mention the specter of an unhappy marriage, is something most earnest young people soberly contemplate.

Though it seems young to me now, I remember being twenty-eight and feeling not young at all. Single again after another collapsed relationship, I did what any self-respecting psychology graduate student who knew she wanted children would do: I went into therapy. Luck always plays a role where questions of love and fertility are concerned, and going into therapy doesn't directly create luck. But it can help us to perceive how we are unconsciously working at cross-purposes with ourselves. For me, understanding that was the most important thing I could do to get out of my own way. A youngish woman, caught in a confusing or unsatisfying pattern of relationships, or unable to consider the question of children with a person she loves, is in a situation that has a particular urgency, an edge. She may be more or less aware of the closing of the reproductive window — not right now, but some day in the not-unimaginably-distant future. The stakes for figuring out how to choose the right kind of person, how to make a relationship work, and how to approach the issue of children begin to feel increasingly high.

The uncertainty about whether we will find someone to love is not unlike the uncertainty about whether we will have children. Women who want these things are up against aspects of life they cannot fully determine or control. They are inevitably vulnerable. And that is a predicament about which women have highly conflicted feelings, especially since there are so many more aspects of our lives today over which we exert greater control than ever before. The writer Alice Rossi captured what it was like to admit how desperately she wanted a baby:

> There's great vulnerability in desperation. How much safer you are if there isn't anything you want too badly. And how much cooler. Cool is, I suppose, the absence of desperation, of urgent desire, of neediness. I had wanted to believe that I was somehow different from all the women who were undergoing one high-tech procedure after another in pursuit of pregnancy. I'd hoped that I was more highly evolved, less sentimental, less traditional. I wasn't. I wanted a baby as badly as anybody did.[17]

That "urgent desire," that "neediness" is in part what women's expanded life choices are supposed to have freed us from. There is something almost unseemly about this raw desire right in the middle of a perfectly civilized, reasonable life. It's how women in an earlier era might have felt about bringing a diaphragm on a first date. It feels at once too vulnerable and too brazen to admit one's desire in advance of the sure chance of fulfilling it. Some refuse to consider that this neediness might pertain to them. Thirty-year-old Evelyn Taylor, reports *Newsweek*, "has no intentions of having children any time soon. She is too busy flying around the country as a sales rep for a large movie company and loving it. Eventually, she'd like to have kids, but not for at least five to 10 years. Fertility is not a concern. 'If Madonna can have a kid at 40, then so can I,' she says. And if she can't she'll adopt."[18] So easily said, so hard in practice. My forty-five-year-old friend tells me, "If you'd asked me in my twenties about having children, I'd have said, no problem, if we can't have them, we'll adopt. I was completely caught unawares by the primal rage I felt at being infertile. I felt like a cavewoman. I remember feeling that if I can't have a baby, I'm going to burn this house down."[19]

Equally interesting as the surprising discovery of this raw "cavewoman" drive is women's desire to see themselves as cool and reasonable about having children. Many seem to feel a sense of self-mastery when they can manage not to care too much, not to feel in too much of a rush. One expression appears to be our ever-rising standards about how established or ready we should be to have children. Middle-class couples often feel it incumbent upon them to buy a house and decorate it in order to be "settled" enough to have a baby. I remember feeling weirdly insecure that my desire for a baby burned brighter than my need to fix up the baby's room — her crib was next to our computer desk and our hideous Naugahyde recliner for her first year. More experienced mothers reassured me that "a baby only needs a box to sleep in," but I still felt out of step and a bit bizarre.

Sometimes, when people decide to wait to try to conceive a baby, the reasons they give are vague. One woman felt she was too irritable and wanted to become less so. One hadn't gotten around to marrying her live-in boyfriend. One was pursuing more stability in her career, even though her career as a free-lance writer was inherently unstable. Women (and men) have deep-seated psychological reasons for feeling conflict about having children; having a baby is one of the most weighty issues we face in life, and all sorts of powerful fantasies, fears, and feelings adhere to it. Yet whatever the psychological conflicts — and there are many possible ones — the social context of the last few decades has helped support our equivocation with the message that independence is progressive, but wanting babies is regressive, even slightly embarrassing. And our equivocation is further underwritten by the practical reality that once a woman has a baby, her job is irrevocably changed, often for the worse. One writer noted how commonly "employers object to women's desire to have their cake and eat it, to reproduce and go on earn-ing."[20] Some women may manage this problem by delaying grat-ification; a baby (the cake), they hope, will be a "reward" for their hard work, their playing by the rules. Yet in terms of fertil-ity, playing by the rules can also operate to women's distinct dis-advantage.

Cryogenics as Liberation

BECAUSE DECISIONS REGARDING CHILDBEARING ARE so personal and lend themselves to the language of "choice," it is easy to overlook the powerful social forces that shape women's deci-sions about when they have children. The sociologist Kristin Luker argued that the social factors that press poor women to have children early are similar to those that push middle- and upper-middle-class women to have them late. Poor women have children early before their prime working years, when they can still count on the help of kin. More affluent women, whose mo-bility and culture tend to mitigate dependence on kin for help with child rearing, often wait to have children until they are es-tablished professionally or more secure economically. Both, however, are "devising individual solutions for a massive social problem" — namely, the lack of a social structure that offers support for women attempting to combine child rearing with paid work during their optimal childbearing years.[21]

Luker astutely points out that both poor and affluent women's strategies for childbearing entail social costs, although "to date, only the costs of early childbearing have been the occasion of public handwringing."[22] Yet the high economic costs of the as-sisted reproduction technologies most often employed by the older childbearing cohort are well documented. The medical costs of late childbearing include those related to the mother's increased health risks, her use of expensive technologies, and the health needs of the babies, who are more likely to be multi-ples (e.g., twins, triplets) and therefore more susceptible to prematurity and low birth weight. In psychological terms, anyone who has struggled with age-related infertility or knows someone who has is aware that it brings with it enormous emotional costs as well.

Yet, all this pain and unpredictability and risk are recast by some as women's ultimate opportunity. Law professor Jane Cohen, who became a mother of IVF twins at age fifty,

> envisions a new "vanguard feminism" where "the capacious arms of feminism wrap themselves around the possibility that women get to choose to *have*, as well as not to have, children." When she teaches about ART [assisted reproductive technologies] and the relevant legal issues, some young women appreciate that "this technology will create great relief later in life, will allow them to sort out career and relationship and *then* children — will allow them to buy time," she says. Although freezing sperm and embryos is commonly practiced, it will be the "dawn of a *new* consciousness" when eggs can be "frozen and put on the shelf," she says. When young women can store their eggs until the right time — "That will change people's lives," she says.[23]

"Some young women" may appreciate this possibility, but what about the others? Those not under the sway of their charismatic law professor's gratitude at being able to complete her family at this late date might pause to wonder whether that is the world they want to work toward, or be a part of. The consumer advocate Judith Sternberg Turiel asks the relevant question: "If the choice were up to them, how would women and their partners prefer to experience childbearing?"[24] Most people would opt for the low-tech method, preferably through having sex, preferably with someone they love. This possibility is not open to everyone, but people tend to endorse its value in general terms. And people tend to agree that, all things being equal, it is preferable to have children at an age where the health risks to the mother and child are minimized.

A medical, case-by-case approach to infertility is a godsend for an individual when it turns out well, but it has nothing to say about the larger social conditions that contribute to age-related fertility problems in the first place. What is framed in an optimistic American vein as the "expansion of women's choices" looks very much like a high-end stopgap for what is a larger-scale social problem. The expensive, treatment-oriented model where law students can bank their eggs and fifty-somethings can get pregnant results in great help to the few. But more general interventions, such as finding ways for women of all classes to more manageably combine paid work and the care of children, would result in greater help to the many.

Given all the emotional, medical, and economic benefits of childbearing that is neither very early nor very late, it seems we would be stumbling over ourselves, trying to rearrange society rather than women's reproductive biology, so as to accommodate that timetable.[25] But yet again, in this domain of central, passionate import to many women, we are caught in a web of vague taboos; slight, constant pressures to move toward certain solutions and away from others. In terms of careers, there are powerful incentives to try to work within, rather than oppose, the status quo, even though the status quo of careers is set up in ways that tend to disadvantage us reproductively, economically, or both. It may be paranoid speculation, but it is not hard to envision a world where, in the presence of inflexible work structures and aggressively marketed fertility treatments, we find ourselves beginning to accept fertility interventions as more and more of a norm. Imperceptibly, fertility technology may come to be viewed not as a last resort but as an "opportunity" to postpone childbearing into one's forties. Grimmest of all — shades of the futuristic movie *Gattica* — by degrees we may find that assisted reproduction has acquired a sheen as the newer and better "option," glimmery in its vague association to celebrities and to technology's cutting edge, pointing somehow in the right direction because it's about "freedom" and "choices." And yet all the while, we will find ourselves increasingly unable to analyze the whole constraining set of assumptions that got us into this way of thinking in the first place.

Childbearing, the Natural and the Sacred

IN ACCOUNTS BY WOMEN ABOUT their infertility, there is a recurring theme. Whatever doubts or trepidations may have beset a woman's decision to have a child, once she attempts to conceive and has trouble, she is startled, sometimes shocked. Her fecundity is something she considered until now her female birthright, an effortless by-product of being a woman. In a way, this reaction exemplifies a habit of mind girls develop of necessity in childhood. Every female child, after all, makes temporary peace with her inability to have a baby. She must wait decades and assumes, if she is inclined to motherhood, that childbearing lies somewhere in her indeterminate future. Her assumption that her equipment will work when she needs it is reinforced throughout her adolescence and young adulthood by the message that she must protect herself from unintended pregnancy through contraception. Whenever a woman decides to have a child, her underlying belief in her eventual ability to fulfill her fertility has already been in place for a long time.[26]

But an intriguing aspect of women's expectation of fertility is what it reveals about our sense of what is "natural" within us. Everyone knows about the stubborn tendency over the ages to identify woman with nature and man with culture, a tendency that has spawned mountains of analysis and critique.[27] Women themselves have an ambivalent relationship to their linkage with "nature." At times it feels limiting, at times freeing; at different moments, we may cherish, take for granted, or seek to control the "natural" within us.

In the 1970s, the natural childbirth movement explicitly affirmed the value of naturalness to the birth process; if a woman was allowed to labor in her own way, it was thought, the wisdom of her body would ease her toward a healthy birth and a transformative personal experience. The "technocratic model" of childbirth, which framed birth as a medical procedure enacted upon a woman, was contrasted with a woman-centered process of tuning in to the body.[28] The opposition of natural childbirth and medicalized birth presented a fairly simple dichotomy where the "natural" was on the side of women's power and the "technological" was on the side of men's. But fast on the heels of the natural childbirth movement, huge advances occurred in assisted reproduction, prenatal diagnosis, and neonatology, and these advances upended assumptions about "the natural" once again. The ability of medical technology to help women conceive and birth children became widely viewed as a method of helping them fulfill a deep, natural desire.

Reproductive technology has also contributed to something of a "moving target of naturalness" where conception and childbirth are concerned. Today, it is possible, and quite common, to use "unnatural" methods of birth control for years, maybe decades, before we attempt to conceive a child. At that point, couples are usually disappointed if sex doesn't result in a pregnancy, and not simply because it is a matter of inconvenience or expense; the naturalness of conception is itself a value that many hold dear. There are various other moments where people feel an emotional, ethical, or spiritual inclination to see "the natural" preserved: in opting for natural childbirth versus pain medication; in vaginal birth versus caesarean; in using or eschewing prenatal diagnosis; or in any number of new frontiers, such as fetal surgery or sex selection. The preserve of the "natural" keeps shifting as the methods of assisted reproduction proliferate. For example, thanks to the technological advances of fertility medicine, it is possible for a woman undergoing IVF to have multiple embryos transferred to her uterus to increase the likelihood that one will be viable. Yet, when multiple fetuses "take," posing a health risk to the mother and each other, some women feel a strong emotional and ethical pull to let "nature take its course" and not to intervene with fetal reduction.

Whereas we tend to fully accept that any achievement in the world requires action, work, and effort, we expect, by and large, that our fecundity will just be there when we want it, that it is an underground stream that can be dipped into at any time. It is something we feel to be an intimate part of us, a "going on being" confirmed by our periods even when we are not actively using it. We are taken aback when it is not.

For many of us, gender stereotypes stubbornly entwine with these contrasting images; we see the "natural," "of service," and "always there" as feminine, and the "cultural," "achieving" and "mastering" as masculine. Women sometimes deal with this division by "doing" their own identity first in the hopes of "being" a mother later, when their identification with their own active mastery is more secure. Although understandable as a response to the pragmatic difficulties posed by the design of education and work, this strategy also bears the imprint of a certain view of femaleness and even, perhaps, a certain kind of fantasy about one's mother. In this fantasy, nature (or mother) is there to serve us, for us to make use of when we need it/her, and to ignore when we don't. We treat our mothers, and our female fecundity, as endlessly available.[29] But what we've learned from feminism and environmentalism is that the female, natural things that are "always" there — fertility, mothers, Earth — do have to be tended; they can in fact be destroyed or used up. Part of our challenge as women is to honor and protect those seemingly passive "waiting" aspects of ourselves that have to do with our female procreative potential.

For women there is profound meaning wrapped up in the "natural" aspects of fertility, conception, and childbirth. To the extent that a woman views her life-giving capacities as sacred, as partaking of the awesome mystery and design of nature, and as involving her in the cycle of life on the most intimate, immediate level, she will attribute great significance to her natural reproductive functions. Interestingly, as more of us turn to fertility treatment to enable this sacred participation, attitudes once viewed as dehumanizing — the objectification of our bodies, a mechanical view of our bodies' products, hormones, eggs — become our ally. In coming to our own ethical interpretations of such issues as prenatal testing, assisted reproduction, and selective abortion, we face whole new domains wherein we need to make sense of the relationship of natural processes and human interventions. It is in this sense that the anthropologist Rayna Rapp has called contemporary women "moral pioneers."[30]

Having Children, Caring for Children

INFERTILITY CAN BE SO PAINFUL to people partly because giving birth to and nurturing a child are both very meaningful aspects of parenthood. But at the same time, we know that the desire to have a baby and the desire to care for a child can be quite distinct. The essayist Katha Pollitt noted, for instance, that historically, women "rich enough to avoid personally raising their children often did, as Rousseau observed to his horror."[31] For a host of economic, historical, and psychological reasons, the tension between having and caring for children is at the core of contemporary maternal anxiety. What does it mean to identify yourself with the role of caring for children — economically, socially, personally? What does it mean to have children and turn their daytime care over to others? What does it mean to care for children who are not biologically your own? Many feel that caring for their children is of great value but feel invisible or undervalued in the world at large. Others endorse the value of parental care in principle but find doing it unrewarding. One woman finally stopped fertility treatments and proceeded to adoption because she realized the most important thing to her was "being a mom, however it happened." Another felt that giving birth to her own biological child was an essential aspect of what she sought in motherhood, but she did not feel that devoting her time to hands-on care of her child was central to her vision of herself as a mother.

In this complicated realm of what it means to have and care

for children, mothers' conflicts take various forms. In an illuminating, if somewhat dramatic, analysis, the sociologist Linda Blum examined the widespread practice of pumping breast milk as one site where mothers play out their conflicts about being available to their children. Contemporary medical opinion holds that breast milk is unequivocally the best food for baby, and this opinion has helped to mold a particular compromise between the baby's needs for breast milk and the mother's need for autonomous activity.[32] Blum demonstrates how pumped breast milk has come to symbolize, or stand in for, the mother's physical presence. A mother is able to maintain the illusion of being "at once exclusive and irreplaceable *but* replaced — at least during her hours working and working-out." Whereas breastfeeding "once seemed . . . a deeply embodied and interdependent act, likened to the marital sex act, [it] has fast become something that can occur without the mother being physically present." This newer view is striking in its "lack of attention to mothers" and *their* experience of the difference between breast pumping and breastfeeding. "The mother in her body, her pleasures and needs, satisfactions and pains, have been largely erased."[33]

Here we see how the breast milk operates as a much more manageable, controllable, concrete stand-in for the whole contested, conflicted arena of the real mother's presence. The powerful feelings a woman has about wanting — or not wanting — to spend time caring for her child, the competing messages about how much time a mother *should* spend with her child, the message that she is not successful if she is not fit or active or gainfully employed — all these anxious concerns are somehow neatly codified in the injunction that if you pump breast milk for your baby while you are away, you are being a fully "present" mother. Further, in treating this disembodied product from the mother as not so different from contact between mother and child, an effort is made to cope with loss by insisting there is none; by declaring, in other words, that nothing is lost when a mother is not actually there with her baby.

If we think for a moment about another set of body products, eggs and semen, that are stimulated, harvested, ejaculated, and joined for the purpose of creating a genetic child of two parents, we can detect within that project as well some of the same contemporary anxieties. Producing one's own genetic child reassures people about a primal connection at precisely the social moment when one of the most wrenching issues parents face is how much time they spend with their children. Something about "knowing" where one's baby came from gives people a sense of a solid starting point for the journey of connection. When long stretches of time together cannot be counted on to build the bond, genetic relatedness seems to take on particular significance.

Some observers have recently wondered whether a higher valuation of having children relative to caring for them is built into the very structure of adoption and infertility treatment. For example, resolving feelings about not being able to have one's own biological baby is commonly viewed as a prerequisite to pursuing adoption. But as the legal scholar Elizabeth Bartholet observes, "It may be impossible to know what part of the pain of infertility relates to a desire to parent, and whether this desire will be satisfied by adoption, without knowing what adoption is about. An understanding of adoption may thus be essential to resolving feelings about infertility."[34] Subtly and inadvertently, the amazing, tantalizing advances in fertility medicine direct our attention toward the importance of having our own biological children and deflect it away from our confused ambivalence about how the practice of caring fits into parenthood. Even as fertility medicine is all about women's desire to mother, its very predication on the biological mother-child connection cannot help but contribute to our societal emphasis on having, as opposed to caring for, children.[35]

Alongside the voluble public discussion of all the risks of adoption — the lack of knowledge about inherited predispositions or diseases, the potential difficulties of attachment, the haunting possibility of a child's lifelong longing for her birth parents — there is another very compelling and moving discussion by adoptive parents about their experience of becoming parents to their children. They speak both of the amazingly chance nature of having become parent to this child, and at the same time of their profound sense of its "rightness." Herself an adoptive mother, Elizabeth Bartholet wrote, "I could not have anticipated that this family formed across the continents would seem so clearly the family that was meant to be, that these children [her two Peruvian adopted sons] thrown together with me and with each other, with no blood ties linking us together or to a common history, would seem so clearly the children meant for me."[36] Researching adoption, the adoptive father and journalist Evan Eisenberg found: "In workshop after workshop I heard parents attest, with wonder still fresh, that their adopted child seemed meant for them from the start, and that they could not imagine loving a 'biological' child more."[37] Stepparents describe a similarly intense and involving journey into parenthood.[38]

However painful and deeply disappointing it is for many people to relinquish the dream of having their own child, that relinquishment is harder when one's family, like everything else in life, is an achievement to be ranked on various scales of success. Our social ethos relentlessly vaunts production over care. It is not simply that we worry we will not have enough time for our children. We also are shaped by, and sometimes endorse, the very split our social arrangements demand from us, the trade-off that gives us status and material goods in exchange for defining ourselves as "producers" rather than "nurturers." An orthopedic surgeon boasted to me in the course of idle cocktail party chatter that his wife had gotten pregnant *right away*, though he evinced no shame at the fact that he and his wife were astonishingly absent from their children's day-to-day lives. One cannot help detecting in this disconnect a sensibility that is supremely keyed to individual "success" but neglectful of relationships. This sensibility may come more easily to those who reap great material or professional rewards for endorsing it; but its diffusion throughout the culture ends up permeating the air that all of us breathe.

Women today are right in the thick of this issue, trying to

make sense of ourselves as producers and nurturers. In some ways, physically birthing her own baby seems to make a woman both, in one fell swoop. Yet, if we were to consider the bond with a child as arising from the practice of caring for him or her, perhaps we would not be so inclined to interpret having a baby within a framework of individual accomplishment. If we gave nurture its due, its full import, there might be more skepticism about treating breastfeeding and breast pumping as commensurate or about the sense that conceiving and birthing the baby is what makes you close to him or her.

A searching discussion of the matter of having versus caring for children has arisen among women who have gone through the agony of infertility and emerged childless on the other side. A forty-six-year-old friend who was divorced in her mid-thirties and spent much of the next few years frantically pursuing pregnancy on her own through various procedures said:

> At forty-three, I was still completely in the grip of needing to have a baby. At forty-six, I feel over it, and it is a relief. I finally got to the point where I said to myself, This isn't only about *having* a baby. The pull to do that is very strong. I think it comes from somewhere deep in our primitive brains. I came to a point where I realized it was really ultimately more about *caring* for a baby and child. And in my case I realized that once I got past the intense desire to have a baby, I didn't feel I was really cut out for caring for my own child, and I do much better caring for other people's children.

Melissa Ludtke, the author of a landmark study of single motherhood, *On Our Own*, described a similar process in her own development. In her mid-forties, she revisited the question of whether to become a mother, a path she had previously pursued through artificial insemination. She noticed that "the powerful emotions that once dominated my decision-making were now partnered with concrete evaluations about whether adopting a child was the only, or even the best way, for me to express my 'mothering' desires. . . . This time around there is an absence of the constantly churning internal and external pressures I felt when I was in my thirties and driven by 'baby hunger.'"[39] At the close of her book, Ludtke anticipates adopting a Chinese girl in the coming year.

Narcissism, Pregnancy, and Love

IN NICOLE HOLOFCENER'S 2002 FILM, *Lovely and Amazing*, the heroine Michelle keeps telling her story of natural childbirth to anyone who will listen. A frustrated artist in a rudderless marriage, Michelle is insecure, and she clings to her unmedicated childbirth as her one accomplishment — a political statement, claim to specialness, and icebreaker rolled into one. In Michelle's endless rehashing of her birth experience, Holofcener captures a kind of narcissism that easily attaches to producing a child. I remember when I was pregnant with my first child, I felt startled and resentful when cars did not stop at crosswalks. Couldn't they see there was a *pregnant woman* trying to cross the street? On some irrational, self-important level, I was surprised to find that their encounter with me and my pregnant belly was not enough to change their disposition of indifference and incivility behind the wheel. Agnes Rossi gets at similar feelings about being able to bear children: "Our language needs a word for the feminine equivalent of machismo. *Feminisa*, or something. Just as the ultimate symbol of machismo is the erect penis, the essence of feminisa is the ability to create a living, breathing human being in the space between one's hipbones. I wanted to do that, wanted to add getting pregnant naturally to my list of accomplishments in life."[40] Or, as the French writer Colette put it, "I am tired of hiding what was never mentioned — namely, the state of pride, of vulgar grandeur, which I enjoyed while ripening my fruit."[41]

Remember Julia Kristeva's distinction between the experience of pregnancy and the experience of parenting a child. In pregnancy, a woman can experience (in Kristeva's fervid phrase) "a fantasy of totality — narcissistic completeness" that is "a sort of instituted, socialized, natural psychosis."[42] The arrival of the child, on the other hand, calls the mother to "the slow, difficult, and delightful apprenticeship in attentiveness, gentleness, forgetting oneself."[43] There can be a "high" to getting pregnant, being pregnant, and having a baby; one could almost call it a mania, for the sense of power and expansiveness it brings. This expansiveness is, in a sense, utterly appropriate to the miracle that pregnancy is. At the same time, it contrasts with the more integrated "human scale" states of mind that go into the daily care of children.

The feelings of specialness and entitlement surrounding pregnancy and bearing children may pack an additional kick in our culture by virtue of the high value we place on ownership as a sign of worth. Children, aside from being people we love, are our ticket to the future, our hope, our royal bloodline, our precious production. No toy, no darling outfit from Baby Gap, should be spared. A friend commented on the parade of luxury strollers that made their appearance (complete with babies) at her college reunion. A problem we all face is that our love for our children is at times difficult to keep separate from the fantasy of narcissistic completeness that our commodity culture continually excites. Whether it is a new car, a bigger house, a smooth midriff (magically unmarred by that once-vaunted pregnancy), or an Ivy League acceptance letter for Jack or Jill, contemporary American culture purveys endless opportunities to pine after an illusory wholeness, distracting us from the source of true wholeness in the commitment and intimacy of love.

A colleague of mine likened the actual nurturing and raising of children to what the psychoanalyst Melanie Klein called the "depressive position."[44] The phrase refers not to depression, but rather to the developmental achievement of being able to love another as a whole, separate person. It involves the capacity to cope with the feelings of loss, disappointment, and guilt that real relationships inevitably bring, and the relinquishment of the illusion that others exist solely for one's own gratification or as projections of one's own mind. For a mother, feelings of totality, specialness, or omnipotence surrounding having a baby must give way to the daily recurring needs for attentiveness and empathy, as well as to the inevitable daily failures. There is the high of having the baby, and then there is the rest of life, with its "slow, difficult, and delightful apprenticeship." We experience this contrast in hormone-tinged form after childbirth when we have the "baby blues."[45] We experience it when we decide to forgo the "high" of having another child for the sake of the love and daily nurture of the children we already have. I have sometimes thought that there is something about the lavish bestowal of gifts at a baby's birth, about the very way their beauty exceeds their functionality, that captures this heightened, expectant moment of miraculous specialness, setting it apart from every moment of parenthood that follows.

It is no wonder that women who want children want all of this, that they want the whole experience; they want it in their bodies, in their minds, in their hands, and in their hearts. But as a society, we should attempt to be as ingenious at giving women the possibility of caring for their babies as we are about helping them to have them.

9

Abortion

WHEN MY HUSBAND PICKED ME up after work during my first pregnancy, I would vomit before I could even say hello. I had to admire, in the glazed aftermath of yet another bout of puking, the sheer will to life displayed by this small cluster of cells. It seemed it would do anything short of killing me to ensure its own survival. I remember learning during my third pregnancy, when I suffered an endless string of flus and colds, that a pregnant woman's immune responses are partly suppressed to lessen the chance she will develop an immune reaction to her own baby.[1] It seemed that as long as I stayed alive, nature didn't much care how sick I felt.

Many women, including myself, are unprepared for how abstract their happiness at being pregnant becomes in the face of those first-trimester physical surges — the midsentence stuporous sleep, the racking waves of nausea. But in that brutal and awe-inspiring contest of bodies, I also sensed the genesis of a relationship in which the struggle for growth in earnest was at the core, and in which my love — already too ethereal a word — was expressed, and even strangely defined, by my strength and resilience in the face of that struggle. That stage of pregnancy was my best lesson in the unsaccharine nature of mother love, its intimacy with creation and destruction.

Pregnancy begins a *relationship*. Most essentially, it launches a relationship between a woman and the potential child she car-ries within. It also initiates a new relationship between a woman and herself — her body, her history, and her future. For these reasons, when a woman considers abortion, the question of whether the fetus should continue to develop does not stand alone; it is a question she wrestles with in the context of whether a relationship should continue to develop between her-self as a potential mother and the fetus as a potential baby.

Some believe that the fetus is a full-fledged person from con-ception. I do not. But the belief that the fetus is not a full-fledged person does not make abortion emotionally easy or morally simple. Awareness of the potential relationship set in motion by pregnancy is one of the most heartrending and ethi-cally fraught issues for a woman considering abortion. Preg-nancy's ineluctably relational nature means that once it begins, it can never be completely negated. A baby comes to term or it doesn't, through choice or fate. It comes to term, and it is kept or relinquished. In any case, in any outcome, there is a relation-ship the woman has to *do something with* — mourn it, celebrate it, try to forget it, embrace it, dismiss it, accept its loss. When a woman feels she must not allow the child and the relationship to develop, it is almost never an easy thing, physically or psycho-logically.[2] Yet women sometimes feel that as difficult, painful, even tragic as it is, they must do it to survive, or to respect them-selves and their situation in life.

This very aspect of the abortion dilemma illuminates a facet of maternal desire. The desire to mother involves the intention and commitment to enter into a relationship of love and care with a child. It represents an attempt to integrate our deepest personal longings and highest human aspirations. There are sit-uations in which a woman does not want to enter into that re-lationship, or she recognizes she does not have the ability to responsibly commit to it. Such a woman confronts the same ba-sic realities as the woman who chooses to keep a pregnancy does. First, each grapples with the enormous importance of a po-tential mother's desire for a child to that potential child's flourishing and fulfillment as a human being. And second, each faces the reality that when a woman bears a child, she channels her emotional and physical energies in ways that are hugely consequential in defining the person she will become. In light of these facts, what a woman *wants* with respect to having a child is of absolutely decisive, even sacred, importance.

Desire and Selfhood

THERE IS A STARK, ALMOST shocking difference between how one feels when one wants to be pregnant and how one feels when one doesn't. The same physiological event can be experienced as a blessing or a catastrophe, as being in harmony with one's body or as being mugged by it. Women's lives are often described as contextual, but this may be the most contextual aspect of all, "the mother of all contexts." The extremes of women's responses in the face of pregnancy, and every ambiguous point in between, puts us face-to-face with how central the issue of *wanting* is to the abortion dilemma.

We have difficulty knowing how to weigh the mother's desire for a child; by its very nature, it seems too capricious, too emotional, and too devoid of principle. And perhaps because this desire is so hard to evaluate, its complexity is flattened both by abortion's opponents and proponents. On the right, the mother's desire is too often dismissed as a selfish concern with "convenience," a touchy-feely, morally insignificant wisp in comparison with the sober matter of fetal life.[3] On the left, it seems desire had best not be inquired after too energetically, for fear that women's ambivalence about their abortions might be used to discredit their decisions and undermine the legitimacy of their right to decide.

In fact, a woman's desire is absolutely central to the morality of abortion, even though the ways we have tended to talk about it have not always helped us to understand why. In the wrong hands, sometimes in women's own, the notion of "wanting" has been facilely assimilated into the "we are empowered and can do whatever we want" school of moral nihilism. But desire is actually more complex than our more casual notions of feeling or preference imply. It is not simply about feelings, however complicated or conflictual; it is also about intentions, the coordinated movement of feeling, thought, and action toward a self-chosen purpose. The critic Adam Gopnik aptly described desire as a "thought-through feeling."[4] The freedom and responsibility to choose the intentions most important to us are central features of what we believe it means to be a person. A woman's desire with respect to something so consuming and momentous as carrying a pregnancy to term involves just these sorts of intentions.

In *Fruitful,* a memoir of her life as a mother and a feminist, the writer Anne Roiphe reflected on the folly of trying to ground the ethics of abortion in when life begins, as she and her friends had tried to do in the days before Roe v. Wade. "We should have drawn the line on whether the fetus was or was not wanted and shaped the debate on that issue," she wrote, "instead of getting mired in metaphysics or theology about the beginning of life."[5] Roiphe speaks of whether the mother wants the fetus; but she is actually implying something much broader about the fact that the potential mother is the person in the best position to assess her desires and make judgments about them. Whether a child is "wanted" functions as a shorthand to convey two related but distinct meanings: a woman's feelings concerning having the baby and her prerogative to evaluate her own feelings and come to her own decision.

A woman's feelings about an unintentional pregnancy are almost always mixed. Even when she is deeply chagrined to be pregnant, she may feel remorse about having an abortion. She may imagine pleasure at mothering a child but see no practical way to support it. She may have no interest in caring for a child but feel swayed by her family's wishes for her to keep it. She may ultimately hope for a child with her partner but feel that to have a child now would threaten the viability of their relationship. She may ambivalently decide to continue the pregnancy and one day find herself very happy about it. When a woman considers her feelings, whatever they are, she also likely considers them in light of her values. It is almost impossible to have feelings about abortion without those feelings becoming interwoven with ethical concern.

Yet whatever a woman feels about an abortion — whether she feels bereft, suicidal, liberated, that she will go to Hell, or all of the above, whether she has an abortion half awake, half asleep, or completely confused about what she wants — her entitlement to make her own decision does not derive from the content of her feelings. It derives from her own ultimate authority to weigh her own competing desires, intentions, and values and to undertake her own course of action.

In this sense, decisions about continuing a pregnancy confront us with the connection, in its most naked form, between a woman's very claim to personhood and her reproductive freedom. The reality of pregnancy is that having a baby one does not inwardly consent to is a traumatic offense to one's integrity as a person; having a baby that one desires is an ultimate fulfillment of oneself as a person. Not being able to have a baby when one wants to is experienced as a great injury to the self. Ending a pregnancy that would have shortchanged one's other commitments is experienced as a wrenching but necessary act of self-preservation. Each instance bears out just how deeply our reproductive fate is enmeshed with our very selves. Whether abortion is legal or illegal, safe or dangerous, women will always have abortions, not only because practical limitations or social stigma urge it, but also because there are situations where to have a baby represents a compromise of herself or her values that a woman will take great risks to avoid.[6]

The trivialization of this connection between a woman's integrity and her procreative choice has at times found expression in *legal* arguments against women's reproductive self-determination. In her article "Are Mothers Persons?" (note the pointed reversal of the more usual question, "Are fetuses persons?"), the philosopher Susan Bordo demonstrates the stunning desecration of women's personhood right under our noses in the realm of reproductive law. The principle of a person's right to physical inviolability has been strenuously protected in cases concerning such issues as whether someone can be legally compelled to donate bone marrow to a dying relative. The import of this protection is not simply physical; it constitutes, Bordo writes, "a protection of the *subjectivity* of the person involved — that is, it is an acknowledgment that the body can never be regarded merely as a site of quantifiable processes that can be assessed objectively, but must be treated as invested with personal meaning, history, and value that are ultimately determinable only by the subject who lives 'within' it." When this "meaning-bestowing function is in danger of being taken away," the law tends to interpret "the situation as a violent invasion of the personal space of the body."[7]

But look what happens, Bordo says, when the body in question is a woman's pregnant or reproductive body. The right to physical integrity and the protection of subjectivity gives way to the abrogation of a woman's will for the sake of saving an unborn child's life. Courts do not order people to make personal sacrifices on the order of a transplant or marrow donation, even to save their own child's life; for, despite the fact that a child's life hangs in the balance — a full-fledged person's life — the potential donor's claim to inviolable subjectivity overrides the potential recipient's need for life-giving support. In contrast, where a woman's specifically *reproductive* decision making is concerned, courts *have* ordered caesarean sections, intrauterine transfusions, and the delivery of babies of terminally ill women against their will. Here we see in sharpest relief a particular bias directed not simply against women but specifically against women's autonomy in pregnancy decisions.

If a woman happens to be poor, pregnant, and of non-European descent, she "comes as close as a human being can get to being regarded, medically and legally, as 'mere body,' her wishes, desires, dreams, religious scruples of little consequence and easily ignored in the interests of fetal well-being."[8] Bordo cites a 1987 study that found that 81 percent of court-ordered obstetrical interventions involved African-American, Asian, or Hispanic women. In the case of Ayesha Madyun, a woman who resisted a caesarean on religious grounds, the judge ruled that "for him *not* to issue a court order forcing her to have the operation would be to 'indulge' Madyun's 'desires' at the expense of the safety of her fetus."[9] This sort of dismissal of religious beliefs by the judicial system is, as the legal scholar Stephen Carter has argued, part of a more general cultural tendency to treat religious convictions as optional and expendable.[10] But even beyond that, such legal opinions essentially deprive the pregnant woman of the right to informed consent, paternalistically declaring how she should interpret the meaning and value of a given procedure. By so doing, they preempt the very act that forms the core of her entitlement to informed consent: that is, her own subjective determination of what a given intervention means to *her*.[11]

Bordo helps us appreciate that coercion in reproductive decisions undermines not simply what individual women want but also their entitlement to subjectivity *itself*. In the polemics of abortion, the pro-life side objects to a woman sacrificing an actual human life merely for the sake of her own "convenience" (that is, reproductive control), whereas the pro-choice side argues that a pregnancy can be terminated with little impact on a woman's autonomous self. The fact is, a woman's personhood cannot be disentangled from her reproductive life so cleanly. "The nature of pregnancy is such," Bordo correctly observes, "that to deprive the woman of control over her reproductive life . . . is necessarily also to mount an assault on her personal integrity and autonomy (the essence of personhood in our culture) and to treat her merely as [a] material incubator of fetal subjectivity."[12]

Pregnancy as Relationship

THE REASON FREEDOM IN REPRODUCTIVE decisions is so important to women's integrity has to do with the kind of relationships pregnancy and motherhood are. If requiring a woman to
carry a baby to term were on the order of insisting she pay a
parking ticket, we wouldn't bat an eye; no morally weighty
abridgment of personal freedom would be involved. Our sense
that coercion in reproductive decisions jeopardizes women's important and legitimate interests in self-determination has to do
with what a woman commits to, psychologically and emotionally, by carrying a baby to term.

It helps to consider the unique character of pregnancy. Most
obviously, pregnancy is unique in that there is no counterpart in
male experience. For the woman herself, it is unique in that it
involves a new relationship between "me" and "other," between
"my body" and "not my body." Women rarely experience pregnancy as a clear matter of "me the mother" and "you (or 'it') the
fetus." Instead, we are intimate with the fetus's otherness early
on, and it is an otherness instantly able to alter our *own* reality.
When we are tired or nauseated, we feel taken over by a stubborn force wresting life from our flesh, our bone, our consciousness. Individual women experience this situation in their own
ways, inflected by their psyche, tradition, history, and circumstances. There is no universal norm that guides a women's experience of it; every pregnancy is different, every woman is different,
and each pregnancy for a given woman is different. But there is a
basic situation that each pregnant woman is faced with and has
to make sense of in her own way, and that is the relationship
between herself and the developing fetus.[13]

The reality of pregnancy is that it is a relationship of great,
and progressively greater, physical and psychological investment. That is abundantly clear when a pregnancy is wanted; it
is why women can become grief-stricken after even an early mis-
carriage, and why women who choose to have prenatal diagnos-
tic testing want to do so as early as possible. Yet even when a

woman does not want to be pregnant, she almost inevitably be-comes increasingly involved psychologically and emotionally as the pregnancy continues. To insist, then, that women carry their pregnancies to term, and give the baby up for adoption if need be, makes deciding against involving oneself in the rela-tionship virtually impossible. By the same token, if a woman were compelled to have an abortion, she would be prevented from deciding *to* involve herself.

Even when women respect the potential of fetal life, one rea-son they choose abortion over giving a baby up for adoption is their awareness at how deeply attached they will become to their developing fetus as pregnancy progresses. For some, the idea that they would actually manage to relinquish the child at birth becomes increasingly unbearable. During my second preg-nancy, I had amniocentesis around halfway through the preg-nancy. The baby was already kicking. I walked around in a moral fog, not even quite sure if it was right to have taken the test, since I could barely allow myself to think of any outcome but keeping the baby, no matter what the test revealed. My experi-ence, which I don't think was unusual, underscores just how emotionally and physically involving the relationship of preg-nancy is. For that reason, among others, many women faced with an unwanted pregnancy decide that ending the pregnancy while it is still mostly a potential relationship, is the more en-durable choice.

In the view of many of abortion's opponents, the ethical rem-edy to an unwanted pregnancy is for a woman to carry the baby to term and either find a way to care for the baby or put it up for adoption. Both of these are honorable, even noble, solutions when they are chosen by a woman herself. But the moment ei-ther solution is coerced, by law or overweening emotional pres-sure, troubling implications follow for both the woman and for her relationship to the child. Consider, for example, a relational "worst case scenario," where continuing a pregnancy is forced on a woman. In a case described by Bordo, a man was granted an injunction against his girlfriend's abortion by a judge who ruled that "since the woman was not in school, was unemployed, and was living with her mother, 'the continuance of her pregnancy would not interfere with either her employment or education.'" He continued, "'The appearance and demeanor of the respondent . . . indicated that she is a very pleasant young lady, slender in stature, healthy, and well able to carry a baby to delivery without an undue burden.'"[14]

The circumstances in which this woman's baby will enter the world are really quite horrifying. Are the feelings of a woman who is compelled by the courts to bear her boyfriend's baby likely to be all that different from her feelings if she were required to have the baby of a rapist? What does it do to the development of one's relationship to a child to have it forced on one, not simply by biological fate, but by one's boyfriend, and then by the law? It seems certain that the mother will feel robbed of her will and compromised in her ability to share parental responsibilities with the child's father. What would it mean to a child to be born into a universe of such contention and total absence of shared goals?

The likely result of such forced childbearing is, in other words, misery for mother and child. But this fact will appear morally relevant only if one considers not just "the life of the unborn" but also what the "born" require to survive and flourish. The judge in the case focused on the former and ignored the latter; by his lights, if the woman was "well able to carry a baby," why shouldn't she also be "well able" to devote her life to that child? For the potential mother, by contrast, her ability and desire to devote herself to caring for the child are absolutely central issues. Caring for the child will require an enormous share of her emotional and practical resources; the relationship with her child will become central to *who she is*. A woman who is rejecting of a pregnancy cannot be forced to find room in her soul to embrace it. If there is a path of discovery that could allow a pregnant woman to transform her resistance into acceptance, it is a path that only she herself can tread.

Only when we understand the relationship as central do we see that a woman's deliberation about abortion necessarily involves her prospects for *caring* for the potential child, in the context of her responsibility to other people in her life, herself, and the wider community. When the abortion dilemma is framed solely in terms of the fetus's right to life, the necessity of this relationship drops out of the picture. But in fact, the fetus's alleged right to life is completely inseparable from another human's commitment of enormous resources, time, and energy. Taking into account a mother's complex and sometimes conflicting obligations to care, we quickly leave the black-and-white world of antiabortion certitude. We enter into the more ambiguous, complicated domain of what obligations a woman has to nurturing *this* potential child and *this* potential relationship, in light of her other obligations and the fact that her resources to care for others and herself are not limitless.[15]

One of the many complexities women face in weighing decisions about pregnancy is that, though legal coercion is actually rarely at issue, psychological pressure can exert an enormously powerful force. One college student sought therapy because she was still suffering from the trauma of an experience of pregnancy and adoption two years earlier. When she became pregnant at seventeen, her devoutly Catholic parents never discussed it with her but silently assumed that she would live at home, carry the baby to term, and give it up for adoption. The young woman described her pain at seeing her biological daughter in the care of the adoptive mother. She felt the mother was well meaning, and the family provided all the signs and symbols of a good home, but in her eyes, the adoptive mother seemed somewhat superficial. She was plagued by thoughts of how the adoptive mother wasn't doing things as she herself would have done.

Relinquishing a child in adoption can be extraordinarily painful in any circumstance. But this young woman's trauma was intensified by her lack of opportunity to talk honestly and sort out her feelings at the time, and to think through and come to a decision for herself. Likewise in cases of abortion, coercion complicates already difficult emotions. In any unintended pregnancy, there is no pain-free solution. But whatever confusion, regret, or grief a woman feels in the process of making her own decision, when her decision is forced, not only are these emotions compounded, but her sense of self-determination and self-respect suffers harm.

What Is Sacred?

THE MYSTERY OF ABORTION IS that while at times unspeakably sad, ending a pregnancy can involve love. A woman can feel strongly that to have a child in a compromised situation, in a situation where she is not prepared to devote her full attention and commitment, is not something she would want to do to someone she loved. This paradox is captured in Gwendolyn Brooks's poem about abortion, when she writes "You were born, you had body, you died," and, only a few lines later, "Believe me, I loved you all."[16] By dint of their biology, women are charged with the knowledge that life involves ruthlessness, even sometimes toward those we love, or those we could love. We bear children, and we are faced at times with terrible decisions about how to value a life — our own and the one growing within us. We rear children, and we become intimate with the psychological realities of relationships, including their pain and conflict and moral complexity. Recalling her illegal abortion in 1938, the activist Lana Phelan said, "I was laying on that gurney just sobbing my heart out, and I'll never forget that woman [her abortionist], she was wonderful. She came around, big black lady, she put her arms around me on the gurney, and she put her face down near mine, and she kind of put her cheek up next to mine. And she said, 'Honey, did you think it was so easy to be a woman?'"[17]

The paradox that we can feel love for a potential life that we choose to end becomes suspect, even incoherent, if we believe that the fetus is a person just like ourselves. For if we regard the fetus as a full-fledged person entitled to rights, the notion of loving a potential life we choose to end becomes indistinguishable from the delusional or grim claim of the murderer to have loved her victim.[18] The passionate disagreements between people about abortion appear to revolve around the rights of the fetus to life on the one hand, and the rights of the woman to self-determination on the other. But perhaps there is a way to think about these issues that does justice to our intuitions both about the sanctity of life and the dignity of the individual.

The philosopher Ronald Dworkin has argued that very few people actually believe, even if they think they do, that fetuses have the right not to be killed and an interest in remaining alive. Most abortion conservatives, for example, permit some exceptions to their anti-abortion stance, in cases such as rape or incest. Yet if a fetus had a right to life on par with already-born individuals, ending that life could never be justified on the basis of a crime of which the fetus itself was innocent. Instead, Dworkin suggests, their objection to abortion is grounded on something else: the belief that individual human life is sacred.[19]

According to Dworkin, people with widely divergent views on abortion hold in common a belief in the sacredness or intrinsic value of a human life. We revere both the "natural miracle" of "any human creature, including the most immature embryo, [as] a triumph of divine or evolutionary creation, which produces a complex, reasoning being from, as it were, nothing."[20] Likewise, we honor the human creative investment, both "the processes of nation and community and language through which a human being will come to absorb and continue hundreds of generations of cultures" and "the process of internal personal creation and judgement by which a person will make and remake himself."[21]

The sacredness of human life lies in both natural creation — of the natural world, the species of the earth, our human bodies — and human creation, the human creative force that feeds art, culture, and human personality. In Dworkin's view, the difference between abortion conservatives and liberals often lies in the aspect of sacredness they deem most important. Abortion conservatives tend to rank the natural creative element above the human, though they acknowledge the latter's importance. Abortion liberals, while recognizing the value of the natural, tend to give greater weight to the human creative contribution.[22] Different positions on abortion can be understood as lying along a continuum of the relative value people place on the natural and human creative contributions to human life.

Any woman considering abortion who regards the embryo not as just a bunch of cells but as a biological wonder and a potential human believes both the natural and human creation to be meaningful and worthy of reverence. Yet many women regard the *confluence* of natural and human creativity that the desire to have a child represents as *itself* a sacred feature of bringing a child into the world. Being ready to fulfill one's procreative potential with a certain person, at a certain time in your shared life, brings to the experience of pregnancy and anticipated childbearing a sense of integration, of being in tune with one's chosen destiny. This integration of human and natural creation is what many women experience as the "highest form" of childbearing. We feel engaged on every level, physical, emotional, intellectual, spiritual; we fully participate in our own life and the life we are creating, in the continuation of the species and the continuation of culture.

Obviously, to require women to carry all pregnancies to term is to thwart their aspiration to this integration. If women do not have reproductive choice, they are frustrated in their ability to exercise their specifically human creativity. This is not because having and caring for children itself frustrates creative aspiration. Rather, it is because preventing women from making their own reproductive decisions curtails their choices with respect to their own human investments. Determining the meaning of having children *for* women, deciding for them when they will have children and when they will not, effectively takes the choice about how they will use their bodies and what work they will do out of their hands.

Women must obviously be in a position to decide for themselves how they will value the natural and human contributions represented by an unborn child. But it is exactly their powerful sense of the *connection* between natural and human creation that makes an abortion decision so complicated and so painful. Women throughout history have been in a position to experience that connection in an immediate way, because it is they who have both birthed and nurtured babies. "Conceiving children is not enough for the continuation of human life," wrote Annie Leclerc; "it is also necessary to feed them, care for them, cajole them, talk to them; it is necessary to live them so that they live."[23] The primal, psychological truth of relationships is that babies are conceived from sex, but unless they are nurtured and brought into the human community, they die. They need the passionate commitment of another human to become fully human. Women know that if they are able or willing to provide that nurture, to commit huge amounts of their own energy, talents, time, and emotion, the fetus will indeed, under most circumstances, become a fully human child. That is part of the difficult context they confront.

The fact that a woman needs to invest *herself* for the child to grow is treated as dispensable and all but morally weightless when the natural and the human contributions to life are cleanly separated and placed in a hierarchical relationship, with "nature's miracle" — conception — as the highest pinnacle. The moral clarity with which some argue the pro-life position seems to depend on treating as part of "nature's miracle" — and thereby erasing — women's investment of their humanity, their time, and their love in enabling the flourishing of an individual human life. In this scheme, any intuition women might have about the value to a child's development of their own *desire* to mother is deemed completely irrelevant. Yet if our aspiration is to create humans in the highest sense, people who can love, reflect on the world, and bring understanding and compassion to their relation to themselves and others, we should acknowledge and honor both the natural and human aspects of creating a child and view their integration as itself sacred.

On the abortion rights side, the importance of a woman's reproductive freedom has justifiably been framed in terms of her rights to self-determination, to personal choice, to the inviolability of her body. But in framing the argument almost solely in those terms, pro-choice rhetoric has forsaken a more inspirational discussion of the profound necessity and liberating potential of a desired motherhood. The birth control activist Margaret Sanger wrote in 1920 that voluntary motherhood was "the most sacred aspect of woman's freedom." Unashamed to engage the spiritual dimension, she contended that a motherhood that was the "fruit of a deep yearning" was a motherhood "ready to obey its own urge to remake the world."[24] Through a desired motherhood, a woman brought integrity and joy to her relationships to herself, her children, her mate, and her larger community. The contemporary pro-choice movement would benefit from conceptualizing abortion not only in terms of rights but also in terms of the sacredness of desired motherhood. Through that effort we might deepen our understanding of maternal desire and find a more encompassing, expressive language to describe the seemingly contradictory aspects of women's reproductive life.

Pro-life Feminism and Saintliness

THERE ARE THOSE WHO FULLY endorse the sanctity of the connection of natural and human creativity and are at the same time passionately against abortion. "Pro-life feminism" has been one label used to refer to the view that a stand against abortion is a stand for respecting women. As the pro-life feminist Sidney Callahan put it, "I can't see separating fetal liberation from women's liberation. Ultimately, I think the feminist movement made a serious mistake — politically, morally, and psychologically — by committing itself to a pro-choice stance, a stance which in effect pits women against their children."[25]

Almost everyone can agree that as a society we devalue caring for children. We can also acknowledge that pro-choice rhetoric has by and large avoided dealing with the common intuition that there is a sacred dimension of conception and fetal life. We can even concede that there is a spiritual opportunity posed by an unplanned pregnancy, and it is possible to respect the spiritual state of women who are able truly to put the life of a potential baby on par with their own. This admiration is not far removed from how we feel about James McBride's mother in his memoir, *The Color of Water*, who overcame the trauma of her early life and her own loss and depression and was able, through faith and love, to raise eight children. Likewise, we tend to regard as enlightened and almost saintly those people who adopt troubled or disabled children, sometimes many of them.

Pro-life feminists legitimately question whether a permissive and even cavalier approach to abortion works to the detriment of women's interests. Their concern derives from a belief in the immense value of women's reproductive capacity and extends to a vision of society organized around true recognition of that value. In that sense, their view converges with that of some ardently pro-choice feminists. Both consider what society might look like if our goal was to give women's concerns the same centrality and respect that men's have traditionally enjoyed. Both find fault with a society that condemns abortion but does little to make the health and welfare of children a primary goal.[26]

However, I find it problematic when pro-life feminists argue backward from the sanctity (and the rights) of fetal life to a prescriptive, utopian view of women's lives. They don't always acknowledge that the key intermediary step must always be women's ultimate responsibility to make their own abortion decisions. We cannot go directly from an opposition to abortion to a certain vision — even if a freer, more respectful vision, according to its advocates — of women's lives. We can only proceed through a respect for women's personhood. It is not enough to insist that women will find their sense of greatest meaning and value in a society that opposes abortion; it is necessary to create a society where women are free to discover that, or not, for themselves.

Recognizing women's right to self-determination entails accepting that society cannot compel saintliness. It is fundamentally unfair to oblige women to be good Samaritans with respect to their pregnancies.[27] Throughout history, women often have not been free to make and take responsibility for their own decisions about sexuality and motherhood, and it has been easy enough to create identities for them, to make them stand for good or evil. When we finally accept that women must be their *own* mediators of their conscience or God's word, we lose a fantasy about the purity of women and a clarity about their rightful destiny. But we gain a fairer, more truthful, more complex view of each other.

10

Midlife

I REMEMBER A NUMBER OF years ago telling some colleagues, ac-complished professional women in their fifties whose children had started college, that I was pregnant with a third child. Their faces melted with delight. They talked about how having chil-dren is the most wonderful thing. Many regretted aloud having stopped at two; even the women with three children wished they'd had a fourth. One colleague, whom I remembered bear-ing down on me a few years before about how children had stalled my career, effused, "That is *exactly* the right thing to do."

I was touched by their unbridled enthusiasm, but I was also taken by surprise. I felt I was seeing a side of these driven women that I hadn't seen before. Had their perspective on child rearing changed? Were they seeing its value in a new way, now that they were further from the daily wear and tear? Perhaps the passage of years had distilled what was most satisfying in their lives. What-ever it was I was observing, it struck me as a sudden change of course. I felt as if I'd seen them traveling in one direction, and now they were traveling the other way.

I thought long and hard about this and realized that what I most needed to understand was not their reaction but my own. Their reactions were really quite simple and expectable. "How wonderful, how great" was what anyone might say on hearing news of an anticipated baby. It didn't commit them to any particular stance on the great referenda on motherhood; it was a caring, supportive gesture. So why did what they had to say surprise me? What expectation did I hold, unbeknownst to myself, that was disconfirmed by their comments?

I began to recognize that I held two ideas, fantasies really, about the views of these women fifteen or twenty years my senior. First, I imagined that their having been so heavily engaged with their work when their children were young meant that tending their children had not been particularly interesting to them. Second, I felt that insofar as my decision to have another baby revealed my desire to spend my time caring for my children, they would judge that desire, seeing it as some sort of weakness, or as a selling short of the feminism we held in common. I imagined they would be disappointed in me for not "managing" better the emotions of motherhood to make room for a highly involving work life, or that they would detect some excessive "leakiness" of maternal emotion in my desire for another child.

Once I exposed these notions to the light of day, I could see that they were rife with distortions. But I also saw that they contained real intergenerational issues on questions of motherhood. Between my mother's generation and my own we have undergone at least two huge shifts in the typical trajectory of middle-class mothers' lives. Women who mothered the children of the baby boom, from post–World War II to the early 1960s, did so largely as stay-at-home mothers. With the frustrations of that experience in mind, they began working toward having more in their lives than marriage and child rearing — that is what Friedan's The Feminine Mystique was all about. Women who came of age in the feminist era of the 1960s and 1970s entered the workforce in unprecedented numbers. Their progress came to be measured increasingly in terms of integration into positions of power in public life; children and their care was, partly for strategic reasons, downplayed. In my generation and those following, the issues are again different. They revolve around the question of how to perform the jobs and professions we —

men *and* women — need to do, while meeting our own and our children's needs for connection and time together. A friend in her fifties took a hopeful perspective: "My mother's generation suffered because they weren't allowed to say that they *didn't* want to be with their children. My generation suffered because we couldn't say that we *did* want to be with our children. Maybe you folks will have it all!"

Women now in their fifties and sixties bore the brunt of the necessary cataclysmic social shift wherein women embarked on the project of becoming integrated into mainstream society. To give birth to themselves, some women had to forgo children. Some had to delay children and were ultimately unable to have them. Some got distracted by a set of ideas that they eventually realized were not helpful to them. And many found a way to nurture their own growth and that of children, to include themselves in the enterprise of nurturing human growth. The vision embodied in that attempt at wholeness, carried out on a massive social scale, is one that we all benefit from and draw upon daily, whether we know it or not, appreciate it or not, deny it or not.

Women coming of age today breathe a different air. A friend was amused when he said to his young daughter, "Look, a woman pilot!" and she didn't understand why he was making a big point about it. I talk with my children about girls' having had no access to education under the Taliban regime, and they look at me with squinting eyes, as if trying to comprehend an otherwordly life form. At the same time, though professional and economic access is now taken for granted in Western democracies at a level unimaginable a couple generations ago, women today have other challenges. Among these is navigating a path they are satisfied with between the demands and opportunities of the workplace and the role of mother.

When young women today assert the importance of mothering in their lives, it is too often misconstrued, especially in the popular press, as a pendulum swing, as a "return" to something, as if it were a simple, unchanged "going back." At its best, however, it is a forward movement, an attempt at a new synthesis that is mindful both of the costs of a motherhood that blots out "one's affective, intellectual, and professional personality" *and* the costs of a work life or professional identity that leaves too little room for one's "personality" as a mother.[1] Though the intent among some well-educated women to stay home with children can seem retrograde to those whose consciousness was formed in the atmosphere of their own mother's frustration, contemporary women have the experiences of their *own* mothers' generation to reflect on and react to. From some this includes a vivid memory of parental unavailability.

When young women today evaluate their choices with reference to mothers who were not frustrated and idle but, rather, busy and professionally fulfilled, new motifs emerge. At a guest lecture I gave to college students, one young woman exclaimed how important work was to her own mother's identity, and how glad she was for her mother's satisfaction. She then added that she herself didn't want children unless she felt sure she was willing and able to devote most of her time to them. Anne Roiphe writes of the reception students at an academically excellent girls' school in Manhattan gave to a successful professional who came to speak to them:

> When she finished [talking], the first question asked was what hour did she get home. The second question asked was who took care of her children during the day. The third question was about what happened if one of her children was sick. The students, most of them daughters of working women, professional women who had left their children in the care of au pairs, nannies from Jamaica or Trinidad, did not take kindly to this lawyer and her accomplishments.[2]

To these reactions, and to the coveting of domesticity expressed by some young women, one might respond, as an older friend did: "How can you throw away everything we fought so hard for? Don't you understand what you are doing?" But in the eternally returning dance of mother-daughter relations, it helps to notice not only the *content* of each generational switch — constrained to mother, free to work, free to mother — but its *form*. The intergenerational tumble of mother-daughter relations is always and forever shaped by the push-pull of love, need, anger, and rebellion. That college student in my lecture wrestled with her choices and her identity with reference to her mother. When I was attributing feelings and opinions about childbearing and children to women older than myself, I was casting them as starkly different from me as a way of working out my own self-definition. That's how we do these things. And the criticism we heap on our mothers, or the conflict we have with mother stand-ins, does not undercut our mothers' utter centrality. Rather, it proves it.

Natalie Angier pursues this paradox with characteristic wit in her book *Woman: An Intimate Geography*. "Women need their mothers," she writes. "They blame their mothers, they dream of killing their mothers, but they keep coming back for more mother time. They want something, even if they can't articulate the desire. They expect something. They expect their mothers to be there for them, for years and years after they have become adults."[3] As Angier reads the anthropological data, this need is anchored in our evolutionary past, specifically in lactating mothers' reliance on mothers and elder female kin to forage the necessary food for her other children. "We need touch, and as a rule the appetite serves us well. In a similar vein, I would argue that a woman's mother-lust, her need for the older female and for other women generally, is also ancient, and also worth heeding."[4]

When seen within an evolutionary time frame, our irritations with our mothers shrink and our reliance on them looms larger. Perhaps the idea that we need to get away from our mothers to find ourselves was a little naive, or at least incomplete. It's one side of the story, a reasonable hypothesis, and it makes sense of the facts as long as our project is becoming independent and self-sufficient in twenty-first-century America. It works more or less well, right up until the moment we have children. Suddenly, the balance of blame and need shift. When our project was independence, keeping the disappointments and irritations alive helped fuel our projection onward and outward. But once children arrive on the scene, our irritations with our mothers are no longer so central to our goals. We yearn for their help, their support, and we are less preoccupied with their limits than grateful for their abilities. Blame and need switch places.

Daniel Stern offers a psychoanalytic angle on the same mother preoccupation that Angier describes. In studying women becoming mothers, he found it "eye-opening" to realize that expectant mothers in therapy "know full well that they have entered into a different psychic zone" having to do with a shifting relationship toward the matrilineal.[5] With the birth of a baby, women's sense of meaning and personal power tend to become more wrapped up with the maternal figures in their lives; they become "more interested in women and less in men, more psychologically involved (consciously or not) with their mothers and less with their fathers."[6] In practical terms, new mothers seek out "benign mother figures,"[7] whether their own mother, a mother they remember from their past, or other women in their current life, to teach and affirm them on their journey into motherhood.

Women in my generation who had their kids in their thirties and try to juggle child rearing with demanding jobs find they are a "sandwich" generation of a new kind. Many of our own mothers raised us closer to extended family. We moved away and made lives elsewhere. Now, looking at our own children, we are painfully aware of the costs of having moved so far away that there is no ongoing help from extended family in raising our kids. A friend admitted to a sly, retro plan to see to it that her own children stayed closer to home so she could help with grandchildren. I remember my bereft wandering around my house after our babysitter moved to Florida; in those moments I felt slightly absurd to have depended so elementally on such a newcomer to my life. I felt both comforted and forlorn when my mother said how much she wished she lived closer so she could care for my children.

When we take account of how important, intergenerationally and even evolutionarily, the mother-daughter bond is, it helps put our intense and contradictory emotions in perspective. Our blame and need of our mothers, our back-and-forth switches between the two, their prickly coexistence, may simply be how things are and have always been. Yes, there are toxic mothers whose very presence can send their daughters into depressive tailspins. But in most cases, things are not that severe. And even when they are problematic, women are often surprised to see how the dynamic shifts when they have children. Not only do we need our mothers in a new way, as help, as support, and sometimes as the (not too overbearing) voice of experience, but we begin to empathize with them, and to understand them better, more viscerally. A friend of mine who is fifty-five said she had recently reached a point in her life where she felt she understood her mother almost completely. Maybe it takes until about that age to have such a degree of understanding. But I notice, even in the ten years since I became a mother, how my various criticisms of my mother have imperceptibly fallen away. I feel the same enjoyment of her now that I remember feeling as a child, just from a different position. Now, we are two grown women who care about our children and each other, and that adds a new note to our mutual sympathy.

This sympathy is the salutary side of the reality that our mother lives on in our own mothering. The psychoanalyst Rosemary Balsam provides an amusing example of its less favorable aspect. A young mother came to her therapy session with her four-month-old boy. She chose to sit on a chair rather than on the couch nearer the therapist, saying, "I don't want to mess it up." Before she nursed her infant, she spread on her lap an enormous plastic-backed towel. After nursing, she used two additional towels, one for his spit up, one for her breasts. Finally she settled in to talk about what she had planned to discuss at this session:

> how her mother was insisting on buying new plastic coverlets for her living room furniture. "I don't know

why. We don't need it. She thinks it's this gift. I hate covers of any kind over furniture! I believe in kids making a mess. They have to enjoy themselves, and Tom and I see eye-to-eye on this one. That's one thing I've always said. I certainly won't be like her that way — covering up every stick of furniture when I was a kid in case I make a mess! I want to think more here about how to stand up to her, to put my foot down. It's *my* house and I'm the mother now, and I'll do what I want to, thank you."[8]

A Short History of Mothers in Midlife

I RECENTLY ATTENDED A BABY shower at which, expectedly, there were lots of babies under the age of one and quite a few newborns. But unexpectedly, when I surveyed the scene, I was struck by the fact that the mothers of these newborns ranged in age from thirty-eight to forty-nine. Given the wide range of ages at which people conceive and bear children, the term "midlife" as any sort of developmental marker begins to sound meaningless. One woman is welcoming her first baby at forty-six, another is preparing for her last child to go to college. (In some cultures, it is not unusual for a woman of forty-five to have children in their twenties and also be mothering a newborn.)[9] In many ways, having your first baby in your midforties instead of your midtwenties *is* a different experience — your knees creak more, you are more in touch with the impermanence of life. But at twenty-five or forty-five, both first-time mothers are embarking on a similarly transforming developmental phase.

The issues commonly associated with mothering in midlife clearly cannot be keyed to any particular chronological age. Rather, they are related to a phase of parenthood. In the midlife parental phase, a mother will experience her children's increasing independence — learning to drive, leaving home — and she will learn to let go. During this time, she herself will age, perhaps go through menopause. These developments will propel her to reflect on her past, evaluate her present, and plan for her future.

In the olden days, when women's psychology was thought to revolve around penis envy, and motherhood represented their compensatory summum bonum, the ending of a woman's reproductive life signaled by the advent of menopause was evidence of the long decline, tolling, like Tennessee Williams's clock, "Loss, loss, loss."[10] This was the lone psychoanalytic narrative; being a woman was all about loss, and after childbearing was complete, even more so. The psychoanalyst Helene Deutsch, a woman with a fulfilling career, emphasized this component above all others. For women who had rigid characters, or who had never been able to fulfill themselves sexually or maternally, the sense of "mortification" was worst. But even for the "motherly" woman, menopause "only intensifies in her something that has always been present, ever since her children left her to pursue their own independent ways. Just as the narcissistic woman is in love with her lost past, the motherly woman is in love with the past of her motherhood, during which she really had her children, because she was indispensable to them. 'Children should always remain little,' thinks many a mother when her grown-up son leaves."[11] A similar note was sounded by an older woman therapist who attended a talk I gave. She said that among older women she knew, there was a "continual process of mourning" the departure of children, which spoke of the timelessness of mothering. She attributed the richness of being a grandparent in part to its arrival after a period of grieving one's own children's departure.

That slant on mothers' response to children leaving home came in for a thoroughgoing revision in the 1970s and 1980s, when therapists began to write about the retrograde inaccuracy of the so-called empty nest phenomenon. "Why do negative stereotypes about the middle years in a woman's life continue to persist, despite all empirical evidence to the contrary?" wondered one therapist. "Neither menopause nor the empty nest, by themselves, are correlated with a decrease in well-being."[12] In 1978 the psychologist Lillian Rubin devoted a book to examining the transitions of women who had spent their young adulthood immersed in raising children and who were now contemplating the next phase of their lives. She found that for the most part, women greeted their renewed freedom with excitement and relief. When a woman was anxious, the anxiety did not arise from seeing her children go, but rather from the void that was left by their absence and the need to find a meaningful new way to channel her energies.[13]

If the first psychological narrative on midlife and menopause, as articulated by Deutsch and others, was one of loss, the second narrative, which gained ascendancy in the 1970s and 1980s, was one of freedom. Today, we are somewhere else, maybe in between. Contemporary forms of balancing the impulses to independence and connection have arisen. The earlier writings on the challenges to women of menopause and the "empty nest" tended to address two relatively distinct groups: women who had borne children early while forgoing other careers, and those who had not borne children while they pursued other careers. One contemporary twist has been the sequential living of these two personae within the same woman. Reflecting the increased number of women who have devoted themselves to work for many years before having children, today we have what amounts to a "mini-genre" of writing by women who in many cases began their adult lives focused on their work and a bit dismissive of those who weren't, and who later, either mourning their childlessness or celebrating the delights of motherhood, write of their own transformation.[14] Ann Crittenden, author of *The Price of Motherhood*, conveyed the message well: "Deep down," she wrote of her pre-motherhood days, "I had no doubt that I was superior, in my midtown office overlooking Madison Avenue, to those unpaid housewives pushing brooms. 'Why aren't they making something of themselves?' I wondered. 'What's wrong with them? They're letting our side down.'"[15]

Later, after she became a mother in her early forties, she felt differently: "I fell hopelessly in love with this tiny new creature, with an intensity that many mothers describe as 'besotted.' I had taken a lot of trips in my life, but this was the most exotic. The world of motherhood was as strange and unfamiliar to me as a hidden Himalayan kingdom. The first surprise came when I realized how hard and yet how incredibly gratifying motherhood was. . . . The second surprise" — a surprise to her new mother-self, but a view completely familiar to her childless self — "came when I realized how little my former world seemed to understand, or care, about the complex reality I was discovering."[16]

This "discourse of surprise" is intriguing on a number of fronts. Crittenden's sense that motherhood is as strange and unfamiliar as a "hidden Himalayan kingdom" — a sense echoed in the writings of other late-bearing mothers — is striking in part because of what it suggests about the writer's identification with her own mother. We all had mothers, with whom most of us lived as children. We observed her life, we experienced her tending to us, we felt toward her in childhood an intense, even consuming love. That that world is experienced as "exotic" not only conveys temporal distance from childhood but also suggests an active refusal of identification with one's mother, at least in her maternal role. Perhaps this can be understood in terms of the sheer energy women who came of age in the 1960s and 1970s felt they had to expend not to recapitulate the limits of their mothers' lives. But when they approach motherhood themselves, later in life, they express astonishment at the riches that they have forgotten or repressed. Sometimes this discovery can take on an almost manic, grandiose quality. Susan Cheever, who bore a daughter at thirty-eight and a son at forty-six, offers a compelling description:

> My passion for Liley was so great that I truly, truly thought she was an exceptional child — one in a million. . . . I won't forget the day I took her to our first babies and mothers class at a school down the street.

There were ten mothers and ten babies enrolled for exercise, crafts, and advice. My daughter was clearly a superior baby. I was actually amazed when the other mothers didn't drop their inferior babies and rush over to admire my baby. This isn't a joke; I was really surprised.[17]

One senses in these accounts that the woman's ardent pleasure in her child and the uninterested posture taken earlier on are two sides of the same coin. Their dramatic divergence illustrates one method of managing the competing impulses toward autonomous achievement and maternal connectedness. Perhaps, earlier on, these women endorsed a split view, in which their own lives were about adventure, sexuality, and ambition, while their mothers' lives were about passivity, self-sacrifice, and anonymity. That stance may have solidified as they correctly perceived that the world of achievement placed unforgiving limits on women who put a priority on motherhood. Somehow, something broke it up — age, development, attainment of goals, a new relationship — and they began to see the world through an entirely new lens.

This question of how to find that elusive balance between mothering and one's other goals preoccupies huge numbers of women in the current childbearing generation as well. Although social conditions change from generation to generation, in some ways the questions stay the same. That is one reason we can't have too many testimonials and memoirs by women that discuss their child rearing years. As Angier eloquently put it, "our constitutional hunger for our mothers" is "like the river of our lives. It flows on, and we must navigate it, and it surges and howls and falls, but it doesn't end and we must ride it."[18] Women need to hear from women farther along in life, they crave counsel from women who have had a chance to reflect on their decisions and evaluate them. Younger women want to know so many things from older women: How did they feel about caring for young children, and how did they reconcile those feelings with whatever other strivings they felt? What prompted them to wait to have children, and how do they evaluate their reasons now? How did they arrange their day-to-day lives with infants and small children? And what do they see now, looking back, as the costs and benefits of their arrangements?

The Professional
Lover of Children

PUBLIC DISCUSSION OF THESE ISSUES is difficult in part because they entail hard choices and an inevitable sense of loss. People understandably try to see their own decisions as the right ones and are sometimes threatened by considering other paths. Into this conflict-ridden cultural arena has emerged the hybrid figure of the professional lover of children. Here we find the busy professional woman — Hillary Clinton, Marian Wright Edelman, Sylvia Ann Hewlett — who passionately supports the cause of children. The professional lover of children satisfies our longing for a cultural image of both the nurturant mother and the mother whose career has never suffered.

In books by Clinton, Edelman, and Hewlett, one finds similar themes. Each came from hardworking, traditional households with strong religious or moral values. They all attribute great importance to their parents' high standards for ethical and scholastic excellence. They deeply appreciate the sacrifices and groundedness of their parents. They all felt connected to the communities or close-knit extended families from which they came. All look back with some yearning to simpler days when societal mores and parental roles were more clear-cut.

Part of what their young lives taught them, and a lesson they fervently wish to impart to others, is the importance of time with children. "The adults in our churches and community . . . ," writes Edelman of her own childhood, "took time and paid attention to us."[19] "The time we spend with children — and what we do with it — is more than an indulgence for parents," writes Clinton. "It is an investment in children's future — an investment we can't make up later."[20] "Time is, of course, at the heart of the enterprise," write Hewlett and her co-author Cornel West in *The War Against Parents*. "Being a 'good-enough' parent requires providing a child with the gifts of love, attention, energy, and resources, generously and unstintingly given over a long period of time."[21] Each iterates, and reiterates, that time is the heart of the matter.

These authors' pleas for changes in social policy are based on personal and political conviction, further fueled by their first-hand experience trying to integrate a work and a family life. Their struggles as working mothers devoted to the well-being of their own and others' children add to their expertise and authority. And yet, any mother caught between the demands of work and raising children cannot help but be curious about how, in the midst of their lives of large-scale ambition, they have managed to practice what they preach with respect to time with children. Most of us endorse the value of spending time with our children in principle. The rub comes in actually doing it. What does their particular juxtaposition of high-powered professionalism and advocacy for children teach us about the culture and about ourselves?

Drawing attention to the social forces that compromise the welfare of children, these advocates' goal is to generate policy solutions. But at times, in their understandable focus on the social causes of children's distress, they give short shrift to the personal level at which each of us wrestles with how we allocate our time and resources, and how we square our beliefs about parental involvement with what we actually do. One form this imbalance takes is the tendency to paint society as devaluing children and the author as their unambivalent champion, relegating the author's own ambivalence to the background. In *It Takes a Village*, Clinton writes lovingly of her own mother as a person who was "terrific at thinking up simple, imaginative activities to do with us. . . . Sometimes my mother and I would spend hours having picnics in our backyard and pointing out the shapes we saw in clouds." The same image is called upon when portraying time with her own daughter: "The simple activities I shared with her became favorites of mine with Chelsea. We often spent hours in the backyard at the governor's mansion, stretched out on a quilt and looking at birds and clouds. We also used to lie on our backs in the front hallway when no one was around, watching the dancing rainbows the sun made as it struck the crystal chandelier."[22]

Clinton's memories evoke her identification with her own nurturing mother, an identification that likely shaped her own maternal style and suffused her with a sense of maternal richness. Because Clinton seems like such a good mother and such a competent professional, she is exactly the kind of person from whom we would most like to hear about the particulars of spending time mothering in the context of demanding professional commitments. Mothers faced with similar dilemmas long to learn more specifics from women like Clinton about their experience of the conflicts and trade-offs they've faced, and are eager for the articulation of a philosophy of child rearing that might reconcile these conflicts. Yet, in some ways, Clinton's sun-dappled images frustrate, floating disembodied above the question of how her pleasure in mothering connected to her choice to spend much of her time engaged in other work.

A tendency to lodge ambivalence in society instead of in oneself, and to cast personal conflict as derived solely from social forces, is evident when certain maternal ideals are written off as oppressive social ideology rather than owned as partly internally, psychologically based. In her book A Lesser Life, Hewlett blames much of her sense of inadequacy and failure as a mother of a newborn on the ideologies that celebrated natural childbirth and the importance of breastfeeding. Though she justly skewers the ideologues' excesses and rigidity, she does not explore why they exerted the power over her that they did. She wanted, perhaps based on what she describes as her father's ambitions for her and her mother's generosity to her children, to be both the consummate professional and the bounteous mother.

She wanted, as many of us do, to realize her ambitions to the fullest both as a mother and as a professional. What does she do when that proves impossible? She treats the ambitions attaching to motherhood — the value of nursing and of spending time caring for one's children — as produced by oppressive ideologies put over on women. The maternal ambitions are thus transposed from an internal value to an external demand, creating an easier, more clear-cut object for her frustration. As she looks back, her *own* wishes regarding natural childbirth, nursing, or time spent caring for her child drop from view; she is mystified by how credulous she was in accepting these misguided prescriptions for motherhood. For example, casting a retrospective glance at her decision to hire part-time rather than full-time care for her newborn, Hewlett writes, "I cannot now understand how I endured the constant physical and psychological stress of trying to combine motherhood and career in this way."[23]

Yet if Hewlett's own work and her own deeply held principles are any guide, the reason she pursued this path is obvious. She believes that parents should spend time with their children. In her own case, her belief in the importance of parents caring for children was in direct and painful conflict with another aspiration, namely to succeed at her chosen career. She feels the difficulties personally — "It is hard to exaggerate how wrenching it is to try to carry out work responsibilities with a baby in attendance" — but she blames the powers that be for forcing her to relinquish her fantasy of doing everything and to hire full-time help. "I did this not out of any consideration for myself or Richard," she hastens to make clear (though she admits, "by this stage both of us were wretchedly tired"), "but because I was encountering tremendous disapproval and hostility at work."[24] The problem of the discourse of the professional lover of children is that by focusing solely on the external causes of the "war on parents" and ignoring the internal dilemmas, it is unable to provide a social analysis that encompasses the "shadow side" of our own ambivalence about devoting our time to our children.

The failure to confront this shadow side accounts for the bombast of one of Hewlett's latest works. Hewlett and West's *The*

War Against Parents is shot through with portentous claims about having "constructed a vision and a movement with the power to heal," and having "found a repository of comfort and strength that has the potential to bridge the deep divides of race, gender, and class."[25] They attribute near messianic significance to their collaboration, persuaded that their own power as symbols — being black and white, male and female — will span divides, heal splits, and resolve differences.[26] The "extraordinary journey" of "giving new status and support to mothers and fathers has extraordinary potential because of the ways in which the parent-child bond is the most fundamental building block in human society." "If we can produce this magic parent power," they write, "we can go to the very heart of our darkness and make the center hold."[27]

The purpose of this larger-than-life rhetoric may be to drum up enthusiasm for their policy recommendations, but it also strikes me as one way of coping with a central personal dilemma. The professional lover of children spends a great deal of time touting the value of time spent with children. In Hewlett and West's worldview, parent-child attachment is not simply that, the product of sustaining but unglamorous hours of involvement; it is "magical parent power." Hewlett and West describe themselves as having been chronically torn between professional aspirations and parental responsibilities. The losses inherent in those choices, instead of being accepted and mourned, are swept up into the "magic" of the solution to end all solutions — the great, grand plan to end parental pain and suffering. An attempt is made to subsume and absorb the real losses into an ever more idealized dream of parental availability. Yet, the grandiloquent claim to healing all divisions is compelling evidence that the basic division, the division of self, is alive and well, and still painful.

All this in no way discounts the book's utility as a set of constructive policy recommendations. But the problem of parental availability to children must be approached on two fronts. The grinding, often frustrating work of shifting policies in government and business is crucial, both because family policies are rife with problems and because changing material conditions is one of the most powerful ways of changing consciousness. At the same time, unless we make sense of the competing strivings in ourselves, we can't offer the necessary social analysis that would heal the splits in the culture. Unless we understand, for instance, what makes persons of privilege, who *have* a choice, choose to spend their time working over taking care of children, we can't very well make sense of the underlying pressures that keep our child-unfriendly cultural ethos in place. On a fundamental spiritual level, the enemy *is* us. When Hewlett and West write, "It's virtually unimaginable today to put together the kind of devotion and attention our parents gave to us," they are not only saying that external pressures make it difficult to realize.[28] They are also saying that in our contemporary culture, *it is hard to imagine oneself as the kind of person* who would be willing or interested in putting together that kind of devotion and attention. It is a crisis of self as much as it is a crisis of society.

Understanding why parents spend so much time away from their children requires that we examine not only the inflexibility of the workplace but also the incentives that are found there, incentives that bring stress but also rewards. This is the question that the sociologist Arlie Hochschild asked in her book *The Time Bind*. At every level of the major corporation she studied, she observed mothers and fathers opting for more work rather than less — more shifts on the factory floor, refusal to take advantage of family leave — even as they admitted the toll it took on their family lives. Hochschild offered a deft analysis of the strategies people used to justify their choices, from "emotional asceticism" — a demand that they and their children "do without" emotionally — to an endlessly deferred image of a "potential self," a version of oneself who will someday go fishing with the kids instead of working weekends. To confront these tendencies, Hochschild argues, requires

> opening a national dialogue on the most difficult and frightening aspect of our time bind: the need for "emo-

tional investment" in family life in an era of familial divestiture and deregulation. How much time and energy ought we to devote to the home? How much time and energy do we dare subtract from work? . . . What is needed . . . is a public debate about how we can properly value relationships with loved ones and ties to communities that defy commodification.[29]

Loss, Love, and Looking Back

SOON AFTER MY YOUNGEST CHILD turned three, I started remembering how it felt to be me before I had children. I began listening to music again. I read novels and felt the characters' lives more acutely. I became reacquainted with the shape and feel of solitariness. It wasn't that I was alone much more often. But I was alone in my head more. I had more psychic room. I was wistful about the loss of a certain naive belief that having my children had constituted a resting point, a final destination. They were changing, I was changing. My daughter's legs were growing gangly, she had precise ideas. The two boys were old enough now to share a perfectly self-sufficient imaginative world. I loved them as deeply, and cared for them as much, but sometimes I noticed a new voice inside saying "It's their life." At an earlier point, this feeling of distance would have felt a bit heartless. Now, in some way I couldn't quite define, it seemed right, both for me and for them.[30]

As our children grow older, they need to assert their difference, but in some ways so do we. When my children reached school age, I was surprised to find myself wanting to pick up lost threads of my life. I wanted to travel to places I had been to twenty years before, I wanted to take up the violin again. A friend said she felt like Rip Van Winkle; now that her children were eleven and seven, she felt more like the young woman she had been at twenty-four than she had at any time in the intervening two decades. These feelings can be as disorienting as they are liberating, for they challenge us to find a vital way of integrating our past, pre-motherhood selves into the structures and commitments of our present lives. Tempting as it may be to blame our children, or our partners, or even patriarchal society for having "put to sleep" important parts of ourselves as we've mothered, the most fundamental issue is what occurs in our relationship to *ourselves*, and that is where we must struggle to find a new integration.

The wedge of distance that grows as one's children grow has mingled in it excitement and sadness, freedom and guilt; we are never sure if we have gotten its dimensions right. At seven, my daughter still found separations wrenching. Was it because I had left her at the age of two, crying, with a caregiver whom I later discovered had been neglectful? Was it, contrariwise, because she had had such a gratifying childhood that she was having a hard time learning how to tough it out? Was it — the most likely possibility — neither? As best we can, we are guided by our feelings in making these judgments, but since we are in the thick of it, our assessments are constantly changing. What seemed like a problem yesterday has evaporated today. What seems just fine today is a concern tomorrow. Our appraisal of our children and ourselves as parents is always changing, never standing still.

A woman on the eve of first-time motherhood faces different but no less preoccupying uncertainties. She is about to embark on a phase of her life that cannot be truly prepared for; but at the same time, she is caught in a thicket of competing models of motherhood in whose terms she often feels she must somehow understand herself. She likely feels subtle, not even conscious, pressure to try to make her experience of having a baby conform to her previous ideas about herself. She may fear the loss of who she is now or of the quality of her relationship to her partner or her work. If she has an intense job, she may expect boredom tending an infant and be surprised by her interest; if she is happy to throw herself into mothering, she may expect rhapsodic communion and be shocked by its ups and downs. To get our bearings in the face of this life change, we may hold on to a shred of our recognizable priorities or resist being surprised by other potential selves.

A perspective that can help us on these roads comes from mothers looking back from the vantage of a life long lived. Somehow experience seems able to soften the edges of doctrine, to temper the rigid "either/or" with a bit of "both/and." It is so helpful, so calming really, to be reminded by older women that life is long, and that there is room for many aspirations. It doesn't resolve the conflicts we face, but it does remind us of the possibility of a roomier perspective at just the moment we feel most powerfully boxed in by the momentous importance, for our family and ourselves, of making the "right decisions." In *Fruitful*, Anne Roiphe writes that even though for most mothers and even grandmothers the "sense of identity, of meaning, lies with our children," child rearing doesn't absorb all one's time for years on end: "There is time enough in one life to find many different kinds of satisfactions and satisfy many different kinds of necessities."[31]

When we are caring for small children and trying to do a job, everything can feel like a source of potential guilt, everything can seem like a veiled referendum on our adequacy as mothers. We live chronically with a sense of doing no job fully, and that itself can be a source of unhappiness for people who derive pride from a job well done. When I talk to people whose children are grown, I find not that they are devoid of guilt, but that they have an empathy for their younger selves, an understanding of their own history, and a respect for the fact that they could not have done things another way, given who they were. One friend, now a grandmother, put it this way:

> I can look back and see times when I was so wrapped up with working out my own stormy adolescence that I wasn't able to be really present for my children, particularly my younger one. It's like when you are growing a plant, and for some period of time you don't water it or give it the right nutrients, and after that, it keeps growing, but you can always see the place where it didn't get

what it needed, the lump or the irregularity, or where it started sprouting off in a different direction. I can see that place in my child, and I know it has to do with what I wasn't able to give her. Throughout life you are always reworking the same issues over and over again, and I am more aware now where I was in that process when I had my children and I know I couldn't have been different, but I also see the costs to them.

Another older friend has one child in college, another finishing high school. Though at times she looks back and wonders about the effect of times she was unavailable, she has a clear-eyed sense of herself:

I realize that I did not feel that I had a choice not to work. It was not a financial issue and not exactly a political issue — my politics are more quiet and private — but a sense that I would somehow be degrading myself as a person and failing myself and my children if I were to be nothing more than a full-time mother. It seemed no more possible to me than washing windows on a sky-scraper (I have a fear of heights, which I have somewhat overcome in order to take my children skiing.)

To nurture herself and her children, she needed to have deeply meaningful work.

I remember once when I was in training as a therapist, and pregnant, a clinical supervisor said, "No patient is as interested in your pregnancy as you are." It captured something about the particular state we enter when we are pregnant and new mothers. We often feel that *everything* we do is of supreme importance. It is a state of mind fully adaptive for the task at hand and stage of life. But a more seasoned parent, one who has been through the babyhood, childhood, and adolescence of her children, sees over and over the ways that her child never really was under her control, never was anyone other than who he or she was going to be. That releases parents from a sense of oppressive importance; it grants them humility and a certain kind of freedom to see things unsentimentally.

What is ultimately reassuring about what older women have to say is that they are no longer as invested as younger women are in taking a stand with respect to their own ambivalence. They are not in the middle of living it. For better or worse, the job is mostly done. And they see what being a mother cost them and what it gave them; they see what they were able to give their children and what they were not, with clearer eyes. Whichever judgment they make about how they lived their children's early years, they talk of it with an attitude of greater acceptance.

I asked one professional friend, a mother of two late-adolescent children, what her feelings were about the amount of time she spent with her children when they were young. She replied:

> When I *really* think about regrets about not having spent more time with them, I realize that much of that regret is bogus. The time I imagine missing is almost always an idealization of leisurely hours in the park, warm and cozy times reading a book or baking a pie. Those regrets omit the boredom of pushing the swing, the exhaustion of repeatedly saying that ten stories are enough, and the work of cleaning up the kitchen after the pie-baking. The reality is that I spent a lot of time with my children when they were little and when they were bigger. But the fact is, there's never enough time.

There is also the pull of nostalgia to reckon with, not only for one's own children's childhood, but for one's fertility. Anne Roiphe captures it well:

> I thought I had long ago banished the wish for another pregnancy from my mind. . . . But I found myself staring at the young Orthodox women who live in my neighborhood, who had four, five, six small children around them. . . . Envy was what I felt for the fertility, for the

bearing of the child, for the round pregnant bellies, for the strollers packed with doubles or children so close in age that neither could walk alone. . . . I knew that as these children grew up they would find sorrow, misunderstandings, conflict with parents and conflict with siblings. . . . On the other hand, how grand they look, those women with their many children.[32]

This is perhaps the feeling of the women I spoke to, the ones with two children who wish they'd had a third, the ones with three who wish they'd had a fourth. When we look back on the capacity to bear and rear children from a time when it is gone, it becomes a distilled essence of joyful fecundity. Around the age of forty, when I knew we would have no more children, I felt a pang whenever I saw a newborn or heard a friend was having a baby. It was an odd new position; to be no longer in the "before" or the "during," but in the "after." I could think it through rationally — we'd had a good run; we had been so lucky; I wanted to concentrate on being as good a mother as I could be to the ones we had — but there was this pang, anyway. I think it is a particularly female window onto mortality. You can only postpone, but never escape, the final reckoning of no more children. Even if you have eight kids, that eighth is your last. Even if you have another child at forty-five, at fifty, at some point you can't have any more. And as primal as the urge feels, one is wary of its species-serving deceptions. That cute being envelops one's time and energy, wears away one's joints and muscles, and at a certain point, the system just doesn't have that much to give.

ONE DAY MY HUSBAND AND I set about the task of hanging family pictures. We couldn't believe they'd lain in boxes for four years, that we had not had one spare afternoon in all that time to hang them. When we unwrapped them and leaned them against a wall, there was a picture of our daughter and son, taken when she was three and he was six months old. We were startled to realize that the picture had been a recent one when we wrapped it for our move. But just in the time it had taken us to set up house, a blink of an eye, it seemed, the picture was from the distant past, another era of our life entirely. I remembered the day the picture was taken, but I didn't remember what my daughter's voice sounded like then, or the precise heft of my little son in my arms. In the absence of memory, what comforted me was time. I knew I had been there, and that I had done with them and for them, day in and day out. For me, simply knowing I was there helped me bear all I had forgotten.

11

Fathers

IN 1903, MY MATERNAL GRANDMOTHER'S father was fatally shot
in a barroom in Lawrence, Massachusetts. My grandmother
Helen was four years old. Michael Moher, her father, was a
twenty-six-year-old bartender and amateur boxer who had
sailed from Ireland with his four brothers and two sisters eleven
years before. As the Lawrence newspaper recounted it, an Italian patron, angered at not having his pail filled with more beer,
later returned to the bar and shot my great-grandfather. From
the front-page story you could take in at a glance the ongoing
tensions between the Irish and the Italian in the industrial mill
town. It also conveyed with astonishing intimacy the tragic human cost. "Mrs. Moher is a frail little woman and is almost prostrated by the blow. . . . 'Poor Mike,' she said . . . 'did not count
on so cowardly an attack. He could defend himself in a fair fight
but to be shot in such a treacherous way; oh, it is awful, awful'
and she burst into tears."[1] She died three years later from what
my grandmother would call "a broken heart," leaving her seven-
year-old daughter and four-year-old son.

In 1935, my mother's father, Helen's husband, died of a bleed-
ing ulcer. My mother was eighteen months old. She doesn't remember him. He worked for the American Tobacco Company.
My mother and her brother speculated that smoking or drink
may have led to his demise, but she never quite felt comfortable
asking her mother to spell things out. The image of her father

that she conjured from her mother's stories was of an easy-tempered man and a good dancer who watched over her from heaven. Till the end of her life, my grandmother sprinkled her rose-tinted tales from the past with allusions to "your father" to my mother, or to us, "your grandfather," in her Boston accent.

In 1967, my parents divorced. I was in second grade. I was listening to Petula Clark's "Downtown" when my father came into our living room, turned off the record player, and convened a family meeting. My mother had told us earlier in the day that we couldn't have friends over that evening because she and Daddy were going to have a talk with us. My siblings and I were nervous, giggly. We thought maybe they were having another baby. They told us they were getting divorced. My father has always been involved, in every way, in my life. But remembering that arc from eager expectation to world-altering sadness can still make me cry.

My own personal twist on the cherished American idea of progress has had a lot to do with fathers. From quite a young age, I discerned a trajectory from my grandmother, who lost her father and mother, to my mother, who lost her father, to myself, who lost living with my mother and father together. Progress in my own life revolved around managing to create an intact family in which father and mother were both alive, present, and involved. This is the "better life for my children" that most preoccupied me, my particular American dream.

At the same time, the legacy of these various paternal losses has given me some insight into how fathers get "written out" of the psyches of women. The absence of the father can be passed down through the generations, with grief, confusion, and denial of need often filling the void. In a not-untypical attitude of the divorced mother — why would the children have any desire or need to see their father? — we hear echoed this denial of a father's importance. This is a problem for individual children and mothers. When children grow up without fathers, they pine but do not necessarily have a clear idea of what they are pining for. When women without fathers become mothers, the pattern is often continued and reinforced. It is also a problem for the culture. The critique of patriarchy, which was intended to dismantle injustices and find less gender-dominated ways for people to live, has inadvertently fueled a minimization of flesh-and-blood fatherhood, in ways that we are just beginning to understand.[2]

It seems we have paid a great deal of attention to the irresponsibility of fathers, whether documenting deadbeat dads or the tenacious "second shift" burden on mothers. But there is a piece of the complex puzzle of fathers' roles in families that is comparatively neglected: the question of how mothers view fathers, and how that itself affects the constellations of fathering and mothering we see today. Specifically, how do the dynamics of maternal desire, lived on a cultural and personal level, influence women's understanding of the role of fathers in children's lives and the role of husbands in their own?

This is a tinderbox, of course, because women often feel deeply wronged, and have suffered from their own lack of social and economic power. At the same time, some aspects of life that women have been more intimate with — particularly caring for children — have comparatively excluded men. If we see caring for children as valuable, then we have to ask, what stands in the way of fathers sharing in it more fully? Scholars have delineated the economic and social factors that create parenting inequalities; the importance of fathers for children, *both* male and female, has been studied as well.[3] But it would also help to examine mothers' feelings and attitudes about fathers and sharing caregiving in order to understand better some of the psychological factors that keep long-standing imbalances in maternal and paternal care in place.

Mothers' Mixed Feelings
About Equally Sharing Child Care

ONE OF THE MOST THOROUGHLY researched and robustly documented findings about married parents' division of household labor is that women still disproportionately manage the child care and housework.[4] Though this state of affairs furnishes a well-known source of wives' resentment, it is more complicated than it appears at first glance. For while mothers may not welcome their "second shift" portion of housework, many do strongly value the role of "primary parent," the parent who oversees the child's activities and provides more hands-on care. This is partly a matter of proclivity — a desire to do the parenting work — but also a matter of identity: women often feel that their identity as mothers rests in large part on this sense of involvement.

This duality presents a quandary for employed and non-employed mothers alike. For non-employed mothers, the challenge is to enact their desire to care for their children, while not assuming the devalued role of "housewife." One woman I know managed this conflict by maintaining a perpetual stance of grievance. She strategically (though perhaps unconsciously) defined her at-home-parent status as the "one-down" position in her marriage. Though it was a role she liked, and one she had chosen for herself, its denigrated status was understood, in her marital economy, to require her husband to "make up" for it by doing his share of housework after he got home from his full-time job. Conversely, during the time I was taking care of our children and not employed outside the house, I felt that the "cost" of being able to do something I very much wanted to do — care for the children — included doing something in which I was less interested — housework.

For a woman in the workforce, especially one who works as much or more than her husband, the challenge is maintaining a sense of her central importance as a mother when she is away many hours each day. One way she may shore up her maternal self-concept is by having comparatively more involvement in the children's lives than the father does. A busy professional friend is married to a man who had such a big success that he no longer needed to work. When I suggested to her that he could be at home, caring for their toddler and managing the other child's activities, she firmly rejected the notion. "I want to be in charge of the lists," was her droll reply. "They're my lists!"

Though she viewed him as a wonderful father, she preferred the nanny for daytime care and herself as the organizational parent.

Mothers' powerful investment in their own importance as caregivers exerts ongoing but rarely articulated effects on family dynamics and cultural ideas. We live in an era of increasingly flexible gender roles, but it seems that in some ways, changing gender roles have themselves heightened mothers' anxieties about their centrality. For example, our avowed conviction is that there is nothing essential or biologically prescribed about mothers assuming the caregiving role. At the same time, we witness a renewed emphasis on the inviolability of the biological connection of mother and child in our contemporary debates about gestational surrogacy, adoption, and foster care.[5] Women everywhere bemoan fathers' lack of participation in parenting and domestic life. Yet we also see a problematic tendency to use the biological beginnings of the mother-child bond, or the preeminent value of the maternal, to support a worldview in which mothers are sufficient and fathers are expendable. I remember hearing a young man on a radio call-in show earnestly ask a feminist pundit what he should do about the gaping loss he still felt because his father left due to divorce when he was a very young child. She suggested that sons don't really need fathers to help them separate and create lives of their own, because nowadays mothers are able to help sons with that. The young man was trying to communicate his longing for a father with whom he could have identified, and from whom he could have received care. The pundit bypassed the emotional content of his question in her eagerness to assert mothers' sufficiency.

What this worldview neglects, of course, is how much children seek and desire paternal care, and how central fathers are to the people our children become. Dr. Seuss addressed this issue back in the 1940s in his children's book *Horton Hatches the Egg*. In that tale, Horton the elephant is recruited to sit on the egg of a mother bird longing for a tropical vacation. The sincere Horton agrees, and he endures storms, drought, and hunters' attempts on his life in order to fulfill his commitment. Meanwhile, we see the mother bird sunning herself, utterly forgetful of those she left behind. As the egg is about to hatch, she swoops back into the picture and tries to take possession of her baby. But when the bird hatches, it is a baby elephant with wings. Horton, by caring for the gestating bird faithfully, becomes a "real" parent. In human terms, a father's presence, his hands-on care, allows children both to identify with the image of a loving father and to conceive of themselves as worthy of a father's love.

Mothers' contradictory feelings about their centrality to children signals, among other things, that they are caught in a conflict between the competing aims of gender equality and maternal identity. They recognize what an amazing and unique opportunity it is to be the central love of a child's life. They ardently desire it, and often feel entitled to it, not necessarily in a selfish or exclusionary way, but in a way that feels true to what they want in life. If they can, they may express this desire by being the primary caretaker of their child. If that is not possible, or not desired, they may be the comparatively more involved caretaker: "My husband works sixty hours per week, but I only work forty." Yet at the same time they may want to be the more hands-on parent, they are also aware of the ways this can disadvantage them, whether through lack of pay and prestige at work, power imbalance in marriage, or having their freedom constrained by their role as primary responder and comforter to their child.

The goal of gender equality implies parity in parents' earning and caregiving roles. But for practical and emotional reasons, many mothers prefer, at least for a time, to assume more of the caregiving role. When they do, two kinds of inequality result: an inequality of earning power, and an inequality of caregiving time. Mothers (and fathers) have mixed feelings about these sources of inequality. At times, and for some people, being the primary earner can feel like a great advantage; at other times, and for some people, being the primary caregiver can. Caregiving and earning are both ways of nurturing a family, but they involve different allocations of time and offer their practitioners different rewards. Whatever family role a woman assumes, whatever role she wants to assume, she will likely find herself confronting at some point or another an incompatibility between what she wants and what is strictly equal.

Divorce:
Economic Equality,
Caregiving Equality

THE TWO MODES OF SUPPORTING a family, caregiving and earning, are central to the sometimes contentious and difficult disagreements that arise when parents divorce. Until relatively recently, divorce settlements typically treated the money earned by the family's major breadwinner, nearly always the father, as legitimately "his," preserving, as Joan Williams put it, "fathers' freedom to seek future emotional and sexual fulfillment at the expense of their existing children."[6] This trend created the well-known spiral of increasing poverty for divorced mothers and increasing affluence for divorced fathers.[7] In my youth, the stories were legion, shared as coming-of-age tales among college roommates: the mother who had to sell her jewelry to put food on the table, or the wealthy father who refused to pay his daughter's college tuition, or the father angry at the tattered clothes that the mother's meager child support couldn't replace. Indeed, one of the striking observations in Judith Wallerstein's studies on the effects of divorce is fathers' tendency to abdicate financial care of their college-age children.[8]

Underlying this legal bias was the misconception that mothering work was "free," and therefore it was due no remuneration. But as feminist economists and legal scholars pointed out, the hours a mother spent caring for her children could have been spent earning money at a job; thus, every unpaid childcare hour could be thought of as a "lost" hour of pay. For divorce settlements to be fair, a woman's contribution to the family economy had to be taken into account, including her opportunity costs. Ann Crittenden suggested that being a mother may be the most satisfying, meaningful, and important job in the world, but women *also* give up a lot to do it. If women are going to give up economic remuneration and professional advancement to care for children, their caregiving work must be recognized in the way we structure the economics of divorce.

Equitable distribution and community property laws have gone some way toward redressing the economic inequities of divorce, though problems still abound.[9] At least in principle, the breadwinner's earnings are generally no longer considered "his," but rather payment for the totality of work performed and goods generated by the entire family system; and consideration is given to nonmonetary contributions to the marriage, such as homemaking and child care. But whereas the potential for *economic* inequality in divorce has received justifiably increased attention, the *caregiving* inequality continues to receive comparatively less. After divorce, mothers disproportionately suffer the consequences of the economic division of labor within the marriage; but fathers are disproportionately vulnerable to the effects of caregiving inequality within the marriage. Equitable divorce settlements should address not only the potential economic inequality in divorce but also the complementary emotional inequality, namely fathers' marginalization from the most satisfying, meaningful, and important job in the world. This marginalization, and the sense of disaffection it can fuel, plays its own role in the characteristic American patterns of family dissolution.

When a marriage is intact, each partner benefits from the other's services. The breadwinner gains from the caregiver's care of their children, and the caregiver gains from the breadwinner's work. Ideally, each experiences some vicarious satisfaction from the other's efforts. When there is a divorce, however, what was once perceived as working for the good of the family is now perceived as a source of inequality. The economic inequality derives from the primary caregiver's relinquishment of paid work. The emotional inequality derives from the primary breadwinner's relinquishment of caring for the children. No one can do

everything, and in a satisfactory marriage, each partner is usually willing to sacrifice something (for example, continued career
advancement or a closer relationship with children) for the sake
of the whole. But divorce often exhausts that goodwill, and the
compromises surface as inequalities.

The high incidence of divorce has generated much discussion
about the need for women to stay competitive in the workforce
and well employed throughout marriage to buffer the potentially devastating financial effects of marital dissolution. But we
hear comparatively little discussion of men's need to "stay competitive" in the caregiving domain, to remain intensively involved in parenting to guard against being marginalized in their
children's lives. Given the value we place on economic clout
and the relatively demeaned status of caregiving, this lack is not
particularly surprising. But it also reflects and maintains a bias,
apparently shared by women and men alike, that men's involvement in fatherhood need not be actively pursued or carefully
protected.

Many reasons might be offered for the virtues of a division of
labor in families. Some may argue, for instance, that maternal
care is preferable when children are very young because they are
more dependent on, or closer to, the mother, or because the father just isn't as interested. But we should acknowledge how
closely intertwined and mutually creating these conditions are,
and also what fathers risk losing out on as a result of this emotional situation. In her research about midlife, the psychologist
Lillian Rubin observed that mothers were often quite relieved,
even happy, when their children left for college or married,
whereas fathers tended to take it much harder. As she understood it, fathers were more pained because they felt they had
never really "lived" their children's childhoods:

> Whatever his feelings about his work, he generally
> spends most of his life at it — most of his emotional and
> physical energy being spent in pursuit of economic secu-
> rity for the family. Consequently, he's not there when

his children take that first step, when they come home from school on that first day. He's not there to watch their development, to share their triumphs and pains. Then, suddenly, one day it's too late. One day they're gone — gone before he ever had a chance to really know them.[10]

In the two decades since Rubin did her research, social norms have raised the standard for how involved fathers *should* be with their children, even if divorce and father absence often mean those norms are unmet. A father today is in a better position to feel and articulate his longing to care for his children than previous generations of fathers were. Still, the extent to which role divisions still favor men's performing as "ideal workers" and women as caregivers means that some of what Rubin describes remains in place.

Fathers sometimes actively collude in their own marginalization, as the sociologist Arlie Hochschild detailed in *The Second Shift*. They can become consumingly identified with their work, detached from relationships in general, fearful of entering the demeaned female arena of caregiving, or comforted by the mother-wife taking care of the family. Social and workplace norms constrict fathers' participation in family life, subtly influencing the construction of masculine identity by conveying that successful manhood involves being a provider. Men often do not consciously think through these pressures, but they unconsciously enact them.

However, the fact that men sometimes seem to "choose" their marginalization doesn't relieve us of the need to consider the effect of the caregiving inequality on men's involvement in family life; nor does it absolve us of the need to understand better the assumptions that underly it. Both men's and women's thinking about this issue is affected, for example, by the pervasive assumption that children need mothers more than fathers. A colleague of mine, a child psychologist who conducts mediation in high-friction custody cases, says she notices a consistent gender breakdown, in which mothers say, "My children need me," whereas fathers usually let it slip that they "want" to be with their children (until they remember the coaching that their attorney has given them, and assert that it is "good for" the children to be with them). It is significant that mothers often do genuinely experience their children as needing them more, and themselves as needing their children more. Do the fathers actually feel their children need them less? Do they feel they need their children less? Or has ideology shaped feeling, such that fathers have a hard time claiming that children need them as much as children need their mothers?

Adding yet another layer of complexity to all this, a mother's claims about her children's need for her may express a possessiveness toward them. A woman I know always supported wholeheartedly the view that men and women should share parenting equally, and she and her husband had managed to meet that ideal better than most. The children counted on both parents equally for planning playdates, doing the food shopping, and carpooling, and they turned to each parent equally for comfort and sharing confidences. Yet when the parents divorced, the woman argued that her status as mother entitled her to a greater portion of time with the children. In a related vein, my unsentimental colleague observed to me: "In mediation I far too often hear the mother in the divorcing couple insist that children are upset because they aren't spending enough time with her. Her solution to every problem is 'they need more time with me.' My thought is usually, we need to figure out a way to get them away from you more so that they don't have to take care of you." My colleague's view may minimize the mother's degree of insight into her children's needs; after all, such a mother has made a profession out of caring for her kids. But the fact remains that many women are strongly identified with the role of mother, in all its capaciousness. And that identification, in turn, affects their powerful and sometimes contradictory feelings about fathers' role as providers.

Father as Caregiver
Versus Father as Provider

ONE EVENING, SOME FRIENDS AND I were out to dinner, intently discussing a career choice that needed to be made by one of the women's husbands by the next day. As the wife laid it out, one job was very close to home, required only a year's commitment, was low pressure, and was relatively low paying. The other job required a forty-five-minute commute and a five-year contract and offered higher prestige, higher pay, and various seductive perks. The jobs were equally interesting. "The first job has everything we've been saying we're looking for," she said. "He'll have more time for the kids, we'll live at a slower pace. It's a step toward a more spiritual life. But then every time he says he's leaning toward that job, I think, wait a minute, what about saving for retirement, what about our mortgage, what about our standard of living? I feel like a total hypocrite."

None of us felt completely innocent; we recognized the basic contradiction. It is easy to believe that men and women should share child care equally or that men should not be immersed in the rat race. Easy to believe, that is, up until the moment when the plan might actually go into effect. Then we have to face wishes that are at some level incompatible: we aspire to gender equality and fairness, but we also want to be supported while we care for our children.

Each of the mothers at the table worked at a job that meant a lot to her: one was a teacher, one was a researcher, and two were therapists. Each was married to a man who worked longer hours and made more money than she did. Each woman liked it that way; it genuinely reflected the balance she wanted in her life. In that sense, each had succeeded in putting together a life she was happy living. Two of the women's husbands were unhappy in their current jobs, but none of the four resented shouldering the larger share of the family's financial burdens, and only one was actively lobbying to be home with the children more.

Seen through a certain lens, these women were still unfairly bearing the opportunity cost of parenthood. It was primarily *their* careers that had been limited when children came along. But these women were glad of that. They all wanted to be the more hands-on parent. Not only that, three of the four had been drawn to careers in the "caring professions," not notable for high pay, partly *because* they had envisioned these careers allowing them to adapt their schedules to child rearing. Seen in that light, the people getting the short end of the stick would appear to be the men. The buck stopped with them when it came to staying afloat financially. They had to work longer hours and had less flexibility in deciding to leave a job they disliked.

Like a gestalt drawing that looks like a rabbit or a duck, depending on our perspective, whether we see the typical woman's or typical man's predicament as preferable depends on what we focus on. If we focus on the unfettered ability to concentrate on work, the sense of effectiveness and accomplishment that comes from working and earning, or the satisfaction and comfort of having a spouse keep the home and children's lives running smoothly, then the men's position looks pretty good. But if we focus on the sense of connection to children, a greater variety of daily tasks, or relatively less responsibility in supporting the family, the women's position looks better.

Whether it is good or right for women to prefer this allocation of family labor, many do. In therapy it is not uncommon to hear a woman patient, while considering the good and bad points of a new love interest, wonder aloud at his capability to support her if they have children, even if she herself has an advanced degree and a highly paid job. In an economic sense, her concern can be understood as a rational calculation of whether she will have to withstand a demotion in living standard or class status if she takes time off to raise children. But it also relates, on a psychological level, to her notions about masculinity and femininity, her own maternal goals, and the meaning she associates with being provided for.

Even if men and women endorse gender equality in principle,

they often have powerful ideas about how providing links up with being a successful man or woman. More generally, people's ideals of gender fairness often accord imperfectly, even badly, with what they need to feel loving, loved, and sexually attracted. One woman, a very accomplished professional in her own right, felt that it was important for her husband to have a higher-paying job so that she could feel she respected him. It was as if his higher standing elicited from her a positive sense of his masculinity, which in turn made him attractive to her. The most non-gender-stereotypic woman I know once told me she had to have a tall boyfriend in order to feel "feminine." The most successfully role-sharing, egalitarian couple I know broke up suddenly, when the husband left his wife for a younger, less accomplished girlfriend. These aren't issues about which we can make social policy; they have to do with the emotional "feel" of whether a relationship works or not.

At the same time we should work to loosen the grip of these social valuations, a certain conservatism is built in to the fact that we each have one life, and we seek to make that life as liveable as possible within the cultural framework we find ourselves in. As the economist Shirley Burggraf noted, "sometimes the balancing act can be worked out and sometimes it can't; but even if it can . . . many people still cherish a degree of gender specialization."[11] A certain sense of difference, even the sense of having something to give the other person that he or she needs but hasn't obtained on his or her own, is often critical to a person's sense of impact and importance as a mate and a lover. That may not be the way it is "supposed" to be, but love and sexuality are rarely politically correct.

Marriage ideally provides more than what you could get in the strict exchange economy of the marketplace. In the best case, it joins fairness with the aspiration of fostering the growth of each partner. Most of us know people whose marriages follow the "cost center" model. Insisting that both members of the couple pull their own economic weight at all times is a buffer against unfairness, but it also constricts the aspirational opportunities that can be furthered by marriage. One spouse's desire to go back to school or change careers is met with the requirement that it not cost the family in time or money; another spouse can take an extended parental leave if it doesn't mean he or she decreases his or her contribution to the family pot. These arrangements insist on equity but at a certain price to flexibility, closeness, and trust.

In long-term relationships, a sense of justice is closely tied to love. If one or the other person does not feel treated fairly, it corrodes the bond. If they insist on strict equity in all things, the feeling of generosity can be diminished, which can also be destructive. Before we have children, we can fairly easily evaluate fairness in our partnerships: if he is cooking, I am doing the dishes; if I am working more, he is cleaning house. But when children arrive, the calculus of fairness becomes more complicated, and often in a particular way: mothers tend to be more riven with conflict between providing and parenting than men do. The most engaged, involved, loving fathers I know readily admit that going to work on Monday morning does not arouse anywhere near as much emotional conflict in them as it tends to arouse in their wives. And because of that, mothers are often less willing or less desirous of trading the care of children for paid employment.

On a practical level, how can we handle this asymmetry? Most obviously, it must be worked through on a personal level, one couple at a time. In my own case, the answer has been "a little of this, a little of that." My husband and I both believed that we would thrive best by sharing child care, in order to share equally the burdens but even more so to have equal access to the pleasures. When we had our first child, I was finishing my PhD and my husband was already an established professional. It became clear to me quite soon that I had a strong desire, the intensity of which made it feel like a need, to spend my time caring for our daughter. My husband took a month of paternity leave, and after that, worked a forty-hour week, working three long days and two short days so as to spend two afternoons with the baby while

I worked. By the time we had our third child, I felt I could not manage being adequately attentive both to my psychotherapy patients and to my children, all of whom legitimately required my physical and emotional presence, so I decided to discontinue clinical practice, at least for a time.

These decisions meant that my husband had to work harder. They also meant that we were moving farther from, rather than closer to, the stated ideal of sharing child care more or less equitably. With increasing numbers of children, the efficiencies of a stay-at-home parent and a working parent were clear to us — both in terms of economics (we didn't have to have business expenses for two separate practices, for example) and in terms of the total familial situation. My husband gave up some of the satisfactions of hands-on care and assumed the full burden of financial provision; he gained a sense of security that the children's care was continuous and good, that I was running the household and family dinners were reliably on the table, and that he was helping me do what I most wanted to do. I gave up the satisfactions and pay from my work as a therapist, a sense of connection to my professional community, and a certain feeling of being on a forward-moving "track" that would meet my ambitions. I gained an ability to focus on nurturing the children, the ease of not balancing multiple roles, and the chance to read and write, thanks to about fifteen hours of babysitting each week.

This situation was on the whole a harmonious one for us, and I think that has to do with what Arlie Hochschild brilliantly characterized as "the economy of gratitude" in marriage. A couple's satisfaction with their division of labor is deeply tied to what counts as "a gift" in their relationship. "When couples struggle," Hochschild wrote, "it is seldom simply over who does what. Far more often, it is over the giving and receiving of gratitude."[12] In our marriage, our division of labor worked in part because we agreed on the nature of "the gift." My husband and I both felt that caring for the children was a good to be prized; because of that, we both tacitly agreed that my husband's hard work was a gift to me. This was the 1990s, after all, and it was no longer considered an entitlement either for a father to work or for a mother to stay home. Couples needed to make an agreement about a division of labor; in our case, the agreement allowed me to do what gratified me, and it allowed him less of that gratification but let him practice a profession that he loved. He in turn felt that my desire and willingness to care for the children was a gift to him and to the family.

Now, of course, it was not all sweetness and light. At times I felt exhausted, put-upon, overworked, ungratified, and generally underappreciated. At the same time, I felt inhibited in my right to complain, since we had agreed, after all, that I had the better deal. I would wonder in those gloomy moments whether looking like a slob, spending one's days in a messy house with no hope of cleaning it up, finishing washing the dishes from one meal only to start in on the next really did constitute the better deal. I would darkly imagine my husband's pleasure at dressing in his suit and pressed white shirt, strolling down the street for a solitary cup of coffee during a break, and greeting friends and colleagues at various professional meetings.

I was most often restored at those times by a good night's sleep and a rational assessment of the inevitability of trade-offs and my own priorities. I had to admit that I had a lot more opportunities in my busy yet unregimented day for a whole variety of satisfactions: cuddling the baby, reading books, walking outside, and seeing friends, to name just a few. But perhaps just as powerful, acting as a subterranean stream to refresh and replenish me, was the value my husband placed on what I was doing and, significantly, his interest in doing the very things I was doing. He was not a man who "couldn't possibly imagine" spending his time taking care of the children, or who "wondered what I did all day." In our family culture, my job had all the value, all the "prestige" his did, maybe a bit more. As a result, I felt appreciated and just as important, I felt understood.[13]

In their study of marriage and the transition to parenthood, psychologists wonder why some couples deal with the arrival of a baby so smoothly and others suffer so acutely. They often find that a key factor in a couple's harmonious transition is whether the father joins the mother in undergoing a transformation, whether he consents to share the world of parenting and she allows him in.[14] I know that for me, my husband's eagerness to enter the world of parenthood with me was one ingredient in our accord. When that sharing doesn't happen, what gets in the way? At times, marital happiness derails when fathers continue to hanker after their wife's exclusive attention or when mothers resist letting their husbands into the parenting "loop." Both are suggestive of a not-universal but familiar tendency among new mothers to be pulled into an intense involvement with their children, which new fathers may perceive as an exclusion or threat. When women have children, they may begin to look to children to satisfy emotional needs that men continue to look to women to satisfy. The research on the transition to parenthood suggests the necessity of dealing constructively with this asymmetry, one that can affect everything from women's experience of sexual and maternal love to their ability to share parenthood to their feelings about whether they "need" men.

Letting Men In

WE ALL KNOW OF SITUATIONS where fathers are absent or virtually so. Volumes have been written about the toll that an overly exclusive mother-child relationship exacts. There is the pathological, claustrophobic variety, where the mother can't stand the child's separate existence. In Mona Simpson's novel *Anywhere but Here*, for example, young Anne is in thrall to her mother, who drives her cross-country to trade on her child-star potential. The father and the stepfather are history, and now mother and daughter are alone, hurtling along the highway. When Anne gets sullen, her mother kicks her out of the car and drives off. Anne describes her experience:

> I lost time then; I don't know if it was minutes or if it was more. There was nothing to think because there was nothing to do. First, I saw small things. The blades of

grass. Their rough side, their smooth, waxy side. Brown grasshoppers. A dazzle of California poppies. . . . [B]y the time I saw her car coming back, I'd be covered with a net of tears, my nose running. I stood there with my hands hanging at my sides, not even trying to wipe my face.[15]

In Anne's complete dependence on her only parent, she bends her perception to adapt to her mother's psychic tyranny.

There are other mother-child relationships that do not exclude all others — the mother has a network of involved friends, teachers, and so on — but simply lack a father. In some cases, a mother stridently dismisses the need of a father. In others, she reveals a gulf between her attachment to her child and her attachment to his father. As the writer Lisa Shea put it, "It wasn't until my son's father and I separated that I understood my notion of family didn't necessarily include being a wife, and that I may have wanted a child more than a marriage."[16] Ironically, sometimes a woman feels men are so dispensable precisely because her own father looms so large. No one quite measures up, or the woman is so fully identified with her father that she has no room for two "fathers" in the picture. In a contemporary twist, the "disappeared" father has been institutionalized in a whole new way by the widespread availability of anonymous sperm donation.[17]

Fathers are important to children not only because every child hungers for masculine, paternal love. Psychological theory also suggests that a crucial step in development is the child's ability to progress from a relationship between two people to a relationship between three people. In this transition, a child moves from her intense relationship with the caregiver to an enlarged circle of relationships that encompasses another person, one who loves not only the child but the caregiver as well. Taking her place in such a triad compels a child to wrestle with a basic limit with which all humans must contend, the boundary between the generations. A child's psychological development depends on recognizing that no matter how much he loves his mother or father, he cannot accede to the position of either's mate. Accepting generational limits is part of the difficult but necessary process of accepting the reality of the "outside world" — the reality that other people have relationships to each other that you cannot control and to which you must adapt. The triad itself may be more central than the sex of the parents. A lesbian or gay couple also provides an opportunity for children to observe and accept their place within a family in which two adults have a relationship with one another.[18]

Fathers and mothers are important to children, then, both in their own right and in their relation to each other. But once women have children, they sometimes find it hard to include men fully. An occasional topic of discussion among some new mothers is that while new fathers feel they've lost their relationship with their wives, new mothers feel burdened by their husbands' need for their attention.[19] Some women, once they have children, tend to feel "delight in motherhood, disappointment in marriage."[20] When marriages dissolve, fathers' sense of exclusion from the mother-child relationship plays itself out in some fairly predictable ways. Some fathers tend to see their attachment to their spouse and children as a "package," and divorce leads them to reject or drift away from their children.[21] Other fathers, reacting to a similar sense of exclusion, find that single parenthood is the first time they become truly involved with their children.

There are many practical, social, and economic reasons for mothers' relatively greater involvement with children, but there are deeper psychological sources as well. One such source may be a somewhat stronger tendency among mothers to turn to their children to gratify emotional needs for intimacy, warmth, and pleasure, needs that men seek to gratify primarily in their relationships with women. In her 1976 book *The Mermaid and the Minotaur*, Dorothy Dinnerstein argued that the ubiquity of female caregiving for babies and small children was at the heart of this asymmetry between women and men.[22] According to her view, the intense first attachment that boys and girls both have with a woman (their mother) meant that in adult heterosexual relationships, a man would be more likely to seek gratification with a woman, at the "source," as it were, to recapitulate his early erotic feelings for his mother. A woman, herself the "source," would find her erotic longing satisfied by a man, but because her earliest relationship also was with a woman, her erotic energies would continue to be more divided between women and men. If and when she had her own baby, a woman would relive the intense closeness she first experienced with her mother with her own child, expressing and satisfying, to some extent, her early erotic feelings for her mother.[23]

Here, the term "erotic" is to be understood broadly, as what Loewald called "the life or love drive," rather than as the focal seeking of sexual sensation.[24] Dinnerstein, like Freud, saw the early mother-child relationship as erotic, and she did not try to water this down. It is intense, it is passionate, but it is not sexually focused; rather, "the feeling, the vital emotional intercourse, between infant and parent is carried by touch, by taste and smell, by facial expression and gesture, and by mutual accommodation of body position."[25] In *The Eros of Parenthood*, Noelle Oxenhandler evokes a similar expansive understanding of the term:

> A mother cradles her baby against her body, she puts his mouth to her breast. She pulls his mouth from her breast, wipes his wet lips, holds him out for a moment at arm's length before nestling him against her shoulder. This is fusion and separateness. She tickles him under his chin and under his arms until his whole body wriggles with sensation; then she stops tickling and strokes his chin with firm, predictable, circular strokes until his body goes soft again. This is excitement and repose.[26]

Dinnerstein suggested, then, that women's erotic life (broadly conceived) was more wrapped up with their relationships with their children than was men's. This, in her view, was a problem, the solution to which was to be found in equalizing men's and women's caregiving roles. Exclusive maternal caregiving, according to Dinnerstein, gave rise to different erotic propensities in women and men and different sexual fears. It made women fearful of betraying their early love for their mother if they freely explored their erotic options or enjoyed sex unencumbered by the search for love. It made men fear the enormous, all-encompassing power of their first female love, and seek relief and control by compartmentalizing love and sex. Equalizing parenting roles, in this scenario, would allow women the greater sexual freedom that men enjoy, and would allow men the greater freedom to express parental love that women enjoy.

Dinnerstein deemed both of these outcomes crucial, but she was most concerned with the ways that unequal parenting roles had hobbled women. She worried that a woman's absorption in maternal activity thwarted her participation in "central human projects" and left her bearing the brunt of all our human ambivalence toward mortality, the flesh, and the loss of our first blissful union. And women's lack of sexual freedom and their ostensibly disabling tendency to fuse sex and love damaged their "brute sense of bodily prerogative, of having a right to one's bodily feelings. A conviction that physical urges which one cannot help having are unjustified, undignified, presumptuous, undercuts the deepest, oldest basis for a sense of worth; it contaminates the original wellspring of subjective autonomy."[27]

Though Dinnerstein gave full voice to the "eros of parenthood," her argument was skewed by a characteristically 1970s belief in the salvific power of sexual liberation. She placed much more emphasis on the notion that women seize their freedom by becoming more like men with regard to sex than on the second implication of her argument, namely that men are liberated by engaging more fully in the pleasures of caregiving. She did not, therefore, fully develop two important insights latent in her work: first, the ways in which mothering expresses "positive" aspects of women's erotic life, and second, the ways that men and women might come together not only through a similarly free orientation to sex but also through a similarly passionate pleasure in parenthood.

With regard to the first issue, Dinnerstein's dispiriting description of the effect of women's inhibited erotic freedom — namely, damage to "a brute sense of bodily prerogative" and a sense that one's urges are "unjustified, undignified, presumptuous" — could as easily be applied today to how some women regard their urges toward motherhood. Now, women are faced not so much with a lack of sexual freedom as with the pervasive supposition that eros has nothing to do with motherhood. When the eros of maternity is itself regarded not as an expression of "the brute sense of bodily prerogative" but rather as some sort of pale derivative, it leaves women confused and oddly ashamed about their powerful attraction to motherhood.

When we take seriously the notion of an "eros of parenthood," we notice that mothering babies and children is, for many women, a source of the same kind of integrating delight that we often associate with a fulfilling erotic relationship. I am not likening the eros of the mother-infant bond to genitally focused sexuality (redolent of potential exploitation). Nor am I recycling the threadbare notion that "women don't want sex, they want motherhood." But both these tempting misinterpretations demonstrate how hard we still find it to recognize and characterize the broader arena of eros in female experience.[28] Incidentally, we may not recognize huge swaths of female erotic experience as such because they appear so "diffuse." Motherhood is one such experience, of course; others are the threading of erotic pleasure through intimate friendships between women, or the self-adornment that passes simply as "feeling and looking one's best." Deriving erotic pleasure from multiple registers of sensual experience was labeled "polymorphous perversity" by Freud, but the psychoanalyst Adria Schwartz suggested the term "polymorphously diverse" to capture more accurately, and less pejoratively, women's multiple avenues of sensuality.[29] The psychoanalyst Dianne Elise asks whether we might better represent female pleasure not as "diffuse" but as "extensive."[30] Both attempt to articulate the kind of eros that plays a part in early mother-child relationships and that comes to affect women's adult sexuality as well as their experience of mothering. As we can see, treating eros and motherhood as separate, even incompatible, has contributed to a general mischaracterization of female erotic experience.

But our tendency to cleanly separate eros and parenthood has also led to an impoverished description of fathers' experience of caring for children and to a lack of exploration of how men might more completely join women in the transformation of parenthood. Practically speaking, men miss out on a large portion of child and infant caregiving. But their life with children is also affected by misunderstandings and stereotypes about the character of paternal love. Fatherly love is not only protective and providing, a love from a slight remove, but it is also tenderly nurturing and intensely felt, a love from "close in." It encompasses not only the moment of fatherly pride at a well-played Little League game but also the warm smile and shared delight while toweling a child after a bath. Not unlike maternal desire, fathers' love for their children remains a glaringly underdeveloped narrative.

What might an expanded view of eros, one that includes the realm of sensual, loving parent-child feeling, mean for the relationships between wives and husbands, mothers and fathers? For women, it suggests that their "extensive" erotic nature, potentially expressed in mothering, is not something infantile that they need to get over or grow out of, but can be every bit as central to their "brute sense of bodily prerogative" and their "subjective autonomy" as their sexual expression is. Becoming a mother is, for many women, a moment of communication about who they really are. If her partner dismisses or ignores its meaning to her, or finds it threatening, a woman can have the disillusioning experience of feeling she is not really known, or loved, or that she has less in common with her partner than she thought she did.[31] For men, viewing caring for children as a source of meaning and pleasure is arguably even more difficult than it is for women, in part because notions of masculinity tend to gather excessively around competition, status, and sexuality. But babies and children also powerfully connect men to their own "life or love drive"; and that truth further clarifies why it is important, as marriage researchers have observed, for men as well as women to open themselves to the changes of parenthood, to be receptive to the transformation of becoming a parent.

To understand better women's psychological barriers to including men fully in family life, we need to think about women's relationship to motherhood less flexibly in one way and more flexibly in another. The women I know who are most frustrated in their mothering are those whose financial or practical situation deprives them, in what they feel is an extreme way, of time to be with and care for their children. Trying to talk women out of this feeling is like trying to dismiss their sexual impulse as "all in their head." In other words, casting mothers' desire to care for their children as an atavistic urge they should outgrow puts women in a position eerily similar to the one they always seem to end up in, namely that whatever they want is somehow wrong. We envy penises because we feel we have nothing. We want sex, and we're insatiable or sluttish. We want motherhood, and we are masochistic, desexed, infantile, or fear success. To think "less flexibly" about women's desire to mother means, in other words, to accord the same honor to their yearning to have and care for their children that we accord to other things we regard as basic human needs.

At the same time, we need to think more flexibly about women's sense of prerogative about their role as primary parent. Given that what we see as essential about ourselves has inevitably passed through limitless acts of social shaping, and given that we are all susceptible to self-serving or self-deceptive distortions in our thinking, it does not suffice for a woman simply to assert her status as "mother" as the basis of her centrality to her children and to leave it at that. Women's sense of prerogative about their role as primary parent has complex, multiple meanings. One woman may express this sense of prerogative by excluding men. Another may feel "delight in motherhood, disappointment in marriage." Still another may allow herself to diagnose a man too quickly as emotionally unavailable, or to relinquish too readily the ideal of shared child care. Each response can serve as a rationale for retreating from the sometimes painful task of forging a collaborative relationship.

Paradoxical as it sounds, coming to a place of parental sharing with one's mate is intimately tied to awareness of one's maternal desire. Only in fully experiencing that desire, as well as our ambivalence and fears, can we open ourselves up to the importance of similar feelings in men. If a woman feels she can legitimately claim a central place for her motherhood only through authority and ownership, through a territorial insistence on her rightful sphere, then the ardent desires and wishes at the heart of that claim go unarticulated. If she sees her motherhood as "just the way things are" or "the way things are supposed to be," she relegates her mothering to the realm of determinism, essentialism, and "instinct," and evades the freedom and desire she could potentially express through it. Too often, that evasion has offered a way for women both to claim the role of primary parent (deriving their satisfactions under the radar screen) and simultaneously resent their oppression. To address the asymmetry, then, in which women attempt to gain from their children what men attempt to gain from women, we need to see women's delight in their children as answering a deeply anchored desire, and at the same time, to invite men more openly into that delight, and more fully into the family circle.

Fairness and Generosity

WHEN I BEGAN WRITING A book in earnest, and began to get paid for it, my husband breathed a sigh of relief. He had gracefully submitted to the yoke of provider, and now he was freed somewhat to think about what he wanted. He loved his work, but he had been working hard, he missed seeing his family more, and now that the breastfeeding phase of our last child was receding further into the past, we found no easily defensible reason why I should still be doing the greater share of child tending. The only real reason was built into the structure of our careers: he was more established and more experienced in his work. As a result, he could command a greater income than I could. That "advantage" had become a mixed blessing.

We both agreed in principle on what should happen — he should work less and take over more of the care of the children. What I didn't anticipate was the difficulty of the adjustment, not so much in practical terms, but inwardly. Of course, change is always hard; some phase of disequilibrium always intervenes before things settle into a new pattern. But the strain arose for reasons specific to the situation as well, because we had certain buried feelings we didn't quite know we had, and they took a while to understand.

First, I noticed that we dawdled a bit over changing our arrangement. I had passing thoughts in the course of my days that rationalized that delay. It seemed a lot of money to be giving up for just a few hours of child care; couldn't we find some less expensive way to arrange things? Or . . . now that I was making some money, shouldn't I have a chance to spend it on what *I* wanted (a new couch, or replacing our ugly windows)? Somehow I was slipping into a frame of mind that consciously I totally rejected: my husband's income was *our* money, but my income was *my* money.

As I was noticing my shameful line of thought, my husband was having his own concerns. He was wondering and worrying what it would do to my opinion of him if he cut back on work. What would his forgoing of income, his declaration of wanting to support the family through his presence rather than his work, and his trading ambition for family involvement mean to me? Would I respect him less? It seemed like such a retro question even to be entertaining. Yet, when I thought about it, I knew women who were outright contemptuous of their husband's lack of ambition or earning power, and the fusion of moneymaking with masculinity certainly pervades the culture. Did I unwittingly endorse it? I realized that I did not fear losing respect for my husband as a man. But his working less did raise an anxiety in me, having to do with another fear, more primitive in some way, of having my "supplies" withdrawn. I saw quite clearly how that fear, albeit irrational, linked up with an inner representation of my husband both as the "good mother" *and* the "good father," nurturing me through supporting me. And I also saw that if I had not become aware of the basic fear, but simply had reacted to it, it would have been easy to grab the handiest socially conventional barb ("You are falling down on your responsibilities") to sting him with and try to pressure him back into the status quo.

One thing that helped shake me out of my temptation to see my husband as simply a player on my internal stage was taking a clear-eyed look at his willingness to recognize, earlier in our life as parents together, the importance to me of having time to care for our babies. I simply could not have done what was most meaningful to me unless he had been willing and able to support the family financially. I believe that new mothers deserve that support, and that society as a whole should be doing a lot more to provide it; but that does not take away from the fact that men don't have to do it, and indeed, many men don't or can't do it.

The basic sense of support and security I feared I'd lose when my husband cut back on work was returned to me tenfold by his greater presence and involvement in the family. As many mothers have attested, when it is working, they feel a unique satisfaction in sharing parenthood and work responsibilities with their partner. For one thing, it is reassuring. When a father is at work and a mother is at home, he can usually feel confident that his children are in the hands of the other person who cares for them most in the world. When both parents are at work, the burden of wondering or worrying about the child care tends to fall disproportionately on the mother. But when she is at work and the father is at home, she is freed in a fuller way to focus on her work. And if her work is not intrinsically engaging, she still can rest easier with the knowledge that putting in her hours at work is not compromising her children's care.

Over and above this sense of reassurance, there is an active sense of pleasure. I take pleasure in seeing my husband doing certain things better with our children than I can, giving them things I can't give them as easily or as well. I enjoy seeing him have the opportunity to express certain sides of himself, or watching his closeness with them. Perhaps I feel most happy seeing how much the children enjoy him and rely on him. When my husband was able to stop working so hard and became the primary caretaker on afternoons when I worked, our son said one morning, "Mom, I love you," but then ran over to my husband and said, "Dad, I love you," and scrambled onto his lap. It was the first time in a long time that he had spontaneously chosen to engage more fully with his father than with me. A parent often misses out on those daily precious moments when he or she is the less hands-on parent.

GIVEN ALL I'VE SAID ABOUT the joys of sharing parenthood and the need to include fathers, a question remains: Is it sexist for a woman to feel she should be the primary caregiver for her baby or child? In answering that question, we must recognize, first, that for many women, it is based on an authentic, powerful, passionate wish. Such women are obliged to be aware of that wish; to do what they can to make certain, as the Buddhist teacher Jack Kornfield put it, that their path is connected to their heart.[32] The error, however, is then to insist that this feeling is based on a mystical, essential core that dictates what *should* happen. Maternal desire should not be a platform from which to make a power bid or a decision by fiat about how things should be arranged. Recognizing maternal desire should work as a springboard, a starting point for uncovering, sorting, and communicating about how we want to live our lives. A father or prospective father needs to go through a similar process.

This requires doing what scares many people when it comes to role division in parenting: namely, having a conversation. Not simply about logistics but also about feelings, doubts, and uncertainties about what one's feelings even are. Voicing fears and hopes is hard not only because traditions run deep, or because parenthood is hard to anticipate, but also because decisions about how to raise our children relate so centrally to our identities and what we each want from life. Some women get the message that they are weak or irresponsible to miss a beat, to *want* to miss a beat, when children come along. Others are disappointed when their husbands expect them to stay home. Whatever the issues for a given couple, becoming parents is one area where unconscious, "default" frameworks can hold enormous, almost blinding, sway. Consciously considering these frameworks can frighten and disorient, and even upend basic assumptions on which a relationship rests. Fearing adjustments, and knowing so little about what to expect, couples can temporarily delude themselves that they will return to "normal" at some point soon after the baby is born. Yet, frightening as it is, expecting a child is also a time of hopefulness, possibility, and transformation. If love is "the will to extend one's self for the purpose of nurturing one's own or another's spiritual growth,"[33] new parenthood presents an opportunity to engage not only in an infant's growth but in one's own and in one's partner's as well.

Take a not unusual contemporary example. A husband and wife were both academic researchers in the same field. When they had a baby, they were committed both to sharing the care of their child and continuing to pursue their work at a similar level. A conference in another city at which the mother was planning to present her work occurred when the baby was five months old. She was still nursing, and she had made the assumption, without really thinking, that she would of course take the baby with her. Though her husband knew how reflexively and "naturally" his wife made this assumption, he initiated a conversation about this arrangement. They had decided to share the baby's care. If that was what they intended to do, he felt their baby should stay home with him, where he was available to care for her in familiar surroundings with no disruption to her routine. This took an adjustment for the mother, in her thinking and her emotions. But on balance she agreed. It was fairer; it did not deeply or lastingly impinge on the basic structure of her relationship with her baby. She would still nurse, though perhaps not quite as often, when she got back. She would be strengthened in her sense of her husband's parental competence, which she had never doubted but on which she'd focused some anxieties. She would have the feeling of sharing something precious with him, not only because she gave to him something she herself had a hard time parting with, but also through their strengthened sense of shared enterprise.

If she had insisted on her "right" to be "the mother," it would have foreclosed an opportunity for understanding each other's wishes and fears, and for saying what needed to be said. The couple therapist Daniel Wile has pointed out that couples having arguments sometimes "employ powerful, irrefutable, culturally sanctioned complaints to try to get across points they are having difficulty getting across."[34] People are tempted to use slogans (her: "You never help with housework"; him: "You're a nag") to justify feelings that they don't quite understand. The heart of a couple relationship, in Wile's view, is "saying what you need to say and feeling that it has gotten across."[35] In this sense, we can see that many of the standard, genderized arguments between men and women — including about parenting — are a way not to know, or not to risk expressing, our greatest vulnerabilities. If this woman had insisted on her "right to be the mother," it might well have arisen from, and obscured, her fear that if she shared care with the father she would feel less close to her baby, or she would feel worse about herself as a mother. Being able to talk about the underlying issues is necessary if we are to express ourselves fully and if we are to feel understood. It also provides the best chance a couple has to feel close and connected.

At a time — early parenthood — when gender roles are both conservative and contested, it is very hard to rouse oneself from the fatigue, the petty resentments, and the stress of baby care to articulate what we really need and want. Yet during this time, couples also yearn for appreciation of the gifts they have given each other. We live at a cultural moment when women feel conflict not only about how involved we want to be in the care of our children but also about the role of men. In some ways the two are connected. Women feel conflicting things, and so we give mixed messages. We can feel exasperated and unsupported and lonely that men are not our full parenting partners, but we may also subtly and not so subtly demand that men provide for us or acknowledge our parental primacy. For women to genuinely help men come into the place of greater family connection, we have to deal honestly with the competing messages we send. One step in this direction is to try to understand and communicate the place maternal desire occupies in our minds and hearts. That process is not about defining our desire as opposed to or in contrast to men's. Rather, it is speaking from the heart about our desires, in true conversation with men.

12

Time with Children

WHEN OUR THIRD CHILD WAS born, it was June. He was a big baby, but he was my first easy birth. He was heavy, and for weeks I'd felt as if he might simply drop out of me. I fretted over the countless possible circumstances of his coming, about where I might be when it started, and with whom, since our second child had come eight minutes after we arrived at the hospital, and could well have been born in the car. But in the end, there was no rush. The baby remained securely settled till his due date. I was four centimeters dilated, and had been for days, when we decided to break my waters. The grandparents had long since arrived, and my husband was able to leave work unhurried. So, at noon on a cloudless spring day, he and I found ourselves driving to the hospital, nervous and almost shy to be alone again with this rite of passage before us, knowing that no words could make a bridge between this luminous, ordinary moment and the fruition, so near at hand, of the deep bloody marriage of our bodies.

That summer, I was happier than I had ever been in my life. I felt calmly ecstatic, in a place of lively rest. Was this the peace that came of having ridden the anxieties and strains and excitements of my fertility and having arrived safely at the other side? I felt light and heavy in my body at the same time, akin to the repose of sated passion. Yet my state of being was more continuous, less drowsy, and more alert. I felt I had satisfied my passion with the universe. We were content with each other; we'd done well.

During the first days of my son's life, while relatives were still there to entertain the older children, I read *The Leopard* while I nursed. It is a book of exquisite melancholy, the story of a magnetic Sicilian prince whose waning years coincide with the twilight of southern Italy's monarchic rule. Di Lampedusa wrote his novel in the last two years of his life, and his descriptions of the parched, unforgiving earth, of the nonchalant cruelties that pass for love, of the prince's last wisps of consciousness, are the product of a mind on intimate terms with life and death. On a still morning when everyone else went down to the park, I sat alone with the baby, listening to his newborn breaths as he slept on my lap and later his snuffling, hungry sucks. I could hear the cooing of the mourning dove perched on the telephone wire above the street, and the crows' cawing farther down the hill. Out the window were drooping sunlit spider webs the children would later inspect and destroy, and butterflies, whose darting, bright lives are measured in days. I could not have been more full; life could not have been more sweet. And at the same time, there was also that ache, at "the rustling of the grains of sand as they slid lightly away,"[1] and at my baby's sleeping breath; that ache of beauty and longing and time and the unbearable fragility and surpassing preciousness of this moment.

Perhaps because I felt full, I could bear to gaze at the naked contours of my yearning. This yearning had no object, at least no visible, earthly one. I have heard it called "the nostalgia for the present." There is the well-known biblical passage from 1 Corinthians: "For now we see through a glass, darkly; but then face to face: now I know in part; but then shall I know even as also I am known."[2] The words capture the expectant yearning, the urge to see behind the veil, which seems to be part of the very fabric of love. When we love, we are never spent, there is always more. Love seems to encompass a feeling of seeking but of never quite reaching. Its yearning is like a question with no final answer; to love life, to love other people, it seems, is to tenderly embrace that question.

. . .

THERE WERE SEVERAL THINGS THAT made the time with my children over that summer and the year that followed so happy. For one, I was able to give myself over to it. After the roller coaster of my three maternity leaves and a move, my clinical practice had diminished by attrition. Though we didn't know what the future would bring, in the short term, while we had an infant and two small children, we could afford to live on one salary. As I am a psychologist, my independent interests also lay in the same direction as parenthood. I felt grounded and constructive when responding to the children's needs and desires, in the countless acts of diapering, feeding, filling cups, fastening shoes, comforting, and answering questions. One source of pleasure was doing different things while in each other's company. I liked reading a book while I was nursing the baby, while the five-year-old was drawing in another room and the two-year-old was pretending to be Prince Philip falling off his horse or building with blocks somewhere near my feet. I felt integrated in those moments — physically engaged with the baby, intellectually engaged with my book, emotionally engaged with my son and daughter and, of course, with the baby and the book, in harmony with everything around me and with life.

At home with the children I made sacrifices, but I did not sacrifice myself. I was one of the personalities, one of the players. We all had our wills, and we all loved one another. How would we make this work? Sometimes I played with them. Sometimes I took care of the household, cooking, cleaning, and dealing with the constant mound of paperwork. Sometimes I read a book, an activity that could feel as absorbing to me as they were. Sometimes they pulled the book out of my hand and said, "Stop reading!" and sometimes they went off and got lost in their own fantasy play.

As sleep deprivation once more receded and professional engagement returned as a valued goal, I felt increasingly compelled to focus my intellectual effort on understanding the most central thing in my life, taking care of children. My decision to write about it was possible because my husband was able and willing to support the family, and it was satisfying because it gave me a way to integrate my life as a psychologist and my life as a mother. Its chief advantage was that it allowed me to pursue my goals — to have time with the children, to engage in intellectual work, and eventually to make an income — in a way that helped me cope with the feeling of being pulled in different directions by my children and my work.

My particular solution to the dilemma of children and work is obviously not available, or attractive, to everyone. But the basic issues it was intended to address in my own life are central to many mothers' lives. Mothers everywhere want more freedom to be responsive to their children; they want the enormous importance of their nurturing to be acknowledged; and they suffer when they are unable to put together an arrangement that satisfies both their economic and psychological need for employment and their sense of the value of caring for children.

Women thinkers a generation before me, blessed like me with education and opportunity, cogently anatomized mothers' oppressions. Adrienne Rich, though she gestured toward the transformative potential of maternal pleasure, trained the force of her analysis on its corruption by patriarchal culture. My own experience drew me to charting the pleasures of caring for babies and small children, the very aspect of motherhood that Rich had intermittently found so painful. Certainly the realm of maternal pleasure is much wider than that; some mothers find their keenest delight in conversation with their older children, others express their maternal gifts in spheres wholly other than the traditional, domestic one. But it was in attempting to analyze my desire to care for my small children, and to place that desire in the broader context of women's aspirations and our social life, that it occurred to me that the radical promise of exploring maternal pleasure had remained unfulfilled.

De Beauvoir asked, all those years ago, "What is a woman?," and her answer reverberated in every subsequent treatment of motherhood. "One is not born, but rather becomes a woman," she wrote, meaning that the defining property of the social category "woman" was not her female physique, but her status as "a person who is not expected to set her own agenda in the world."[3] Ever since, it has been hard to rescue our willingness to take care of others from the taint of inauthenticity, to see it as anything other than a refusal of risk or freedom. It has been hard, in other words, to see our desire and choice to care for children as one way we set our own agenda in the world.

It may once have been true that the price of a woman's social acceptance was that she leave her ambitious, striving self outside the door. But today, she is as likely to be urged to leave outside, or at least politely hide, her intensely emotional concern about caring for her children. Virtually every area of women's reproductive and caregiving lives has been distorted by the fear that if we admit the importance of having and caring for children, we somehow risk losing our opportunities, our freedom, and even our dignity as persons. Over the years, feminist writing has cast a skeptical eye on the meaning to mothers themselves of taking care of children. Psychoanalytic writings have at times implied that caring for children and desire have little to do with one another. Debates about day care gingerly step around the complicated fact that for many women, caring for their children is a way to connect both to their children and to themselves. Theories of adolescent girlhood slight the role that mothers' satisfaction in caregiving plays in helping daughters to value themselves and their own maternal potential. An array of psychological and social forces contribute to women's confusion and ambivalence about their desire to mother, which in turn render their attitudes toward fertility and the specter of infertility particularly charged. Maternal desire is all but absent from the arguments on either side of the abortion rights issue, regarded as irrelevant or politically dangerous. And with respect to the role of fathers, our efforts to share parenting more equally are impeded not simply by structures of work and entrenched gender socialization but also by the conflicting feelings mothers have, and the mixed messages they send, about the meaning they attach to caring for children.

The project of understanding maternal desire has only just begun. For so long, "maternal" and "desire" seemed contradictory; in conjoining them, we can begin to develop a psychological language for the autonomous goals and creative intentions that women have expressed in mothering all along. We may disagree on many questions confronting women, but we can all endorse the fundamental value of women's ability to interpret their own desires and become authors of their own lives. Giving maternal desire the centrality in our thinking that it has in our experience can only help us toward that goal.

I HAVE BEEN SPEAKING THROUGHOUT about time with children. And I have been speaking of how availability to children can allow for a certain quality of time together. But of course, this is precisely the kind of time that many parents lament not having. Surveys document that not having enough time for their children ranks high as a source of parental dissatisfaction.[4] A friend commented that she realized she and her husband never fought about money, but they often fought about time. "Time-saving techniques" are a women's magazine staple. Scholarly studies like Hochschild's *The Second Shift* and Schor's *The Overworked American* confirm our impression that our time for emotional connection with our families has eroded. There are plenty of obvious reasons for this: longer commutes, the need to take on more jobs to make ends meet, the throwing back on the individual of things that used to be taken care of by the government or workplace, such as retirement planning or school lunches. Looming largest, perhaps, is our society's ongoing inability to adjust to the loss of domestic labor as women have "transferred the major portion of their labor to the marketplace."[5]

Yet some researchers call into question the widely held belief in our "time famine," observing that Americans have reduced their work hours and gained free time in the last thirty years.[6] Studying what people actually do moment-to-moment with their day, Robinson and Godbey found gains in free time from 1965 to 1995 among women and men, the employed and unemployed, whites and blacks, married people and single people, parents and nonparents, and the young, middle-aged and elderly.[7] These researchers argue that our speeded-up pace of life, responsible for our perception of "time famine," has been erroneously attributed to more hours of work.[8] In their view, there is a conspicuous discrepancy between people's actual balance of work and free time and their perception of it.

In light of these findings, Robinson and Godbey ask what is fueling our subjective sense of "time famine," even as we enjoy relative time "plenty." One gloomy undercurrent is that people's free time is often available in fragments, and instead of using fifteen minutes here or there to have a conversation, find a recipe, pay some bills, or play with a child, they choose to spend it watching TV. If Robinson and Godbey's findings are correct, watching television turns out to be how Americans spend a huge amount of the additional free time they have gained in the last thirty years. But the researcher's question spurs us to consider larger issues than simply the activities, however mindnumbing, that Americans spend their time on. It encourages us to consider that scarcity of time is not only a factual reality, but also a psychological construction. As such, it encodes perceptions and carries messages of the culture. Part of understanding the conflicts we have about time with children entails decoding some of these messages.

The reigning metaphor by which we live is that time is money.[9] We speak of saving time, wasting time, investing time. In the middle and upper classes, a worker's time is quite valuable in monetary terms, disposing people to think in terms of the cost of not working, the cost of leisure time, and the cost of not using their time efficiently. People try to increase the "yield" on their time by what Robinson and Godbey call "time deepening": trying to fit more into a given unit of time by speeding up an activity (zooming down the supermarket aisles, driving fast), choosing activities that can be done quickly (ordering take-out instead of cooking), or doing more than one activity at once (eating and drinking while doing income taxes or watching a movie on an airplane trip). We peg our sense of value to time's efficient use, and we become annoyed if others "waste" our time. The person with the least time to spare is the most important, though in many cultures that person would simply be considered rude.[10]

"Time deepening" underlies the notion of "quality time," which is an attempt to accomplish "efficiently" in a smaller unit of time the same parent-child closeness and engagement achieved by leisurely companionship. People have become understandably skeptical of the notion of quality time in recent years, because they sense that how cared for people, especially children, feel in relationships is strongly affected by their loved one's actual presence. We may pride ourselves on our ability to multitask, but at a certain point multitasking and caregiving collide. Without a certain level of attentiveness to loved ones, people risk multitasking their way right out of relationships.

Still, the view that time, like money, is a commodity (one we never have enough of) pervades our relationships with our children, just as it pervades our lives in general. Observe, for instance, some of the adaptations parents, especially affluent ones, make to the worth of their time in the marketplace. Catalogues purvey toys, documents sociologist Allison Pugh, intended to mechanically supply "parents in absentia": a Winnie the Pooh doll that "reads" to a child, a radio-controlled pitcher that allows a child to teach himself to bat, an electronic dog whose "red eyes flash, in approval."[11] Parents exploit the vast differential in first world and third world wages by hiring caregivers who leave their own children in their home country under the care of someone else.[12] Our "time is money" mind-set works at cross-purposes with what is inherently valuable in human relationships, expressing the devaluation of care that operates on a global scale and affects us all.

Related to this is the tendency to view as a "weakness" a posture of humility before the mystery of time's workings. Books like *The Rules* counsel women on strategies for obtaining a husband and children, seemingly harkening back to a "simpler" time when gender traditionalism prevailed. But they also advocate a thoroughly contemporary bid for control, saying, in effect, that women have no time for mystery, for ambiguity, for the development of feeling. To have patience for love is to be a wimp. They unabashedly treat men as product, with no appreciation of the irony that this guarantees they will be treated in exactly the same way.[13] They try to apply the lessons of our culture — be in charge, succeed in the free market — to women's traditional "disempowered" receptivity.

Where children are concerned, many a child therapist finds herself depressed by the number of parents who come in seeking help for their child, because the child has not excelled on their timetable. It is somehow the mark of a successful parent to insist that their children are accelerated in everything, not simply keeping up with their peers but surpassing them.[14] We see the effects in the children's faces. A third-grade boy wears the slightly smug, slightly scared expression of someone who knows he's supposed to be special but isn't quite sure why. A friend of mine worries that her son feels "too normal" in his class of super-high achievers. Another friend tells me that her child's school has a "community service" requirement built into the curriculum, which everyone understands to be a résumé padder for gaining secondary school admission. She worries it is teaching the children not so much compassion as a bloated sense of self-congratulation.

These tendencies in our thinking about time and achievement can be understood as part of a more general orientation identified over twenty-five years ago by the psychoanalyst Erich Fromm, the orientation toward "having," as opposed to "being." When we are oriented to having, our agenda is to possess. In the having mode, we define ourselves through our property, in which we include not only our material possessions, but also our bodies, our egos, our relationships, our feelings, our experiences, and our problems. This orientation is so basic to how we as a culture think about time, money, things, and ourselves that we hardly notice it. We consume not only material goods, but also information, education, and experiences, and we define ourselves by what we consume. In the case of women, the slogan "having it all" expresses deeply valued aspirations in terms of a checklist of acquisitions (partner, children, home, job). We treat our ego and its cravings as real and legitimate. The success of our economic system in part derives from harnessing the enormous power and self-regenerating nature of human craving. It incites craving through its success at creating endlessly imaginative new ways to satisfy it.

When we are oriented to being, our agenda is to be "at one with." We are concerned not so much with things as with *processes* of living, knowing, and loving. We seek after authentic relatedness with other people. We seek to get beyond appearances, and plumb the depths. Spiritual visionaries from many traditions have made the distinction between having and being a central one in their systems of human development. They have sought to discern the nature of true human freedom, which they see as related to freeing inner activity from ego boundedness and craving. As Fromm characterizes this distinction,

> the process going on in persons who are aware of themselves in depth, or who truly "see" a tree rather than just look at it, or who read a poem and experience in themselves the movement of feelings the poet has expressed in words — that process may be very productive, although nothing is "produced." Productive activity denotes the state of inner activity; it does not necessarily have a connection with the creation of a work of art, of science, or of something "useful."[15]

An unlikely messenger of the being mode is one of my favorite children's books, *Peek-A-Boo!*, by Janet and Allan Ahlberg.[16] As in many books for children, nothing much is accomplished.

A baby plays peek-a-boo with his family throughout the day — when he wakes up, at breakfast, during chores, at the park, at supper, at bath, and at bedtime. What charms me as a reader is how messy the house is. The mother and father in every frame are tending to the tasks of life — washing windows, ironing, cooking, feeding children, bathing the baby — with no illusion of completion; around them are a jumble of children's toys and shoes, heaps of dirty laundry, open drawers, and sponges soaking in the sink. The pictures burst with the *process* of living, with the thousand undone jobs that betoken the priority of responsiveness over efficiency that makes for a happy family. A starker contrast to the pristine, lifeless tableaux of *Martha Stewart Living* could not be found. Though Martha's surfaces seduce, you need no more than a nanosecond to determine which emotional world you'd rather live in.

Many of our child rearing practices are steeped in a preoccupation with having. Traces can be found all around us. Take, for instance, the top-selling *Baby Einstein* and *Baby Mozart* videos, intended to jump-start your six-month-old's mental ability. The videos' content is cute and innocuous (if suspiciously hypnotic), but the fantasy their promotional strategy attempts to induce is creepy: if you sit your child down and give him something to consume passively, out will come a process — that is, thinking. These videos are the infant equivalent of the language tapes you put under your pillow to "learn French as you sleep" or the vibrating waistband you wear to "take off pounds effortlessly." There is no shortcut where process is concerned. But the product's appeal is that it taps into the illusion that you can pay money to buy a *thing*, and it will magically induce a (thinking) *process*, without the human interaction or teaching and without the work or time that are essential to that process.[17]

Trapped in the paradigm of having, we have trouble seeing what is so misguided about our contemporary efforts to imbue children with self-esteem. We note that children don't feel good enough about themselves, so we heap them with praise, we give every kid a medal at the school Olympics, and declare "every child a winner." But the open secret about this shortcut is that true self-esteem arises in the context of being cared for by others, being truly educated by one's teachers, and doing the hard work of self-development. In an era when, as historian Elisabeth Lasch-Quinn puts it, "norms that once characterized life among only the most deprived Americans have become universal,"[18] the real work of caring and teaching that lead to an internal sense of worth are in ever shorter supply and are increasingly treated as expendable. After all, why bother paying the high price of true caring and teaching when you can paper over the problem with a gold star?

It may be a cliché, but it seems that the children with the most stuff are often the ones whose parents are around the least. Perhaps material possessions are the guilty parent's attempt to make up for his or her absence. But I also think it has to do with a worldview oriented toward having, which underlies both the acquisition of toys for the children and titles for the adults. Such children are indoctrinated into a world that replaces relationships to people with relationships to things. Especially in some sectors of the upper middle class, one observes a redefinition of family life that says nothing is lost when both parents are away from their babies and small children for most of the day. These parents tend to employ a great deal of household help, and when tensions erupt between them about who is doing what, the solution is, as often as not, hiring more help. Rather than struggle with inconvenient longings, they deny that they have given anything up, like the academic I know whose life was consumed with getting tenure and yet who believed that he had sacrificed no time with his three children in the process. Or they behave as if their children don't really need them, like the mother who felt it wasn't really worthwhile to be home with her baby until he was old enough for her to "teach him things." Often as not, though, they revise their stories to suit their goals. The mother who thinks she should be home when her son gets older finds that now that he is in preschool, she really doesn't need to be home after all. The stories shift to fit the circumstances because there is an underlying resistance to kneeling down in front of the mystery of the "other," to getting down on the floor and discovering something genuinely new.

THE CULTURAL ETHOS OF "HAVING" puts parents in an odd position with respect to the nurture of children. First off, it pulls us toward material acquisition and away from time with children. Second, it encourages us to view our children as our most valuable commodities. Note, for example, the text on a billboard for the financial company Citicorp: "Your most important asset is the one who is asking you when you are going to raise his allowance."[19] But even more broadly, it subtly favors the tendency to see people and relationships less as ends in themselves than as "assets," accomplishments, or instrumental means to some other end. Citicorp's ad copy, jarring as it is, is not half so jarring as the advertiser's confidence that we will be attracted by its message, that the vision of parenthood it presents is one we will aspire to make our own.

This is one contemporary way in which becoming a mother presents a crisis to women. Within the paradigm of having, we feel responsible, even virtuous, when we can manage to conceptualize our activities as quantifiable accomplishments. But relating to children is stubbornly resistant to that formula, and the more time a mother spends doing it, the more some recess of her conscience may charge her with "accomplishing nothing." Thus it is that a general societal problem is experienced by individual women as a problem of personal identity.

A high-achieving woman became pregnant and was exceedingly happy. But within a very few weeks, once past the iffy first trimester, her joyful anticipation gave way to an intense preoccupation with how time off tending a baby would allow others to view her as weak or inferior for having "dropped out of the race." Each time she began to accept her uncertainty and tried to honor what she was authentically grappling with, she would become absorbed with how to forestall the loss of others' respect and to manage a semblance of "staying on track." Her superego seemed to have become a chorus of name-calling peers all too ready to deride her for going nowhere. And at those moments, she feared she would no longer have anything of value if she left her job and stayed home with her baby; what her job gave her — status, power, prestige, and a voice in the world — were central to her sense of success as a human being.

Even when a prospective mother tries to question her own assumptions, resisting the dominant ethos is tricky, because to a significant degree, women's equality and autonomy have been defined in terms of our refusal of traditional roles and our claiming our rightful piece of the economic pie. A full-page ad in the *New York Times* on "Take Your Daughter to Work Day" extols the corporate sponsors whose support means that "more girls aged 9–15 would rather sit on the board of directors of a doll manufacturer than actually play with one [*sic*]."[20] Indeed, women's advancement is cast as synonymous with minimizing the value of caring work and rejecting the "passivity" of the orientation it relies on. Years ago, college seniors at Wellesley protested the choice of Barbara Bush as a graduation speaker on the grounds that her only qualification was her husband's political success. As economist Shirley Burggraf observed, the students "seemed not to understand . . . the extent to which their lives were literally built on their own mothers' contributions. Many of the protesting students probably would have never made it to Wellesley, or even have been born, if their mothers and grandmothers hadn't done the kind of work that Barbara Bush did."[21] It is obviously wrong to divide the sexes, as we have historically, into "having, doing" males and "being" females. Yet this dichotomy is alive and well in the Wellesley students' impression that mothers don't "do" anything worthy of recognition. The students appeared to accept the basic terms of the hierarchy that places women's caring work at the bottom rung, though presumably they intended to escape that devalued status themselves.

At the same time that the culture gives women the message that only by collaborating with the values of the marketplace

can they garner security, independence, and self-respect, we de-
monize "the working mother" for her cold-hearted self-interest
and tell punitive morality tales about the costs of her choices.
This is just one more means by which women are co-opted into
shouldering the burden of society's incongruous values, a point
that was cogently argued by sociologist Sharon Hays in her book
The Cultural Contradictions of Motherhood. Of course, this double
message falsely dichotomizes the world of women and mothers
into acquisitive "working" mothers and affiliative "non-working"
mothers. Women's paid employment obviously fulfills many
purposes in addition to the economic, including affiliation and
the enactment of deeply held social values. The categories of
"working" and "non-working" mother too often function as code
for other variables entirely.

The pull of our acquisitive culture is also not uniquely relevant to working mothers, much as the popular press might paint
it that way. It exerts an enormous pull on stay-at-home mothers
as well. At the extreme affluent end of the spectrum, it is not a
rarity for "stay-at-home" mothers to have their children in all-
day child care while they fill their time with shopping or staying
fit. These women, and the husbands whose all-consuming careers support their lifestyles, have voted with their feet to put
things before people. But this is a relatively small sector of society. Most mothers who do not work have taken that path precisely because they believe there is value in the parental care of
children. As Sharon Hays found, many mothers endorse the
value of intensive mothering in part as an explicit protest against
the dehumanizing aspects of the marketplace.[22]

But these mothers' situation with respect to our culture of commodities is also ambiguous. First of all, unlike the women of *Lysistrata*, who withheld sex from their husbands until they stopped
making war, the stay-at-home mother's hands-on care of her children often *requires* her partner to don his armor and step into the
fray of overwork. Moreover, we are all so immersed in metaphors
of "productivity" and "results" that the stay-at-home mother must
fight the impulse to write herself a job description that defines

her effectiveness in terms of her children's measurable accomplishments. The pull for full-time mothers to try to give their mothering work the sheen of productivity is particularly strong, perhaps, because they feel vulnerable, inwardly and outwardly, to the charge that caring for kids amounts to "doing nothing," to a waste of their skills and earning power. The spouse of a well-educated stay-at-home mother made a particularly pointed version of this charge. He said her prestigious college should have admitted someone else who would have actually *used* the degree, as if "using her degree" to be a good mother to his children wasn't use enough! (His stance was particularly ironic given the fact that children's school performance is related to their mother's level of education.[23]) In the current atmosphere, it is not surprising that women who devote their time to caring for children might seek to convince themselves and the world of the "value added" by their presence at home.

The "responsible" stay-at-home mother, then, feels pulled to schedule a roster of activities for her toddler, launching him on the path of being "well-rounded" and herself on the path of high-intensity child-focused chauffeuring.[24] We earnestly evaluate the local baby gym class's techniques for enhancing sensorimotor skills, only dimly aware that its glossy brochure is a crass marketing ploy to convince parents that children need pricey classes to acquire skills they will develop naturally anyway. The marketplace machinery that creates needs in order to fill them is up and running in babyhood, and one's sense of being a "good parent" often becomes tied to whether, how much, and what one consumes on behalf of one's child.

The whole point of those gym classes, of course, is for children to run around on equipment they don't have at home and to have fun. We all know that. But the way they are pitched reveals a facet of the weirdly constraining ethos of parenting today, whereby the responsible parent will look with suspicion on something that is "just" for fun. Piano lessons and music classes are routinely advertised as enhancing math skills. We have a hard time escaping the dictate of our conscience that all our actions must be means to some other end. When we give our children piano lessons to improve their math skills, we feel we are being good parents. Even when our goal is intrinsic — we are taking a hike for the sheer pleasure or beauty of it, for instance — we often explain it to ourselves as instrumental ("I need the exercise") to still our fear that perhaps otherwise it is a "waste."

Why is it depressing to measure children's success, or our own, in terms of quantifiable "packets" of experience? What is grating about watching a mother cooing back and forth with her baby while she changes a diaper suddenly burst into a lesson in counting? It is something about her overeager intrusion of teaching into a moment of communion. One feels the mother attempting to take their fullest moment of being "at one" and colonizing it in the lesser project of skills acquisition. Amid all our talk of productivity, the true waste is this: at the one time in our lives when our children offer us the unconditional gift of being loved beyond measure, we retreat, as if we can't even let ourselves feel it unless we make some gesture toward proving we've earned it. We struggle mightily to turn the miracle of being into having, hoping somehow to stanch the waterlike flow of moments that burble by without ever allowing us to possess them.

FOR MOTHERS, ALL THIS AMOUNTS to a turning away from our intrinsic value to our children, and a shielding of our eyes against the blinding knowledge of our amazing, undeserved importance. We may distract ourselves by offering things in our place, as if our human presence were not infinitely more valuable than a stimulating toy. We may manage our anxiety in the face of this awesome reality by grabbing at whatever ideological security blanket best comforts us: railing against unrealistic models of "intensive mothering" as victimizing women, touting maternal duty and saying nothing of maternal joy, claiming that children don't need all the attention that the soft-hearted or the traditional say they do. Yet whatever position we take, it serves in part to help us cope with the gap between our enormous aspiration and our sense of insufficiency in living motherhood as intensely as we can. I remember as a graduate student attending a weekend meditation retreat, where every breath, every glance at a flower, seemed to bring me back to the problem of death. When it was my turn for a brief meeting with the Zen master, I told him of my thoughts. He responded simply: "Better now than in the oxygen tent." The early years of our children's lives give us a unique opportunity to embrace living fully, in all its fatigue, moodiness, laughter, inconvenience, pleasure, and mess. There is a huge list of reasons why such equanimity is hard to attain, from shifts in roles to conflicts between work and family to the pervasive pressures of a materialistic culture to the fear of death. But it is worth asking ourselves: what can we do to help ourselves claim the joy?

A FIRST STEP THAT ANY of us can take is to sit with the problem, whatever form it takes in our lives. We need to listen to the stirrings of our own soul, take responsibility for all our different feelings, and work toward greater discernment of our desire amid the clamor of voices. How do we do that? First, we notice. We notice the clench in our stomach or the low-level spaciness we feel when we leave our baby for the day. We ask ourselves what we can learn from it. We notice our sense of relief when we get out the door and leave our screaming toddler. We turn that sense of freedom over in our minds, trying to learn all we can about its sources. We notice our thought that we are doing "nothing" caring for a baby all day, or the way thoughts about what we need to get done tumble forward when we sit down to read our child a story. We notice what the pressure of too little time feels like, the way it scatters our attention, wears away at our sense of effectiveness, prompts us to try to move the discomfort outside ourselves by looking for someone or something to blame. Noticing does not make bad feelings go away, but it creates slightly more breathing space for our intimate experience, giving us a moment of honest specificity amid the self-persecuting half-truths that usually clog our minds. It can make us more compassionate toward ourselves, and less lonely.

We try to notice things about our children too. We try to decipher their signs and signals from a centered place, neither reading too much into their ups and downs nor denying their significance. We try to notice what they are asking from us, and how they are asking. We try to figure out whether the way they ask (whining, demandingness, tantrums) is making it hard for us to give them what they want or need. A child played on a beach during vacation. He had been there with a nanny for several hours. His mother arrived, and the child soon fell to whining. Minutes later, exasperated, the mother presented him with an ultimatum: "Stop whining, or I'm leaving." It was a heartbreaking scene to witness because it was clear the child was whining because he wanted his mother's attention. Unable or unwilling to receive what he was trying to tell her, the mother turned his (irritating) behavior against him. They missed each other by a mile. Sometimes our children ask for things we can't give, like more of our time. But again, there is value in being aware of their feelings and our own, and in letting our children know we understand their feelings rather than denying them out of anxiety or sadness.

We also try to notice the larger stories we tell ourselves about our lives, the values our choices express. Economic need is obviously a driving force behind mothers' and fathers' employment and the time they spend away from their children. Money is a necessity; it pays for food and shelter, it can make the difference between the life we grew up with and a better life for our children. Money also buys advantages, from safe neighborhoods to SAT prep courses. And discretionary spending really does make one feel better. It meant a lot to me when I could get rid of that Naugahyde recliner and decorate my baby's room. A woman in Juliet Schor's *The Overspent American* was willing to simplify her life in many ways, but she refused to give up her hair-coloring appointments.[25] Such seemingly superficial uses of money can confer an almost primal sense of pride and satisfaction.

At the same time, it is useful to recognize the social and psychological factors that influence the perception of economic need. We need to notice the scaffolding of assumptions that sanction our choices — assumptions about what is necessary to our happiness, what we can't do without, what is central to our membership in a social group — and make sure that they are assumptions we wish consciously and intentionally to endorse. We need to look closely at our situation to discern what constitutes a real constraint and what constraints are not as rigid as they seem.

All of us, from the affluent couple on their third remodel to the working-class couple at Costco, lugging home their widescreen TV, are so thoroughly influenced by consumerism that it is hard to separate what we need from what we've been conditioned to desire. But it is still worth trying to distance ourselves from our usual assumptions, to ask ourselves what exactly constitutes a material necessity, and to think about it directly in reference to the question of family time. We can even use the exercise as an opportunity for self-knowledge. Over the years, my pock-marked kitchen floor and my overgrown backyard have both served as objects of spiritual contemplation. Each time they have tormented me with an inchoate sense of failure, each time I have felt like fixing them would be the surest route to fixing myself, I have tried to take a step back and calmly recall that the choice not to spend time making money to improve my surroundings was the same choice that allowed me to spend time with the children. I have even comforted myself with the thought that the time I didn't devote to calling contractors or leafing though landscaping books probably was better spent showing the kids how to prepare soil and plant seeds in our mangy flower bed.

But lest I or anyone be lured into a Candide-like complacency, tending our own garden in this best of all possible worlds, we should not forget that being a parent at this cultural moment, regardless of how much time we spend with our children, pitches us into a host of unsettling quandaries. Private school versus public school, diverse city versus homogeneous suburb, commitment to the human family versus "not in my backyard." My husband and I have three children, something the environmentalist and writer Bill McKibben has respectfully pointed out is itself ethically questionable. Joy Williams wrote that "in terms of energy consumption, when an American couple stops spawning at two babies, it's the same as an average East Indian couple stopping at sixty-six, or an Ethiopian couple drawing the line at one thousand."[26] The preferred emblem of these dilemmas for the liberal middle class is the vexatious question of the car. Do we buy the gas-guzzling monstrosity that provides two extra seats, so that the children can have friends over without prevailing, yet again, upon the transportational generosity of their parents? Or do we buy the more socially responsible station wagon with the pop-up seat that the Insurance Institute for Highway Safety rates as "inferior"? Belch out 12.2 tons of greenhouse gas per year or live with the risk of being bulldozed by a truck? The choice almost makes us nostalgic for the deluded innocence represented by the family station wagon, which, in the days before seat-belt enforcement, functioned as a traveling clubhouse, with children scrambling between the seats and "way back" at will. In this, as in many other more consequential decisions, we confront a central tension of parenthood, between our concern for the greater good and our commitment to the health and happiness of our own. Lurking within this tension is the temptation to absolve ourselves of guilt over the planet, because after all, aren't we already pouring all our available energy into caring for others?

Children can, if we let them, expand our fellow feeling. As a friend said when I revealed years ago feeling wistful at the end of childbearing, "The point isn't whether you keep having children. It's being able to find a way for the experience of love that you have toward your own children, a love that feels like it can't be matched, to widen and deepen your love for others." And that is why, once we are no longer drowning in diapers, no longer struggling to compose a shopping list, let alone a letter to our representative in Congress, no longer stricken with fear that our job security or professional standing depends on not making waves, it is worth considering how we might bring the knowledge we gained from tending children into the cultural conversation. There is evidence of such efforts all around us. We see it in the beautiful, rigorous scholarship that has been informed by women's and men's personal experiences of having and caring for children. We see it in grassroots efforts to ease the way of those who come after, like the group of older mothers in my community, volunteering their time to improve the day care options for the county's poorer mothers. We see it in the individual effort of a parent who pushes the policies of his or her workplace in a slightly more flexible direction. And we find it in ourselves when we respect that there are many ways to mother well, when we refuse to judge our own or others' maternal choices in terms of rigid ideals, and when we manage to live by the knowledge that mothering is not about perfection but about love, acceptance, responsibility, and engagement, toward our children and ourselves.[27]

Finally, it is important to notice when we are "choosing away" from spending time with our children and to ask ourselves what that is about. What are some of the powerful ideas that tip the balance of people's choices away from time with children? I remember that around the time when our children were two, four, and seven years old, there was one day each week, Tuesdays, when the babysitter worked all day, from 8 A.M. till 5 P.M. Every other day of the week, I ended my workday by 2 P.M., or I didn't work at all. I came to notice what I called "the Tuesday effect." At around 5:30 or 6 P.M. on Tuesdays, I would frequently have the thought "Oh boy, it's exhausting to be with these kids all day!," only then to realize that I was having this thought *only* on the day when I *wasn't* with them for much of the day. I came to wonder about that.

I knew that at other points in my work life, I had managed to strike an energizing balance between work and caring for children. I would work for a certain number of hours, feel effective and refreshed, and then come home and feel brightened and alert playing with my child. Each activity served to feed the other. And I have read of other women who feel their workday releases them to enjoy their children in the evening. But what I was noticing with the Tuesday effect was more akin to what Arlie Hochschild described in her book *The Time Bind*. She found it was not a simple matter of "lack of time" that deprived children of their parents, but rather that people were "choosing against" time with family by putting in more time at work. Their sense of meaning and effectiveness gradually clustered more and more in their work identity, and home became less and less rewarding. They felt less effective at home; the emotional needs were more unruly, less easily dispatched.[28] Similarly for me, the more I worked on a given day, the more my center of gravity was in my work and the less I could find exactly what there was to enjoy in taking care of my children.

We can use these feelings as a pretext to insist that work simply *is* more interesting, child care simply *is* more boring. Or we can take it as an opportunity to explore what is getting in the way of fully participating in our own family life. Do we have problems with our spouse that we are not confronting? Does the sheer pace at work make the more meandering tempo of childhood seem unbearably slow? Are we so tied to a narrow notion of achievement that time with children seems unproductive? Do we feel vaguely bad about ourselves for our detachment or ineffectualness at home, a feeling we are only able to banish while at work?

The hard truth is that our ability to appreciate something is affected by the time we devote to it. Whether it is a person or a pursuit, one way we treasure it is through the time we give to it. The more time we spend on a relationship (with a child, with nature, with a piece of music), the more we know and the more we appreciate, and the more facets there are to love. In some ways, the speed at which we live our lives is implicated in the degradation of our capacity to appreciate. As Robinson and Godbey write, "While efficiency, at least as envisioned in American society, always starts with *wanting* more, appreciating may start both with *valuing* more what is already here and with wanting less."[29]

Paradoxically, though our perpetual busyness can be seen to reflect our ever-rising standard for what is necessary to a good life — up-to-date appliances, new cars, state-of-the-art computers, travel — we seem less and less able as a society to provide for the true necessities of people's lives, namely health care, a working wage, the comforts of home, good care for our children, and restorative leisure.

If we notice ourselves choosing away from spending time nurturing our children, each of us needs to ask, Have I set up my life so as to rationalize shying away from any activity, any spiritual practice, that would put me closer to the burning center of my life, to authentic connection? To what extent are my activities oriented toward maintaining my sense of control, or managing my fear of want and insecurity, or stoking my vanity, in a way that is leading me away from experiencing the depth of love I could? The theologian Thomas Merton wrote: "Love affects more than our thinking and our behavior toward those we love. It transforms our entire life. Genuine love is a personal revolution. Love takes your ideas, your desires, and your actions and welds them together in one experience and one living reality which is a new *you*."[30] This is how people talk about becoming parents. This is how women talk about becoming mothers. This is the explosion in one's heart as old as time.

I RIDE BIKES WITH MY children to school in the morning, the oldest on a two-wheeler, the middle one on training wheels, and the youngest in a cart attached to the back of my bike. One day after dropping off the older ones, I climb the hill to the bike path with my solid three-year-old in tow. As I begin mentally carving up my day, wondering how I will fit in my errands, my work, I am suddenly returned to myself by the beauty of the morning — the mist, our chatting, the pumping of my heart. Every time he asks me a question, it makes a difference how I answer it, not so much by the facts I offer but in the way I attend, in the way I keep faith with his earnest effort to make sense of the world. His thirst for knowledge and my power to slake it move me. It lets me notice once again what our time together means for us both. It feels good and right to hallow this morning, this hour. The liberation of the heart which is love, I think, as we whizz along the bike path and count our friends the ducks.

ACKNOWLEDGMENTS

MANY PEOPLE HAVE HELPED ME during the years of writing this book, and I am deeply thankful to all of them. For reading chapters, talking over ideas, and for sustaining support and friendship, I thank John Adler, Anne Becker, Daniel Becker, Meryl Botkin, Susan Coates, Rachel Conrad, Katrin Borland de Marneffe, Dianne Elise, Toni Vaughn Heineman, Stephen Hinshaw, Jeanne Burns Leary, and Mary Margaret McClure. Particular thanks to Gary Kamiya for his comments on the entire draft, and to Leslie Ann Fuchs, Laura Klein, and Kate Moses for their enthusiasm and crucial early feedback.

Friends, acquaintances, colleagues, and scholars I've admired from afar all came to my aid in myriad ways, offering the chance reference or anecdote, taking time to answer my e-mails, or consulting with me about some aspect of their expertise. I am grateful to them all for their assistance. I particularly wish to thank Karen Betzner, Karen Breslau, Ellen Burkhart, Lee Rubin Collins, Carolyn Pape Cowan, Diane Doucette, Richard Fabian, Renée Carroll Ghosh, Tracy Haughton, Alan Heineman, Susan Hill, Linda James, Nancy Kaplan, Lynne Layton, Alicia Lieberman, Vivian Steir Rabin, Maria Rivera, Rebecca Rogers, Alan Rubenstein, Rebecca Saletan, Donald Schell, Stephen Seligman, and Judith Sternberg Turiel. An unexpected pleasure of working on this book has been reconnecting with old friends and trading perspectives on parenthood. For their insights and camaraderie, I thank Amy Givens, Patricia Howard Hudson, Hester Kaplan, Lizzie Leiman Kraiem, Liz Schein Krengel, Jessica Marshall, and Erika Peterson Munson. Though for reasons of discretion they remain unnamed, I am also hugely indebted to all the people I have encountered in the course of work and parenthood who have shared with me their struggles and their stories.

For their scholarly example, their encouragement, and their contribution to my intellectual development, I thank my teachers, particularly Nancy Chodorow, Philip Cowan, Carol Gilligan, and the late Enrico Jones. My gratitude also goes to my children's many excellent teachers and caregivers, at school, at preschool, and at home. Dara Blachman, Susanna Bonetti, and Lynne Foster helped me track down references, and I thank them for their diligence.

I can't say enough wonderful things about my agent, Tina Bennett, who is supremely gifted as both editor and advocate. Our work together has been a professional high point, and I thank her for her integrity, guidance, and good humor at every step of the way. I have also been blessed to work with my editor, Judy Clain, whose responsiveness, vision, and extraordinary fluidity between emotion and intellect have made for a highly satisfying collaboration. My sincere thanks also go to Judy's assistant, Claire Smith, and to all the superb professionals at Janklow & Nesbit and Little, Brown.

I am fortunate to have an extended family who lavish me with unwavering loyalty, interest, and pride. I offer my enduring appreciation to them all. I am especially thankful to my parents-in-law, Kathleen Jacobson Becker and John Becker, for their generous care; to my stepparents Barbara Rowe de Marneffe and Anthony Ferranti, for the many gifts they have shared with me and our family; and most of all, to my devoted parents, Nancy Edmonds Ferranti and Francis de Marneffe, who gave me life and taught me to love it.

For their steadfast support and enfolding affection, I am grateful to my friends Debra Fine, Maureen Katz, Elizabeth Lloyd Mayer, Sheila Sammon Milosky, and Susan Morrison. Among these cherished companions I count my brother, Peter de Marneffe, on whom I can always rely for a great conversation, and my sister, Colette de Marneffe, my inspiration and best friend.

Finally, from my deepest heart, I thank my beloved children, for being who they are, and my husband, Terry Becker, for everything.

Preface

1. DINNERSTEIN, *Mermaid and Minotaur*; Chodorow, *Reproduction of Mothering*; Gilligan, *In a Different Voice*; and Leclerc, *Parole de Femme*.
2. FIRESTONE, *Dialectic of Sex*.
3. FREUD, "Analysis Terminable and Interminable"; and Horney, "Flight from Womanhood."

1. The "Problem" of Maternal Desire

1. BREUER and FREUD, "Studies on Hysteria." For a deft, definitive guide to Freud's writings on women, see Young-Bruehl, *Freud on Women: A Reader*. In *The History of Sexuality*, the philosopher Michel Foucault brilliantly demonstrated how incessant, seemingly "free" social discussion of sex served to regulate and define sexual expression. Similarly, though it may seem that people "can't stop talking about motherhood," their very volubility may serve to obscure, and even discount, important aspects of maternal experience.
2. GEORGE ELIOT [Mary Ann Evans], *Felix Holt*, chap. 27.
3. LUKER, *Dubious Conceptions*, 170.
4. WOLF, "Future Is Ours to Lose," 154.
5. See, for instance, Danielle Crittenden, *What Our Mothers Didn't Tell Us*.
6. BARTHES, *Mythologies*, 11.
7. "Regression": See, for instance, Sandra Scarr, quoted in Chira, *Mother's Place*, 13. "Baby care manuals": See, for instance, Chira, *Mother's Place*, chap. 3; and Eyer, *Motherguilt*.
8. FALUDI, *Backlash*, especially chaps. 4 and 11.
9. MIEDZIAN, *Boys Will Be Boys*, 4, quoted in Shalit, *Return to Modesty*, 216. Not unusually, Miedzian's offhandedly dismissive comment about caring for children and home is followed, in the body of the book, by a critique of "our national lack of interest in and lack of respect for child-rearing" (71).

10. Because my argument concerns the ways mothers are subtly and not so subtly encouraged to downplay their desire to care for their children, my examples and vignettes tend to illustrate that side of the dilemma. This emphasis should not be taken to mean that there are not equally valid and painful dilemmas from the other side; that, for instance, a mother may feel duty-bound to care for her children and inhibited in expressing her other desires or needs.

11. For instance, Stern, *Interpersonal World of the Infant*; and Beebe and Lachmann, *Infant Research and Adult Treatment*.

12. Among the most trenchant recent accounts for the general reader, see Burggraf, *Feminine Economy and Economic Man*; Folbre, *Invisible Heart*; and Ann Crittenden, *Price of Motherhood*. For a liberal political perspective on similar issues, see Harrington, *Care and Equality*.

13. Examples include Cusk, *Life's Work*; Alden, *Crossing the Moon*; Ann Crittenden, *Price of Motherhood*; and Maushart, *Mask of Motherhood*.

14. For more historical context, see Ehrenreich and English's classic work *For Her Own Good*; and Dally, *Inventing Motherhood*.

15. Brooks, "the mother." This poem appears by special consent of the Brooks Permissions, with the understanding that Gwendolyn Brooks did not want this work to promote the causes or arguments made by those on either side of abortion rights issues.

16. On changing attitudes toward family time, see, for instance, Radcliffe Public Policy Center, "Life's Work." On fathers with primary custody, see, for instance, Goldberg, "Single Dads Wage Revolution." On child support, see, for instance, Harden, "'Dead Broke' Dads' Child-Support Struggle."

17. In making an argument in an arena as sensitive as motherhood, one runs the risk of seeming either to take an overly personal viewpoint that leaves out other equally valid perspectives or, conversely, to try to speak for everyone, thereby blurring the crucial differences between mothers of diverse personalities, tastes, classes, and cultural identifications. My aspiration here is perhaps best understood as a response to the need for "clear, accessible, stimulating general hypotheses" identified by the philosopher Susan Bordo in *Unbearable Weight*, 223.

2. Feminism

1. Among many examples are Juliet Mitchell, *Psychoanalysis and Feminism*; Olsen, *Tell Me a Riddle*; Faludi, *Backlash*; Ludtke, *On Our Own*; and Hays, *Cultural Contradictions of Motherhood*.

2. Orenstein, *Flux*, 5.

3. See Rich, *Of Woman Born*; especially chap. 9, "Motherhood and Daughterhood"; and Friedan, *Feminine Mystique*, 72.

4. The examples I mention emphasize the theme of reparation to the mother as an act of love, an impulse first limned in the psychoanalyst Melanie Klein's classic article "Contribution to the Psychogenesis of Manic Depressive States." But some feminist "love letters" are celebrations of the

mother-daughter bond, such as Cixous's "Laugh of the Medusa" and Leclerc's *Parole de Femme*.

5. I focus in this book on the psychological effects; the economic effects have been thoroughly detailed by Burggraf, *Feminine Economy and Economic Man*; Folbre, *Invisible Heart*; and Ann Crittenden, *Price of Motherhood*, among others.

6. For an excellent discussion of these differences and the general feminist differences between "gender minimizers" and "gender maximizers," see Blum's *At the Breast*. For a fascinating historical perspective, see Snitow, "Gender Diary."

7. For a discussion of how de Beauvoir saw her own situation with respect to other women's, see Deirdre Bair, *Simone de Beauvoir*, chap. 28.

8. JARDINE, "Death Sentences," 90.

9. MOI, "While We Wait," 1023–28. Moi argues that the inadequate English translation distorts de Beauvoir's views on motherhood. Other authors maintain that de Beauvoir held a negative view of motherhood, both personally and philosophically. See, for instance, Catherine Rodgers, "Elisabeth Badinter and *The Second Sex*."

10. DE BEAUVOIR, *Second Sex*, 575.

11. DE BEAUVOIR, *Second Sex*, 572–73.

12. DE BEAUVOIR, *Second Sex*, 575.

13. DE BEAUVOIR, *Second Sex*, 553. For a penetrating critique of the idea that agency is the essential quality that defines the individual, see Benhabib, "Generalized and Concrete Other."

14. In a thoroughly rewarding study of *The Second Sex*, the philosopher Nancy Bauer argues that a necessary task, as de Beauvoir conceived it, was to resist projecting the subject/object split onto males and females, and instead, for each individual to accept and take responsibility for his or her ambiguity as both subject and object. Thus, Bauer writes: "On Beauvoir's view the essential struggle is with myself: I struggle to let go of a fixed picture of myself, to risk letting the other teach me who I am." This is as apt a characterization as any one of the *positive* opportunities provided by motherhood; but it is one that de Beauvoir doesn't explicitly pursue. See Bauer, *Simone de Beauvoir*, 236.

15. FRIEDAN, *Feminine Mystique*, 67.

16. FRIEDAN, *Feminine Mystique*, 67.

17. For example, Lasch (*Women and the Common Life*, 94) contended that *The Feminine Mystique* was a critique of suburban isolation disguised as a critique of the sexual division of labor. Daniel Horowitz, a biographer of Friedan, argued in *Betty Friedan* that she downplayed her radical Marxist roots and pandered to bourgeois psychology.

18. For a discussion that places Friedan's point of view in historical context, see Ehrenreich and English, *For Her Own Good*, 21: "Betty Friedan, the best-known sexual rationalist of our period, found the home a 'trap' and housewives stunted in mind and spirit. But in recoiling, justifiably, from 'woman's sphere' (and not so justifiably, from the women in it), sexual rationalism rushes too eagerly into the public sphere as men have

defined it." Friedan addressed this issue in her later book, *The Second Stage*.

19. FRIEDAN, *Feminine Mystique*, 346.
20. Campaign speech by Ralph Nader in Dearborn, Michigan, broadcast on *The Newshour with Jim Lehrer* November 2, 2000.
21. HAYS, *Cultural Contradictions of Motherhood*, 18.
22. RICH, *Of Woman Born*, 194–95.
23. Rich acknowledged the basic contours of this dilemma: "Because the conditions of life for many poor women demand a fighting spirit for sheer physical survival, such mothers have sometimes been able to give their daughters something to be valued far more highly than full-time motherhood. But the toll is taken by the sheer weight of adversity, the irony that to fight for her child's physical survival the mother may have to be almost always absent from the child, as in Tillie Olsen's story 'I Stand Here Ironing.' For a child needs, as that mother despairingly knew, the care of someone for whom she is 'a miracle'" (*Of Woman Born*, 247).
24. RICH, *Of Woman Born*, 246–47.
25. RICH, *Of Woman Born*, 246.
26. EHRENREICH and ENGLISH, *For Her Own Good*, 5.
27. COTT, *Bonds of Womanhood*, chap. 1. The studies I cite in this section focus mostly on middle-class women in the northeastern United States.
28. RYAN, *Cradle of the Middle Class*, 106; and Lasch, *Women and the Common Life*, 93–120.
29. SKLAR, *Catharine Beecher*, chap. 11.
30. SMITH-ROSENBERG, "Female World of Love and Ritual," 59–60.
31. COTT, *Bonds of Womanhood*, 200–201; and Smith-Rosenberg, "Beauty, Beast, and Militant Woman," 126.
32. DOUGLAS, *Feminization of American Culture*, 254.
33. WELTER, "Cult of True Womanhood," 151–74.
34. Quoted in Cott, *Bonds of Womanhood*, 88.
35. See, for example, Aries, *Centuries of Childhood*; and Stone, *Family, Sex, and Marriage*.
36. SCHOR, *Overworked American*, 92.
37. SCHOR, *Overworked American*, 93.
38. See, for example, Ozment, *Ancestors*. Parents have clearly practiced different parenting styles across different historical periods, social classes, and cultural groups. That some of these styles may be more phenotypically nurturing or affectionate does not necessarily mean that the other styles betray a lack of care or love. Parenting styles tend to be adapted to preparing children for the challenges they can expect in their given culture. See Small, *Our Babies, Ourselves*, chap. 2.
39. See, for example, Ryan, *Cradle of the Middle Class*, 231–32; and Cott, *Bonds of Womanhood*, 200.
40. MARILYNNE ROBINSON, *Death of Adam*, 94.
41. WOLF, *Beauty Myth*, 15.
42. A number of authors have discussed parental attention in terms of transmitting middle-class status to children. See, most notably, Ehrenreich, *Fear of Falling*.

43. DE BEAUVOIR, *Second Sex*, 587.

44. About Friedan's attitude toward housework, Daphne Merkin wrote: "Although [Friedan] vehemently attacked the way the media encouraged women to dust, iron, bake, and vacuum away their best years — 'Occupation: Housewife' was her derisive term — it was unclear whom she had in mind to take care of the 'details of life' when evolved women stopped attending to them, unless it was less evolved women" ("Sister Act," 81).

45. SCHOR, *Overworked American*, 94–95.

46. SCHOR, *Overworked American*, 98.

47. Housework, for the record, is not universally regarded as dreary. Writers like David Sedaris and Caroline Carreños have described its satisfactions, and lawyer-turned-housekeeping-expert Cheryl Mendelson had this to say in her book *Home Comforts*: "Your own housework can be a joy to you because of the way it is integrated into your life and because of your intense identification with your home and its contents. It does not feel the same to the hired worker. This is similar to the way the feelings of parents about their own children make their experience in taking care of them profoundly different from that of their friends, relatives, and hired caretakers" (806).

48. See Glenn, "Social Constructions of Mothering," 7; and Joan Williams, *Unbending Gender*, chap. 5.

49. For further analysis of this phenomenon, see Parreñas, *Servants of Globalization*; and Ehrenreich and Hochschild, *Global Woman*. Also see Hondagneu-Sotelo, *Doméstica*, for a discussion of the experience of Mexican and Central American women.

50. For discussion of this point, see Collins, *Black Feminist Thought*, 54–55; and Joan Williams, *Unbending Gender*, 167–68.

51. ANN CRITTENDEN, *Price of Motherhood*, 8, 79.

52. JOHNSON, *One Minute Mother*.

53. FALUDI, *Backlash*, 312–31.

54. For an extensive analysis of this issue, see Ireland, *Reconceiving Women*.

55. POLLITT, *Reasonable Creatures*, 43. Pollitt articulates her perspective on "difference" feminism in her essay "Marooned on Gilligan's Island" in *Reasonable Creatures*, 42–62.

56. KAMINER, *True Love Waits*, 42. There are many critical analyses of the concept of femininity, notably Susan Brownmiller's *Femininity*.

57. KAMINER, *True Love Waits*, 5–6. Kaminer's concern references a long-standing tension within feminism between treating women as individuals and treating them as a class with certain common characteristics. For a historical perspective on this tension, see Cott, *Grounding of Modern Feminism*.

58. KAMINER, *True Love Waits*, 109–10.

59. Though Kaminer legitimately critiques the way we too often move from a recognition of reproductive differences ("only women get pregnant") to a set of gender stereotypes ("women are caring, sharing, and nurturing"), she makes the mistake of viewing any articulation of women's intense identification with mothering as just one more capitulation to gender stereotypes. When women's reproductive roles are discussed

solely in terms of biological necessity and cultural stereotypes, what gets left out is a psychological account of maternal desire, and a recognition of its ongoing, powerful role in how we view equality and difference. Accounts that neglect maternal desire are also unable to observe the ways in which the mantle of "woman's nature" is used as a cover, a shorthand, or a more emotionally neutral way of talking about these deeply held desires. See Kaminer, *Fearful Freedom*, 212–13, and chap. 10. For a nuanced discussion of feminist themes of equality and difference, see Joan W. Scott, "Deconstructing Equality-Versus-Difference."

60. Harper's Forum, "Giving Women the Business," 50.

61. GILLIGAN, *In a Different Voice*, 2.

62. Joan Williams argues that, although they are often lumped together, the view that women are entitled to special legal treatment under some circumstances ("special treatment") and the view that women as a group share a different perspective on morality ("different voice") are "logically independent. Although many special treatment feminists believe that women really are different, others do not. . . . The logical independence of these debates means that one can imagine someone who does not believe that women share an ethic of care but who does support a statute designed to give mothers pregnancy disability leave" (*Unbending Gender*, 179).

 As lesbian, gay, and single parents become more commonplace, it is even more obvious how little bearing self-identification as "feminine" in a conventional sense has on the quality of care or the commitment people bring to mothering or parenting.

63. MORRISON, in Moyers and Tucher, *World of Ideas*, quoted in Bassin et al., *Representations of Motherhood*, 2.

64. ERDRICH, *Blue Jay's Dance*, 11–12.

65. At the extreme, one can see the depth of this human need in the fact that throughout the ages, taking children away from their parents has been a way to break spirits. For a biopsychological perspective on the human need to give care, see Taylor, *Tending Instinct*. For a classic and controversial sociobiological look at specifically maternal capacities, see Alice Rossi, "Biosocial Perspective on Parenting."

66. *Newsweek*, March 23, 1970, 72.

67. SWISS and WALKER, "Smart Women, Smart Choices," *Working Mother*, 22.

68. GREER, *Female Eunuch*.

3. Psychoanalysis

1. In her book *Mothers of Psychoanalysis*, Janet Sayers points out that each of these early women psychoanalysts contributed to the development of theory in ways having very much to do with their own experiences of being mothered and mothering, lending credence to the notion that there are "as many theories of psychoanalysis as there are analysts" (33).

2. LANGER, *Motherhood and Sexuality*, ix–x. Langer alludes to Lundberg and Farnham, *Modern Woman*.

3. SAYERS, *Mothers of Psychoanalysis*, 33.

4. ROAZEN, *Helene Deutsch*, 134, 136.
5. ROAZEN, *Helene Deutsch*, 135; and Sayers, *Mothers of Psychoanalysis*, 34, 40.
6. DEUTSCH, "Two-Year-Old Boy's First Love," 159–64.
7. For Deutsch's discussion of the "tragedy of motherhood," see Deutsch, *Motherhood*, 302–17.
8. DEUTSCH, *Motherhood*, 291.
9. DEUTSCH, *Motherhood*, 282.
10. DEUTSCH, *Motherhood*, 292–93.
11. Quoted in Quinn, *Mind of Her Own*, 170.
12. QUINN, *Mind of Her Own*, 171.
13. QUINN, *Mind of Her Own*, 172.
14. HORNEY, "Flight from Womanhood," 60.
15. At a panel on life choices and social service at my 2002 high school reunion, a woman in her late sixties captured something important about the psychological and emotional effect of women's restriction to the domestic sphere at a time when marrying and childbearing very young was the norm. Though she was happy at the time, she felt she had been unable to really "live" her motherhood, to embrace it consciously or actively choose it, because it was only when she was older that she "woke up" and figured out for herself what she thought about life, values, and politics.
16. In Chodorow's account, a baby's awareness of self and other and his very awareness of reality are initiated by his growing awareness of his mother's difference. It is the mother's independent action that brings about the infant's awareness of self and other: "The infant achieves differentiation of self only insofar as its expectations of primary love are frustrated. If the infant were not frustrated, it would not begin to perceive the other as separate" (*Reproduction of Mothering*, 69). Thus, the frustration of the infant's wishes for merger catalyzes the development of a boundaried, independent sense of self.
17. BALINT, "Love for the Mother and Mother-Love," 256, quoted in Chodorow, *Reproduction of Mothering*, 85. Balint's view rests on her assumption that "the relation between mother and child *is built upon* the interdependence of the reciprocal instinctual aims" (256). She asserts that just as babies and children see their mothers through the lens of their own gratification, so too do mothers; for example, even after children have grown, mothers insist on thinking of their children as their "little ones." "Is this not yet another proof," she writes, "of the remoteness of maternal love from reality? Just as the child's love is remote because he never imagines his mother as a being with divergent, that is to say, self-interests?" (256).
18. CHODOROW, *Reproduction of Mothering*, 87.
19. Chodorow's own thinking has obviously also developed during this period as well, as evidenced in *Femininities, Masculinities, Sexualities* and *Power of Feelings*. However, her 1978 book stands as a cultural artifact, worthy of analysis in its own right due to its enduring impact on our ideas.
20. GERGELY, "Reapproaching Mahler," 1202–3. For reviews of recent relevant

research, see Gergely, "Reapproaching Mahler" and Beebe and Lachmann, *Infant Research and Adult Treatment*, chap. 4.

21. STERN, *Interpersonal World of the Infant*, 10.

22. SANDER, "Infant and Caretaking Environment." See also Sander, "Thinking Differently"; and Stern, *Interpersonal World of the Infant*, 104.

23. SANDER, "Thinking Differently," 20.

24. BEEBE and LACHMANN, *Infant Research and Adult Treatment*, chap. 5.

25. STERN, *Interpersonal World of the Infant*, 103. This process is referred to as
"affect regulation" in psychological writings and is a topic of extensive
research. See, for instance, Fonagy et al., *Affect Regulation*.

26. Our current appreciation of this dialectical aspect of merger and autonomy
was prefigured by the writings of Hans Loewald. See *Papers in Psychoanalysis*. Similar themes emerge in Stern, *Interpersonal World of the Infant*, 125–27, and Kaplan, *Oneness and Separateness*. For an innovative
cognitive-developmental model of some of the mechanisms involved in
psychological differentiation, see Gergely and Watson, "Social Biofeedback Model of Parental Affect-Mirroring." In earlier psychoanalytic
thinking, when fusion was cast as the "primitive" state and autonomy
the "mature" one, the roots of psychopathology were often located in
"fixations" at infantile stages. For a refutation of this now-discredited
view, see, for instance, Eagle, *Recent Developments in Psychoanalysis*,
chap. 3.

27. Gergely has pointed out that while Mahler's concept of symbiosis misappre-
hends the infant's ability to perceive difference between self and other,
it is accurate in the classical biological sense of denoting the "close
coexistence between two organisms in which some of the vital life functions of one of the participants is fulfilled or facilitated by the activities
of the other" ("Reapproaching Mahler," 1206).

28. For a discussion of the psychological processes involved in such experiences, see Stern, *Interpersonal World of the Infant*, 104–11.

29. CHODOROW, *Reproduction of Mothering*, 59.

30. For a discussion of the problems of according a causal developmental role to
fantasy in this way, see Stern, *Interpersonal World of the Infant*, 253–55.
For a discussion of the theoretical confusions embedded in the psychoanalytic concept of "primary narcissism," see Laplanche and Pontalis,
Language of Psychoanalysis, 337–38.

31. This view is attributed notably to Melanie Klein, among others. See Seligman, "Integrating Kleinian Theory."

32. A series of papers by attachment theorists Carol George and Judith Solomon have delineated how underdeveloped in writings about attachment the mother's side of the attachment relationship is, with respect to
her strong motivation for caregiving and its relationship to her other
motives and goals. See, for example, George and Solomon, "Development of Caregiving"; Solomon and George, "Defining the Caregiving
System"; and George and Solomon, "Representational Models of Relationships."

33. For a full description of how this comes about, see Benjamin, *Bonds of Love*,
chaps. 1 and 2.

34. MAHLER, PINE, and BERGMAN, *Psychological Birth of the Human Infant*, chap. 6.

35. "Separation consists not so much of losing mother's presence," Benjamin writes, "as losing control of her coming and going" ("Omnipotent Mother," 134–35).

36. BENJAMIN, *Bonds of Love*, 34.

37. BENJAMIN, *Bonds of Love*, 39.

38. BENJAMIN, *Bonds of Love*, 35.

39. See, for example, Benjamin, *Bonds of Love*, 212–13, "Omnipotent Mother," 134–36, and *Like Subjects, Love Objects*," 37–38.

40. BENJAMIN, *Bonds of Love*, 213.

41. Benjamin's account draws on ideas put forward by the pediatrician and psychoanalyst D. W. Winnicott in his essay "Use of the Object." Winnicott suggests that it is through destroying the mother in fantasy — a characteristically human, and developmentally necessary, mental act — that the infant is able to discover that she is a real other, existing "outside the arena of subjective phenomena" (87). One of Benjamin's key goals is to use Winnicott's insight to work out a developmental, psychological account of the problem of recognition in Hegel's philosophy. I am obviously not addressing the import of that project here, except perhaps insofar as I worry that the attempt to fit the mother-child relationship at rapprochement to the contours of Hegel's master-slave relationship distorts our picture of certain aspects of maternal experience.

    Those familiar with Benjamin's work may think my emphasis on the reality component of her description of rapprochement — the mother's coming and going, her role in the world — minimizes the psychological situation that is the true focus of her analysis. I am not taking issue here with her psychological model per se, nor with the importance of the mother's "survival" as conceptualized by Winnicott. Rather, I am questioning Benjamin's addition of a particular feminist cast to this issue of "survival," such that it is no longer understood primarily in its psychological sense as the mother's ability not to withdraw or retaliate or close down or break down (abilities generally available to any emotionally healthy mother), but is explicitly linked to, or implicitly elided with, the position that women gain a sense of self ("survive"), in the eyes of themselves, children, and men, through their involvement in the outside world. Of course, any given mother's well-being has much to do with the context of her mothering, and Benjamin has contributed a great deal to our understanding of the basic maternal dilemma of finding a way to balance connectedness and separateness in familial and public domains. But I believe that Benjamin's implication that women's psychological autonomy depends on their roles in the outside world and the leave-taking those roles entail is more politically based than theoretically necessary.

42. EHRENSAFT, *Spoiling Childhood*, chap. 4.

43. BENJAMIN, *Bonds of Love*, 82. See also Hegel, *Phenomenology of Mind*, 229–40.

44. BENJAMIN, *Bonds of Love*, 79.

45. BENJAMIN, *Bonds of Love*, 96.

46. See, for example, Peters, *When Mothers Work*.

47. GERHARDT, SWEETNAM, and BORTON, "Intersubjective Turn in Psycho-analysis," 26. The authors continue, "In this context, not only is the mother unable to lead the child down the path of individuation during this critical moment, but her own unconscious dynamics exert a regressive pull on the child toward attachment and merger." Note the same conflation of attachment and merger that was observable in Chodorow, *Reproduction of Mothering*, 59.

48. BENJAMIN, *Bonds of Love*, 23.

49. Some writings that do approach these issues include: Bassin, "Maternal Subjectivity"; Stern, *Motherhood Constellation*; Stern and Bruschweiler-Stern, *Birth of a Mother*; and Nachman, "Maternal Identification." For an intriguing view of the conflict between desire and procreation in Freudian theory, see Dimen, "Strange Hearts."

50. BOWLBY, *Attachment* and *Secure Base*. For an historical look at the development of attachment theory and research, and a gripping portrait of the personalities involved, see Karen, *Becoming Attached*.

51. AINSWORTH, et al. *Patterns of Attachment*.

52. Securely and insecurely attached children are similar in that they both exhibit an organized pattern of behavior toward their caregiver. More recently, a third major attachment category, disorganized attachment, has been conceptualized by Mary Main and her colleagues to include those children whose behavior is anomalous and disoriented. For overviews of the organized and disorganized categories of attachment and references to relevant work, see Main, "Organized Categories"; and Hesse and Main, "Disorganized Infant, Child, and Adult Attachment."

53. For in-depth discussion of this point, see Slade, "Development and Organization of Attachment," 1149–50. As a child grows, her specific behavioral expressions of attachment behaviors obviously change; a baby may need to be held, a teenager may need a phone call. But throughout development, a child's "internal working model" of attachment — the relational pattern of expectations and contingencies laid down in early interactions with a caregiver — remains a powerful template that guides her basic approach to relationships and attachment seeking. Under some circumstances, for instance when a parent becomes less responsive due to depression or more responsive due to increased social support, a child's attachment status may also change. See Bretherton and Mulholland, "Internal Working Models," 93; and Hesse, "Adult Attachment Interview," 411.

54. The seminal paper introducing the Adult Attachment Interview (AAI) was Main, Kaplan, and Cassidy's "Security in Infancy, Childhood, and Adulthood." For a comprehensive review of AAI theory and research, see Erik Hesse, "Adult Attachment Interview." The association of infant behavior in the Strange Situation and adult AAI responses is a robust finding that has been replicated numerous times. See Hesse, "Adult Attachment Interview," 406–8, for a summary of findings.

55. See Hesse, "Adult Attachment Interview," 425–26; and Pearson et al., "Earned- and Continuous-Security."

56. FONAGY and TARGET, "Mentalization," 95. See also Fonagy et al., "Attachment, the Reflective Self, and Borderline States"; and Slade, "Development and Organization of Attachment," 1154–55. For a foundational paper on the relationship between reflectivity, flexibility of attention, coherence of discourse, and caregiver responsiveness, see Main, "Metacognitive Knowledge, Metacognitive Monitoring."

57. Reported in Fonagy and Target, "Mentalization," 94. Fonagy emphasizes the mother's shift to an incompatible state, but Susan Coates considers the crucial component of the mother's communication to be her recognition of the child's emotional state followed by a shift in affect that the child can then join (conversation with the author, May 18, 2002).

58. LYONS-RUTH, "Rapprochement or Approchement," 9.

59. LYONS-RUTH, "Rapprochement or Approchement," 12.

60. LYONS-RUTH, "Rapprochement or Approchement," 6.

61. TRONICK, "Emotions and Emotional Communication." See also Beebe and Lachmann, *Infant Research and Adult Treatment*, chaps. 7 and 8.

62. Further, the ability to talk about these disruptions and misunderstandings together as children get older appears to be something that characterizes secure attachment relationships. See Bretherton and Mulholland, "Internal Working Models," 97, 101.

63. BEEBE and LACHMANN, *Infant Research and Adult Treatment*, 85–86.

64. JAFFE et al., "Rhythms of Dialogue in Infancy." "Coordination" can be understood as the "degree of predictability of one person's behavior from that of the other," or "whether or not two parallel streams of behavior are correlated" (Beebe and Lachmann, *Infant Research and Adult Treatment*, 32, 99).

65. BEEBE and LACHMANN, *Infant Research and Adult Treatment*, 103

66. See Beebe and Lachmann, *Infant Research and Adult Treatment*, 103, for a fuller description of the meaning of these findings.

67. MATHIOT, "No Time to Hurry," 4.

68. DEUTSCH, *Motherhood*, 296–97.

69. LANGER, *Motherhood and Sexuality*, x. Along similar lines, Erik Erikson wrote that "procreative patterns, in varying intensity, pervade every state of excitement and inspiration, and *if integrated*, lend power to all experience and all communication" ("Womanhood and Inner Space," 306).

4. Pleasure

1. The picture is on the cover of *Mothering*, no. 100, May/June 2000. In her article on Renaissance images of the Virgin Mary, Margaret R. Miles wrote: "Depictions of the nursing Virgin and child in which the child twists around to engage the viewer's eye employed an established visual device for inviting the viewer to participate in the pictured scene" ("Virgin's One Bare Breast," 202). Miles cites Baxandall, *Painting and Experience*.

2. LECLERC, *Parole de Femme*, 148 (my translation). For a thorough treatment of the mammalian bases of maternal feelings, see Hrdy, *Mother Nature*.
3. For a riveting portrait of motherhood in conditions of extreme poverty, see Scheper-Hughes, *Death Without Weeping*.
4. HAYS, *Cultural Contradictions of Motherhood*, xv.
5. A woman's experience of her reproductive body, in particular its uncontrollability or "leakiness" (menstruation, vaginal secretion, leaking breasts during lactation) can become symbolized in ways that fuel a sense of oneself as too "female," too emotional, or as unable to "contain" one's thoughts or think clearly. See Kalinich, "Sense of Absence."
6. The conflict embedded here is fed both by the ways in which the structures of work are inimical to parenthood and by the ways in which parenthood and family have become, in some sense, the last outpost of community and shared emotional engagement. Marriage, religion, and neighborhood no longer offer the continuity that they once did; nor, it seems, do they continue to provide as compelling avenues for expressing and supporting community feeling as do children.
7. "'[Childbirth produces] more pronounced changes than at any time other than death,' says Raphael Good, an Ob-Gyn and psychiatrist at the University of Miami" (*Newsweek*, July 2, 2001, 26).
8. These were Frost's words: "My poems — I should suppose everybody's poems — are all set to trip the reader head foremost into the boundless" (quoted in Bomford, *Symmetry of God*, 52).
9. DeCASPER and FIFER, "Of Human Bonding," 1174–76. The interpretation of this research is drawn from Stephen A. Mitchell, *Relationality*, 8–9.
10. STERN, *Interpersonal World of the Infant*, 141.
11. PINKER, *Language Instinct*, 279.
12. FERNALD, "Human Maternal Vocalization," cited in Pinker, *Language Instinct*, 279.
13. STEPHEN MITCHELL, *Relationality*, 8. My discussion of Loewald is indebted to Mitchell's astute reading.
14. LOEWALD, "Psychoanalysis as an Art," 363.
15. LOEWALD, "Primary Process," 185.
16. BOMFORD, *Symmetry of God*, 150.
17. Bomford writes: "The mystical journey is an attempt by the conscious mind to enter the realm that otherwise is wholly unconscious" (*Symmetry of God*, 58–59).
18. St. Augustine addressed God as "The Beauty, both so ancient and so new," in *Confessions*, book 10, chap. 27 (quoted in Bomford, *Symmetry of God*, 12).
19. For a beautiful essay that touches on similar themes, see Lear, "Introduction of Eros." Lear writes (134–35):

In response to Aristophanes, Socrates tells a story which he says he once heard from a priestess who taught him "the art of love." Diatoma, the priestess, questions Socrates, and from their dialogue it emerges that eros can neither be an immortal god nor a mere mortal. Rather, eros lives in an "intermediate region," between the divine and human realms, and shuttles back and forth as a messenger. . . . On this interpretation, eros bridges the gap between the transcendent and the immanent realms. Eros would thus create a "transitional space" whereby mundane life is invested with deep value and meaning.

. . . Eros, for Loewald, constitutes the field through which meanings flow. Mother, one might say, plays the roles both of divine and messenger.

20. ERDRICH, *Blue Jay's Dance*, 134.

21. In an essay "My Milk," writer Anne Enright describes a way in which breast-feeding an infant "precedes" language: "I suspect, as I search the room for the hunger by the fireplace, or the hunger in her cry, that I have found a place before stories start. Or the precise place where stories start. How else can I explain the shift from language that has happened in my brain? This is why mothers do not write, because motherhood happens in the body, as much as the mind." Also see Balsam, "Mother Within the Mother," 467–69. D. W. Winnicott referred to mothers' mental state in the weeks after giving birth as "primary maternal preoccupation," in "From Dependence Towards Independence," 85–86.

22. See Stern et al., "Non-Interpretive Mechanisms in Psychoanalytic Psychotherapy."

23. Regarding the not completely conscious quality of these interactions, note Stern's finding that in 32 percent of affect attunements with their babies, mothers reported conscious awareness of what they were doing; in 24 percent, they reported being entirely unaware, and in 43 percent, only partly aware (*Interpersonal World of the Infant*, 149).

24. In the discussion that follows, I will not be dealing with the most obvious, overarching goal of mothering: ensuring the survival of the human species.

25. See Csikszentmihalyi, *Flow*.

26. STERN, *Interpersonal World of the Infant*, 148.

27. Csikszentmihalyi writes: "This growth of self occurs only if the interaction is an enjoyable one, that is, if it offers nontrivial opportunities for action and requires a constant perfection of skills" (*Flow*, 65). For a deeply thoughtful philosophical perspective on the goals that structure mothering activity, see Ruddick, *Maternal Thinking*.

28. See Csikszentmihalyi, *Flow*, 62–66.

29. CSIKSZENTMIHALYI, *Flow*, 66.

30. See Moi, *Sexual/Textual Politics*, 161–73, for a lucid guide to Kristeva's complex terminology.

31. KRISTEVA, "About Chinese Women," 156.

32. KRISTEVA, "Women's Time," 206.

33. In Nina Winter's *Interview with the Muse*, Weldon said: "Another thing that seems quite helpful to the creative process is having babies. It does not distract at all from one's creativity. It reminds one that there is always more where that came from and there is never any shortage of ideas or of the ability to create. The process of being pregnant and then of hav-

ing the baby and getting up in the night only puts one more in touch with this fecund part of oneself" (42).

34. D.W. Winnicott describes this process in "Note on the Mother-Foetus Relationship."

35. Kristeva, "Women's Time," 192. See also Moi, "Introduction."

36. Miles, "Jesus Before He Could Talk."

37. Kristeva, "Stabat Mater," in Female Body in Western Culture, 115.

38. Kristeva, "Stabat Mater," in Female Body in Western Culture, 110. See also Weir, "Identification with the Divided Mother," 81–84.

39. Kristeva, "Stabat Mater," in Kristeva Reader, 163.

40. Weir, "Identification with the Divided Mother," 82.

41. Bomford, Symmetry of God.

42. Weir, "Identification with the Divided Mother," 88.

43. Weir, "Identification with the Divided Mother," 89.

44. Slade et al., "Mothers' Representations of Their Relationships." Page numbers for quotations are 612, 614, and 613 respectively.

45. For a more extensive description of how a mother's autonomous-secure, dismissing, or preoccupied approach to attachment affects her child, see Fonagy et al., "Attachment, the Reflective Self, and Borderline States."

46. Coates, "Having a Mind of One's Own," 122–23.

47. Coates, "Having a Mind of One's Own," 122.

48. Peri and Moses, Mothers Who Think.

49. Quoted in Lambert, "Image and the Arc of Feeling."

50. Although, as Jonathan Lear has written: "From a psychoanalytic point of view, everyone is poetic; everyone dreams in metaphor and generates symbolic meaning in the process of living. Even in their prose, people have unwittingly been speaking poetry all along" ("Introduction of Eros," 31).

51. Kristeva, "Women's Time," 206.

52. Quoted in Graybeal, "Kristeva's Delphic Proposal," 35.

53. Csikszentmihalyi, Flow, 143.

54. Quoted in Csikszentmihalyi, Flow, 148.

5. Ambivalence

1. Lamott, "Mother Anger," 94–95.

2. Quoted in Chira, A Mother's Place, 62.

3. Janna Malamud Smith treats what may be the most primal impediment to maternal enjoyment, anxiety about successfully safeguarding and protecting one's young, in her book Potent Spell.

4. Csikszentmihalyi uses the expression "unselfconscious self-assurance" in Flow, 203.

5. See, for example, Parker, Mother Love/Mother Hate.

6. Pearson, I Don't Know How She Does It, 263.

7. Ann Crittenden, Price of Motherhood.

8. Lewin, "Study Says Little Has Changed."

9. Nancy Chodorow made this point in Reproduction of Mothering, as did Dorothy Dinnerstein, more apocalyptically, in Mermaid and Minotaur.

Arlie Russell Hochschild took up the issue of equality in household work in *Second Shift*.

10. MAHONY, *Kidding Ourselves*, 139–48. Mahony offers a savvy set of negotiating principles that she argues are crucial to women's ability to realize equitable division of labor in marriage.

11. For a trenchant discussion of the mixed motives mothers bring to their overburdened "second shift" lives, see Maushart, *Mask of Motherhood*, 222–26.

12. FOLBRE, *Invisible Heart*, 35.

13. GRIGORIADIS, "Baby Panic," 22.

14. CHODOROW, "Preface to the Second Edition," in *Reproduction of Mothering*.

15. KATIE ROIPHE, "Grandmother's Biological Clock," 80.

16. HRDY, *Mother Nature*, xii–xiv.

17. The psychoanalyst Carolyn Ellman suggests that when a girl is the particular object of her father's devotion, she may deny competition and envy toward her mother, feeling "she is the favorite and there is no other. In this state, there is no envy, since the mother hardly exists" ("Empty Mother," 646). Note also in this connection Janine Chasseguet-Smirgel's classic paper "Freud and Female Sexuality," in which she argues that men deny women power because they feel women, in their capacity as mothers, have so much of it. As women have gained access to positions of cultural and economic power occupied previously by men, they may perceive their power, as men traditionally have, as a way to deny or deflect the (sometimes excessive) power mothers exert. They may also develop difficulties, similar to men's, around opening up to the "maternal," a stance they are compelled to revisit when they themselves become mothers.

18. ELLMAN, "Empty Mother," 651.

19. ELLMAN, "Empty Mother," 652.

20. By denying that "something" to her mother in fantasy — whether power, creativity, desire, babies — she effectively denies it to herself too, through guilt and fantasized punishment.

21. For example, beauty is the particular focus of envy in *Snow White*, whereas greed and envy of food is prominent in *Hansel and Gretel*.

22. There is an extensive body of psychoanalytic writing on the dynamics of envy, beginning with Melanie Klein's classic work, *Envy and Gratitude*. For consideration of the particular place of envy in female development, see, for example, Burke, *Gender and Envy*; and Adrienne Harris, "Aggression, Envy, and Ambition."

23. Quoted in Grigoriadis, "Baby Panic," 24.

24. WASSERSTEIN, "Competitive Moms," 259.

25. PARKER, *Mother Love/Mother Hate*, 59.

26. PARKER, *Mother Love/Mother Hate*, 6–7. Because ambivalence is a universal psychological experience, Parker is concerned to emphasize that in mothering, "ambivalence itself is emphatically not the problem; the issue is how a mother manages the guilt and anxiety ambivalence provokes" (6).

27. See Parker, *Mother Love/Mother Hate*, 135–37.

28. See, for example, Parker, *Mother Love/Mother Hate*, 2.

29. QUINDLEN, "Playing God on No Sleep," 64.

30. See Csikszentmihalyi, *Flow*, for an illuminating discussion of the relationship between boredom, anxiety, challenges, and skills (52, 72–77).

31. WINNICOTT, "Transitional Objects and Transitional Phenomena," 14, and "Playing," 53.

32. WINNICOTT, "Capacity to Be Alone," 30, 34. Peter Fonagy summarized the idea this way: "Winnicott proposes that the child needs to be able to play alone in the presence of the mother if a stable true sense of self is to emerge. She must be sufficiently unobtrusive for the child to forget her and to focus on self-exploration, which lies at the root of solitary play. A defended or unavailable caregiver will force the child to think about the parent and thus not be able to remember himself" (*Attachment Theory and Psychoanalysis*, 98–99).

33. See, for example, Parker, *Mother Love/Mother Hate*, 24; Benjamin, *Bonds of Love*, chap. 5; Thurer, *Myths of Motherhood*; and Douglas and Michaels, *Mommy Myth*.

34. WINNICOTT, "Hate in the Counter-transference," 74; Joyce, *Ulysses*, 197; Paglia, *Sexual Personae*, 313; and Kimball, "Ambiguities of Milan Kundera," 10.

35. KIMBALL, "Ambiguities of Milan Kundera," 10. In a related vein, literary scholar Ann Douglas, discussing nineteenth-century American writing, described sentimentalism as "a cluster of ostensibly private feelings which always attains public and conspicuous expression. . . . Involved as it is with the exhibition and commercialization of the self, sentimentalism cannot exist without an audience" (*Feminization of American Culture*, 254).

36. Quoted in Phillips, *Winnicott*, 3.

37. Too often, a mother's aspiration to provide this kind of experience for her child is seen as focusing on the child at the expense of herself. That interpretation not only fails to see how focusing on the child is an aspiration for herself; it also minimizes how the authentic emotional communication in their relationship, enabled in part by the time they have together, is vitally important to her as well. For further discussion of Winnicott's concept of true and false self, see "Ego Distortion." See also Phillips, "On Risk and Solitude."

38. GHENT, "Masochism, Submission, Surrender," 108.

39. Another psychoanalyst, the late Doris Bernstein, articulated a critical distinction between being willing to endure pain for its own sake, and for an end that one has judged to be worthwhile. She wrote that a "woman's ability to tolerate pain (childbirth, etc.) must be differentiated from a masochistic wish for pain. So, too, the capacity to make self-sacrifices (as, for instance, in caring for her children) must be viewed as a pleasurable living up to an ego ideal, not as an expression of masochism" (*Female Identity Conflict*, 166). Also see Erikson, "Womanhood and the Inner Space": "It is obvious that woman's knowledge of pain makes her a 'dolorosa' in a deeper sense than one who is addicted to small pains.

She is, rather, one who 'takes pains' to understand and alleviate suffering and can train others in the forbearance necessary to stand unavoidable pain" (310).

40. CHODOROW and CONTRATTO, "Fantasy of the Perfect Mother," 88. Chodorow and Contratto suggest that feminists fall into the more general cultural pattern of mother-blame, "simply add[ing] on to this picture the notion that conditions other than the mother's incompetence or intentional malevolence create this maternal behavior" (89–90).

41. For a lonely defense of *Leave It to Beaver*, see bell hooks, *All About Love*, 26–28.

42. A. S. BYATT, *Still Life*, 187.

43. A. S. BYATT, *Still Life*, 161.

44. A. S. BYATT, *Still Life*, 163.

45. A. S. BYATT, *Still Life*, 166.

6. Child Care

1. For child care workers' perspectives on these same issues, see Ehrenreich and Hochschild, *Global Woman*.

2. From Payne, *Between Ourselves*, 181–84.

3. MASLOW, *Motivation and Personality*, chap. 4.

4. For example, statistics on day care staff turnover for 1997 revealed that 20 percent of centers reported losing 50 percent or more staff over the previous year. By staff category, 27 percent of teachers and 39 percent of assistants had left their job the previous year. See Vandell and Wolfe, "Child Care Quality."

5. See Clarke-Stewart, *Daycare*, 100–2.

6. POLLITT, *Subject to Debate*, xv.

7. GROSS, "Women and Their Work." For an insightful discussion of how polarized concepts of work and family fail to capture mothers' experience, see Garey, *Weaving Work and Motherhood*.

8. See Joan Williams, *Unbending Gender*, chap. 5.

9. ANN CRITTENDEN, *Price of Motherhood*, 17.

10. ANGIER, "Primate Expert Explores Motherhood's Brutal Side."

11. BURGGRAF, *Feminine Economy and Economic Man*, 13.

12. HRDY, *Mother Nature*, 50–52, 109–13.

13. CHIRA, *Mother's Place*, 123. For sources supporting this claim, see Chira, *Mother's Place*, notes to chap. 6. Also see Clarke-Stewart and Fein, "Early Childhood Programs."

14. CHIRA, *Mother's Place*, 124.

15. SCARR, "American Child Care Today," 100.

16. SCARR, "American Child Care Today," 99.

17. SCARR, "American Child Care Today," 105.

18. For a discussion of the downside of for-profit day care centers, including cutting corners on staff pay, training, and staff-to-child ratios, see Clarke-Stewart, *Daycare*, 54–55.

19. SCARR, "American Child Care Today," 106.

20. MICHEL, *Children's Interests/Mothers' Rights*.

21. MARILYNNE ROBINSON, *Death of Adam*, 4.

22. JOAN WILLIAMS, *Unbending Gender*, 38. In her view, "a subjective sense of authenticity and repose about one's 'choices' may reflect no more than a decision to bring one's life into alignment with the expectations and institutions of domesticity."

23. JOAN WILLIAMS, *Unbending Gender*, 5.

24. MAHONY, *Kidding Ourselves*, 139–48.

25. JOAN WILLIAMS, *Unbending Gender*, 49. The statistic is from the *Washington Post*, cited on 286. The Packard Foundation report "Caring for Infants and Toddlers" cited 1999 findings that put the figure at 68 percent of mothers and 69 percent of fathers (reported in Lewin, "Study Says Little Has Changed").

26. BRAZELTON and GREENSPAN, *Irreducible Needs of Children*, 48.

27. JOAN WILLIAMS, *Unbending Gender*, 37.

28. Joan Williams offers a nuanced and sustained critique of the "full commodification model," a phrase coined by economist Barbara Bergman to refer to the "traditional feminist strategy [in which] women's equality is for women to work full time, with child care delegated to the market" (*Unbending Gender*, 40).

29. CHIRA, *Mother's Place*, 17.

30. CHIRA, *Mother's Place*, 214.

31. LEAR, *Open Minded*, 43. See chap. 2, "Knowingness and Abandonment."

32. LEAR, *Open Minded*, 43.

33. LEWIN, "Now a Majority."

34. CYNTHIA LEE STARNES, Letter to the Editor, *New York Times*, October 28, 2000.

35. Information about the study can be obtained at the NICHD website: www.nichd.nih.gov/od/secc/index.htm. The site provides a listing of the published scientific papers based upon the study's data. In broad terms, the NICHD study suggests that if a family has a good income and the mother is well educated, a child has a good chance of doing well, whether she is in day care or not. With respect to the amount of child care, no consistent direct relationship has been found between hours spent in child care and children's cognitive, language, or social development. A higher quantity of hours spent in child care has been found to have a small but statistically significant effect on the probability of less harmonious mother-child relationships and more problem behaviors at two years old. In terms of quality of care, lower-quality care has been found to be modestly associated with less harmonious mother-child relationships, more problem behaviors, and lack of school readiness. Higher-quality care, as might be expected, has been associated with the opposite effects: more harmonious relationships, less problem behavior, and greater school readiness.

36. I am focusing only on those aspects of the findings that relate specifically to the mother-child relationship, but I do not want to leave the reader with the impression that those findings comprise the bulk of the study.

Consult the NICHD website for more information about the variables the study has measured.

37. NICHD Early Child Care Research Network, "Effects of Infant Child Care." "Minimal amounts of childcare" were defined in the statistical analysis as ten hours or fewer per week.

38. NICHD Early Child Care Research Network, "Child Care and Mother-Child Interaction." For a review of the research linking attachment security to caregiver sensitivity, see Belsky, "Interactional and Contextual Determinants," 251–54.

39. NIH News Alert, "Only Small Link Found." Regarding this issue, the study itself points out: "The meaningfulness of these effects rests on the extent to which such small degrees of difference in maternal sensitivity or the child's engagement with the mother relate to meaningful differences in children's developmental outcomes at these and later ages. They may not." NICHD Early Child Care Research Network, "Child Care and Mother-Child Interaction in the First Three Years of Life," 1409.

40. SHELLENBARGER, "Here's the Bottom Line."

41. BROOKS-GUNN, HAN, and WALDFOGEL, "Maternal Employment and Child Cognitive Outcomes."

42. The children whose school readiness was most adversely affected by early and full-time maternal employment included, intriguingly, three quite different groups: boys, children with married parents, and children whose mothers had been rated as insensitive when the children were six months old.

43. Initially, day care research tended to draw on an attachment paradigm, which suggested that child care was problematic because it meant repeated separations from the mother, which the child then interpreted as an abandonment or rejection, affecting in turn the security of the child's attachment to the mother. In contrast to this "maternal separation model," the NICHD research design relies more heavily on a "quality of mothering model." In this model, the mother's employment, and the time away from the child that it requires, affects the quality of the mother-child interaction, which in turn may affect the child's security of attachment to the mother. See Jaeger and Weinraub, "Early Nonmaternal Care and Infant Attachment," for a fuller discussion of these models.

44. McLAUGHLIN and KRAUS, *Nanny Diaries*, 26.

45. BASS, "Price of Success."

46. LAIBLE and THOMPSON, "Mother-Child Discourse" and "Mother-Child Conflict in the Toddler Years"; and Dunn, Brown, and Beardsall, "Family Talk About Feeling States."

47. WINNICOTT, "Morals and Education," 100.

48. See, for example, Ahnert and Lamb, "Shared Care," 1044–45.

49. There is also broad variability in how mothers experience being apart from or together with their children. Some feel all right about giving up a little closeness for more autonomy. Some feel out of touch without a great deal of hands-on interaction with their children. The psychoanalyst Patricia Nachman has researched mothers' subjective experience of closeness and

distance with their children, including "how mothers convey their availability in terms that go beyond that of physical presence." She concluded that the "mother's imagination about closeness and distance are important factors in formulating new ways of thinking about the separation-individuation process and the conditions that contribute to the child's experience of maternal availability" ("Maternal Identification," 223).

50. CUSK, *Life's Work*, 206.
51. Quoted in Chira, *Mother's Place*, 13.
52. SCARR, PHILLIPS, and McCARTNEY, "Working Mothers and Their Families," 1405.
53. LEACH, *Your Baby and Child*, 8.
54. See, for example, Eyer, *Motherguilt*, chap. 3; and Peters, *When Mothers Work*, 42–43. For a rebuttal of the claim that the research method used for studying attachment is "unscientific," see Belsky, quoted in Karen, *Becoming Attached*, 328.
55. Quoted in Hrdy, *Mother Nature*, 485.
56. BOWLBY, *Maternal Care and Mental Health*, 67–68, quoted in Karen, *Becoming Attached*, 63–64.
57. CHIRA, *Mother's Place*, 51.
58. LEACH, *Your Baby and Child*, 8.
59. The psychologist Judith Harris caused a stir some years ago with her book *Nurture Assumption*, which claimed that parents had negligible effects on their children's personality characteristics over and above their genetic contribution. But the one parental influence that Harris conceded had to do with happiness: "People sometimes ask me, 'So you mean it doesn't matter how I treat my child?' They never ask, 'So it doesn't matter how I treat my husband or wife?' and yet the situation is similar. I don't expect that the way I act toward my husband is going to determine what kind of person he will be ten or twenty years from now. I do expect, however, that it will affect how happy he is to live with me and whether we will still be good friends in twenty years" (341).
60. CHIRA, *Mother's Place*, xviii.
61. LECLERC, *Parole de Femme*, 148 (my translation).

7. Adolescence

1. Psychologists have recently questioned the characterization of adolescence as predominantly a time of turbulence. See Arnett, "Adolescent Storm and Stress."
2. See Erikson, "Womanhood and the Inner Space," 291–318.
3. ANNE ARCHER, interviewed in Bonavoglia, *Choices We Made*, 108. See also Dalsimer, *Female Adolescence*, a psychoanalytic study of adolescent heroines from literature, in which Dalsimer observes: "Juliet's soliloquy and Anne Frank's diary give voice to the welcoming of approaching womanhood and of newly awakened sexuality. It is this possibility that has, I believe, been the most serious omission from traditional psychoanalytic theory about female adolescence" (139–40).

4. APTER, *Altered Loves*, 87–88.
5. See, for example, Orbach, *Fat Is a Feminist Issue*, 50; Wolf, *Beauty Myth*, 204–5; Debold, Wilson, and Malave, *Mother-Daughter Revolution*, chaps. 2 and 5; Brown and Gilligan, *Meeting at the Crossroads*, 219–21; Gilligan, Rogers, and Brown, "Soundings," 327; and, not least, the founding text of the genre, Rich, *Of Woman Born*. For a critical discussion, see Hirsch, "Feminist Discourse/Maternal Discourse," 165.
6. BRUMBERG, *Body Project*.
7. All quotes are from Kuczynski, "She's Got to Be a Macho Girl."
8. KUCZYNSKI, "She's Got to Be a Macho Girl."
9. BELL, "Objects of Affection, Subjects of Desire."
10. Ozment's chapter "Parental Advice" in his book *Ancestors*, 77–103, documents various historical examples of parents' advice to young adult children that conform much more closely to the tenor of *Little Women* than to what we tend to offer today.
11. WINNICOTT, "Morals and Education," in *Maturational Processes*, 100.
12. KUCZYNSKI, "She's Got to Be a Macho Girl."
13. KUCZYNSKI, "She's Got to Be a Macho Girl."
14. GARDNER, "Mom vs. Mom," 25.
15. COLIN, "My Lunch with Paul Auster."
16. *CosmoGirl* cover shown is illustration for Kuczynski, "She's Got to Be a Macho Girl."
17. BORDO, *Unbearable Weight*, 171.
18. BORDO, *Unbearable Weight*, 178.
19. The general interpretation I am offering is obviously speculative and empirically untested, as is true of most social theory on eating disorders. Aside from the psychodynamic factors involved, newer evidence suggests that genetic factors exert an effect, as well as a number of social factors, including media influence, the pressures of peer group membership, and even the impact of immigration and the process of cultural assimilation. For a review, see Becker et al., "Genes (and/or) Jeans?" Whatever the genetic contributions prove to be, eating disorders have flourished at unprecedented levels in recent decades, a phenomenon that has prompted thinkers in diverse fields to reflect on the sociocultural factors involved.
20. CHERNIN, *Hungry Self*, 42.
21. Chernin writes of herself, "Many women of my age have difficulty thinking of themselves as mothers. No matter how hard we have tried, we have never succeeded wholeheartedly in embracing the maternal role" (*Hungry Self*, 74).
22. CHERNIN, *Hungry Self*, 47–48.
23. BULLITT-JONAS, *Holy Hunger*, 45.
24. See Apter, *Altered Loves*, chap. 2.
25. In a study that relates eating disorders to the capacity for reflection, Catherine Steiner-Adair asked thirty-two female secondary school students to describe their perception of cultural values and images of women, as well as their own personal ones. Of her respondents, 60 percent took a personal perspective on cultural images of women and defined an ideal

image of their own. The other 40 percent offered rigidly perfect cultural ideals, which they endorsed as their own personal ideals. None of the first group scored in the eating disordered range of an eating attitudes test, but virtually all of the second group did.

The interesting implication of Steiner-Adair's finding is not so much the attitudes themselves that each group endorsed but rather what they imply about their reflective capacity. Unable to take a critical distance from cultural ideal images, the 40 percent group — Steiner-Adair dubbed them "Super Women" — responded as if there were no such thing as an internal reality that interpreted external reality. See Steiner-Adair, "Body Politic."

26. GOLDSTEIN and KORNFIELD, *Seeking the Heart of Wisdom*, 38.

27. GOLDSTEIN and KORNFIELD, *Seeking the Heart of Wisdom*, 36.

28. Accessible Buddhist discussions of desire are found in Boorstein, *It's Easier Than You Think;* and Salzberg, *Heart as Wide as the World*, among many others.

29. MUSICK, *Young, Poor, and Pregnant*, 109–10.

30. This psychological observation has a socioeconomic analogue in the finding that as women's literacy and education levels rise, fertility rates decline. For a discussion of this phenomenon from an economic perspective, see Sen, *Development as Freedom*, especially chap. 8.

31. DEAN, *Teenage Pregnancy*, 126–30, 163.

32. DEAN, *Teenage Pregnancy*, 106–7.

33. DEAN, *Teenage Pregnancy*, 158.

34. DEAN, *Teenage Pregnancy*, 125.

35. The groundwork for these trends, other research suggests, may be laid in earlier childhood. Fonagy et al. found that "mothers in a relatively high-stress (deprived) group characterized by single-parent families, parental criminality, unemployment, overcrowding, and psychiatric illness would be far more likely to have securely attached infants if their reflective functioning was high" (*Attachment Theory and Psychoanalysis*, 27, reporting findings from Fonagy et al., "Theory and Practice of Resilience").

36. DEAN, *Teenage Pregnancy*, 117. Dean writes in her conclusions: "Family environments in which husbands and wives value their relationships with each other and in which husbands (fathers) are consistently present and active in their children's lives seem to be especially important in supporting favorable psychological outcomes for children. That this would be a primary finding in a study focusing almost exclusively on mothers and daughters attests to the importance of men in the lives of mothers and children" (200).

37. MACHUNG, "Talking Careers, Thinking Job." Machung's findings contrast somewhat with Folbre's observation referred to in chap. 5, 129. Whereas both Machung's female interviewees and Folbre's students expected to take time out of their careers to raise children, Folbre's students did not admit the impact of that choice on their future earnings. One possible reason for this difference might be that Folbre asked her question in the public setting of a college course on the political economy of women,

whereas Machung conducted one-on-one research interviews. In public before their peers, Folbre's students may have been less willing ("almost embarrassed") to articulate their own conflicting goals regarding work and eventual motherhood than were the students in Machung's more private interview setting.

38. ORENSTEIN, *Flux*, 19.
39. MAYER, "Women, Creativity, and Power," 121.
40. Michelangelo's *Night*, Florence, San Lorenzo, New Sacristy. Pictured in Salmi, *Complete Works of Michelangelo*, 116.
41. Recent research suggests that the association of anorexia nervosa with high socioeconomic status has yet to be empirically demonstrated, and that bulimia nervosa may in fact be correlated with lower socioeconomic status. See, for instance, Gard and Freedman, "Dismantling of a Myth." For a review of the association of eating disorders and ethnicity, see Smolak and Striegel-Moore, "Challenging the Myth of the Golden Girl."

8. Fertility

1. SILBER, *How to Get Pregnant*, 57; and Nofziger, *Fertility Question*.
2. ASRM's advertising campaign was discussed by Kalb, "Truth About Fertility," 42.
3. "InterNational Council on Infertility Information Dissemination Protests the New Infertility Public Service Campaign by the American Society for Reproductive Medicine," INCIID.org, August 6, 2001, Arlington, VA.
4. Judith Sternberg Turiel catalogues these risk factors in *Beyond Second Opinions*, 317–20.
5. See, for example, Kalb, "Truth About Fertility," 42.
6. A quote from the psychic "Maureen," in Alden, *Crossing the Moon*, 282.
7. Judith Sternberg Turiel points out that some women can easily imagine a satisfying life without children, but once they decide to pursue pregnancy, the quest to conceive can become all-consuming, taking on a life of its own (conversation with author, March 22, 2003). For psychoanalytically informed explorations of the ways that culture and emotion interact in the creation of personal meaning, see Chodorow, *Power of Feelings*; and Stephen A. Mitchell, *Relationality*. For a view of emotion as largely created through cultural and linguistic practices, see Lutz, *Unnatural Emotions*.
8. ALDEN, *Crossing the Moon*, 3.
9. ALDEN, *Crossing the Moon*, 17.
10. DOWNS, *Fertility of American Women*. For an exploration of the affirmative decision not to have children, see Safer, *Beyond Motherhood*.
11. COLLINS, "Mother At Last," 57.
12. For a psychoanalytic discussion of the effects of these cultural forces on women's psyches, see Layton, "Working Nine to Nine," and "Relational No More."
13. LOPATE, "Lake of Suffering," 108–9.

14. SHACOCHIS, "Missing Children," 41.
15. SHACOCHIS, "Missing Children," 45.
16. DANIELLE CRITTENDEN, *What Our Mothers Didn't Tell Us*, chap. 2.
17. AGNES ROSSI, "In Vitro," 63.
18. *Newsweek*, August 13, 2001, 42.
19. For written accounts that touch on similar feelings, see Bartholet's *Family Bonds*, in which she chronicles in painful detail the eight-year obsession with becoming pregnant that preceded her decision to adopt; and Bialosky and Schulman's edited collection, *Wanting a Child*.
20. From Sullerot, *Women, Society, and Change*, quoted in Martin, *Woman in the Body*, 100.
21. LUKER, *Dubious Conceptions*, 172–73.
22. LUKER, *Dubious Conceptions*, 17.
23. HODDER, "New Fertility," 98–99.
24. TURIEL, *Beyond Second Opinions*, 291.
25. Turiel gives some specific suggestions in *Beyond Second Opinions* (149):

> First, information about fertility, contraceptive choices, pelvic inflammatory disease (PID), and prevention and treatment of sexually transmitted diseases would be widely available to teenagers as well as adults. Women and men in their twenties and early thirties would have employment and educational choices that include flexible schedules, job sharing, part-time work, generous maternal and paternal leaves, and work-at-home options (especially with widespread use of personal computer networks); high-quality childcare at or near work sites; affordable health care that emphasizes prevention of infertility — and that provides health care for children. Such changes could help reduce the pressure on young women to choose between children and career, reducing also the number of potential patients who, for reasons of physiology, truly need to rely on fertility treatment as their only hope of pregnancy.

> The improbability that our society will realize such a humane social program for safeguarding women's interests is tied, as Katha Pollitt has pointed out, to the absence of a larger movement of social justice. See her *Subject to Debate*, xxi.

26. For further discussion of the girls' psychological development with respect to motherhood and fertility, see Pines, *Woman's Unconscious Use of Her Body*, especially "Emotional Aspects of Infertility and Its Remedies"; and Kestenberg, *Children and Parents*, part 1.
27. For one example among many, see Griffin, *Woman and Nature*.
28. For two admirably cogent and complex articulations of this view, see Martin, *Woman in the Body*; and Davis-Floyd, *Birth as an American Rite of Passage*. The dichotomy between patriarchal-technological and woman-centered-natural with which Davis-Floyd initially approached her research yielded to more nuanced appreciation of individual differences over the course of her study.
29. For the fullest development of this idea, see Dinnerstein, *Mermaid and*

Minotaur. Steiner-Adair discusses fantasies of limitless bounty with respect to both women and the earth in "Politics of Prevention," 390. The fantasy of female fecundity as "always there" does not depend on whether an individual's mother was indeed present and involved. Even when a girl experiences her relationship with her own mother as dangerous or destructive, the illusion of fertility as eternally available appears to hold emotional power. See Chodorow, "'Too Late'"; and Pines, *Woman's Unconscious Use of Her Body.*

30. RAPP, *Testing the Woman.*

31. POLLITT, *Reasonable Creatures,* 46.

32. There is some controversy on this point. Though the health benefits of breastfeeding are widely endorsed, Sandra Steingraber investigates the threats to breast milk posed by environmental toxins in *Having Faith.*

33. BLUM, *At the Breast,* 53. Blum adds: "Psychoanalyst Michelle Friedman points out that the breast milk takes on a fetishized quality when it is so often emphasized apart from, and as equivalent to, the embodied, relational practice." In psychoanalytic terms, a "fetish" can be understood as a thing, or a part of a person, that we focus on because it is less frightening than a whole person. As psychoanalyst Louise Kaplan has written, "The fetish is designed to divert attention from a whole story by focusing attention on a detail." The sexual fetish, Kaplan further explains, is a way to cope with a sense of loss; it is "constructed to represent absences of losses of every kind — castrations, deprivations, separations, illnesses, abandonments, annihilations, deaths — as well as to represent the powers that can diagnose, protect, ameliorate, heal, remedy, fix, and resurrect" (*Female Perversions,* 122–23).

34. BARTHOLET, *Family Bonds,* 31.

35. In a related vein, in Hodder, "New Fertility," 97, Elizabeth Bartholet says our society is

> "completely inconsistent and schizophrenic" regarding the significance of the biological link. Although "adoption regulation is premised on the notion that biology is everything," with its focus on the rights of the birth mother (and father), "our tolerance of a free market in the ART realm seems premised on the attitude that biology doesn't matter at all," she says. "Therefore it's OK to induce men to give sperm for money, and have laws set up so that they have no responsibility for the child. Therefore it's perfectly legal, at least so far, for women to be induced to come in and 'sell' their eggs."

36. BARTHOLET, *Family Bonds,* xiv–xv.

37. EISENBERG, "Adoption Paradox," 82.

38. See, for example, Waterman, *Birth of an Adoptive, Foster, or Step-mother.*

39. LUDTKE, *On Our Own,* 432–34.

40. AGNES ROSSI, "In Vitro," 62.

41. COLETTE, *L'Etoile Vesper,* quoted by de Beauvoir in *Second Sex,* 560.

42. KRISTEVA, "Women's Time," 206.

43. KRISTEVA, "Women's Time," 206.

44. I am indebted to Lisa Buchberg, DMH, for this insight.

45. The "baby blues" often follow childbirth, but some women find their sad, anxious, or fearful feelings postpartum do not subside, but become more intense and longer lasting. Two organizations that provide public education and advocacy about postpartum depression, as well as referrals for women in need, are: Depression After Delivery, Inc., 91 East Somerset St., Raritan, NJ 08869, (908) 541–9712, 800–944–4PPD, www.depressionafter delivery.com; and Postpartum Support, International, 927 N. Kellogg Ave., Santa Barbara, CA 93111, (805) 967-7636, www.postpartum.net.

9. Abortion

1. For a review article on the normal immunological suppressions, and enhancements, of pregnancy, see Priddy, "Immunologic Adaptations During Pregnancy."

2. There are abortions, to be sure, that are conducted in a seemingly offhand or callous way. Some affluent teenage girls, Naomi Wolf writes, treat it as "a rite of passage"; they "choose abortion because they were careless or in a hurry or didn't like the feel of latex" ("Our Bodies Our Souls," 851).

3. For example, Robert Bork wrote that "the vast majority of all abortions are for convenience." He supports his contention with the finding that among the top reasons women gave for their abortions were: "concerned about how having a baby could change her life (76%);" "can't afford baby now (68%)"; and "has problems with relationship or wants to avoid single parenthood (51%)." Concluding that "the reasons most women give for having an abortion are 'social,'" Bork attempts to dismiss any reason that has to do with women's actual situations ("Inconvenient Lives"). See also Luker, *Abortion and the Politics of Motherhood*, 203.

4. GOPNIK, "Double Man," 91.

5. ANNE ROIPHE, *Fruitful*, 50–51.

6. This is harrowingly illustrated in Cynthia Gorney's monumental history of the American conflict over abortion, *Articles of Faith*.

7. BORDO, "Are Mothers Persons?," 73–74.

8. BORDO, "Are Mothers Persons?," 76.

9. BORDO, "Are Mothers Persons?," 78.

10. See Carter, *Culture of Disbelief*.

11. BORDO, "Are Mothers Persons?," 79.

12. BORDO, "Are Mothers Persons?," 94.

13. For a philosophical treatment of these issues, see Young, "Pregnant Embodiment."

14. BORDO, "Are Mothers Persons?," 93.

15. For the source of this argument, see Bolton, "Responsible Women and Abortion Decisions."

16. BROOKS, "the mother." This poem appears by special consent of the Brooks Permissions, with the understanding that Gwendolyn Brooks did not

want this work to promote the causes or arguments made by those on either side of abortion rights issues.

17. GORNEY, *Articles of Faith*, 78.
18. For a riveting treatment of the question of a mother murdering her child out of love, see Toni Morrison's novel *Beloved*.
19. DWORKIN, *Life's Dominion*, chaps. 1 and 2.
20. DWORKIN, *Life's Dominion*, 83.
21. DWORKIN, *Life's Dominion*, 84.
22. Kristin Luker catalogues many of the social characteristics that differentiate women who hold pro-choice and pro-life views. She illustrates that the relative weight women accord to natural and human creation tends to reflect how they have chosen to invest their own energies. See *Abortion and the Politics of Motherhood*, chap. 8.
23. LECLERC, *Parole de Femme*, 108–9 (my translation).
24. SANGER, *Woman and the New Race*.
25. Harper's Forum, "Is Abortion the Issue?," 36.
26. See, for example, Wolf, "Our Bodies Our Souls," 859–60; and MacKinnon, "Reflections on Sex Equality Under Law," discussed in Dworkin, *Life's Dominion*, 56–57.
27. This argument is made in Judith Jarvis Thomson's classic paper, "Defense of Abortion."

10. Midlife

1. KRISTEVA, "Women's Time," 206. The complete quotation is apposite: "The arrival of the child . . . leads the mother into the labyrinths of an experience that, without the child, she would only rarely encounter: love for an other. . . . The ability to succeed in this path without masochism and without annihilating one's affective, intellectual, and professional personality — such would seem to be the stakes to be won through guiltless maternity. It then becomes a creation in the strong sense of the term."
2. ANNE ROIPHE, *Fruitful*, 66–67.
3. ANGIER, *Woman*, 255.
4. ANGIER, *Woman*, 257.
5. STERN, *Motherhood Constellation*, 172–73.
6. STERN and BRUSCHWEILER-STERN, *Birth of a Mother*, 132–33.
7. STERN and BRUSCHWEILER-STERN, *Birth of a Mother*, 131.
8. BALSAM, "Mother Within the Mother," 473–74.
9. SCHULTZ, "Big Belly in Cambodia."
10. TENNESSEE WILLIAMS, *The Glass Menagerie*: "The time is short and it doesn't return again. It is slipping away while I write this and while you read it, and the monosyllable of the clock is Loss, loss, loss, unless you devote your heart to its opposition."
11. DEUTSCH, *Motherhood*, 484. For a recent reconsideration of the issue, see Bemesderfer, "Revised Psychoanalytic View of Menopause."
12. TALLMER, "Empty-Nest Syndrome," 242.
13. RUBIN, *Women of a Certain Age*.
14. See, for example, Fleming, *Motherhood Deferred*, and feminist reconsidera-

tions of children and fertility, such as Greer, *Sex and Destiny;* and Friedan, *Second Stage*.

15. ANN CRITTENDEN, *Price of Motherhood*, 3.
16. ANN CRITTENDEN, *Price of Motherhood*, 11.
17. CHEEVER, *As Good as I Could Be*, 55.
18. ANGIER, *Woman*, 255.
19. EDELMAN, *Measure of Our Success*, 5.
20. CLINTON, *It Takes a Village*, 108.
21. HEWLETT and WEST, *War Against Parents*, 30.
22. CLINTON, *It Takes a Village*, 101–2.
23. HEWLETT, *Lesser Life*, 22.
24. HEWLETT, *Lesser Life*, 22.
25. HEWLETT and WEST, *War Against Parents*, xi.
26. HEWLETT and WEST, *War Against Parents*, xi.
27. HEWLETT and WEST, *War Against Parents*, 53.
28. HEWLETT and WEST, *War Against Parents*, 19.
29. HOCHSCHILD, *Time Bind*, 249.
30. Rozsika Parker (*Mother Love/Mother Hate*, 103) helps make sense of this experience when she writes:

> Mother and child face the task of negotiating a sequence of separations from the moment of birth onwards. However, while children move with more or less difficulty towards an ever-increasing sense of themselves as individuals separate from their mothers, women evolve from one maternal identity to another. Thus they move from being a mother supporting a head, to a mother pushing a buggy, to a mother holding a hand to a mother waving a hand, to a mother waiting for a hand to hold. *But always a mother.*

31. ANNE ROIPHE, *Fruitful*, 211.
32. ANNE ROIPHE, *Fruitful*, 205–6.

11. Fathers

1. *Lawrence Telegram*, Lawrence, MA, June 4, 1903.
2. For example, infant-parent researcher Alicia Lieberman, in her paper, "Attachment Theory and Research," wrote:

> Attachment theory has been pivotal in increasing our awareness of early relationships as indispensable building blocks for the young child's unfolding personality. It is the first theory that allowed for systematic scientific documentation of the importance of love as an essential ingredient for healthy emotional development in infancy and early childhood. At the same time, because the primary focus of attachment theory and research is the mother-child relationship, an unintended side effect has been that, by omission rather than by commission, the importance of fathers in the child's emotional landscape has not received the attention it deserves.

3. On social inequities, see Burggraf, *Feminine Economy and Economic Man;* Ann Crittenden, *Price of Motherhood;* and Folbre, *Invisible Heart.* On fathers, see Pruett, *Fatherneed;* Parke and Brott, *Throwaway Dads;* and Popenoe, *Life Without Father.*

4. See, for example, Cowan and Cowan, *When Partners Become Parents,* chap. 5; Thompson and Walker, "Gender in Families"; Perkins and DeMeis, "Gender and Family Effects"; and Heymann, *Widening Gap.* For a discussion of how women assume the time commitment of emotional care as well, see Ruddick, "Care as Labor and Relationship"; and Alexandrov, "Seeking and Giving Emotional Care."

5. The Baby M case in the late 1980s, which pitted the interests of a (working class) birth mother paid for her surrogacy against the (professional) biological father to whom she was contractually bound to relinquish the child, catalyzed a feminist groundswell of support for protecting the rights of gestational and birth mothers. For a particularly intelligent discussion of the Baby M case, see Pollitt, "Contracts and Apple Pie."

6. JOAN WILLIAMS, *Unbending Gender,* 127.

7. See, for example, Bianchi, Subaiya, and Kahn, "Gender Cap in Economic Well-Being."

8. See Wallerstein, Lewis, and Blakeslee, *Unexpected Legacy of Divorce,* 251–53.

9. For examples, see Joan Williams, *Unbending Gender,* chap. 4; and Ann Crittenden, *Price of Motherhood,* chaps. 7 and 8.

10. RUBIN, *Women of a Certain Age,* 36.

11. BURGGRAF, *Feminine Economy,* 126.

12. HOCHSCHILD with MACHUNG, *Second Shift,* 18.

13. For a discussion of how, by contrast, fathers' lack of support can contribute to maternal ambivalence, see Parker, *Mother Love/Mother Hate,* 10–11. For research on how a father's realistic appraisal of the challenges of caring for children contribute to a mother's acceptance of her own ambivalence, see Boulton, *On Being a Mother.*

14. See, for example, Gottman and Silver, *Seven Principles for Making Marriage Work,* 212; Shapiro, Gottman, and Carrere, "Baby and Marriage"; and Cowan and Cowan, *When Partners Become Parents,* 101–2.

15. SIMPSON, *Anywhere But Here,* 3–4.

16. SHEA, "Mother of One," 197.

17. For an illuminating study of how mothers of children created by anonymous and known sperm donors think about and talk about the fathers of their children, see Hertz, "Father as an Idea."

18. See Heineman, "Boy and Two Mothers."

19. In her 1949 article "Love for the Mother and Mother-Love" (256), Alice Balint had this to say:

> Pregnancy, giving birth, suckling, and fondling are instinctual urges to a woman, and these she satisfies with the help of her baby. Physical proximity lasting as long as possible is pleasurable to both mother and child. In fact, I believe—turning again to anthropology — that those rules which separate man and wife after the birth of a child, often for many

months, have their origin in the desire of the woman to enjoy without disturbance the new relationship with her infant.

In most human societies, a woman's need for care after birth has been met by other women in her social group (see Kitzinger, *Ourselves as Mothers*). In American society today, many women rely on their husbands for emotional and pragmatic support while caring for infants, and many in fact take pleasure in their husband's nurturing of them postpartum. Beyond the direct gratification of being cared for by her husband, that pleasure may in part recapitulate being cared for by her mother, especially in times of vulnerability. I remember, in the days after the all-night labor that preceded giving birth to our first child, waking up from a stuporous nap when my husband entered the room, and reflexively uttering, "Mom?" In my twilight state of semiconsciousness, he and she were briefly fused.

20. SHEA, "Mother of One," 197.
21. POPENOE, *Life Without Father*, 32, 186. See also Belsky and Kelly, *Transition to Parenthood*, 244.
22. Nancy Chodorow explored this theme from a different angle in her essay "Oedipal Asymmetries and Heterosexual Knots."
23. An obvious problem with Dinnerstein's formulation is its neglect of the fluidity of gender identifications for both men and women. For example, a man can identify with his mother as he nurtures his new baby; that identification is not closed off to him simply because he is a man. For a useful critique of the assumptions about infant psychology and gender categories that underlie Dinnerstein's thesis, see Flax, "Reentering the Labyrinth."
24. From Loewald, "Review," 62, quoted in Lear, "Introduction of Eros," 124.
25. DINNERSTEIN, *Mermaid and Minotaur*, 31.
26. OXENHANDLER, *Eros of Parenthood*, 6.
27. DINNERSTEIN, *Mermaid and Minotaur*, 73.
28. For a thoughtful articulation of the fluidity between maternity and sexuality, see Traina, "Maternal Experience."
29. FREUD, "Three Essays on the Theory of Sexuality"; and Schwartz, *Sexual Subjects*, 52–53, quoted in Elise, "Generating Gender," 164.
30. ELISE, "Woman and Desire," 128.
31. At the same time, women have to be careful not to fall into the expectation that men are supposed to be transformed just the same way they themselves are. Women are sometimes prone to seeing fathers as mothers manquées, becoming exasperated when fathers fail to act in all important particulars like mothers. The kind of shared transformation I am getting at is not about dissolving difference; if anything, it involves a heightened attention to the experience of each individual.
32. The phrase "we must make certain our path is connected with our heart" is from Kornfield, *Path With Heart*, quoted in hooks, *All About Love*, 80.
33. HOOKS, *All About Love*, 4, quoting M. Scott Peck, *The Road Less Traveled*.

34. WILE, *After the Honeymoon*, 165.
35. WILE, *After the Honeymoon*, 47.

12. Time with Children

1. DI LAMPEDUSA, *Leopard*, 277–78.
2. "Nostalgia for the present" is a phrase recollected from a commentary on the Chinese philosopher Chuang-Tze, the source of which I was unable to locate. The 1 Corinthians 13:12 quotation is from the King James version of the Bible.
3. DE BEAUVOIR, *Second Sex*, 301; and Bauer, *Simone de Beauvoir*, 171.
4. GALINSKY, *1997 National Study*.
5. BURGGRAF, *Feminine Economy and Economic Man*, 11.
6. ROBINSON and GODBEY, *Time for Life*. The authors critique the methods of data interpretation used by Hochschild and Schor, 49–55. My reading of the research on time use indicates that there is a great deal of controversy about methods and interpretation. See, for instance, Janny Scott, "Working Hard."
7. ROBINSON and GODBEY, *Time for Life*, 128–29.
8. ROBINSON and GODBEY, *Time for Life*, 55.
9. For a discussion of the "time is money" metaphor, see Lakoff and Johnson, *Metaphors We Live By*, 7–9.
10. ROBINSON and GODBEY, *Time for Life*, 38–42.
11. PUGH, "When Is a Doll More Than a Doll?," 11–14. Pugh also points out that the catalogues' relentless emphasis on play as a means of developing skills implies that there is something inferior about "just play," which in turn feeds into the notion that "there is such a thing as 'wasted' time in childhood" (22).
12. See Parreñas, *Servants of Globalization*.
13. *The Rules*, in fact, appears to celebrate women's treatment as product (to wit, chap. 4's title, "But First the Product—You!," 15).
14. See, for example, Elkind, *Hurried Child*.
15. FROMM, *To Have or To Be?*, 91.
16. AHLBERG and AHLBERG, *Peek-A-Boo!*
17. The appeal of the product works on two levels. Whereas its stated purpose is to expose babies to "the greatest forms of human expression" because "your baby's potential is immense," its practical purpose is often to pacify babies while mothers are busy. ("Now that he is crawling and no longer content to chill out in his bouncy seat, *Baby Einstein* is the only thing he will sit still for," reports one mother on www.babyeinstein.com.)
18. LASCH-QUINN, "Mothers and Markets." She continues:

> Divorce, full-time day care, overwork, reliance on outside experts to cope with the ordinary challenges of everyday life, simultaneous full-time work schedules for both parents of young children, and the reduction of child rearing to the crass baseline of supervision: these are just a few tendencies that have come to be accepted as normal for middle-

class families. The full costs of this change are only now being fully felt, and fully admitted.

19. Billboard in Union Square, San Francisco, March 27, 2002.
20. Advertisement sponsored by the Ms. Foundation for Women, *New York Times*, section C, April 26, 2002.
21. BURGGRAF, *Feminine Economy and Economic Man*, 129.
22. HAYS, *Cultural Contradictions of Motherhood*, 18.
23. U.S. Department of Education. *Digest of Education Statistics 2000*.
24. For a fascinating study of class differences with respect to child rearing approaches, see Lareau, *Unequal Childhoods*.
25. SCHOR, *Overspent American*, 128.
26. McKIBBEN, *Maybe One; and* Joy Williams, "Case Against Babies," in *Best American Essays 1997*, 211.
27. The psychologist Wendy Mogel points out that relaxing our own standards of parental excellence makes for greater happiness. "Plan nothing," she suggests, "disappoint your kids with your essential mediocrity and the dullness of your home. Just hang around your children and wait to see what develops. Strive to be a 'good enough' parent, not a great one. It can make everyone in the family relax and paradoxically make life richer" (*Blessing of a Skinned Knee*, 57). A national advocacy organization whose explicit mission is to foster respect for individual mothers' choices and recognize the value of all mothers' work, paid and unpaid, is Mothers and More, found at www.mothersandmore.org.
28. See Hochschild, *Time Bind*, chap. 4.
29. ROBINSON and GODBEY, *Time for Life*, 316.
30. MERTON, *Love and Living*, 28, quoted in hooks, *All About Love*, 187. The phrase "the liberation of the heart which is love" is the Buddha's, from Salzburg, *Lovingkindness*, 1, quoted in hooks, *All About Love*, 83.

AHLBERG, JANET, and ALLAN AHLBERG. *Peek-A-Boo!* New York: Viking, 1990.

AHNERT, LIESELOTTE, and MICHAEL E. LAMB. "Shared Care: Establishing a Balance Between Home and Child Care Settings." *Child Development* 74, no. 4 (2003): 1044–49.

AINSWORTH, MARY, M. C. BLEHAR, E. WATERS, and S. WALL, eds. *Patterns of Attachment: A Psychological Study of the Strange Situation.* Hillsdale, NJ: Erlbaum, 1978.

ALDEN, PAULETTE BATES. *Crossing the Moon: A Journey Through Infertility.* St. Paul, MN: Hungry Mind Press, 1996.

ALEXANDROV, ELINA O. "Seeking and Giving Emotional Care: When Is Marriage a Safe Haven for Working Parents?" Working Paper no. 25, Center for Working Families, University of California at Berkeley, CA, April 2001.

ANGIER, NATALIE. "Primate Expert Explores Motherhood's Brutal Side." *New York Times*, Science section, February 8, 2000.

———. *Woman: An Intimate Geography.* Boston: Houghton Mifflin, 1999.

APTER, TERRI. *Altered Loves: Mothers and Daughters During Adolescence.* New York: St. Martin's Press, 1990.

ARIES, PHILIPPE. *Centuries of Childhood: A Social History of Family Life*, translated by Robert Baldick. New York: Alfred A. Knopf, 1962.

ARNETT, JEFFREY JENSEN. "Adolescent Storm and Stress, Reconsidered." *American Psychologist* 54, no. 5 (1999): 317–26.

BAIR, DEIRDRE. *Simone de Beauvoir: A Biography.* New York: Summit Books, 1990.

BALINT, ALICE. "Love for the Mother and Mother-Love." *International Journal of Psycho-Analysis* 30 (1949): 251–59.

BALSAM, ROSEMARY H. "The Mother Within the Mother." *Psychoanalytic Quarterly* 64, no. 3 (2000): 465–92.

BARTHES, ROLAND. *Mythologies*, translated by Annette Lavers. New York: Hill & Wang, 1987.

BARTHOLET, ELIZABETH. *Family Bonds: Adoption and the Politics of Parenting.* Boston: Houghton Mifflin, 1993.

BASS, ALISON. "The Price of Success." *Boston Globe Magazine*, July 22, 2001.

BASSIN, DONNA. "Maternal Subjectivity in the Culture of Nostalgia: Mourning and Memory." In *Representations of Motherhood*, edited by Donna Bassin, Margaret Honey, and Meryle Mahrer Kaplan, 162–73. New Haven, CT: Yale University Press, 1994.

BASSIN, DONNA, MARGARET HONEY, and MERYLE MAHRER KAPLAN, eds. *Representations of Motherhood.* New Haven, CT: Yale University Press, 1994.

BAUER, NANCY. *Simone de Beauvoir, Philosophy, and Feminism.* New York: Columbia University Press, 2001.

BAXANDALL, MICHAEL. *Painting and Experience in Fifteenth-Century Italy.* New York: Oxford University Press, 1972.

BECKER, ANNE E., PAMELA KEEL, EILEEN P. ANDERSON-FYE, and JENNIFER J. THOMAS. "Genes (and/or) Jeans?: Genetic and Socio-Cultural Contributions to Risk for Eating Disorders," *Journal of Addictive Diseases.* Forthcoming.

BEEBE, BEATRICE, and FRANK M. LACHMANN. *Infant Research and Adult Treatment: Co-Constructing Interactions.* Hillsdale, NJ: The Analytic Press, 2002.

BELL, LESLIE. "Objects of Affection, Subjects of Desire: Twenty-Something Women and the Contradictions of Sexuality." Unpublished doctoral dissertation, University of California at Berkeley.

BELSKY, JAY. "Interactional and Contextual Determinants of Attachment Security." In *Handbook of Attachment: Theory, Research, and Clinical Applications*, edited by Jude Cassidy and P. R. Shaver, 249–64. New York: Guilford, 1999.

BELSKY, JAY, and JOHN KELLY. *The Transition to Parenthood: How a First Child Changes a Marriage — Why Some Couples Grow Closer and Others Apart.* New York: Delacorte Press, 1994.

BEMESDERFER, SANDRA. "A Revised Psychoanalytic View of Menopause." *Journal of the American Psychoanalytic Association*, 44, suppl. (1996): 351–69.

BENHABIB, SEYLA. "The Generalized and the Concrete Other: The Kohlberg-Gilligan Controversy and Moral Theory." In *Feminist Social Thought: A Reader*, edited by Diana Tietjens Meyers, 736–56. New York: Routledge, 1997.

BENJAMIN, JESSICA. *The Bonds of Love: Psychoanalysis, Feminism, and the Problem of Domination.* New York: Pantheon, 1988.

———. *Like Subjects, Love Objects: Essays on Recognition and Sexual Difference.* New Haven, CT: Yale University Press, 1995.

———. "The Omnipotent Mother: A Psychoanalytic Study of Fantasy and Reality." In *Representations of Motherhood*, edited by Donna Bassin, Margaret Honey, and Meryle Mahrer Kaplan, 129–46. New Haven, CT: Yale University Press, 1994.

BERNSTEIN, DORIS. *Female Identity Conflict in Clinical Practice.* Northvale, NJ: Aronson, 1993.

BIALOSKY, JILL, and HELEN SCHULMAN, eds. *Wanting a Child.* New York: Farrar, Straus & Giroux, 1998.

BIANCHI, SUZANNE M., LEKHA SUBAIYA, and JOAN R. KAHN. "The Gender

Gap in the Economic Well-being of Nonresident Fathers and Custodial Mothers." *Demography* 36, no. 2 (May 1999): 195–203.

BLUM, LINDA M. *At the Breast: Ideologies of Breastfeeding and Motherhood in the Contemporary United States.* Boston: Beacon Press, 1999.

BOLTON, MARTHA BRANDT. "Responsible Women and Abortion Decisions." In *Having Children: Philosophical and Legal Reflections on Parenthood*, edited by Onora O'Neill and William Ruddick, 40–51. New York: Oxford University Press, 1979.

BOMFORD, RODNEY. *The Symmetry of God.* London: Free Association Books, 1999.

BONAVOGLIA, ANGELA, ed. *The Choices We Made: Twenty-Five Women and Men Speak Out About Abortion.* New York: Random House, 1991.

BOORSTEIN, SYLVIA. *It's Easier Than You Think: The Buddhist Way to Happiness.* San Francisco: HarperCollins, 1995.

BORDO, SUSAN. "Are Mothers Persons?: Reproductive Rights and the Politics of Subjectivity." In *Unbearable Weight: Feminism, Western Culture, and the Body*, 71–97. Berkeley: University of California Press, 1993.

——. *Unbearable Weight: Feminism, Western Culture, and the Body.* Berkeley: University of California Press, 1993.

BORK, R. "Inconvenient Lives." *First Things* 68 (December 1996): 9–13.

BOULTON, MARY GEORGINA. *On Being a Mother: A Study of Women with Pre-School Children.* New York: Tavistock Publications, 1983.

BOWLBY, JOHN. *Attachment.* Vol. 1 of *Attachment and Loss.* New York: Basic Books, 1980.

——. *Maternal Care and Mental Health.* Geneva: World Health Organization Monograph Series 12, 1951.

——. *A Secure Base: Parent-Child Attachment and Healthy Human Development.* New York: Basic Books, 1988.

BRAZELTON, T. BERRY, and STANLEY I. GREENSPAN. *The Irreducible Needs of Children: What Every Child Must Have to Grow, Flourish, and Learn.* Cambridge, MA: Perseus Publishing, 2000.

BRETHERTON, INGE, and KRISTINE A. MULHOLLAND. "Internal Working Models in Attachment Relationships: A Construct Revisited." In *Handbook of Attachment: Theory, Research, and Clinical Applications*, edited by Jude Cassidy and P. R. Shaver, 89–111. New York: Guilford, 1999.

BREUER, JOSEF, and SIGMUND FREUD, "Studies on Hysteria." In *The Standard Edition of the Complete Psychological Works of Sigmund Freud*, edited by James Strachey, 2: 3–181. London: Hogarth Press, 1955.

BROOKS, GWENDOLYN. "the mother" (1945). In *The Norton Anthology of African American Literature*, edited by Henry Louis Gates Jr. and Nellie Y. McKay, 1579–80. New York: Norton, 1997.

BROOKS-GUNN, JEANNE, WEN-JUI HAN, and JANE WALDFOGEL. "Maternal Employment and Child Cognitive Outcomes in the First Three Years of Life: The NICHD Study of Early Child Care." *Child Development* 73, no. 4 (2002): 1052–72.

BROWN, LYN MIKEL, and CAROL GILLIGAN. *Meeting at the Crossroads: Women's Psychology and Girls' Development.* Cambridge, MA: Harvard University Press, 1992.

BROWNMILLER, SUSAN. *Femininity.* New York: Simon & Schuster, 1984.

BRUMBERG, JOAN JACOBS. *The Body Project: An Intimate History of American Girls.* New York: Random House, 1997.

BULLITT-JONAS, MARGARET. *Holy Hunger: A Memoir of Desire.* New York: Alfred A. Knopf, 1999.

BURGGRAF, SHIRLEY P. *The Feminine Economy and Economic Man: Reviving the Role of Family in the Post-Industrial Age.* Reading, MA: Addison-Wesley, 1997.

BURKE, NANCY, ed. *Gender and Envy.* New York: Routledge, 1998.

BYATT, A. S. *Still Life.* New York: Scribners, 1985.

CARTER, STEPHEN L. *The Culture of Disbelief: How American Law and Politics Trivialize Religious Devotion.* New York: Basic Books, 1993.

CHASSEGUET-SMIRGEL, JANINE. "Freud and Female Sexuality: The Consideration of Some Blind Spots in the Exploration of the 'Dark Continent.'" *International Journal of Psycho-Analysis* 57 (1976): 275–86.

CHEEVER, SUSAN. *As Good as I Could Be: A Memoir About Raising Wonderful Children in Difficult Times.* New York: Simon & Schuster, 2001.

CHERNIN, KIM. *The Hungry Self: Women, Eating, and Identity.* New York: HarperPerennial, 1986.

CHIRA, SUSAN. *A Mother's Place: Taking the Debate About Working Mothers Beyond Guilt and Blame.* New York: HarperCollins, 1998.

CHODOROW, NANCY J. *Femininities, Masculinities, Sexualities: Freud and Beyond.* Lexington: University Press of Kentucky, 1994.

———. "Oedipal Asymmetries and Heterosexual Knots." In *Feminism and Psychoanalytic Theory,* 66–78. New Haven, CT: Yale University Press, 1989.

———. *The Power of Feelings: Personal Meaning in Psychoanalysis, Gender, and Culture.* New Haven, CT: Yale University Press, 1999.

———. *The Reproduction of Mothering: Psychoanalysis and the Sociology of Gender.* Berkeley: University of California Press, 1978; 2nd ed., 1999.

———. "'Too Late': Ambivalence About Motherhood, Choice, and Time." *Journal of the American Psychoanalytic Association* 51, no. 4 (2003): 1181–98.

CHODOROW, NANCY J., and SUSAN CONTRATTO. "The Fantasy of the Perfect Mother." In *Feminism and Psychoanalytic Theory,* 79–96. New Haven, CT: Yale University Press, 1989.

CIXOUS, HÉLÈNE. "The Laugh of the Medusa." In *New French Feminisms: An Anthology,* edited by Elaine Marks and Isabelle de Courtivron, 245–64. New York: Schocken Books, 1980.

CLARKE-STEWART, ALISON. *Daycare.* Revised Edition. Cambridge, MA: Harvard University Press, 1993.

CLARKE-STEWART, ALISON, and GRETA FEIN. "Early Childhood Programs." In *Handbook of Child Psychology, Vol. 2: Infancy and Developmental Psychobiology,* edited by Paul Mussen, 917–1000. New York: Wiley, 1983.

CLINTON, HILLARY RODHAM. *It Takes a Village: And Other Lessons Children Teach Us.* New York: Simon & Schuster, 1996.

COATES, SUSAN W. "Having a Mind of One's Own and Holding the Other in Mind: Commentary on Paper by Peter Fonagy and Mary Target." *Psychoanalytic Dialogues* 8, no. 1 (1998): 115–48.

COLIN, CHRIS. "My Lunch with Paul Auster." *Salon.com*, July 23, 1999.

COLLINS, KAREN. "A Mother At Last." *Harper's Bazaar*, January 2003, 57.

COLLINS, PATRICIA HILL. *Black Feminist Thought: Knowledge, Consciousness, and the Politics of Empowerment*. New York: Routledge, 1990.

COTT, NANCY F. *The Bonds of Womanhood: "Woman's Sphere" in New England, 1780–1835*. New Haven, CT: Yale University Press, 1977.

———. *The Grounding of Modern Feminism*. New Haven, CT: Yale University Press, 1987.

COWAN, CAROLYN PAPE, and PHILIP A. COWAN. *When Partners Become Parents: The Big Life Change for Couples*. New York: Basic Books, 1992.

CRITTENDEN, ANN. *The Price of Motherhood: Why the Most Important Job in the World Is Still the Least Valued*. New York: Metropolitan Books, 2001.

CRITTENDEN, DANIELLE. *What Our Mothers Didn't Tell Us: Why Happiness Eludes the Modern Woman*. New York: Simon & Schuster, 1999.

CSIKSZENTMIHALYI, MIHALY. *Flow: The Psychology of Optimal Experience*. New York: HarperPerennial, 1990.

CUSK, RACHEL. *A Life's Work: On Becoming a Mother*. New York: Picador, 2001.

DALLY, ANN. *Inventing Motherhood: The Consequences of an Ideal*. New York: Schocken Books, 1982.

DALSIMER, KATHERINE. *Female Adolescence: Psychoanalytic Reflections on Literature*. New Haven, CT: Yale University Press, 1986.

DAVIS-FLOYD, ROBBIE E. *Birth as an American Rite of Passage*. Berkeley: University of California Press, 1992.

DEAN, ANNE L. *Teenage Pregnancy: The Interaction of Psyche and Culture*. New York: The Analytic Press, 1997.

DE BEAUVOIR, SIMONE. *The Second Sex*, translated by H. M. Parshley. New York: Vintage Books, 1974.

DEBOLD, ELIZABETH, MARIE WILSON, and IDELISSE MALAVE. *Mother-Daughter Revolution: From Betrayal to Power*. Reading, MA: Addison-Wesley, 1993.

DECASPER, A., and W. FIFER. "Of Human Bonding: Newborns Prefer Their Mothers' Voices." *Science* 208 (1980): 1174–76.

DEUTSCH, HELENE. *Motherhood*. Vol. 2 of *The Psychology of Women*. New York: Grune & Stratton, 1945.

———. "A Two-Year-Old Boy's First Love Comes to Grief" (1919). In *Neuroses and Character Types: Clinical Psychoanalytic Studies*, 159–64. New York: International Universities Press, 1965.

DI LAMPEDUSA, GIUSEPPE TOMASI. *The Leopard*. 1958. Reprint, New York: Pantheon, 1991.

DIMEN, MURIEL. "Strange Hearts: On the Paradoxical Liaison Between Psychoanalysis and Feminism." In *Freud: Conflict and Culture*, edited by Michael Roth, 207–20. New York: Alfred A. Knopf, 1998.

DINNERSTEIN, DOROTHY. *The Mermaid and the Minotaur: Sexual Arrangements and Human Malaise*. New York: Harper Colophon Books, 1976.

DOUGLAS, ANN. *The Feminization of American Culture*. New York: Anchor Press/Doubleday, 1988.

DOUGLAS, SUSAN, and MEREDITH MICHAELS. *The Mommy Myth: The Idealization of Motherhood and How It Has Undermined Women*. New York: The Free Press, 2004.

Downs, Barbara. *Fertility of American Women: June 2002.* Current Population Reports P20-548. U.S. Census Bureau, Washington, DC, 2003.

Dunn, Judy, Jane Brown, and Lynn Beardsall. "Family Talk About Feeling States and Children's Later Understanding of Others' Emotions." *Developmental Psychology* 27, no. 3 (1991): 448–55.

Dworkin, Ronald. *Life's Dominion: An Argument About Abortion, Euthanasia, and Individual Freedom.* New York: Alfred A. Knopf, 1993.

Eagle, Morris. *Recent Developments in Psychoanalysis: A Critical Evaluation.* Cambridge, MA: Harvard University Press, 1984.

Edelman, Marian Wright. *The Measure of Our Success: A Letter to My Children and Yours.* Boston: Beacon Press, 1992.

Ehrenreich, Barbara. *Fear of Falling: The Inner Life of the Middle Class.* New York: Pantheon, 1989.

Ehrenreich, Barbara, and Deirdre English. *For Her Own Good: 150 Years of the Experts' Advice to Women.* New York: Anchor Press/Doubleday, 1978.

Ehrenreich, Barbara, and Arlie Russell Hochschild, eds. *Global Woman: Nannies, Maids, and Sex Workers in the New Economy.* New York: Metropolitan Books, 2003.

Ehrensaft, Diane. *Spoiling Childhood: How Well-Meaning Parents Are Giving Children Too Much — But Not What They Need.* New York: Guilford, 1997.

Eisenberg, Evan. "The Adoption Paradox." *Discover,* January 2001, 80–89.

Eliot, George [Mary Ann Evans]. *Felix Holt, the Radical* (1866). New York: Penguin, 1995.

Elise, Dianne. "Generating Gender: Response to Harris." *Studies in Gender and Sexuality* 1, no. 2 (2000): 157–65.

———. "Woman and Desire: Why Women May *Not* Want to Want." *Studies in Gender and Sexuality* 1, no. 2 (2000): 125–45.

Elkind, David. *The Hurried Child: Growing Up Too Fast Too Soon.* Cambridge, MA: Perseus Publishing, 2001.

Ellman, Carolyn. "The Empty Mother: Women's Fear of Their Destructive Envy." *Psychoanalytic Quarterly* 69, no. 4 (2000): 633–57.

Enright, Anne. "My Milk." *London Review of Books* 22, no. 19, October 5, 2000.

Erdrich, Louise. *The Blue Jay's Dance: A Birth Year.* New York: HarperPerennial, 1995.

Erikson, Erik. "Womanhood and the Inner Space" (1968). In *Women and Analysis: Dialogues on Psychoanalytic Views of Femininity,* edited by Jean Strouse, 291–318. New York: Grossman Publishers, 1974.

Eyer, Diane E. *Motherguilt: How Our Culture Blames Mothers for What's Wrong with Society.* New York: Times Books, 1996.

Faludi, Susan. *Backlash: The Undeclared War Against American Women.* New York: Anchor Books/Doubleday, 1991.

Fein, Ellen, and Sherrie Schneider. *The Rules: Time-Tested Secrets for Capturing the Heart of Mr. Right.* New York: Warner Books, 1995.

Fernald, Anne. "Human Maternal Vocalization to Infants as Biologically

Relevant Signals: An Evolutionary Perspective." In *The Adapted Mind: Evolutionary Psychology and the Generation of Culture*, edited by J. H. Barrow, L. Cosmides, and J. Tooby, 391–428. New York: Oxford University Press, 1992.

FIRESTONE, SHULAMITH. *The Dialectic of Sex: The Case for Feminist Revolution*. New York: Bantam Books, 1972.

FLAX, JANE. "Reentering the Labyrinth: Revisiting Dorothy Dinnerstein's *The Mermaid and the Minotaur*." *Signs: Journal of Women in Culture and Society* 27, no. 4 (2002): 1037–57.

FLEMING, ANNE TAYLOR. *Motherhood Deferred: A Woman's Journey*. New York: Putnam & Sons, 1994.

FOLBRE, NANCY. *The Invisible Heart: Economics and Family Values*. New York: The Free Press, 2001.

FONAGY, PETER. *Attachment Theory and Psychoanalysis*. New York: Other Press, 2001.

FONAGY, PETER, GYORGY GERGELY, ELLIOT L. JURIST, and MARY TARGET. *Affect Regulation, Mentalization, and the Development of the Self*. New York: Other Press, 2002.

FONAGY, PETER, MIRIAM STEELE, HOWARD STEELE, ANNA HIGGITT, and MARY TARGET. "Theory and Practice of Resilience." *Journal of Child Psychology and Psychiatry* 35 (1994): 231–57.

FONAGY, PETER, MIRIAM STEELE, HOWARD STEELE, TOM LEIGH, ROGER KENNEDY, GRETTA MATTOON, and MARY TARGET. "Attachment, the Reflective Self, and Borderline States: The Predictive Specificity of the Adult Attachment Interview and Pathological Emotional Development." In *Attachment Theory: Social, Developmental, and Clinical Perspectives*, edited by Susan Goldberg, Roy Muir, and John Kerr, 233–78. Hillsdale, NJ: The Analytic Press, 1995.

FONAGY, PETER, and MARY TARGET. "Mentalization and the Changing Aims of Psychoanalysis." *Psychoanalytic Dialogues* 8 (1998): 87–114.

FOUCAULT, MICHEL. *The History of Sexuality*. New York: Random House, 1978.

FREUD, SIGMUND. "Analysis Terminable and Interminable" (1937). In *The Standard Edition of the Complete Psychological Works of Sigmund Freud*, edited by James Strachey, 23: 216–53. London: Hogarth Press, 1964.

———. "Three Essays on the Theory of Sexuality" (1905). In *The Standard Edition of the Complete Psychological Works of Sigmund Freud*, edited by James Strachey, 7: 123–243. London: Hogarth Press, 1953.

FRIEDAN, BETTY. *The Feminine Mystique*. New York: Dell, 1970.

———. *The Second Stage*. New York: Summit Books, 1981.

FROMM, ERICH. *To Have or To Be?* New York: Harper & Row, 1976.

GALINSKY, ELLEN. "The 1997 National Study of the Changing Workforce. Families and Work Institute, 1997." www.familiesandwork.org/nationalstudy.html.

GARD, MAISIE C. E., and CHRIS P. FREEDMAN. "The Dismantling of a Myth: Socioeconomic Status and Eating Disorders." *International Journal of Eating Disorders* 20, no. 1 (1996): 1–12.

GARDNER, RALPH, JR. "Mom vs. Mom." *New York*, October 21, 2002, 21–25.

GAREY, ANITA ILTA. *Weaving Work and Motherhood*. Philadelphia: Temple University Press, 1999.

GEORGE, CAROL, and JUDITH SOLOMON. "The Development of Caregiving: A Comparison of Attachment Theory and Psychoanalytic Approaches to Mothering," *Psychoanalytic Inquiry* 19 (1999): 618–46.

———. "Representational Models of Relationships: Links Between Caregiving and Attachment." *Infant Mental Health Journal* 17 (1996): 198–216.

GERGELY, GYORGY. "Reapproaching Mahler: New Perspectives on Normal Autism, Symbiosis, Splitting and Libidinal Object Constancy from Cognitive Developmental Theory." *Journal of the American Psychoanalytic Association* 48, no. 4 (2000): 1197–1228.

GERGELY, GYORGY, and JOHN WATSON. "The Social Biofeedback Model of Parental Affect-Mirroring." *International Journal of Psycho-Analysis* 77 (1996): 1197–1228.

GERHARDT, JULIE, ANNIE SWEETNAM, and LEANN BORTON. "The Intersubjective Turn in Psychoanalysis: A Comparison of Contemporary Theorists: Part 1: Benjamin." *Psychoanalytic Dialogues* 10, no. 1 (2000): 5–42.

GHENT, EMMANUEL. "Masochism, Submission, Surrender: Masochism as a Perversion of Surrender." *Contemporary Psychoanalysis* 26 (1990): 108–36.

GILLIGAN, CAROL. *In a Different Voice: Psychological Theory and Women's Development*. Cambridge, MA: Harvard University Press, 1982.

GILLIGAN, CAROL, ANNIE P. ROGERS, and LYN MIKEL BROWN. "Soundings." In *Making Connections: The Relational Worlds of Adolescent Girls at Emma Willard School*, edited by Carol Gilligan, Nona P. Lyons, and Trudy J. Hanmer. Troy, NY: Emma Willard School, 1989.

GLENN, EVELYN NAKANO. "Social Constructions of Mothering: A Thematic Overview." In *Mothering: Ideology, Experience, and Agency*, edited by Evelyn Nakano Glenn, Grace Chang, and Linda Rennie Forcey, 1–29. New York: Routledge, 1994.

GOLDBERG, CAREY. "Single Dads Wage Revolution One Bedtime Story at a Time." *New York Times*, June 17, 2001.

GOLDSTEIN, JOSEPH, and JACK KORNFIELD. *Seeking the Heart of Wisdom: The Path of Insight Meditation*. Boston: Shambhala, 1987.

GOPNIK, ADAM. "The Double Man: Why Auden Is an Indispensable Poet of Our Time." *New Yorker*, September 23, 2002.

GORNEY, CYNTHIA. *Articles of Faith: A Frontline History of the Abortion Wars*. New York: Simon & Schuster, 1998.

GOTTMAN, JOHN M., and NAN SILVER. *The Seven Principles for Making Marriage Work*. New York: Crown, 1999.

GRAYBEAL, JEAN. "Kristeva's Delphic Proposal: 'Practice Encompasses the Ethical.'" In *Ethics, Politics, and Difference in Julia Kristeva's Writing*, edited by Kelly Oliver, 32–40. New York: Routledge, 1993.

GREER, GERMAINE. *The Female Eunuch*. New York: Bantam Books, 1972.

———. *Sex and Destiny: The Politics of Human Fertility*. New York: Harper & Row, 1984.

GRIFFIN, SUSAN. *Woman and Nature: The Roaring Inside Her*. New York: Harper & Row, 1978.

GRIGORIADIS, VANESSA. "Baby Panic." *New York*, May 20, 2002, 20–25.

GROSS, JANE. "Women and Their Work: How Life Inundates Art." *New York Times*, Money and Business section, August 23, 1998.

HARDEN, BLAINE. "'Dead Broke' Dads' Child-Support Struggle." *New York Times*, January 29, 2002.

Harper's Forum. "Giving Women the Business: On Winning, Losing, and Leaving the Corporate Game." *Harper's* magazine, December 1997, 47–58.

———. "Is Abortion the Issue?: Strong Sentiments in Search of a Discussion." *Harper's* magazine, July 1986.

HARRINGTON, MONA. *Care and Equality: Inventing a New Family Politics.* New York: Alfred A. Knopf, 1999.

HARRIS, ADRIENNE. "Aggression, Envy, and Ambition: Circulating Tensions in Women's Psychic Life." *Gender and Psychoanalysis* 2 (1997): 291–325.

HARRIS, JUDITH RICH. *The Nurture Assumption: Why Children Turn Out the Way They Do.* New York: The Free Press, 1998.

HAYS, SHARON. *The Cultural Contradictions of Motherhood.* New Haven, CT: Yale University Press, 1996.

HEGEL, GEORG FRIEDRICH W. *The Phenomenology of Mind*, translated by J. Baillie. New York: George Allen & Unwin, 1964.

HEINEMAN, TONI VAUGHN. "A Boy and Two Mothers: New Variations on an Old Theme or a New Story of Triangulation? Beginning Thoughts on the Psychosexual Development of Children in Non-Traditional Families." *Psychoanalytic Psychology* 21, no. 1 (2004).

HERTZ, ROSANNA. "The Father as an Idea: A Challenge to Kinship Boundaries by Single Mothers." *Symbolic Interaction* 25, no. 1 (2002): 1–31.

HESSE, ERIK. "The Adult Attachment Interview: Historical and Current Perspectives." In *Handbook of Attachment: Theory, Research, and Clinical Applications*, edited by Jude Cassidy and P. R. Shaver, 395–433. New York: Guilford, 1999.

HESSE, ERIK, and MARY MAIN. "Disorganized Infant, Child, and Adult Attachment: Collapse in Behavioral and Attentional Strategies, *Journal of the American Psychoanalytic Association* 48, no. 4 (2000): 1097–1127.

HEWLETT, SYLVIA ANN. *A Lesser Life: The Myth of Women's Liberation in America.* New York: William Morrow, 1986.

HEWLETT, SYLVIA ANN, and CORNEL WEST. *The War Against Parents: What We Can Do for America's Beleaguered Moms and Dads.* Boston: Houghton Mifflin, 1998.

HEYMANN, JODY. *The Widening Gap: Why America's Working Families Are in Jeopardy and What Can Be Done About It.* New York: Basic Books, 2000.

HIRSCH, MARIANNE. "Feminist Discourse/Maternal Discourse: Speaking with Two Voices." In *The Mother/Daughter Plot: Narrative, Psychoanalysis, Feminism.* Bloomington: Indiana University Press, 1989.

HOCHSCHILD, ARLIE RUSSELL. *The Time Bind: When Work Becomes Home and Home Becomes Work.* New York: Metropolitan Books, 1997.

HOCHSCHILD, ARLIE RUSSELL, with ANNE MACHUNG. *The Second Shift: Working Parents and the Revolution at Home.* New York: Viking, 1989.

HODDER, HARBOUR FRASER. "The New Fertility." *Harvard Magazine*, November/December 1997, 54–64, 97–99.

HONDAGNEU-SOTELO, PIERRETTE. *Doméstica: Immigrant Workers Cleaning and Caring in the Shadows of Affluence.* Berkeley: University of California Press, 2001.

HOOKS, BELL. *All About Love: New Visions.* New York: William Morrow, 2000.

HORNEY, KAREN. "The Flight from Womanhood: The Masculinity-Complex in Women as Viewed by Men and Women" (1926). In *Feminine Psychology,* edited by Harold Kelman, 54–70. New York: Norton, 1973.

HOROWITZ, DANIEL. *Betty Friedan and the Making of "The Feminine Mystique": The American Left, the Cold War, and Modern Feminism.* Amherst: University of Massachusetts Press, 1999.

HRDY, SARAH BLAFFER. *Mother Nature: A History of Mothers, Infants, and Natural Selection.* New York: Pantheon, 2000.

INCIID.org. "InterNational Council on Infertility Information Dissemination Protests the New Infertility Public Service Campaign by the American Society for Reproductive Medicine." August 6, 2001, Arlington, Virginia.

IRELAND, MARDY. *Reconceiving Women: Separating Motherhood and Female Identity.* New York: Guilford, 1993.

JAEGER, ELIZABETH, and MARSHA WEINRAUB. "Early Nonmaternal Care and Infant Attachment: In Search of Process." *New Directions for Child Development* 49 (1990): 71–90.

JAFFE, JOSEPH, BEATRICE BEEBE, STANLEY FELDSTEIN, CYNTHIA CROWN, and MICHAEL D. JASNOW. "Rhythms of Dialogue in Infancy." *Monographs of the Society for Research in Child Development* 66:2, serial no. 265 (2001): 1–132.

JARDINE, ALICE. "Death Sentences: Writing Couples and Ideology." In *The Female Body in Western Culture: Contemporary Perspectives,* edited by Susan Rubin Suleiman, 84–96. Cambridge, MA: Harvard University Press, 1986.

JOHNSON, SPENCER. *One Minute Mother: The Quickest Way for You to Help Your Children Learn to Like Themselves and Want to Behave Themselves* (One Minute Series). New York: Quill, 1995.

JOYCE, JAMES. *Ulysses.* New York: Random House, 1946.

KALB, CLAUDIA. "The Truth About Fertility." *Newsweek,* August 13, 2001, 40–48.

KALINICH, LILA J. "On the Sense of Absence: A Perspective on Womanly Issues." *Psychoanalytic Quarterly* 62, no. 2 (1993): 206–28.

KAMINER, WENDY. *A Fearful Freedom: Women's Flight from Equality.* Reading, MA: Addison-Wesley, 1990.

———. *True Love Waits: Essays and Criticism.* Reading, MA: Addison-Wesley, 1996.

KAPLAN, LOUISE. *Female Perversions: The Temptations of Emma Bovary.* New York: Doubleday, 1991.

———. *Oneness and Separateness: From Infant to Individual.* New York: Simon & Schuster, 1978.

KAREN, ROBERT. *Becoming Attached: First Relationships and How They Shape Our Capacity to Love.* New York: Oxford University Press, 1998.

KESTENBERG, JUDITH. *Children and Parents: Psychoanalytic Studies in Development*. New York: Aronson, 1975.

KIMBALL, ROGER. "The Ambiguities of Milan Kundera." *The New Criterion*, 4, no. 5, January 1986, 5–13.

KITZINGER, SHEILA. *Ourselves as Mothers: The Universal Experience of Motherhood*. Reading, MA: Addison-Wesley, 1995.

KLEIN, MELANIE. "A Contribution to the Psychogenesis of Manic Depressive States" (1934). In *Contributions to Psycho-Analysis 1921–1945*. London: Hogarth Press, 1950.

———. *Envy and Gratitude*. New York: Basic Books, 1957.

KORNFIELD, JACK. *A Path with Heart: A Guide Through the Perils and Promises of Spiritual Life*. New York: Bantam Books, 1993.

KRISTEVA, JULIA. "About Chinese Women." In *The Kristeva Reader*, edited by Toril Moi, 138–59. New York: Columbia University Press, 1986.

———. "Stabat Mater." Translated by Arthur Goldhammer. In *The Female Body in Western Culture*, edited by Susan Rubin Suleiman, 99–118. Cambridge, MA: Harvard University Press, 1985.

———. "Stabat Mater." Translated by Léon S. Roudiez. In *The Kristeva Reader*, edited by Toril Moi, 161–86. New York: Columbia University Press, 1986.

———. "Women's Time." In *The Kristeva Reader*, edited by Toril Moi, 187–213. New York: Columbia University Press, 1986.

KUCZYNSKI, ALEX. "She's Got to Be a Macho Girl." *New York Times*, section 9, November 3, 2002.

LAIBLE, DEBORAH J., and ROSS A. THOMPSON. "Mother-Child Conflict in the Toddler Years: Lessons in Emotion, Morality, and Relationships." *Child Development* 73, no. 4 (2002): 1187–1203.

———. "Mother-Child Discourse, Attachment Security, Shared Positive Affect, and Early Conscience Development." *Child Development* 71, no. 5 (2000): 1424–40.

LAKOFF, GEORGE, and MARK JOHNSON. *Metaphors We Live By*. Chicago: University of Chicago Press, 1980.

LAMBERT, CRAIG. "Image and the Arc of Feeling." *Harvard Magazine*, January/February 2001, 39–43.

LAMOTT, ANNE. "Mother Anger: Theory and Practice." In *Mothers Who Think: Tales of Real-Life Parenthood*, edited by Camille Peri and Kate Moses. New York: Villard, 1999.

LANGER, MARIE. *Motherhood and Sexuality*, translated by Nancy Caro Hollander. New York: Guilford, 1992.

LAPLANCHE, J., and J.-B. PONTALIS. *The Language of Psychoanalysis*. New York: Norton, 1973.

LAREAU, ANNETTE. *Unequal Childhoods: Class, Race, and Family Life*. Berkeley: University of California Press, 2003.

LASCH, CHRISTOPHER. *Women and the Common Life: Love, Marriage, and Feminism*. New York: Norton, 1997.

LASCH-QUINN, ELISABETH. "Mothers and Markets." *New Republic Online*, March 6, 2000.

LAYTON, LYNNE. "Relational No More: Defensive Autonomy in Middle-Class

Women." *Annual of Psychoanalysis*, vol. 32: *Psychoanalysis and Women*, edited by Jerome Winer and James Anderson. Forthcoming.

———. "Working Nine to Nine: The New Women of Prime Time." *Studies in Gender and Sexuality*. Forthcoming.

LEACH, PENELOPE. *Your Baby and Child: From Birth to Age Five*. New York: Alfred A. Knopf, 1992.

LEAR, JONATHAN. "The Introduction of Eros: Reflections on the Work of Hans Loewald." In *Open-Minded: Working Out the Logic of the Soul*, 123–47. Cambridge, MA: Harvard University Press, 1998.

———. *Open-Minded: Working Out the Logic of the Soul*. Cambridge, MA: Harvard University Press, 1998.

LECLERC, ANNIE. *Parole de Femme*. Paris: Grasset, 1974.

LEWIN, TAMAR. "Now a Majority: Families with Two Parents Who Work." *New York Times*, October 24, 2000.

———. "Study Says Little Has Changed in Views on Working Mothers." *New York Times*, September 10, 2001.

LIEBERMAN, ALICIA. "Attachment Theory and Research: Reflections on How Scientific Knowledge Influences Public Perceptions." Unpublished manuscript, 1997.

LOEWALD, HANS. "Primary Process, Secondary Process, and Language." In *Papers on Psychoanalysis*, 178–206. New Haven, CT: Yale University Press, 1980.

———. "Psychoanalysis as an Art and the Fantasy Character of the Psychoanalytic Situation." In *Papers on Psychoanalysis*, 352–71. New Haven, CT: Yale University Press, 1980.

———. "Review of 'The Regulatory Principles of Mental Functioning' by Max Shur." In *Papers on Psychoanalysis*, 58–68. New Haven, CT: Yale University Press, 1980.

LOPATE, PHILLIP. "The Lake of Suffering." In *Wanting a Child*, edited by Jill Bialosky and Helen Schulman, 106–19. New York: Farrar, Straus & Giroux, 1998.

LUDTKE, MELISSA. *On Our Own: Unmarried Motherhood in America*. New York: Random House, 1997.

LUKER, KRISTIN. *Abortion and the Politics of Motherhood*. Berkeley: University of California Press, 1984.

———. *Dubious Conceptions: The Politics of Teenage Pregnancy*. Cambridge, MA: Harvard University Press, 1996.

LUNDBERG, FERDINAND, and MARYNIA FARNHAM, *Modern Woman: The Lost Sex*. New York: Harper Brothers, 1947.

LUTZ, CATHERINE. *Unnatural Emotions: Everyday Sentiments on a Micronesian Atoll and Their Challenge to Western Theory*. Chicago: University of Chicago Press, 1988.

LYONS-RUTH, KARLEN. "Rapprochement or Approchement: Mahler's Theory Reconsidered from the Vantage Point of Recent Research in Early Attachment Relationships." *Psychoanalytic Psychology* 8 (1991): 1–23.

MACHUNG, ANNE. "Talking Careers, Thinking Job: Gender Differences in Career and Family Expectations of Berkeley Seniors." *Feminist Studies* 15, no. 1 (1989): 35–58.

MacKinnon, Catharine A. "Reflections on Sex Equality Under Law." *Yale Law Journal* 100 (1991): 1281–1328.

Mahler, Margaret, Fred Pine, and Anni Bergman. *The Psychological Birth of the Human Infant.* New York: Basic Books, 1975.

Mahony, Rhona. *Kidding Ourselves: Breadwinning, Babies, and Bargaining Power.* New York: Basic Books, 1995.

Main, Mary. "Metacognitive Knowledge, Metacognitive Monitoring, and Singular (Coherent) vs. Multiple (Incoherent) Models of Attachment: Findings and Directions for Future Research." In *Attachment Across the Life Cycle,* edited by C. M. Parkes, J. Stevenson-Hinde, and P. Marris, 127–59. London: Routledge, 1991.

———. "The Organized Categories of Infant, Child, and Adult Attachment: Flexible vs. Inflexible Attention Under Attachment-Related Stress." *Journal of the American Psychoanalytic Association* 48, no. 4 (2000): 1055–96.

Main, Mary, Nancy Kaplan, and Jude Cassidy, "Security in Infancy, Childhood, and Adulthood: A Move to the Level of Representation." In *Growing Points of Attachment Theory and Research,* edited by Inge Bretherton and Everett Waters. Monographs of the Society for Research in Child Development 50 (1–2) serial no. 209 (1985): 66–104.

Martin, Emily. *The Woman in the Body: A Cultural Analysis of Reproduction.* Boston: Beacon Press, 1989.

Maslow, Abraham H. *Motivation and Personality.* 2nd ed. New York: Harper & Row, 1970.

Mathiot, Shelley. "No Time to Hurry." *Parenting from the Heart: Motherwear's Magazine for Nurturing Families,* no. 41 (1999): 3–4.

Maushart, Susan. *The Mask of Motherhood: How Becoming a Mother Changes Everything and Why We Pretend It Doesn't.* New York: The New Press, 1999.

Mayer, Elizabeth Lloyd. "Women, Creativity, and Power." *Contemporary Psychoanalysis* 39, no. 1 (2003): 114–24.

McBride, James. *The Color of Water: A Black Man's Tribute to His White Mother.* New York: Riverhead Books, 1996.

McKibben, Bill. *Maybe One: A Personal and Environmental Argument for Single Child Families.* New York: Simon & Schuster, 1998.

McLaughlin, Emma, and Nicola Kraus. *The Nanny Diaries: A Novel.* New York: St. Martin's Press, 2002.

Mendelson, Cheryl. *Home Comforts: The Art and Science of Keeping House.* New York: Scribners, 1999.

Merkin, Daphne. "Sister Act." *The New Yorker,* June 14, 1999.

Merton, Thomas. *Love and Living,* edited by Naomi Burton Stone and Patrick Hart. New York: Farrar, Straus & Giroux, 1979.

Michel, Sonya. *Children's Interests/Mothers' Rights: The Shaping of America's Child Care Policy.* New Haven, CT: Yale University Press, 2000.

Miedzian, Myriam. *Boys Will Be Boys: Breaking the Link Between Masculinity and Violence.* New York: Doubleday, 1991.

Miles, Jack. "Jesus Before He Could Talk." *New York Times Magazine,* December 24, 1995, 28–33.

MILES, MARGARET R. "The Virgin's One Bare Breast: Female Nudity and Religious Meaning in Tuscan Early Renaissance Culture." In *The Female Body in Western Culture: Contemporary Perspectives*, edited by Susan Rubin Suleiman, 193–208. Cambridge, MA: Harvard University Press, 1985.

MITCHELL, JULIET. *Psychoanalysis and Feminism: Freud, Reich, Laing, and Women*. New York: Pantheon, 1974.

MITCHELL, STEPHEN A. *Relationality: From Attachment to Intersubjectivity*. Hillsdale, NJ: The Analytic Press, 2000: 1005–35.

MOI, TORIL. Introduction to "Women's Time." In *The Kristeva Reader*, edited by Toril Moi, 187–88. New York: Columbia University Press, 1986.

———. *Sexual/Textual Politics: Feminist Literary Theory*. New York: Routledge, 1985.

———. "While We Wait: The English Translation of *The Second Sex*." *Signs: Journal of Women in Culture and Society* 27, no. 4 (2002): 1005–35.

———, ed. *The Kristeva Reader*. New York: Columbia University Press, 1986.

MOGEL, WENDY. *The Blessing of a Skinned Knee: Using Jewish Teachings to Raise Self-Reliant Children*. New York: Scribners, 2001.

MORRISON, TONI. *Beloved*. New York: Plume, 1988.

MOYERS, BILL, and ANDIE TUCHER. *A World of Ideas: Public Opinions from Private Citizens*. New York: Public Affairs Television, 1990.

MUSICK, JUDITH S. *Young, Poor, and Pregnant: The Psychology of Teenage Motherhood*. New Haven, CT: Yale University Press, 1993.

NACHMAN, PATRICIA. "Maternal Identification: A Description of the Process in Real Time." *Journal of the American Psychoanalytic Association* 46 (1998): 209–28.

NICHD Early Child Care Research Network. "Child Care and Mother-Child Interaction in the First Three Years of Life." *Developmental Psychology* 35, no. 6 (1999): 1399–1413.

———. "The Effects of Infant Child Care on Infant-Mother Attachment Security: Results of the NICHD Study of Early Child Care." *Child Development* 68, no. 5 (1997): 860–79.

NIH News Alert, November 7, 1999. "Only Small Link Found Between Hours in Child Care and Mother-Child Interaction." www.nichd.nih.gov/new/releases/timeinchildcare.cfm.

NOFZIGER, MARGARET. *The Fertility Question*. Summertown, TN: The Book Publishing Company, 1982.

OLSEN, TILLIE. *Tell Me a Riddle*. New York: Delta/Seymour Lawrence, 1994.

ORBACH, SUSIE. *Fat Is a Feminist Issue*. New York: Galahad Books, 1982.

ORENSTEIN, PEGGY. *Flux: Women on Sex, Work, Love, Kids, and Life in a Half-Changed World*. New York: Doubleday, 2000.

OXENHANDLER, NOELLE. *The Eros of Parenthood: Explorations in Light and Dark*. New York: St. Martin's Press, 2001.

OZMENT, STEVEN E. *Ancestors: The Loving Family in Old Europe*. Cambridge, MA: Harvard University Press, 2001.

PAGLIA, CAMILLE. *Sexual Personae: Art and Decadence from Nefertiti to Emily Dickinson*. New Haven, CT: Yale University Press, 1990.

PARKE, ROSS D., and ARMIN A. BROTT. *Throwaway Dads: The Myths and Bar-*

riers That Keep Men from Being the Fathers They Want to Be. New York: Houghton Mifflin, 1999.

PARKER, ROZSIKA. *Mother Love/Mother Hate: The Power of Maternal Ambivalence.* New York: Basic Books, 1995.

PARREÑAS, RHACEL SALAZAR, ed. *Servants of Globalization: Women, Migration, and Domestic Work.* Stanford, CA: Stanford University Press, 2001.

PAYNE, KAREN, ed. *Between Ourselves: Letters Between Mothers and Daughters.* Boston: Houghton Mifflin, 1983.

PEARSON, ALLISON. *I Don't Know How She Does It: The Life of Kate Reddy, Working Mother.* New York: Alfred A. Knopf, 2002.

PEARSON, JANE, DEBORAH COHN, PHILIP COWAN, and CAROLYN PAPE COWAN, "Earned- and Continuous-Security in Adult Attachment: Relation to Depressive Symptomatology and Parenting Style." *Development and Psychopathology* 6, no. 2 (1994): 359–73.

PECK, M. SCOTT. *The Road Less Traveled.* New York: Simon & Schuster, 1978.

PERI, CAMILLE, and KATE MOSES, eds., *Mothers Who Think: Tales of Real-Life Parenthood.* New York: Villard, 1999.

PERKINS, H. WESLEY, and DEBRA K. DeMEIS. "Gender and Family Effects on the 'Second Shift' Domestic Activity of College-Educated Young Adults." *Gender and Society* 10, no. 1 (1996): 78–93.

PETERS, JOAN K. *When Mothers Work: Loving Our Children Without Sacrificing Ourselves.* Reading, MA: Addison-Wesley, 1997.

PHILLIPS, ADAM. "On Risk and Solitude." In *On Kissing, Tickling, and Being Bored: Psychoanalytic Essays on the Unexamined Life,* 27–41. Cambridge, MA: Harvard University Press, 1993.

———. *Winnicott.* Cambridge, MA: Harvard University Press, 1988.

PINES, DINORA. *A Woman's Unconscious Use of Her Body.* New Haven, CT: Yale University Press, 1994.

PINKER, STEVEN. *The Language Instinct: How the Mind Creates Language.* New York: William Morrow, 1994.

POLLITT, KATHA. "Contracts and Apple Pie: The Strange Case of Baby M." In *Reasonable Creatures: Essays on Women and Feminism,* 63–80. New York: Alfred A. Knopf, 1994.

———. *Reasonable Creatures: Essays on Women and Feminism.* New York: Alfred A. Knopf, 1994.

———. *Subject to Debate: Sense and Dissents on Women, Politics, and Culture.* New York: The Modern Library, 2001.

POPENOE, DAVID. *Life Without Father: Compelling New Evidence That Fatherhood and Marriage Are Indispensable for the Good of Children and Society.* New York: The Free Press, 1996.

PRIDDY, KRISTEN D. "Immunologic Adaptations During Pregnancy." *Journal of Obstetric, Gynecologic, and Neonatal Nursing* 26, no. 4 (1997): 388–94.

PRUETT, KYLE D. *Fatherneed: Why Father Care Is as Essential as Mothercare for Your Child.* New York: The Free Press, 2000.

PUGH, ALLISON. "When Is a Doll More Than a Doll? Selling Toys as Reassurance for Maternal and Class Anxiety." Working Paper no. 28, Center for Working Families, University of California at Berkeley, April 2001.

QUINDLEN, ANNA. "Playing God on No Sleep." *Newsweek,* July 2, 2001, 64.

QUINN, SUSAN. *A Mind of Her Own: The Life of Karen Horney.* New York: Summit Books, 1987.

Radcliffe Public Policy Center. "Life's Work: Generational Attitudes Toward Work and Life Integration." Murray Research Center, 2000.

RAPP, RAYNA. *Testing the Woman, Testing the Fetus: The Social Impact of Amniocentesis in America.* New York: Routledge, 1999.

RICH, ADRIENNE. *Of Woman Born: Motherhood as Experience and Institution.* New York: Norton, 1995.

ROAZEN, PAUL. *Helene Deutsch: A Psychoanalyst's Life.* Garden City, NY: Anchor Press/Doubleday, 1985.

ROBINSON, JOHN P., and GEOFFREY GODBEY. *Time for Life: The Surprising Ways Americans Use Their Time.* University Park: The Pennsylvania State University Press, 1997.

ROBINSON, MARILYNNE. *The Death of Adam: Essays on Modern Thought.* Boston: Houghton Mifflin, 1998.

RODGERS, CATHERINE. "Elisabeth Badinter and *The Second Sex:* An Interview." *Signs: Journal of Women in Culture and Society* 21, no. 1 (1995): 147–62.

ROIPHE, ANNE. *Fruitful: A Real Mother in the Modern World.* Boston: Houghton Mifflin, 1996.

ROIPHE, KATIE. "A Grandmother's Biological Clock." *New York Times Magazine,* February 8, 1998, 80.

ROSSI, AGNES. "In Vitro." In *Wanting a Child,* edited by Jill Bialosky and Helen Schulman, 60–68. New York: Farrar, Straus & Giroux, 1998.

ROSSI, ALICE. "A Biosocial Perspective on Parenting." *Daedalus* 106, no. 2 (1977): 1–31.

RUBIN, LILLIAN. *Women of a Certain Age: The Midlife Search for Self.* New York: Harper & Row, 1979.

RUDDICK, SARA. "Care as Labor and Relationship." In *Norms and Values: Essays on the Work of Virginia Held,* edited by J. G. Haber and M. S. Halfo, 3–25. Lanham, MD: Rowman & Littlefield Publishers, 1998.

———. *Maternal Thinking: Toward a Politics of Peace.* Boston: Beacon Press, 1995.

RYAN, MARY P. *The Cradle of the Middle Class: The Family in Oneida County, New York, 1790–1865.* Cambridge: Cambridge University Press, 1981.

SAFER, JEANNE. *Beyond Motherhood: Choosing a Life Without Children.* New York: Pocket Books, 1996.

SALMI, MARIO, comp. *The Complete Works of Michelangelo.* New York: Reynal & Company, n.d.

SALZBERG, SHARON. *A Heart as Wide as the World: Living with Mindfulness, Wisdom, and Compassion.* Boston: Shambhala, 1997.

SANDER, LOUIS W. "Infant and Caretaking Environment: Investigation and Conceptualization of Adaptive Behavior in a System of Increasing Complexity." In *Explorations in Child Psychiatry,* edited by E. J. Anthony, 129–65. New York: Plenum Press, 1975.

———. "Thinking Differently: Principles of Process in Living Systems and the

Specificity of Being Known." *Psychoanalytic Dialogues* 12, no. 1 (2002): 11–42.

SANGER, MARGARET. *Woman and the New Race.* New York: Brentano's, 1920.

SAYERS, JANET. *Mothers of Psychoanalysis: Helene Deutsch, Karen Horney, Anna Freud, Melanie Klein.* New York: Norton, 1991.

SCARR, SANDRA. "American Child Care Today." *American Psychologist* 53, no. 2 (1998): 95–108.

SCARR, SANDRA, DEBORAH PHILLIPS, and KATHLEEN MCCARTNEY. "Working Mothers and Their Families." *American Psychologist* 44, no. 11 (1989): 1402–9.

SCHEPER-HUGHES, NANCY. *Death Without Weeping: The Violence of Everyday Life in Brazil.* Berkeley: University of California Press, 1992.

SCHOR, JULIET B. *The Overspent American: Upscaling, Downshifting, and the New Consumer.* New York: Basic Books, 1998.

———. *The Overworked American: The Unexpected Decline of Leisure.* New York: Basic Books, 1991.

SCHULTZ, KIRI. "Big Belly in Cambodia." *hip Mama* 21 (1999): 12–14.

SCHWARTZ, ADRIA E. *Sexual Subjects: Lesbians, Gender, and Psychoanalysis.* New York: Routledge, 1998.

SCOTT, JANNY. "Working Hard, More or Less: Studies of Leisure Time Point Both Up and Down." *New York Times*, section A, July 10, 1999.

SCOTT, JOAN W. "Deconstructing Equality-Versus-Difference: Or the Uses of Poststructuralist Theory for Feminism." In *Feminist Social Thought: A Reader*, edited by Diana Tietjens Meyers, 758–70. New York: Routledge, 1997.

SELIGMAN, STEPHEN. "Integrating Kleinian Theory and Intersubjective Infant Research Observing Projective Identification." *Psychoanalytic Dialogues* 9, no. 2 (1999): 129–59.

SEN, AMARTYA. *Development as Freedom.* New York: Alfred A. Knopf, 2000.

SEUSS, DR. [Theodor Seuss Geisel]. *Horton Hatches the Egg.* New York: Random House, 1940.

SHACOCHIS, BOB. "Missing Children." In *Wanting a Child*, edited by Jill Bialosky and Helen Schulman, 40–59. New York: Farrar, Straus & Giroux, 1998.

SHALIT, WENDY. *A Return to Modesty: Discovering the Lost Virtue.* New York: The Free Press, 1999.

SHAPIRO, ALYSON FEARNLEY, JOHN M. GOTTMAN, and SYBIL CARRERE. "The Baby and the Marriage: Identifying Factors That Buffer Against Decline in Marital Satisfaction After the First Baby Arrives." *Journal of Family Psychology* 14, no. 1 (2000): 59–70.

SHEA, LISA. "Mother of One." In *Wanting a Child*, edited by Jill Bialosky and Helen Schulman, 195–99. New York: Farrar, Straus & Giroux, 1998.

SHELLENBARGER, SUE. "Here's the Bottom Line on All Those Reports of Child Care's Impact." *Wall Street Journal*, section B, June 23, 1999.

SILBER, SHERMAN J. *How to Get Pregnant.* New York: Charles Scribner's Sons, 1980.

SIMPSON, MONA. *Anywhere But Here.* New York: Vintage, 1992.

SKLAR, KATHRYN KISH. *Catharine Beecher: A Study in American Domesticity.* New Haven, CT: Yale University Press, 1973.

SLADE, ARIETTA. "The Development and Organization of Attachment: Implications for Psychoanalysis." *Journal of the American Psychoanalytic Association* 48, no. 4 (2000): 1145–74.

SLADE, ARIETTA, JAY BELSKY, J. LAWRENCE ABER, and JUNE L. PHELPS. "Mothers' Representations of Their Relationships with Their Toddlers: Links to Adult Attachment and Observed Mothering." *Developmental Psychology* 35, no. 3 (1999): 611–19.

SMALL, MEREDITH F. *Our Babies, Ourselves: How Biology and Culture Shape the Way We Parent.* New York: Anchor Press/Doubleday, 1998.

SMITH, JANNA MALAMUD. *A Potent Spell: Mother Love and Power of Fear.* Boston: Houghton Mifflin, 2003.

SMITH-ROSENBERG, CARROLL, "Beauty, the Beast, and the Militant Woman." In *Disorderly Conduct: Visions of Gender in Victorian America.* New York: Oxford University Press, 1986.

———. "The Female World of Love and Ritual." In *Disorderly Conduct: Visions of Gender in Victorian America.* New York: Oxford University Press, 1986.

SMOLAK, LINDA, and RUTH H. STRIEGEL-MOORE. "Challenging the Myth of the Golden Girl: Ethnicity and Eating Disorders." In *Eating Disorders: Innovative Directions for Research and Practice,* edited by Ruth H. Striegel-Moore and Linda Smolak, 111–32. Washington, DC: American Psychological Association, 2001.

SNITOW, ANN. "A Gender Diary." In *Conflicts in Feminism,* edited by Marianne Hirsch and Evelyn Fox Keller. New York: Routledge, 1990.

SOLOMON, JUDITH, and CAROL GEORGE. "Defining the Caregiving System: Toward a Theory of Caregiving." *Infant Mental Health Journal* 17 (1996): 183–98.

STEINER-ADAIR, CATHERINE. "The Body Politic: Normal Adolescent Development and the Development of Eating Disorders." In *Making Connections: The Relational Worlds of Adolescent Girls at Emma Willard School,* edited by Carol Gilligan, Nona P. Lyons, and Trudy J. Hanmer, 162–82. Troy, NY: Emma Willard School, 1989.

———. "The Politics of Prevention." In *Feminist Perspectives on Eating Disorders,* edited by Patricia Fallon, Melanie Katzman, and Susan Wooley, 381–94. New York: Guilford, 1994.

STEINGRABER, SANDRA. *Having Faith: An Ecologist's Journey to Motherhood.* New York: Perseus Publishing, 2001.

STERN, DANIEL N. *The Interpersonal World of the Infant: A View from Psychoanalysis and Developmental Psychology.* New York: Basic Books, 1985.

———. *The Motherhood Constellation: A Unified View of Parent-Infant Psychotherapy.* New York: Basic Books, 1995.

STERN, DANIEL N., and NADIA BRUSCHWEILER-STERN. *The Birth of a Mother: How the Motherhood Experience Changes You Forever.* New York: Basic Books, 1998.

STERN, DANIEL N., LOUIS W. SANDER, JEREMY P. NAHUM, ALEXANDRA M. HARRISON, KARLEN LYONS-RUTH, ALEC C. MORGAN, NADIA BRUSCHWEILER-

STERN, and EDWARD Z. TRONICK. "Non-Interpretive Mechanisms in Psychoanalytic Psychotherapy: The 'Something More' Than Interpretation," *International Journal of Psycho-Analysis* 79 (1998): 903–21.

STONE, LAWRENCE F. *The Family, Sex, and Marriage in England, 1500–1800.* New York: Harper & Row, 1977.

SULLEROT, EVELYNE. *Women, Society, and Change.* New York: World University Library, 1971.

SWISS, DEBORAH J., and JUDITH P. WALKER. "Smart Women, Smart Choices." *Working Mother,* December 1996, 22–26.

TALLMER, MARGOT. "Empty-Nest Syndrome: Possibility or Despair." In *The Psychology of Today's Woman,* edited by Toni Bernay and Dorothy W. Cantor, 231–52. Cambridge, MA: Harvard University Press, 1986.

TAYLOR, SHELLEY. *The Tending Instinct: How Nurturing Is Essential to Who We Are and How We Live.* New York: Times Books/Henry Holt, 2002.

THOMPSON, LINDA, and A. J. WALKER. "Gender in Families: Women and Men in Marriage, Work, and Parenthood." *Journal of Marriage and the Family* 51 (1989): 845–71.

THOMSON, JUDITH JARVIS. "A Defense of Abortion." *Philosophy and Public Affairs* 1, no. 1 (fall 1971): 47–66.

THURER, SHARI L. *The Myths of Motherhood: How Culture Reinvents the Good Mother.* Boston: Houghton Mifflin, 1994.

TRAINA, CRISTINA L. H. "Maternal Experience and the Boundaries of Christian Sexual Ethics." *Signs: Journal of Women in Culture and Society* 25, no. 2 (2000): 369–405.

TRONICK, EDWARD Z. "Emotions and Emotional Communication in Infants." *American Psychologist* 44, no. 2 (1989): 112–19.

TURIEL, JUDITH STERNBERG. *Beyond Second Opinions: Making Choices About Fertility Treatment.* Berkeley: University of California Press, 1998.

U.S. Department of Education, National Center for Education Statistics. *Digest of Education Statistics 2000,* NCES 2001-034. By Thomas D. Snyder and Charlene M. Hoffman, Washington, DC, 2001.

VANDELL, DEBORAH LOWE, and BARBARA WOLFE. "Child Care Quality: Does It Matter and Does It Need to Be Improved?" *Office of the Assistant Secretary for Planning and Evaluation, U.S. Department of Health and Human Services.* Washington, DC, May 2000.

WALLERSTEIN, JUDITH, JULIA LEWIS, and SANDY BLAKESLEE. *The Unexpected Legacy of Divorce: A 25 Year Landmark Study.* New York: Hyperion, 2000.

WASSERSTEIN, WENDY. "Competitive Moms." *Harper's Bazaar,* September 2002, 259–60.

WATERMAN, BARBARA. *The Birth of an Adoptive, Foster, or Step-mother: Beyond Biological Mothering Attachments.* London: Jessica Kingsley, Ltd., 2003.

WEIR, ALLISON. "Identification with the Divided Mother: Kristeva's Ambivalence." In *Ethics, Politics, and Difference in Julia Kristeva's Writing,* edited by Kelly Oliver, 79–91. New York: Routledge, 1993.

WELTER, BARBARA. "The Cult of True Womanhood: 1820–1860." *American Quarterly* 18 (1966): 151–74.

WILE, DANIEL B. *After the Honeymoon: How Conflict Can Improve Your Relationship.* New York: Wiley, 1988.

WILLIAMS, JOAN. *Unbending Gender: Why Family and Work Conflict and What to Do About It*. New York: Oxford University Press, 2000.

WILLIAMS, JOY, "The Case Against Babies." In *The Best American Essays 1997*, edited by Ian Frazier. Boston: Houghton Mifflin, 1997.

WINNICOTT, D. W. "The Capacity to Be Alone" (1958). In *The Maturational Processes and the Facilitating Environment*, 29–36. New York: International Universities Press, 1965.

——. "From Dependence Towards Independence in the Development of the Individual" (1963). In *The Maturational Processes and the Facilitating Environment*, 83–92. New York: International Universities Press, 1965.

——. "Ego Distortion in Terms of True and False Self" (1960). In *The Maturational Processes and the Facilitating Environment*, 140–52. New York: International Universities Press, 1965.

——. "Hate in the Counter-transference." *International Journal of Psycho-Analysis* 30 (1949): 69–74.

——. "The Location of Cultural Experience" (1967). In *Playing and Reality*, 95–103. New York: Tavistock Publications, 1971.

——. "Morals and Education" (1963). In *The Maturational Processes and the Facilitating Environment*, 93–105. New York: International Universities Press, 1965.

——. "A Note on the Mother-Foetus Relationship." In *Psycho-Analytic Explorations*, 161–62. Cambridge, MA: Harvard University Press, 1989.

——. "Playing: Creative Activity and the Search for the Self." In *Playing and Reality*, 53–64. New York: Tavistock Publications, 1971.

——. "Transitional Objects and Transitional Phenomena" (1953). In *Playing and Reality*, 1–25. New York: Tavistock Publications, 1971.

——. "The Use of an Object and Relating Through Identifications" (1969). In *Playing and Reality*, 86–94. New York: Tavistock Publications, 1971.

WINTER, NINA. *Interview with the Muse: Remarkable Women Speak on Creativity and Power*. Berkeley: Moon Books, 1978.

WOLF, NAOMI. *The Beauty Myth: How Images of Beauty Are Used Against Women*. New York: Anchor Press/Doubleday, 1991.

——. "The Future Is Ours to Lose." *New York Times Magazine*, May 16, 1999.

——. "Our Bodies Our Souls." In *Vice and Virtue in Everyday Life*, 4th edition, edited by Christina Sommers and Fred Sommers, 843–60. New York: Harcourt Brace, 1997.

YOUNG, IRIS MARION, "Pregnant Embodiment: Subjectivity and Alienation." *Journal of Medicine and Philosophy* 9 (1984): 45–62.

YOUNG-BRUEHL, ELISABETH, ed. *Freud on Women: A Reader*. New York: Norton, 1990.

abortion, 237–254, 316; casual attitudes toward, 364n2; debate on, 17, 365n22; and fetal life, 238, 240, 247–249, 253; and intention, 240–241; and law, 241–243, 245–246; as love, 248; and maternal desire, 238–241; and pregnancy, 219, 244–248; and relationship, 240, 248; and the sacred, 248–252; and saintliness, 252–254; selective, 229; and selfhood, 239–243. *See also* reproductive rights

adolescence, 182–210; and connectedness, 198–201; and control, 186–192, 209; female, 15–16, 188–191, 201–205, 209; and mother-daughter relationship, 133, 182–185, 198–201, 209–210, 316; and motherhood, 206–208; pregnancy in, 201–205, 209; and sexuality, 185–186, 190–191, 359n3; and weight, 192–197

adoption, 107, 121, 229; vs. abortion, 245; and biology, 363n35; vs. childbearing, 233–234; and connectedness, 93, 231–232; and fertility, 221–222, 231–232, 362n19; forced, 247–248; and mother-child bond, 284

Adult Attachment Interview (AAI), 77, 109–110, 348n54

affect attunement, 96–98, 103, 351n23

affect regulation, 346n25

Afghanistan, 257

Ahlberg, Allan, 322

Ahlberg, Janet, 322

Ainsworth, Mary, 76

Alcott, Abigail, 35–37

Alcott, Louisa May, 36, 189

Alden, Paulette Bates, 217

allomothers, 154–156

ambivalence, 118–146, 353n26, 367n13; and abortion, 239–240; and achievement, 125; toward childbearing, 217–219; toward child care, 153–154, 177, 231, 316; and creativity, 136–140; and fertility, 215–219; toward ideal day care, 154–156; and ideals of motherhood, 140–146; internal vs. external sources of, 270; maternal role and weight, 192–197; of men, 222; and mother-daughter relationship, 131–136; perspective on, 277; toward roles, 126–130; toward sharing child care, 282–286, 311; and work-family conflict, 122, 131–132

American Society of Reproductive Medicine (ASRM), 213

amniocentesis, 244–245

"the angel in the house," 33–38

anger, 118–120, 137, 141, 177, 193; at infertility, 203, 222; at men, 192–193; in mother-daughter relationship, 133, 182–183, 196, 259

Angier, Natalie, 259–260, 266

Annunciation (painting; Fra Angelico), 107

Anywhere but Here (Simpson), 297–298

Apter, Terri, 184–185, 198

"Are Mothers Persons?" (Bordo), 241

assisted reproductive technologies (ART), xi, 223–226, 228–229, 231, 363n35; in vitro fertilization (IVF), 212–213, 227. *See also* sperm donation

Atkinson, Ti-Grace, 51

attachment, 75–83, 132, 168, 231, 300, 348n43, 348n53, 357n43, 366n2; and autonomy, 78, 80, 82; in child development, 77, 367n2; to child vs. father, 298; and communication, 349n62; and day care, 357n43; and empathy, 78, 81; of father, 203, 205; and happiness, 178–179; and language, 109–111; models of, 203–205, 348n52, 352n45; patterns of, 76–77; and rapprochement phase, 79–80; and recognition, 75–83; and reflectiveness, 360n35; research on, 76–80, 109–110, 165, 181; and responsiveness, 76, 78–81, 174; vs. separateness, 68–70; and solitude, 354n32; and subjectivity, 78, 110; theories of, 271, 346n32, 366n2; and translation function, 109–110; and weight, 193

Auster, Paul, 191

autonomy: and attachment, 78, 80, 82; and breastfeeding, 230; vs. connectedness, 83, 191, 198–201, 264, 266; with connectedness, 74, 86, 205; and control, 187; and female development, 214; and gender roles, 16, 66; individuality in, 357n49; and maternal desire, 317; vs. merger, 346n26; and mother-child relationship, 67–68, 71–75; and mother-daughter relationship, 131, 184–185, 205, 259–260; vs. motherhood, 11, 16, 32, 57–58, 126, 218; and mother-infant bond, 65–71; vs. neediness, 221–222; and pregnancy, 203, 219; and reproductive rights, 242–243; and sentimentality, 142; and sexuality, 130; subjective, 301, 303; and work, 325–326; and work-family conflict, 55, 57

Baby Einstein (video), 322, 369n17
Baby M case, 367n5
Baby Mozart (video), 322
"Baby Panic" (Grigoriadis), 129
Backlash (Faludi), 10, 42–43
Balint, Alice, 65, 70, 367n19
Balsam, Rosemary, 261
Barthes, Roland, 7
Bartholet, Elizabeth, 231–232, 362n19, 363n35
Bauer, Nancy, 341n14
the Beatles, 104, 109
Beebe, Beatrice, 81
Bell, Leslie, 189
Beloved (Morrison), 365n18
Bend It Like Beckham (film), 55–56
Benjamin, Jessica, 63–64, 71–75, 79–80, 83, 85, 133–134, 197, 347n41
Bergman, Barbara, 356n28
Bernstein, Doris, 354n39

birth control. See contraception
Blair, Anita, 46–47
Blum, Linda, 230
body, control of, 187–188, 192–197, 350n5
Bomford, Rodney, 99–100, 108
The Bonds of Love (Benjamin), 63, 71–75
Bordo, Susan, 193, 200, 241–243, 245
Bork, Robert, 364n3
Bowlby, John, 76, 179
Brazelton, T. Berry, 164, 179–180
breastfeeding, 60–61, 63, 84, 306, 351n21, 363nn32,33; as ideology, 269–270; and pleasure, 90–91, 230; vs. pumping breast milk, 230, 233
Brooks, Gwendolyn, 17, 248, 340n15, 365n16
Brumberg, Joan Jacobs, 187
Bullitt-Jonas, Margaret, 198
Burggraf, Shirley, 155, 293, 325
Bush, Barbara, 325–326
Byatt, A. S., 145–146

Callahan, Sidney, 252
capitalism, 34, 53–54
caregivers: fathers as, 291–297; mothers as, 283–284, 308, 310; pay rates for, 153–154, 320; recruitment of, 155; relationships with, 147–149, 156–157, 176; turnover of, 149–153; women as, 161, 283–284, 289, 308, 310, 367n4. See also child care; day care

Carreños, Caroline, 343n47
Carter, Stephen, 243
Chadha, Gurinder, 55
Chasseguet-Smirgel, Janine, 353n17
Cheever, Susan, 265–266
Chernin, Kim, 195–198
childbirth: vs. child care, 236; experience of, 94; natural, 226–227, 234, 269–270, 363n28
child care, 147–181; vs. achievement, 317, 324–328, 334; ambivalence about sharing, 282–286, 311; ambivalence toward, 153–154, 177, 231, 316; appreciation of, 296–297; attitudes toward, 339n9; barriers to sharing, 304–305; and being vs. having, 328; and caregiver turnover, 149–152; vs. childbearing, 3, 18, 229–234, 236; vs. childbirth, 236; and child development, 168–169; and class, 153–155, 370n24; and community, 333; devaluation of, 252; and divorce, 288; vs. economic equality, 285–286; economic factors in, 18–19, 151–154, 305–307; economic value of, 286–287; and education, 18–19; and fathers, 127–128, 291–297, 316; feminism on, 35; and fertility, 215, 229–234, 316; full commodifica-

tion model of, 356n28; and gender roles, 25, 284; and happiness, 176–181; and housework, 38–42, 51, 283; and legal coercion, 247; and maternal intentionality, 171–176; middle-class, 370n18; and mothers' choice, 160–167; and mothers' needs, 170–171; paradox of, 152–157; research on, 168–171, 181; and responsiveness, 168–171; restrictions of, 28; and self-esteem, 149–150, 152; setting limits in, 72–74, 80; sharing, 127–128, 158, 282–286, 294–297, 300–301, 304–311, 316–317; social policies on, 177, 333, 362n25; standards of, 163–164; and work, 25, 127–128, 153–154; and work-family conflict, 150–157, 283–284, 307–308, 316–317. *See also* caregivers; day care

child development, 168–169, 346n30; and attachment, 77, 366n2; and generational boundaries, 298–299; and having vs. being, 323; and moral sense, 9, 175, 189–190; and mother-child interaction, 13–14; rapprochement phase in, 71–72, 75, 79–80, 347n41

Child Development journal, 169

childhood, concept of, 36

Children's Interests/Mothers' Rights (Michel), 159

Chira, Susan, 156, 165, 181

Chodorow, Nancy, ix, 63–71, 83, 130, 143–144, 352n9

Chuang-Tzu, 369n2

class, 153–155, 165, 370n24; and domesticity, 40–41; and eating disorders, 361n41; and men as providers, 292–293; and mother-daughter relationship, 342n23; and parenting, 271, 342nn38,42, 370n18; and reproductive rights, 242–243; and timing of childbearing, 223; working, 21, 154. *See also* middle class

Cleaver, June, 144

Clinton, Chelsea, 269

Clinton, Hillary, 267–269

Coates, Susan, 110, 349n57

Cohen, Jane, 224

Colette, 234

The Color of Water (McBride), 253

competition, 132–136, 138, 191

connectedness: and adolescence, 198–201; and adoption, 94, 231–232; vs. autonomy, 83, 191, 198–201, 264, 266; with autonomy, 74, 86, 205; and breastfeeding, 230; of fathers, 292; and ideals of motherhood, 141; individuality in, 357n49; and language, 93–101; in mother-daughter relationship, 205; need for, 162; and pleasure,

91–93; and responsiveness, 174; vs. separateness, 347n41; and sexuality, 188; social, 100–101; and teenage pregnancy, 203; and time, 317–318; and video, 180; and work, 84, 172–173

conservatism, xii, 7, 10, 30, 167; and abortion debate, 17, 249; "family values" of, 25; on stay-at-home mothers, 152, 173

consumerism, 34–35, 187, 235, 329; and having vs. being, 321–324; and stay-at-home mothers, 30, 326–327; and time, 319–320, 331–332

contraception, 11, 26, 46, 226–227

Contratto, Susan, 143–144

CosmoGirl magazine, 192

creativity, 94, 218, 317, 351n33; and ambivalence, 136–140; and domesticity, 35, 41; and flow experience, 104; natural vs. human, 249–251; and pregnancy, 106; and transitional space, 138–140; and "woolgathering," 146

Crittenden, Ann, 41, 126, 154, 264–265, 286–287

Crittenden, Danielle, 220

Crossing the Moon (Alden), 217

Csikszentmihalyi, Mihaly, 102, 105, 113, 122, 351n27

The Cultural Contradictions of Motherhood (Hays), 326

Cusk, Rachel, 177

daughters. *See* father-daughter relationship; mother-daughter relationship

day care, 7, 10, 50, 158, 356n35, 357n43; ambivalence toward, 154–156, 177, 316; effects of, 169–171; and feminism, 23, 26; for-profit, 355n18; ideal, 154–156; and maternal desire, 157–160, 316; and mothers' needs, 12–14, 316; policies on, 150, 153–155; recommendations on, 164, 166–167; reliability of, 147–149, 151, 355n4; and sharing child care, 127–128; standards of, 158–160; subsidized, 149, 154; videotaping of, 180

Dean, Anne, 203–206

The Death of Adam (Robinson), 160

de Beauvoir, Simone, 26–29, 32, 38, 51, 315–316, 341nn7,9,14

depression, 122, 196–197, 364n45; postpartum, 364n45

Deutsch, Helene, 59–62, 87, 263–264

di Lampedusa, Giuseppe, 313

Dinnerstein, Dorothy, ix, 299–302, 353n9

divorce, 281, 284, 286–290, 299

domesticity, 161–162, 164–165, 258, 356n22; vs. autonomy, 64, 83; and class, 40–41; cult of, 33–38, 165; vs. feminism, 42–43, 52–53

Douglas, Ann, 354n35
Dworkin, Ronald, 249

eating disorders, 193–194, 359n19, 359n25,
    361n41; and mother-daughter relationship,
    195–198, 200
economic factors: and assisted reproductive
    technologies, 363n35; and child care, 18–
    19, 30, 151–152, 305–307; in child care
    paradox, 153–154; and devaluation of care-
    giving, 24–25; in divorce, 286–287; and
    equality, 285–290, 325; and fathers, 291–
    297; and gender roles, 6, 35, 66; and having
    vs. being, 321; and housework, 38; and
    mother-daughter relationship, 342n23; in
    motherhood, 8, 11, 21, 126, 340n5, 350n3;
    and pleasure, 91; poverty, 286, 350n3; and
    sharing child care, 305–307; and special
    status for women, 43–47; and time, 319–
    320, 330–331; and women's power, 353n17;
    in women's work, 5, 30; in work-family
    conflict, 160–161, 206–207, 222–223, 331
Edelman, Marian Wright, 267
education, 18–19, 153, 184, 356n35, 360n30;
    children's achievement in, 327–328; chil-
    dren's readiness for, 169, 174, 181, 357n42;
    and female development, 214, 220; and
    forced pregnancy, 246; vs. love, 190; and
    maternal instinct, 88–89; and maternal
    sensitivity, 169; and nature, 228; and
    teenage pregnancy, 203; of women, 6–7,
    11, 35, 257; and work-family conflict, 206
Ehrenreich, Barbara, 33
Ehrensaft, Diane, 73
Eisenberg, Evan, 232
Eliot, George (Mary Ann Evans), 6
Elise, Dianne, 302
Ellman, Carolyn, 132–134, 353n17
employment. See work, paid
English, Deirdre, 33
Enright, Anne, 351n21
environmentalism, 228
equality: economic, 325; economic vs. care-
    giving, 285–290; emotional, 127; feminism
    on, 44–47, 51; and full commodification
    model, 356n28; gender, 5–7, 22, 24, 64,
    157–158, 285–286, 291–297; and mother-
    hood, 46–47, 126–127; vs. rigid equity,
    293–294; and role of fathers, 291–297; in
    shared parenting, 22, 127–128, 282, 285–
    286, 300–301; in workforce, 51, 157–158,
    325
Erdrich, Louise, 48, 100
Erikson, Erik, 183, 349n69, 354n39
eros, 299–302, 350n19. See also sexuality

The Eros of Parenthood (Oxenhandler), 300
ethnicity, 40–41

Faludi, Susan, 10, 42–43
"The Fantasy of the Perfect Mother"
    (Chodorow and Contratto), 143–144
father-child relationship, 207, 288–290, 298
father-daughter relationship, 62, 281, 353n17
fathers, 22, 280–311; absent, 182, 280–281,
    297; and attachment, 203, 205; devalua-
    tion of, 62, 282; and divorce, 281, 284,
    286–290, 299; expendability of, 284, 299;
    as househusbands, 127, 163; as ideal work-
    ers, 161–162; importance of, 289–290, 299,
    360n36, 366n2; marginalization of, 207,
    287–289; and maternal ambivalence,
    367n13; and maternal desire, 282, 303–
    304; in midlife, 288–289; and mother-child
    relationship, 367n19; and mother-daughter
    relationship, 131, 133, 260; mothers' rela-
    tionship with, 297–305, 360n36, 367n13,
    369n31; parenting roles of, 65–66; and pa-
    ternal desire, 305, 308; as providers, 327; as
    providers vs. caregivers, 291–297; sharing
    child care with, 127–128, 282–286, 305–
    308, 316; and sperm donation, 298,
    368n17; transformation of, xiii, 369n31;
    and work-family conflict, 272–273
The Female Eunuch (Greer), 54–55
The Feminine Mystique (Friedan), 23, 29–30, 256
femininity: vs. achievement, 26–27; and con-
    trol of body, 350n5; and empowerment,
    208–209; vs. masculinity, 193–194, 228; and
    men as providers, 292–293; and mother-
    hood, 42–49, 344n62; psychoanalysis on, 62
feminism, xi, xii, 15, 23–56; antidomesticity,
    42–43, 52–53; and Baby M case, 367n5; on
    day care, 23, 26; difference vs. equality, 45–
    47; and fertility, 212, 224; foremothers in,
    26–32; and gender minimizers vs. maximiz-
    ers, 340n6; historical perspective of, 33–38;
    on housework, 35, 38–42, 343n44; and
    individualism, xiii, 49, 55, 343n57; inter-
    generational differences in, 19–20; and ma-
    ternal desire, 12; and mother-blame,
    355n40; on mother-child relationship,
    340n4, 347n41; and motherhood, 10, 143–
    144, 316–317; and nature, 7–8, 228; phases
    of, 6, 256–258; polarization within, 24–25;
    pro-life, 252–254; protectionist vs. equality,
    44; and psychoanalysis, 63–75; special treat-
    ment vs. different voice, 344n62; on work-
    ing woman, 25, 41, 49–56, 167, 356n28
fertility, 211–236; and adoption, 221–222,
    231–232, 362n19; and age, 213–214, 220,

224–225; and ambivalence, 215–219; and
child care, 229–234, 316; and control, 221–
222; and education, 360n30; and men, 215,
218–219; and mother-daughter relationship, 363n29; and nature, 226–229; nostalgia for, 277–278; and policy, 362n25; and
postponement of childbearing, 215–223;
rates of, 211; and work-family conflict,
214–215, 218. *See also* assisted reproductive
technologies
The Fertility Question (Nofziger), 211
Firestone, Shulamith, xi
"The Flight from Womanhood" (Horney), 62
Flow (Csikszentmihalyi), 122
flow experience, 101–105, 113–115
Flux (Orenstein), 23, 206–207
Folbre, Nancy, 129, 206
Fonagy, Peter, 78, 354n32
foster care, 284
Foucault, Michel, 339n1b
Fra Angelico, 107
France, 149
Freud, Sigmund, xii, xiii, 4, 62, 300, 302
"Freud and Female Sexuality" (Chasseguet-
Smirgel), 353n17
Friedan, Betty, 6, 23, 29–30, 32, 38, 42–43,
256, 341n17, 343n44
Fromm, Erich, 321–322
Frost, Robert, 94
Fruitful (Roiphe), 240, 275

Gattica (film), 225
gender: and control, 16; and equality, 5–7, 22,
24, 28, 157–158, 285–286, 291–297; feminism on, 24, 47; and having vs. being, 326;
hierarchy of, 173; and identity, 289,
368n23; minimizers vs. maximizers of,
340n6; and motherhood, 5, 48–49; and nature vs. culture, 228; and parenting, 22,
271, 285–286, 291–297, 369n31; and social
policy, 46; and stereotypes, 44, 48, 228,
343n59; and work-family conflict, 317
gender roles: vs. achievement, 26–27; and ambivalence, 126–130; and autonomy, 16, 66;
balance of, 287–288; and child care, 25, 66,
284, 308–311; and denial of pleasure, 329;
division of labor by, 22, 293–296, 341n17,
353n10; economic, 6, 35, 66; and femininity, 43; feminism on, 26, 51; history of, 6–11;
ideology of, 4, 29; and industrialization, 6,
33; and inequality, 64; as oppression, 10,
51–52; and self-control, 16, 187; separate
spheres of, 34, 89, 341n18; transformation
of, 6–7; and work-family conflict, 54
George, Carol, 346n32

Ghent, Emmanuel, 143
Gilligan, Carol, ix, 42–43, 47, 208
Godbey, Geoffrey, 318–319, 334
Goldstein, Joseph, 201–202
Goodall, Jane, 155
Gopnik, Adam, 240
Graham, Jorie, 112
Greenspan, Stanley, 164
Greer, Germaine, 54–55
Grigoriadis, Vanessa, 129, 134

Harris, Judith, 358n59
Hays, Sharon, 30, 326
Hegel, G. W. F., 347n41
Hesse, Erik, 179
Hewlett, Sylvia Ann, 42–43, 267–270
Hochschild, Arlie, 272–273, 289, 295, 317,
334, 353n9
Holofcener, Nicole, 234
Holy Hunger (Bullitt-Jonas), 198
homework, 139–140
homosexuality, 299, 344n62
Horney, Karen, xii, xiii, 59–60, 62–63
Horton Hatches the Egg (Dr. Seuss), 284–285
housework, 115, 283, 343n47; and child care,
38–42, 51, 283; devaluation of, 283; femi-
nism on, 35, 38–42, 343n44; vs. ideal
worker, 161–163; pay for, 41–42
How to Get Pregnant (Silber), 211
Hrdy, Sarah Blaffer, 132, 154–156
The Hungry Self (Chernin), 195

identity, x, xii, 16, 254; and achievement,
324–326; and adolescence, 183; and childbearing, 217–218; children as, 275; and
fathers, 285; and fertility, 213, 215; and
gender, 289, 368n23; maternal, 57, 152,
239, 258, 285–286, 290, 366n30; and
mother-daughter relationship, 135, 184–
185; vs. motherhood, 58, 126–127; and nature, 228; and sharing child care, 283, 309–
311; and work, 163, 289, 334
In a Different Voice (Gilligan), ix, 47
independence. *See* autonomy
industrialization, 6, 33
Industrial Revolution, 33–35
infants, 37, 66–67, 95–96. *See also* mother-
infant bond
intergenerational differences, 255–261; and
child development, 298–299; and feminism, 19–20; and mother-daughter relationships, 135, 258–259; and work-family
conflict, 256–258
InterNational Council on Infertility Information Dissemination (INCIID.org), 212–213

Internet, 212–213
in vitro fertilization (IVF), 212–213, 227
The Irreducible Needs of Children (Brazelton and Greenspan), 164
It Takes a Village (Clinton), 268–269

Jardine, Alice, 27
"Jesus Before He Could Talk" (Miles), 107
Jones, Barbara, 46–47
Joyce, James, 141

Kaminer, Wendy, 43–46
Kimball, Roger, 141–142
KinderCare Learning Centers, Inc., 158
Kitzinger, Sheila, 121
Klein, Melanie, 195, 235, 340n4, 353n22
knowingness, 165–166
Kornfield, Jack, 201–202, 308
Kristeva, Julia, 105–109, 112–113, 199, 234–235, 365n1
Kuczynski, Alex, 188
Kundera, Milan, 142

Lachmann, Frank M., 81
Lamott, Anne, 119, 177
Langer, Marie, 59–60, 88–89
language, 108–109; and attachment, 109–111; and connectedness, 93–101; and newborns, 81–82, 95–96; primary- vs. secondary-process in, 97–98, 105; research on, 95–97, 103; semiotic vs. symbolic, 105, 109
Lasch-Quinn, Elisabeth, 323
laws: and abortion, 241–243, 245–246; divorce, 286–287; and motherhood, 21; and special status for women, 43–47, 344n62
Leach, Penelope, 178–180
Lear, Jonathan, 165, 350n19, 352n50
Leave It to Beaver (TV program), 144
Leclerc, Annie, ix, 91, 181, 251
The Leopard (di Lampedusa), 313
A Lesser Life (Hewlett), 269–270
Lieberman, Alicia, 366n2
Little Women (Alcott), 189–191
Loewald, Hans, 96–100, 105, 199, 300, 351n19
Lopate, Philip, 218–219
"Love for the Mother and Mother-Love" (Balint), 65
Lovely and Amazing (film), 234
Ludtke, Melissa, 233–234
Luker, Kristin, 223
Lyons-Ruth, Karlen, 79–80
Lysistrata (Aristophanes), 327

McBride, James, 253
Machung, Anne, 206

McKibben, Bill, 332
Madyun, Ayesha, 243
Mahler, Margaret, 71, 79–80, 346n27
Mahony, Rhona, 127, 163
Main, Mary, 348n52
Martha Stewart Living magazine, 322
Maslow, Abraham, 150
masochism, 143
maternal desire: and abortion, 238–241; absence of, 209; vs. biologism, 167; in day care debate, 157–160; and fathers, 282, 303–304; and gender stereotypes, 343n59; and identity, 57; intensity of, 221–222; and mother-daughter relationship, 186; and paradox of child care, 153, 155–156; in political debate, 316–317; as problem, 3–22; and reproductive rights, 251–252; as sentimental ideal, 144–145; and sharing child care, 294, 305, 308, 311; as social construct, 130
maternal instinct, 87–89
Maternal Thinking (Ruddick), 47
Mayer, Elizabeth Lloyd, 208
meaning: and adolescence, 183, 186; and children, 275, 316; vs. cliché, 113; creation of, 9, 14, 32, 58, 93, 100, 109–117, 165; and culture, 361n7; and eros, 351n19; for fathers, 303; and happiness, 180; interpersonal, 100; and language, 98–99; and mother-daughter relationship, 190, 260; motherhood as making, 32, 58, 111–117; and reproductive rights, 242; and work, 334
Medea, 120
media, 3, 18, 165; and eating disorders, 359n19; on effects of child care, 169; popular, 53–54, 90, 192, 322; sexuality in, 189; television, 144, 318
men, 222, 226, 303–304, 368n23; anger at, 192–193; dispensability of, 298; emotional needs of, 64, 297, 299–300; and eros of parenthood, 301–302; and experience of pregnancy, 244; as fathers, 207, 288; and fertility issues, 215, 218–219; and housework, 40; as ideal workers, 161–163, 289; and identity, 289; and income, 307; nurturing by, 303, 307, 368n23; and parenthood, 22, 65–66, 303–304; and power, 105, 108, 208–209; as providers, 292–293; relationships with, 220, 289; and work-family conflict, 206–207, 289, 294. *See also* fathers
Mendelson, Cheryl, 343n47
menopause, 263–264
Merkin, Daphne, 343n44
The Mermaid and the Minotaur (Dinnerstein), 299

Merton, Thomas, 335

Michelangelo, 208–209

middle class, 39, 184, 222, 256, 342n42, 370n18; and cult of domesticity, 34–35, 37; and feminism, 29, 32; and having vs. being, 323; and Industrial Revolution, 33–34; and work-family conflict, 21, 50

midlife, 255–279; and end of childbearing, 273–279; and intergenerational differences, 255–261; motherhood in, 262–267; mothers vs. fathers in, 288–289

Miedzian, Myriam, 10, 39

Miles, Jack, 107

"Missing Children" (Shacochis), 219

Mitchell, Stephen, 97

Modern Woman, The Lost Sex (Lundberg and Farnham), 59–60

Mogel, Wendy, 315, 370n27

Moher, Michael, 280

Morrison, Toni, 48, 365n18

"Mother Anger: Theory and Practice" (Lamott), 119

mother-child relationship: and attachment, 75–83, 300, 348n47, 357n43, 366n2; attunement in, 66–67; and autonomy, 67–68, 71–75; and child care, 168–170; and child development, 13–14, 348n47; and control, 71–75; and cult of domesticity, 35; and day care, 356n35, domination in, 71–72, 83; and empathy, 65, 174–175; erotic nature of, 299–302; and father, 297–299, 367n19; and femininity, 194; flow experience in, 101–104; and foster care, 284; and happiness, 179–181; and intentions, 173–176; intimacy in, 67, 299–300; language in, 96–98; and maternal ideals, 144; and mother's selfhood, 67–68, 72, 180, 347n41, 354n37; pleasure in, 13–14, 299–300, 367n19; and rapprochement, 347n41; research on, 64–66, 71, 75, 81–82, 88; and sharing child care, 284; women's need for, 170–171; and work, 347n41, 357n43

mother-daughter relationship: and adolescence, 133, 182–185, 198–201, 209–210; ambivalence in, 131–136; anger in, 133, 182–183, 196, 259; autonomy in, 131, 184–185, 205, 259–260; and child care, 316; and class, 342n23; and eating disorders, 195–198, 200; and envy, 132–136, 353n22; and father, 131, 133, 260, 367n19; feminism on, 340n4; and fertility, 363n29; guilt in, 132–133, 195, 353n20; and identity, 135, 184–185; and intergenerational differences, 135, 258–259; and meaning, 190, 260; and moral sense, 189–190; and motherhood, 259–262, 269; and mothers as

models, 30–31; mother's choices in, 184–185; vs. mother-son, 65–66; and nature, 228; psychoanalysis on, 62; reflectiveness in, 199–200, 205, 209; and self-development, 195–197, 205; and self-esteem, 132, 196, 209; and surprise at motherhood, 265; and teenage pregnancy, 203–205; and valuing the internal, 191; and work-family conflict, 131–132, 260, 266

motherese, 96

motherhood: as achievement, 32, 136; vs. achievement, 58, 195–197, 207–208, 266; and adolescence, 206–208; as adventure, viii; and anxiety, 352n3; vs. autonomy, 11, 16, 32, 57–58, 126, 218; biology of, 155; brevity of, 20–21; as choice, 11, 52, 64, 160–167, 252, 345n15; competition in, 132–136, 138; and control, 58, 85, 163; costs of, 207, 258; devaluation of, 21, 197, 201; and dialogue, 105–106; economic factors in, 8, 11, 21, 30, 126, 340n5, 350n3; and empty nest, 263–264; and equality, 46–47, 126–127; eros of, 301–302; and femininity, 42–49, 344n62; feminism on, 10, 23, 27–29, 316–317; first-time, 274–275; and guilt, 44, 47–48, 53; ideals of, 123, 137, 140–146; as identity, 47–48; vs. identity, 58, 126–127; ideology of, 92, 316; vs. individuality, 16–18, 27–28; individuality in, 12, 369n31; and marginalization, 125; as meaning-making activity, 32, 58, 111–117; midlife, 262–267; models of, 30–31, 209, 274; and morality, 9, 175, 189–190; and mother-daughter relationship, 259–262, 265, 269; as opportunity, 28; as paid work, 20; and patriarchy, 30, 63, 274; pleasure in, 9, 27, 30, 35–36, 265–266, 268–269; as protest against consumerism, 326; and psychoanalysis, 344n1; psychological basis of, 15, 21, 28, 51, 64–71; as regression, 19–20; and relationship, 9–10, 27, 50, 59; and reproductive rights, 46–47; and selfhood, 5–6, 15, 33, 47–49, 61–62, 70–71, 75, 86, 130, 163, 217, 274–275; as self-sacrifice, 8–10, 125; sentimentality about, 141–143; and sexuality, 48, 188–189, 266; as skill, 113–114, 138; and social values, 122–123; stereotypes of, 48; surprise at, 265; surrogate, 284; transformation by, xiii, 130, 194; and women's rights, 254; and work-family conflict, 4–5, 16, 49–56, 70–71, 92–93, 314

Motherhood and Sexuality (Langer), 59–60

mother-infant bond, 65–71, 178, 302, 345nn16,17, 346n27; language in, 81–82, 95–96

Mothering magazine, 90
Mother Nature (Hrdy), 155
mothers: allo-, 154–156; as artists, 27, 41, 113,
  217; birth, 367n5; blame of, 355n40; as caregivers, 283–284, 308, 310; choices of, 160–
  167; faux stay-at-home, 152; good enough
  vs. perfect, 145–146; imitation of, 122; intentions of, 171–176; as models of resistance, 30–32; needs of, 160, 170–171; older,
  262–267, 333; parenting roles of, 65–66;
  "perfect," 143–145; poverty of divorced,
  286; power of, 353n17; primate, 155–156;
  professional, 4–5, 88, 121, 132, 258; as role
  models, 23, 30–31, 209, 274; single, 111–
  112, 233–234; stay-at-home, xii–xiii, 167,
  173, 175, 180, 188, 191, 256; stay-at-home
  vs. working, 125, 151–152, 175, 326–327;
  working-class, 21, 154
*Mothers Who Think: Tales of Real-Life Parent-
  hood* (Peri and Moses), 111
music, 104
Musick, Judith, 202–203, 206

Nachman, Patricia, 357n49
Nader, Ralph, 30
The Nanny Diaries (McLaughlin and Kraus),
  171–172, 200
National Infertility Association
  (RESOLVE.org), 212
National Partnership for Women and Fami-
  lies, 167
nature, 7–8, 226–229, 249–251
New York Times, 167
NICHD (National Institute of Child Health
  and Human Development) Study of Early
  Child Care, 168–169, 180
Nofziger, Margaret, 211
Nurture Assumption (Harris), 358n59

Of Woman Born (Rich), 23, 30–32
Olsen, Tillie, 342n23
The One Minute Mother (Johnson), 42
On Our Own (Ludtke), 233
Orenstein, Peggy, 23, 206–207
Our Bodies, Ourselves, 212
The Overworked American (Schor), 39–40, 317
Oxenhandler, Noelle, 300

Paglia, Camille, 141
parenting: and attachment, 77–78; and class,
  271, 342nn38,42, 370n18; and community,
  350n6; eros of, 301–302; by fathers, 65–66;
  and gender, 22, 271, 285–286, 291–297,
  369n31; having vs. being in, 322–324; individuality in, 12, 369n31; influence of,
  358n59; middle-class, 342n42, 370n18;

pleasure in, 301–302; vs. pregnancy, 234–
  235; sensitivity in, 200–201; shared, 10, 22,
  127–128, 282, 285–286, 300–301, 304–305,
  309–311; styles of, 342n38; transformation
  by, xiii, 303–304; transition to, 296–297; by
  women, 83, 304–305
Parker, Rozsika, 136–137, 366n30
Parole de Femme (Leclerc), ix
patriarchy, 30, 32, 63, 185, 196, 274, 282,
  363n28
Pearson, Allison, 125
Peek-A-Boo! (Ahlberg and Ahlberg), 322
penis envy, 62, 263, 304
Perkins, Charlotte Gilman, 41
the personal as political, 26
Phelan, Lana, 248
Pinker, Steven, 96
Plath, Sylvia, 149–150
pleasure, 32, 90–117, 180, 202, 308, 329; barriers to, 91–93, 115–116, 121; and breastfeeding, 90–91, 230; for fathers, 303; and flow
  experience, 101–104; and language, 94–101;
  and meaning-making, 111–117; in midlife
  motherhood, 265–266; in mother-child relationship, 13–14, 299–300, 367n19; in mother-
  daughter relationship, 199; in motherhood, 9,
  27, 30, 35–36, 265–266, 268–269; and mothers' choices, 161; in parenting, 301–302; and
  polymorphous sensuality of women, 302–303;
  and pregnancy, 240; and translation, 104–
  111; vs. work, 92–93, 115–116, 329
policy, public: and child care, 177, 333,
  362n25; of companies, 22; on day care, 150,
  153–155; gender-neutral, 46; on maternity
  leaves, 86–87; and motherhood, 21, 46; and
  relationships, 293; and work-family conflict,
  225, 268, 270–272, 362n25
political correctness, 166
Pollitt, Katha, 152, 229, 362n25
pregnancy, 106, 209, 250, 276; and abortion,
  219, 244–248; adolescent, 201–205, 209;
  and autonomy, 203, 219; and competition,
  134; de Beauvoir on, 27–28; and employment rights, 46–47; and fetal life, 244, 253;
  forced, 245–246; as investment, 244–245,
  247, 251; and mother-daughter relationship, 203–205; and narcissism, 234–236;
  nostalgia for, 277–278; vs. parenting, 234–
  235; and postpartum depression, 364n45;
  and prenatal testing, 244–245; and psychoanalysis, 62; psychology of, 106–107; as
  relationship, 237–238, 244–248; and
  selfhood, 203–205, 219, 239–243; and sick-
  ness, 121, 237; unintended, 91–92, 226,
  240, 247–248, 253; and weight gain, 192
The Price of Motherhood (Crittenden), 126, 264

primary narcissism, 346n30
primates, 155–156
psychoanalysis, 11–12, 57–89, 316, 344n1, 346n26, 352n50; and feminism, 63–75; on relationships, 58–59; women pioneers in, 59–63
public domain, xii, xiii, 6, 29, 34, 89, 341n18
Pugh, Allison, 319

Quindlen, Anna, 138
Quinn, Susan, 62

race, 40–41, 242–243, 271
Rapp, Rayna, 229
recognition: and attachment, 75–83; and mother-daughter relationship, 133–134; and responsiveness, 78–81, 142–143
reflectiveness, 199–200, 205, 209, 349n56, 360nn25,35
relationships: and abortion, 240, 248; and achievement, 324; vs. achievement, 207–208, 232–233; adult, 205; attachment, 203–205, 348n53; with caregivers, 147–149, 156–157, 176; and childbearing, 216, 220; vs. commercial values, 30, 326–327; communion in, 103; and control, 188; and creativity, 138–140; as developmental achievement, 235–236; and division of labor, 293–296; economy of gratitude in, 295; erotic, 300–302; and female adolescence, 190–191; and femininity, 194; and forced pregnancy, 245–246; and generational boundaries, 298–299; genetic, 231; having vs. being in, 321–324; homosexual, 299; long-term, 189; with men, 220, 289; and men as providers, 292–293; merger vs. separation in, 65–71; mother-father, 274, 297–305, 310–311, 360n36, 367n13, 369n31; and motherhood, 9–10, 27, 50, 59; and neediness, 221; new, 120–121; nurturing, 309; parent-child, 36–37, 131–132, 136, 271; pleasure in, 32; vs. political resistance, 31; of pregnancy, 237–238, 244–248; psychoanalysis on, 58–59; and public policy, 293; and reproductive rights, 251–252; with self, 112–113, 120; and sharing child care, 304–305, 309–311; and time, 319, 335; between women, 132–136, 266–267, 302; and work, 172; and work-family conflict, 50, 273. See also father-child relationship; father-daughter relationship; marriage; mother-child relationship; mother-daughter relationship; mother-infant bond
religion, 100, 201–202; power hierarchy in, 108; and reproductive rights, 242–243, 247; and separate spheres, 34, 37; and transcendence, 94, 99, 351n19; and Virgin Mary, 107–108, 349n1
The Reproduction of Mothering (Chodorow), 63–71, 130
reproductive rights, 26, 28, 46–47; vs. coercion, 244, 247–248; and creativity, 250–251; and fetal rights, 248–249; and selfhood, 239–243, 253–254. See also abortion
RESOLVE.org (National Infertility Association website), 212
responsiveness, 88, 168–172, 175, 322, 349nn56,57, 357n42; and attachment, 76, 78–81, 174; and flow experience, 103–104; and recognition, 78–81, 142–143
Rich, Adrienne, 23, 30–32, 49
Roberts, Julia, 126
Robinson, John P., 318–319, 334
Robinson, Marilynne, 37, 160
Roe v. Wade, 240
Roiphe, Anne, 240, 258, 275, 277
Roiphe, Katie, 131
role models, viii–ix, 30–31, 209, 274
Rossi, Agnes, 234
Rossi, Alice, 221
Rousseau, Jean-Jacques, 229
Rubin, Lillian, 264, 288–289
Ruddick, Sara, 47
The Rules (Fein and Schneider), 320

Sander, Louis, 66–67
Sanger, Margaret, 252
Sayers, Janet, 344n1
Scarr, Sandra, 157–158, 178
Schor, Juliet, 36, 39–40, 317, 330
Schwartz, Adria, 302
The Second Sex (de Beauvoir), 26–29
The Second Shift (Hochschild), 289, 317
Sedaris, David, 343n47
self, 188, 201; and attachment, 76, 78, 82; and avoidance of pregnancy, 219; of child, 277; vs. children, 17, 25; commercialization of, 354n35; development of, 7, 15–17, 25, 195–197, 215, 217–218, 351n27; and end of childbearing, 274; expression of, xii, xiii, 8, 13, 25, 75, 82; and female adolescence, 186, 203–205; and fertility, 215; and first-time motherhood, 274–275; and flow experience, 103–104; and mother-child relationship, 67–68, 72, 180, 345n16, 347n41, 354n37; and mother-daughter relationship, 195–197, 205, 210; and motherhood, xii, xiii, 5–6, 15, 33, 47–49, 61–62, 75, 86, 130, 163; and other, 88, 138–139, 347n41; perspective on younger, 275–276; and recognition, 142–143; relationship to, 112–113; and reproductive rights, 239–243, 248; sense of, 15,

self (*cont.*)
76, 78, 86, 103–104, 130, 163, 196, 203–
205, 210, 345n16, 354n32; and sentimentality, 142–143; and time with children, 314;
and work, 4–5, 13, 121; and work-family
conflict, 50, 53–55, 270–272
self-esteem, 149–150, 152, 160, 170; and having vs. being, 323; and masochism, 143; and
mother-daughter relationship, 132, 196,
209; and profession, 4–5, 121
self-image, 70–71, 76
self-sacrifice, 20, 27, 173, 179, 266, 354n39;
and mother-daughter relationship, 185,
196; motherhood as, 8–10, 125
sentimentality, 10, 34, 141–145, 191, 354n35
separateness, 366n30; vs. attachment, 68–70;
vs. autonomy, 74; and loss, 83–87; vs. merger,
65–71; and mother-child relationship, 71–75
servants, 40–41, 323
Seuss, Dr. (Theodor Geisel), 284–285
sexuality, xiii, 4, 15, 33, 55, 254, 339n1; adolescent, 185–186, 190–191, 359n3; and autonomy, 130; and breastfeeding, 230; vs.
child care, 304; vs. eros, 300; and integration, 349n69; vs. love, 301; and the maternal, 183–184, 186; and men as providers,
292–293; and motherhood, 48, 188–189,
266; and polymorphous sensuality of
women, 302–303
Shacochis, Bob, 219
Shea, Lisa, 298
Shellenbarger, Sue, 169
Silber, Sherman, 211
Simpson, Mona, 297–298
skills, 113–114, 138, 351n27
slavery, 40–41
Socrates, 350n19
Solomon, Judith, 346n32
specialness, sense of, 45, 108, 201, 234–236;
and legal status of women, 43–47, 344n62
sperm donation, 298, 368n17. *See also* assisted
reproductive technologies
Spock, Dr. Benjamin, 179
Spoiling Childhood (Ehrensaft), 73
Stern, Daniel, 67, 96–98, 102–103, 260
Still Life (Byatt), 145–146
"Strange Situation," 76
supermom ideal, 10–11, 53–54
Sweden, 157
The Symmetry of God (Bomford), 99

"Take Your Daughter to Work Day," 191, 325
Target, Mary, 78
Taylor, Evelyn, 221
television, 144, 318

test tube babies. *See* assisted reproductive
technologies
"Through a glass darkly . . ." (1 Corinthians),
313
time, 354n37, 367n4, 369n11; and achievement, 320–322; changed sense of, 99–100;
with children, 267–268, 270, 272–273, 277,
290, 304, 312–336; commodification of,
319–320; and connectedness, 317–318; and
consumerism, 331–332; cultural attitudes
toward, 317–320; and intention, 175–176;
for motherhood, 9, 11; passage of, 278–279;
perceived lack of, 318, 330; and pregnancy,
106–107; "quality," 317, 319; and work,
175–176
The Time Bind (Hochschild), 272–273, 334
time deepening, 319
time famine, 318
Tolstoy, Leo, 183
transcendence, 94, 99, 351n19
transitional space, 138–140, 351n19
translation function, 100, 104–111, 199; and
Virgin Mary, 107–108
True Womanhood, cult of, 35
Turiel, Judith Sternberg, 224
"A Two-Year-Old Boy's First Love Comes to
Grief" (Deutsch), 60

Unbending Gender (Williams), 161
unconscious, 94, 97–101, 106, 120
urbanization, 6, 33

Vieira, Meredith, 114
Virgin Mary, 107–108, 349n1

Wallerstein, Judith, 286
The War Against Parents (Hewlett and West),
268, 270–272
War and Peace (Tolstoy), 183
Wasserstein, Wendy, 136
weight, control of, 192–197, 209. *See also* eat-
ing disorders
Weir, Allison, 108
Weldon, Faye, 106, 351n33
West, Cornel, 268, 270–272
What Our Mothers Didn't Tell Us
(Crittenden), 135
Wile, Daniel, 310
Williams, Joan, 161–164, 286
Williams, Joy, 332
Williams, Tennessee, 263
Winnicott, D. W., 138–142, 146, 175, 190,
347n41, 351n21
Wolf, Naomi, 7, 11, 15, 364n2
Woman: An Intimate Geography (Angier), 259

women: adolescent, 15–16, 188–191, 201–205, 209; as attachment figures, 178–179; autonomy of, 242–243; as caregivers, 161, 283–284, 289, 308, 310, 367n4; castration of, xii; child status of, 46; devaluation of, 24; development of, 184–185, 214, 220; domestic labor of, 318; education of, 6–7, 11, 35, 257; emotional needs of, 299–300; and empty nest, 263–264; historical roles of, 6–11; images of, 359n25; and men, 220, 289, 292–293; mother-lust of, 259; and mother role, 290; and nature, 226–229; nature of, 6, 22; objectification of, 27–28, 228–229; older, 266–267, 275, 277; and pain, 354n39; polymorphous sensuality of, 302–303; as primary parents, 304–305; pro-choice vs. pro-life, 365n22; and psychoanalysis, 59–63; psychology of, viii, 60, 62, 214–215, 218, 263–264; in public domain, 6, 29, 105; relationships between, 34, 132–136, 266–267, 302; restrictions on, 345n15; rights of, 55, 254, 301; roles of, 6, 167; self-determination of, 253–254; separate spheres of, 34, 89, 341n18; as servants, 41, 43; sexuality of, xiii, 33, 55, 188, 254, 301; special status for, 43–47, 344n62; submissiveness of, 43, 71, 83, 143; work as progress for, 5–7, 35, 167; working, 25, 41, 49–56, 167, 356n28

work, paid: and autonomy, 52, 325–326; and breastfeeding, 230; and childbearing, 222–223; and child care, 7, 25, 127–128, 153–154; and connectedness, 84, 172–173; costs of, 258; and divorce, 288; vs. domesticity, 41; equality in, 51, 157–158, 325; and female development, 214, 220; flexibility in, 86–87; and flow experience, 113–115; and forced pregnancy, 246; glass ceilings in, 6; and ideal workers, 161–163, 289; and identity, 163, 289, 334; and Industrial Revolution, 34; intellectual, 40; and intention, 171–172; and mother-child relationship, 347n41, 357n43; and mother-daughter relationship, 135; need for, 13, 170–171, 276; planning for, 206–207; and pleasure, 92–93, 115–116, 329; and pregnancy, 46–47; professional, 4–5, 88, 255–256; as progress for women, 5–7, 29–30, 35, 167; and school readiness, 357n42; and selfhood, 4–5, 13, 20, 121; and sharing child care, 127–128; and sharing housework, 283; and status, 325; structure of, 50, 164, 350n6; and time, 7, 175–176, 272–273, 319–320, 330–331; traditional female, 155; underpaid, 153–154; of welfare vs. middle-class mothers, 21; women's access to, 19, 64, 257

work-family conflict: and achievement, 29–30, 113–116, 123, 206–207; and ambivalence, 122, 131–132; and autonomy, 55, 57; balance in, 19, 148, 162, 181, 314, 334; and child care, 150–157, 283–284, 307–308, 316–317; and cultural assumptions, 325–326; denial of, 129–130; economic factors in, 160–161, 206–207, 222–223, 331; and fathers, 272–273; and fertility, 214–215, 218; and first-time motherhood, 274–275; and full commodification model, 356n28; and gender socialization, 317; and guilt, 178, 275; and happiness, 180–181; and intention, 172–173, 175–176; and intergenerational differences, 256–258; and men, 206–207, 289, 294; and midlife motherhood, 264–265; and mother-daughter relationship, 131–132, 260, 266; and motherhood, 4–5, 16, 49–56, 70–71, 92–93, 314; and mothers' choice, 160–167; and paradox of child care, 153–157; vs. pleasure, 115–116, 329; among primates, 155–156; and professional lovers of children, 267–273; in psychoanalysis, 60; and public policy, 225, 268, 270–272, 362n25; and role of fathers, 291–297; and selfhood, 50, 53–55, 270–272; and sharing child care, 283–284, 307–308, 316–317; and women vs. men, 206–207, 289, 294

Working Mother magazine, 53–54

Your Baby and Child (Leach), 179–180

Daphne de Marneffe, PhD, is a clinical psychologist experienced in treating adults and children. Educated at Harvard and UC Berkeley, she has lectured nationally on the subject of maternal desire, and her scholarly work has been published in psychoanalytic and feminist journals. Since the birth of her third child in 1998, Dr. de Marneffe has divided her time between caring for her young children and developing the ideas presented in this book. She lives with her family in California.

maternal desire

On Children, Love, and the Inner Life

by Daphne de Marneffe

A reading group guide

A conversation with
Daphne de Marneffe

How did you come to write Maternal Desire?

It began with a deep feeling in me that having a child, relating to that child, and caring for that child was unbelievably precious — a physically and emotionally transforming joy, a sacred thing. At the same time, when we had our first child, I had painful thoughts going through my head — insecurities, questions. What kind of person was I, that my baby compelled me so much more than anything else? Was there something wrong with me that I felt almost physically incapable of taking up where I left off professionally? I gradually began to wonder about the questions themselves. I sensed that there was more than my own idiosyncratic psychology at work here. I became interested in what, at this moment in society, made questions like mine so pressing for many professional women. Were there subtle social pressures that urged mothers not to identify with these kinds of feelings? Were educated women today encouraged to structure their identities apart from maternal desire? I felt if I could understand some of the social and psychological context of my feelings, I could help other women becoming mothers today to find more satisfaction in their lives, both mothering and work. Those thoughts and feelings were the beginnings of the book.

Maternal Desire *is a very personal book, but also contains a lot of research and scholarship on mothering. Why did you combine the two?*

I wanted to let becoming a mother change me, and I also wanted to use this experience to reexamine the rest of my life. For me, the "rest of my life" included my relationship not only to my husband and my work, but also to the traditions of feminism and psychology I had spent fifteen years studying, as well as the social and cultural world in which I was becoming a mother. The very act of writing the book was integrating for me, a process of knitting together different aspects of myself. It was fully anchored in the day-to-day of caring for babies and young children, but it also grew out of my interest in acting as a "participant-observer," that is, immersing myself in the emotions and experience of the moment, and being able to stand back and reflect on it.

My goal was not simply to present some ideas, but to give the reader a certain kind of *experience.* I wanted her to find her feelings about motherhood acknowledged and described, and then for her to feel invited to think about those feelings in a broader psychological and social context, as a means of making the most satisfying and meaningful choices in her life. I wanted her to experience herself as an agent, rather than as a victim, with respect to her maternal feelings.

That attempt to address the whole person, by the way, is similar to what we do as parents. And it is not unlike what therapists do in therapy. We try to help our children, or patients, be aware of their feelings and have the greatest possible freedom in thinking about them and making good choices with respect to them. When readers have told me that reading the book was like a good therapy session, I have taken it as a great compliment.

It was also one of the book's central goals to examine the ways in which intellectual ideas and cultural trends infuse our personal experience of motherhood. I wanted to give some intellectual heft to the idea of maternal pleasure, which is usually interpreted simplistically or sentimentally. The book's mix of the personal and the scholarly counters the stereotype that maternal feeling is mushy and unthinking, and the mistaken notion that if we really prized thinking, we wouldn't spend our time caring for children. The truth is, we can be deeply moved and affected emotionally by motherhood, and we can — and should — also think about that experience and its implications.

In some ways, the desire to mother is the most obvious and natural thing in the world. Why did you feel the need to write about it?

Calling it "the most obvious thing in the world" is a way to dismiss its complexity. Various philosophers — Foucault and Barthes, to name a couple — have drawn attention to the ways in which the idea of "naturalness" actually conceals all sorts of ideological interests and pressures. I think this operates where motherhood is concerned as well. When women's urge to mother is talked about as the "most obvious thing in the world," not in need of analysis or explanation, one or several ideas are usually hiding there: for example, a collapse of individual differences, an attempt to prescribe behavior by universalizing it, an attempt to constrict the arena of women's subjectivity and freedom by reducing women's priorities and values to their biology or genes, or an attempt to trivialize real desires under the mantle of "sentimentality."

Because such tendencies are so reflexive and pernicious where motherhood is concerned, it is hard to rescue and consider anew women's desire to mother as an expression of self, as a search for meaning. That is what my book tries to do: to disentangle something authentic from all the clichés, and to describe it in a fresh, useful way.

You devote a lot of attention to how psychoanalysis and feminism have viewed motherhood. Why?

Psychoanalysis has come a long way since Freud, and it enhances our understanding of motherhood in at least two important ways. First, it fleshes out the insight that individuals — and societies — have feelings and perceptions that they disavow or attribute to others as a way to escape the discomfort of internal conflict. The more aware we can be of our multiple and conflicting feelings about our motherhood, the more we can own our experience, be more responsive to ourselves, and lead richer lives. Owning our own feelings also expands our empathy for others, which can certainly help quiet the so-called Mommy Wars.

Second, exciting developments in psychoanalytically informed research on early attachment and parent-child interaction give us new ways to conceptualize what has until recently aroused little scientific interest: mothers' pleasure and satisfaction in caring for children, and the ways this pleasure contributes to a woman's own growth as a person, as well as her child's. I discuss this research in the book because I think it is so important to develop an account of how relating to one's child brings to life not only one's child's personality, but parts of oneself.

As to the goals of feminism, I believe that a crucial next step is taking the psychological and emotional meanings of caring for children seriously. We need to investigate deeply and carefully not only what women lose by caring for children, such as economic security, but also what they gain. Motherhood is not only a condition that harms women's material prospects or conflicts with their ambition, but also a life choice and a use of time that reflects many people's deeply held values and desires. If we don't think about that fact with the seriousness it deserves, we end up taking the familiar but unrewarding position that mothers' intense investment in caring for their children is some sort of throwback, or feminine deficit, or problem that needs to be cured. From the point of view of humanity, the last thing we need is to convince ourselves that parents and children don't need rich and satisfying relationships with each other.

You mention parents here, rather than just mothers. How do you see the role of fathers? What about "paternal desire"?

Almost everything I talk about in this book is applicable to fathers. A father's enjoyment of, and devotion to, his children can be every bit as intense as a mother's. I think most of us know families where the father is the more nurturing of the parents, or where the parents are both very nurturing, but in different ways. Any way a family can arrange itself so as to satisfy the emotional lives of its members is a good family, it seems to me.

With respect to gender arrangements in marriage and parenthood, usually the argument is made — and it's an important argument — that women need to have the same opportunities in the work world as men, and men need to contribute to housework at the level that women do. This is one dimension of fairness, but it isn't the only one. Women should have as much opportunity in their work lives as men have, but men should also have as much opportunity to care for their children as women have. If we begin to see the care of children not as something to hand off and escape, but rather something to treasure and enjoy, we can start talking about gender equality in some new ways.

Do you believe that mothers with young children — or fathers for that matter — should stay home to care for them?

I wrote this book as a person for whom spending time caring for children was important and as someone who also wanted a meaningful work life. I believe children crave parental love and attention and flourish when they have a lot of it. I think that is a belief that many, if not most, mothers of young children share. *Maternal Desire* considers this matter both from the point of view of what desires mothers seek to satisfy in caring for children, and what is painful when the desire isn't there, or is in conflict with other aspirations or practical circumstances.

I set out to describe, in an emotionally evocative and intellectually rigorous manner, the ways that caring for children can be a source of meaning and pleasure; to put that idea on the table, so that people could look at it more clearly, and consider it with less confusion and conflict. It has been disappointing when people have refused to engage the deeper argument and have instead represented it as the hackneyed prescription that "mothers should stay home." It's ironic, because one of my central purposes was to analyze and critique precisely this kind of simplistic thinking about motherhood. If anything, that response has reminded me how important — and at times how difficult — it is not to fall into either/or thinking, to maintain a complex picture of something as emotionally charged as motherhood.

You seem to suggest that the moment people begin to talk about what is positive and pleasurable about motherhood, they are accused of idealizing it.

Motherhood, like any important relationship, contains love and hate, anger and goodwill, frustration and satisfaction. There is always a tension between the needs of the self and the needs of the other. Relationships are between real people, not between ideals. Emphasizing only the pleasant side does tend to yield an idealized picture.

At the same time, pleasure and happiness in motherhood is a worthy human goal, an aspiration that many women deeply cherish. It is extraordinarily sad when a mother can't find joy or satisfaction in her mothering. It is a devastating, formative human experience for children, a life-defining lack. It is also extremely painful to mothers. If we care about women's happiness and fulfillment, then we should care about what makes it hard for them to experience joy in their mothering — not only because being a mother capable of joy has benefits for children, but because it benefits the mother herself. At times you hear the objection that there is something inherently life-narrowing for women to spend time caring for children. I am interested in that contradiction. How could something that is so necessary to children's happiness simultaneously compromise women's own?

A colleague suggested recently to me that maybe there is a tragic dimension to, or at least an unresolvable conflict between, the child's wish and need for the mother's presence, and the mother's wish or need to devote her energies to other callings, whatever they are. Just in terms of the limits on creative energy, whoever takes care of children is going to suffer in their ability to accomplish other things. A mother's bond to her child can change her relationship to her work forever. There is truth in that. But whether that change feels more like a loss or a gain depends a great deal on the individual.

Maternal Desire *explores the satisfactions of mothering, but not everyone experiences the same degree of satisfaction or the same amount of pleasure.*

After I finished writing, I noticed a possible tension between my autobiographical anecdotes, which focused for the most part on the pleasures of time with young children, and my theoretical position, that maternal desire should be understood as an important aspect of women's psychology. I could imagine a reader who felt that the way I wrote of my own experience leaned toward the prescriptive, that I saw my own experience as "the answer" to the more general intellectual and social questions that I raised. Or she might see me as implying that fully acknowledging one's own maternal desire would — or should — lead one to spend more time with one's children, an option which is simply not open to many mothers.

I intended to evoke readers' awareness of their own desires, not to offer my personal path as a one-size-fits-all response to such an awareness. In fact, I explicitly meant to explore how difficult it is to recognize diverse simultaneous realities; how difficult it is, in other words, to hold in mind and give voice to the equally compelling truths that many mothers feel an intense desire to care for their children and that many mothers are constrained in their ability to express that desire, and that there is great variability between women as to the intensity or presence of that desire.

A colleague asked me, "Why talk so forcefully about the pleasures of motherhood when it stands to make a mother who needs to work feel guilty or criticized for something she can't help?" But I reject the idea that we should obscure one aspect of experience in favor of another. That kind of evasiveness carries its own dangers. If we don't talk frankly about the sense of pleasure and meaning women find in maternal activity, we cannot honestly assess the pain they feel when they are deprived of it (a pain particularly acute for mothers who have no choice in their work lives). Nor are we likely to galvanize the outrage necessary to challenging those who resist shifting family policies in a more humane direction.

This book focuses mostly on mothering babies and young children. What do you have to say to mothers of older children?

When I give talks to mothers of young children, women with a four-year-old and a one-year-old, for instance, I am fascinated to find that that period of life feels like ancient history to me now. I began the book when my oldest was five, my middle one was two, and I was expecting my youngest. I couldn't have written the book at any other period, because it depended for its perspective on immersion in that phase of life.

Mothering older children is a different territory, I can now say from experience — my children are now twelve, nine, and six — but similar themes persist as well. A friend who read my book felt a longing to relive her children's babyhood, and to feel more present, less anxious, less torn. It helped her to realize that the opportunity had not passed her by; she could bring that sense of pleasure to mothering her older children. Every phase gives amazing opportunities for sharing, and love and growth. I think in parenthood, as in every other part of our lives, we need to cultivate "nostalgia for the present," to see the here and now as incredibly precious.

It's also true that the countervailing pulls of family time and work commitments rarely go away, they just keep shifting. An ongoing issue of parenthood is how to make enough time and psychic space for satisfying family relationships. Preserving time with one's family is akin to preserving open space in nature. It seems that by not developing land, we are "doing nothing," but in fact it takes energy and devotion and discipline not to fill up open space, just as it takes those things not to fill up all our hours with activity that takes us away from our children.

What do you hope readers take from this book?

What I hope for most is that the reader will feel invited to reflect on her life, because the book is meant to help people explore their inner experience. We change and grow through conversation — with ourselves, with friends, with books. I want reading this book to be like having a conversation about what one most deeply wants in life.

I think that how we choose to spend our time when our children are young is enormously important, for them and for us. It is worth careful thought and a weighing of our desires and theirs. I recently read an interview with the novelist Anne Tyler where she said, "Marriage is like parenthood: every last one of us is an amateur at it." With motherhood, I want the sense of struggling toward a personal truth, and the value of that struggle, to come through.

Questions and topics for discussion

1. Do you think that motherhood and a mother's right to enjoy mothering need to be defended, particularly at this time? Do you agree that motherhood is taboo in some circles?

2. De Marneffe takes pains to emphasize the difference between so-called natural instincts and pervasive social ideologies that have acted to normalize women's behavior. How does she tread this line? Her detractors might say that because de Marneffe emphasizes the importance of motherhood to women, she jeopardizes the progress the women's movement has made in decoupling women from their historical role. After reading this book, how would you respond to such a criticism?

3. What do you consider the foundations of a strong parent-child relationship? How do you think the experiences of motherhood and childhood change as increasing numbers of women bear children later in life?

4. De Marneffe at one point notes that every feminist has her own set of feminist beliefs because our convictions are so intertwined with personal experience. Do you consider yourself a feminist? From what material have you built your own version of feminism?

5. If you have children, how do you relate to de Marneffe's description of maternal desire? If you are not a mother, how

does this book make you think about your own impulses to have or not have children?

6. Why do we speak of a mothering impulse rather than a parenting impulse? Do you think this book has important things to say to men as well as women?

7. Were you the child of a stay-at-home mother, or did you mother have a job outside the home? How does this help you think about what kind of parent you want to be? Based on your experience, what do you think is best for children?

8. De Marneffe argues for a nuanced understanding of motherhood and the social role of women, in contrast to the voice that calls motherhood an impediment to women's independence. Is it only at this point, decades after the 1970s "women's liberation" movement, that critiques like de Marneffe's can begin to surface?

9. Have you ever felt guilty for wanting to mother? If you are a working mother, have you felt the need to deemphasize your motherhood in your work-life interactions? Does this book help you claim your identity as a mother?

Daphne de Marneffe's suggestions for further reading

As a reader and a writer, I depend a lot on essays with heart, analyses of social and psychological life that manage to convey both an austere commitment to truth and a deep humanity. Among my favorite general essay collections are *Mythologies* by Roland Barthes and *The Death of Adam* by Marilynne Robinson. Two such books from philosophy and psychology are *Open Minded: Working Out the Logic of the Soul* by Jonathan Lear and *Papers on Psychoanalysis* by Hans W. Loewald.

For those looking for a particularly humane and searching study of female psychology through the lenses of culture, body image, and feminism, I highly recommend *Unbearable Weight: Feminism, Western Culture, and the Body* by Susan Bordo. Those struggling with aspects of fertility and childbearing, and anyone who enjoys good writing, will appreciate *Wanting a Child*, edited by Jill Bialosky and Helen Schulman. The ambivalence of becoming a mother is beautifully rendered by Rachel Cusk in *A Life's Work*.

There are many useful books on child development and child-rearing, but some I have found especially illuminating are *The Interpersonal World of the Infant* by Daniel N. Stern, *The Emotional Life of the Toddler* by Alicia F. Lieberman, *The Blessing of a Skinned Knee* by Wendy Mogel, and *A Mind at a Time* by Mel Levine.

My book's intent is to treat maternal desire as one of many legitimate aspects of self that women can feel, think about, and make choices about. But I, like many readers, have an enduring fascination with novels that touch on aspects of the exquisite conflicts among women's competing desires. Some favorites are *Anna Karenina* by Leo Tolstoy (in a new translation by Richard Pevear and Larissa Volokhonsky), *The Good Mother* by Sue Miller, *Evening* by Susan Minot, *The God of Small Things* by Arundhati Roy, *Wintering* by Kate Moses, and the fiction of Tessa Hadley.